P9-CMF-655

Courtesy U.S. Naval Academy Museum

JOHN PAUL JONES. From a bust by Jean Antoine Houdon in the crypt of the Chapel, United States Naval Academy.

The

UNITED STATES NAVY

A History

By CARROLL STORRS ALDEN, PH.D.
Former Head of the Department of English, History, and Government, United States Naval Academy

And ALLAN WESTCOTT, PH.D.
Senior Professor of the Department of English, History, and Government, United States Naval Academy

J. B. LIPPINCOTT COMPANY
CHICAGO · PHILADELPHIA · NEW YORK

E
182
.A353
1943

973
Alden

COPYRIGHT, 1943, BY J. B. LIPPINCOTT COMPANY

LIBRARY
FLORIDA STATE COLLEGE FOR WOMEN
TALLAHASSEE, FLORIDA

Printed in the United States of America

PREFACE

IN EVERY war, the need for safeguarding our shores, shipping, and sea communications has called for a tremendous naval expansion, which could never have been achieved without the backbone of a strong, well-trained, permanent navy. But after every war, there has been a call from many to disband the fleet and scrap the ships. As a matter of fact, not only in the stress of emergency but in the normal growth of the Republic—its extension of maritime trade, its scientific and industrial progress, and its westward expansion—the Navy has had an important part. If the present history were to have an additional sub-title, it would be "Our National Navy." More and more, both the personnel of the Navy and the people of the Nation have come to realize the increasing breadth of its mission. It is not only "our first line of defense"; it has a significant bearing on our commercial and economic interests and, in peace and war, on our political relations with other powers. This broad mission of the Navy the authors have sought constantly to keep in view.

A second fundamental idea they have stressed is one that logically follows: the full measure of power is to be gained only by co-operation. Our first squadron in the Revolution was commanded by a Marblehead skipper who later rendered outstanding service in the Continental Navy, but who was commissioned and sent out by General Washington, chief in command of the Army. His mission was not only to interrupt

5-19-44 Stech. 4.13
97526

enemy sea communications but to provide our Army with sorely needed military supplies. Later in the war, the operations of Arnold's little makeshift flotilla on Lake Champlain had a vital effect on the land war; and the French fleet off the Virginia Capes made possible the victory at Yorktown. Similarly, the work of Macdonough in the War of 1812 and of DuPont, Foote, Farragut, and Porter in the Civil War attained their highest success in combined operations. On the other hand, two signal disasters of our arms may be attributed in large measure to lack of co-operation—the loss of the Norfolk Navy Yard in 1861 and the widespread destruction eighty years later at Pearl Harbor.

A new standard of combined operations was established in the First World War when the Navy safeguarded the Army in the convoys that carried over two million men to the battlefields of France, and from almost nothing developed a very creditable air power that operated by sea and land. Today the branches of our military forces are of necessity in still closer co-ordination, working together on land and sea and in the air, and in co-operation with our allies. In both the past and the present, the authors have sought to link naval activities with the general military strategy and the achievement of national aims.

To carry the naval story down to the year 1943 has meant increased compression and more condensed treatment of events that have lost some of their earlier importance. The references at the ends of chapters suggest works in which the subject matter is treated in greater detail, but no attempt has been made to indicate all the sources which the authors have used and to which credit is due. To fellow workers in the field of naval history and to our colleagues and others who have assisted us, the authors express their obligation and deep gratitude. Acknowledgement is also due Miss Helen Noel, who drew the maps and diagrams included in this book, and to Mr. Fred A. Walker, who made the drawings heading each chapter.

CARROLL STORRS ALDEN
ALLAN WESTCOTT

CONTENTS

LIST OF MAPS AND DIAGRAMS

The United States Navy

BEGINNINGS OF THE NAVY

I

An old and well-established tradition of Great Britain insures her colonies of protection by the Royal Navy. And because of the strength of the Royal Navy no colony in early times, nor in the present century—until several have risen to virtual independence in the dominion status—has gone to the expense of building a navy of its own. The Thirteen Colonies in North America had at various times their enemies on the sea as well as on the land, and could not but be vitally interested in the results of King William's War and of the French and Indian War, but they did not feel it necessary to supply a force to safeguard their own ships and harbors. Further, since commissions in the Royal Navy were not easy to obtain, it was extremely rare that a youth in a colonial family had naval training.

Immediately after Lexington and Concord steps were taken to improvise a navy. The Second Continental Congress had sources of no small importance to draw on. Pioneers are commonly strong and resourceful, and those of America had been disciplined and hardened in the struggle for life, in the wilderness and on the wild Atlantic. And, as it was easy to recruit a rough army from farmers and woodsmen, so it was practicable to improvise a navy from men of the merchant ships and fishing fleets. Each branch showed the lack of proper equipment; and the discipline, as is commonly the case with irregulars, was much better adapted for raids or brief operations than for ex-

LIBRARY
FLORIDA STATE COLLEGE FOR WOMEN
TALLAHASSEE, FLORIDA

tended campaigns. But the astonishing fact is that the "minutemen" boldly stood their ground against British regulars, and the extemporized fighting ships made daring raids almost within sight of ships of the Royal Navy.

Commerce in the Colonies

The Thirteen Colonies in 1760 contained about 1,500,000 people, white and black, and of these 473,000 lived in New England. It was the men of Massachusetts (including her northern frontier in Maine), New Hampshire, Rhode Island, and Connecticut who especially gave themselves to maritime activities. At the beginning the settlers in the northern colonies were a farming rather than a seafaring community. But their land, which was not as fertile as that of the middle and southern colonies, gave them only a meager subsistence. Thus, instead of feeling the lure of open country to the west, they were virtually driven back to the ocean. The sea supplied them with fish, and even as early as the middle of the seventeenth century furnished them with another highly important means of livelihood. Though they could not grow the abundant harvests of wheat, corn, tobacco, and rice raised elsewhere, they discovered they could make a good living by carrying these products for the people of other colonies and bringing to them what they required, and later doing the same, in lesser degree, for people in various distant lands. Also they carried and found a market for their own products—fish, lumber, and manufactured articles. Shipbuilding in Massachusetts began in 1631 with the launching of Governor Winthrop's *Blessing of the Bay* on the Mystic River, and within thirty years it became a leading industry in Newbury, Ipswich, Gloucester, Salem, and Boston.[1]

Reports of colonial commerce in 1771 show that the middle colonies exported 1,000,000 bushels of wheat and corn, and 36,000 tons of flour and bread, most of which went to the West

[1] S. E. Morison, *Maritime History of Massachusetts*, p. 14.

Indies. New England shipped to the same market cattle, hogs, sheep, and poultry; potatoes and turnips; 22,000 barrels of salted meats and 300,000 quintals of dried fish; besides large quantities of lumber, 42,000,000 feet of pine and oak, 62,000,000 shingles, whole houses in sections, as well as boats and cart wheels. The Sugar Islands were an excellent market; for the planters had found it cheaper to buy food for the slaves rather than divert labor to grow it, and followed the same policy to obtain building materials and manufactured articles.

On the return voyage from the West Indies, American ships brought in equally profitable cargoes, the article most often imported being molasses; in 1771, 4,159,008 gallons of it came to the colonies, one-half of which was utilized for making rum, distilled chiefly in Philadelphia, New York, Newport, Boston, and Medford. Besides molasses they brought in 2,160,790 gallons of West India rum and 213,201 gallons of heavy wine—six-sevenths Madeira and the rest port. Later, a small part of the rum, 5 per cent, was exported, chiefly to Africa to be bartered for negro slaves, ivory, and palm oil, and most of the remainder to Newfoundland to fortify the fishermen. It was the people at home, however, who made the commerce profitable—4,000,000 gallons of rum, besides the heavy wines, being consumed by them in twelve months. Our colonial ancestors were indeed a hardy stock.

In the articles exported to Great Britain, tobacco had long held a position of importance, and whatever may be said against the narcotic it certainly saved the colony of Virginia from early extinction. Rice and indigo from the southern colonies found a good market, also naval stores, tar, pitch, turpentine, and lumber of all kinds. New England supplied lumber and furs, and in return imported large quantities of salt, which was not produced in the North. Nearly 1,500,000 bushels of this commodity were brought in annually. The colonists had a great liking for spices of all kinds, and in twelve months consumed 150,000 pounds of pepper and paprika alone. Further, they imported from Great Britain forty to fifty different kinds of textiles, and in a single year a quarter of a million British-made hats, twenty-five thousand leghorn and chip hats for ladies' wear, shoes, boots, silk garters, fans, and one hundred kinds of drugs.[2] Life in those days was not so simple as is sometimes imagined.

This extensive commerce was significant, for it furnished a livelihood to American shipowners and merchants and produced thousands of hardy seamen, indispensable in building a navy.

Loyalty, Jealousy, and Division

The colonies in their early years were left very much alone. They bore nominal allegiance to the Crown, but until 1660 there was virtually nothing that independence could offer that was not theirs. In the eighteenth century, government in England became more definitely organized, and many of the charters and grants that had been so carelessly given were recalled. Thus in 1754 all but four of the colonies had become royal. From northeastern Massachusetts (Maine) to Georgia the people were loyal, but they demurred over the increasing regimentation and the application of the new order.

But however much the colonists objected, they were slow in drawing together and making a united resistance. They did not join in defending themselves against the common enemies in the Western Hemisphere. The French and Indian War was waged for definite American objectives: protection of settlers living on the frontiers, safeguarding of the fur trade, possession of the Ohio Valley, and title to the western lands. The colonies could not but be vitally interested in the outcome. Yet only Massachusetts, Connecticut, and New York contributed their quota of troops and money, and all drew back and let the British army and navy do most of the actual fighting. Further,

[2] E. Channing, *A History of the United States*, III, 108–111.

many of their merchants continued their normal foreign trade, even with the enemy.

On the instance of the Lords of Trade in London, in 1754, commissioners of seven colonies met in Albany to discuss Indian affairs and to work out a plan of union. Benjamin Franklin, who was one of the commissioners, produced what was known as the Albany Plan of Union. It promised to strengthen the defense and security of the colonies and bore considerable resemblance to the later Articles of Confederation. But although the commissioners all agreed to the plan, not one of the colonies would accept it. The people at home thought it represented too great a surrender of power. The New England colonies could work tolerably well together, but not with New York; New York, Maryland, and Virginia resented the lack of protection Pennsylvania gave to the western frontier and her policy of nonresistance; each colony was interested in its own problems, but suspicious and jealous of the other colonies as they dealt with theirs. The real union of the English settlers in North America and their descendants was destined to be of slow growth.

Merchant captains and fishermen in only a very few ports took a prominent part in the independence movement. They lived a life that was somewhat apart; they found navigation acts at times inconvenient, but they evaded them; they did not fancy customs restrictions, and they had no scruples in ignoring them and resorting to smuggling. As a class they had their limitations. They were plain people and could furnish no officer comparable to Washington, no leaders of political thought comparable to Franklin, Jefferson, John Adams, and Hancock. They were accustomed to the organization of a single ship, and they would loyally support a captain. But beyond this they had not been trained. Their captains had no idea of how to follow a commodore. A squadron might be assembled and a commander in chief appointed, but the squadron seldom held together for more than a few days or was effective for more than a single project.

Unified Feeling against English Coercion

When thus for a century and a half the dominant trends in the Thirteen Colonies had been so individualistic, how could these people have merged into a confederation capable of standing the strain of a seven years' war for independence and how could they have developed a navy that challenged the great Royal Navy and carried war even into British waters?

The opposition to England that led directly to the American Revolution was in the beginning a small minority movement. But the agitators were outspoken and they possessed strong feeling. Being highly aggressive, they exerted an influence quite beyond that of the conservatives. Soon some of the moderates were won over. Then the general feeling became inflamed as the British government took a stronger stand and sent agents who resorted to force. After the first shots were fired, people had to take sides, and the loyalists diminished in number. The colonists then exhibited a oneness of feeling such as had never existed in the Western Hemisphere before.

This consciousness of a common cause followed close after the "Intolerable Acts," most drastic of which was the closing of the port of Boston, June 1, 1774. Parliament had regarded this retaliatory act as mild. For royal authority had been repeatedly flouted by the colonists, and finally the imperial monopoly granted to the great East India Company had been treated with contumely as the costly cargoes of tea in three ships were thrown overboard in Boston Harbor. But the people of Massachusetts looked upon the Boston Port Act as threatening their very life—they could not be excluded from the sea without losing their main dependence. The measure, instead of cowing them, drove them into open rebellion. And it was the fishermen and sailors of Massachusetts who were affected beyond any others. With the "minutemen" they were ready to fight at the first call.

Boston thus became the headquarters of revolution. Before her people could have felt the real force of the restrictions, a great wave of sympathy swept through the central and southern colonies. Money and food poured into Boston. A flock of sheep was driven from Connecticut by Israel Putnam. One thousand barrels of flour came from Philadelphia, 9,000 bushels of wheat and corn from Virginia, and cargoes of rice from Charleston.

The seamen and fishermen, not only of Boston but of Gloucester and Salem, Portsmouth, Providence, Philadelphia, and Baltimore, had already decided on which side they stood. That any of their people should be barred from the sea aroused their fighting spirit.

They lacked naval organization and training, but they were strong and resourceful and they had fighting spirit. Many had sailed in privateers in the French and Indian as well as the European wars, and they required little training in this guerrilla-type of fighting. Some had engaged in the famous expedition against Louisbourg in 1745—organized in Massachusetts, which sent a considerable force of transports and provincial cruisers and privateers, although the real naval support came from four ships of respectable size from the Royal Navy. They were daring and aggressive and they wanted only a semblance of official authorization before they sailed out in quest of British supply ships that already had been dispatched with munitions and equipment for the forces dealing with the insurrection. The seamen and fishermen were plain people, but their hearts were stout. These were the men who converted their vessels into warships, almost overnight, and formed our first navy.

References

Andrews, C. M., *The Colonial Period of American History,* Vol IV, 1938.

Channing, E., *A History of the United States,* Vols. II, III, 1905.

Cooper, J. F., *The History of the Navy of the United States of America,* 2 vols., 1839.

Knox, D. W., *A History of the United States Navy,* 1936.

Maclay, E. S., *A History of the United States Navy,* 3 vols., 1894–1907.

Morison, S. E., *The Maritime History of Massachusetts,* 1921.

Parkman, Francis, *A Half Century of Conflict,* Vol. II, 1892.

THE WAR OF INDEPENDENCE II

The Marine Committee

THE MONTH OF October, 1775, was momentous in our naval history. It was marked by the decision of the Second Continental Congress to fit out four armed vessels. This was the beginning of the Continental Navy. Delegates from Rhode Island had brought with them instructions urging the fitting out of a fleet to protect the coast. The proposal at once gained the support of maritime New England and encountered opposition from the agriculturally minded southern colonies. John Adams of Massachusetts, who strongly favored it, reports that Mr. Chase of Maryland declared, "It is the maddest idea in the world to think of building an American fleet; its latitude is wonderful; we should mortgage the whole continent." The Naval Committee appointed to report on the practicability of the project consisted of three New Englanders, one of them John Adams. They lost no time in expressing their approval, but action was strategically delayed until the feeling was more generally favorable. On the thirtieth of the month Congress fully committed itself by ordering the vessels recommended by the committee, voting, four days later, $100,-000 to meet the expense. Already the Naval Committee of three members had been enlarged to seven, and it was soon superseded by the Marine Committee of thirteen members, one for each colony. It included such outstanding figures as John

Hancock, Samuel Adams, Stephen Hopkins, Robert Morris, Richard Henry Lee, Joseph Hewes, and Henry Laurens.

The Marine Committee might be termed the original Navy Department. It was an executive as well as a legislative body. It reported to Congress on the ships required and secured the authorization to build them and fit them out. It purchased merchant vessels that could be converted into warships, and secured ammunition and naval stores. It attended to the appointment of officers, at first making all the appointments itself and later acting with the Naval Boards,[1] naval commissioners in foreign ports, and captains of the ships concerned. It established the Marine Corps November 10, 1775, organizing the First and Second Battalion of American Marines. It prepared a code of rules to promote discipline in the fleet—the forerunner of "Naval Regulations."

From the beginning the mass of details proved too great for this committee and it wisely delegated many duties to the boards and agents acting under it. The committee suffered also by being too large. But whatever its members may have remarked on their own limitations, the Marine Committee was without question the power that directed naval affairs during the first four years of the war, the period when the Continental Navy was at its height. In December, 1779, a Board of Admiralty of five members took over the duties of the Marine Committee, and this lasted for a year and a half. Then the Agent of Marine, Robert Morris, was given charge of all naval affairs.

Privateers

Throughout the Revolution three distinct naval organizations prevailed: the privateers, the state navies, and the Con-

[1] Two Naval Boards, one at Boston and the other at Philadelphia, were authorized by Congress. Each was composed of three persons "well skilled in maritime affairs" to attend to the construction or purchase, fitting out, provisioning, and manning of naval vessels in its district, as well as their repair. These boards were to keep the Marine Committee informed of the arrival and departure of Continental war vessels, settle naval accounts, pay officers and men, and audit the accounts of prize agents.

tinental Navy. The privateers had the largest numbers of ships and men; and though often ill prepared and uncertain in operation, they caused heavy losses to British merchants and shipowners.

Massachusetts, by action of its General Court, began to issue letters of marque on November 1, 1775, and other states followed. The largest number of American privateers, however, were those that received their authorization from the Continental Congress. Altogether there were not less than 2,000 privately armed vessels that played their part in the war, mounting 18,000 guns and operated by 70,000 men.

Many a seaman in Providence or Philadelphia had already felt the lure of privateering, having tried it in the French and Indian War. The possible returns from a successful cruise, on which a single prize amounting to fifty or a hundred thousand dollars was to be divided between the shipowner and officers and men, often proved demoralizing. The share that came to the captain, whose pay according to the schedule of the Continental Navy was thirty-two dollars a month, made him wealthy for the rest of his life, and even a seaman, whose pay was six and two-thirds dollar a month, might receive a thousand dollars. The dream of sudden wealth was hard to resist, and in consequence Continental frigates or brigs, which held to the published pay schedule for the most part, could not get a full complement in ports where privateers had shipped every sailor for miles around.

It happened also that officers of the Continental Navy, when their assignments were delayed, not infrequently filled in the time by taking out a privateer that was ready. Thus, Joshua Barney, a lieutenant at the beginning of the Revolution and an outstanding captain in the War of 1812, first came to public notice when he commanded a privateer. He was captured and confined in Mill Prison, England. After making his escape, he commanded the *Hyder Ally,* a merchant ship armed with sixteen 6-pounders, which was fitted out as a privateer by merchants of Philadelphia. In this he engaged the *General Monk,* larger and stronger, and after a hotly contested battle of thirty minutes made her a prize and took her in to Philadelphia. John Barry, who rendered brilliant service in the Continental Navy, also tried privateering when he was not otherwise occupied and took several prizes. Thomas Truxtun, who attained distinction in the naval war with France at the close of the century, with the *Independence,* 10 guns, took a merchantman armed with 16 guns; later in the *Mars,* 24 guns, he cruised in the English Channel and sent his prizes into Quiberon Bay. Stephen Decatur, Sr., father of the officer of the same name who won fame in the Tripolitan War and the War of 1812, did not hesitate, in his privateer, to engage the British cruiser *Active* and captured her. Silas Talbot, though holding a commission as an officer in the Army, in the little *Argo,* a sloop of 100 tons, armed with twelve 6-pounders, put out from Providence and took five prizes practically without fighting. After this he boldly engaged the British privateer *Dragon,* three times his size and armed with fourteen 6-pounders. This time he had a real battle, and when the enemy struck, the *Argo* required prompt attention to prevent her sinking. Hardly had temporary repairs been made when the lookout reported the *Hannah,* 200 tons, armed with twelve 12-pounders and two 6-pounders. This he also took and sent her into New Bedford with the *Dragon.* These were the exploits of a colonel in the Army. It is no wonder that Congress commissioned him a captain in the Navy, and he continued as a naval officer even after the war.

American privateersmen were bold. They attacked British commerce with success in the West Indies and even in British home waters. They had to their credit the capture of nine or more small cruisers of the Royal Navy. Exact figures of their total captures are not to be had, but it is estimated that they took more than seven hundred prizes during the first two years of the war. On the other hand, the British had about as many privateers as the states, and they made many captures—both of American merchantmen and of privateers. But the losses sustained by American shipowners were less, for their ships were smaller. Privateers in their raids on commerce played a role not unlike that of submarines in recent warfare. They caused a sharp rise in British insurance rates and placed a heavy burden on shipowners and merchants. They served to make the war unpopular in England, and thus had a highly important influence.

The State Navies

With the exception of New Jersey and Delaware all of the states maintained armed vessels to protect their harbors and commerce. Massachusetts led in numbers and activity, and after Massachusetts no other state sent out so many deep-sea craft as South Carolina. The state navies combined had more ships than the Continental Navy, but their vessels were for the most part smaller and not so well armed. Together with a few large ships mounting 10 to 20 guns there were many designed solely for defense, intended to operate only in the rivers and shallow waters of the coast, and including galleys, with or without sails, floating batteries, and fire ships.

The early service of the Massachusetts and South Carolina navies was the intercepting of British supply ships and securing powder that was so much needed by the Continental Army. They continued throughout the war to take prizes, Massachusetts about seventy, South Carolina thirty-five or more, and Connecticut thirty. Some of the prizes were recaptured, and the successes of the state navies were often offset by the captures made by the British.

The one ambitious operation undertaken by ships of this category was the Penobscot Expedition, which departed with great acclaim but proved to be the outstanding naval fiasco of the war.

The coast of Maine, commonly spoken of as the "Eastern Coast" of Massachusetts, was hard to defend. In 1779 the British had established a base for sending out marauding expeditions near the present site of Castine at the mouth of the Penobscot, and they had stationed there some eight hundred men. Massachusetts took measures to end the menace. Furnishing three brigantines of its own navy and thirteen privateers, it secured the co-operation of New Hampshire, which contributed one vessel of its state navy, and also of the Continental Navy, which supplied three ships and a ranking officer, Captain Dudley Saltonstal, to command the expedition. Thus the fleet comprised twenty armed vessels with 2,000 men. Also it was accompanied by twenty transports, bearing 1,000 of the state militia.

Such extensive preparations could not be kept secret and information reaching New York caused the sending of a British fleet. The initial attack by the American force on arrival was not a surprise, and it was resisted successfully by the force stationed on the Penobscot. As a second attack was about to begin, the fleet from New York, commanded by Sir George Collier, appeared. This consisted of ten vessels and 1,600 men, fewer in numbers than the American force but superior in strength, for it included a ship of the line of 64 guns. The two fleets were scarcely within range when the American force was seized with panic. Offering practically no resistance, they fled up the river, ran their ships ashore, and set fire to them. Soldiers and sailors then made their way on foot through the forest back to Massachusetts. The American losses amounted to 474 men, the British, 13. The affair afforded a lesson which history shows is hard for our people to grasp: an assembly of ships is not a fleet, and a military force of men individually capable and strong but without organization and training is ineffective.

The Continental Navy

In the American Revolution the Continental Navy provided the backbone of the naval fighting force. Its ships were the "regulars," and notwithstanding small numbers they were at times truly effective. The Continental Navy had a rudimentary organization. It worked under the Naval and Marine Committees and had their support so far as they were able to give it. It was handicapped by not coming into existence until after fighting had begun. It was an improvised force, two-thirds of its ships being made-over merchantmen and the crews being drawn from merchant vessels, fishing craft, whalers, or even from the Army. Because so many sailors were absorbed by the privateer service, it never had the manpower the colonies should have supplied. At its maximum, in the fall of 1776, it had twenty-seven ships in commission—a small force to oppose the great Royal Navy, which at the opening of the Revolution had 270 ships and at the close 480. And the disproportion was heightened by the greater average size of the British ships and their heavier guns. To venture forth on the high seas against such odds required men of splendid courage.

Washington's Fleet

The first armed ships that sailed under Continental control and pay were those fitted out by General Washington in the fall of 1775 to meet his needs while laying siege to Boston. On the second of September the schooner *Hannah,* commanded by Nicholson Broughton, a captain in the Army, with orders signed by Washington was sent out with instructions to take all vessels sailing to or from Boston in the service of the British Army. In the following months six schooners and a brigantine were added, and Captain John Manly, a real sailor from Marblehead, was appointed commander in chief of the fleet. Washington still exercised its management. Altogether it captured thirty-five prizes—the best the *Nancy,* taken by Manly in the *Lee,* 4 guns, with a complement of fifty officers and men. In the *Nancy* he took 2,000 muskets, 100,000 flints, 30,000 round shot, 30 tons of musket shot, etc., stores that in 1775 were a godsend to the Continental forces, who would have waited eighteen months for the manufacture of a like quantity at home. In June, 1776, this fleet with the *Defense,* of the Continental Navy, captured four British transports loaded with supplies and more than 350 Scottish troops.[2]

Fleet of Esek Hopkins

Let us return now to the activities of the Naval Committee, which, as related, authorized the fitting out of the first four ships. The committee worked with dispatch and, in less than a week after it had been empowered to go ahead, had appointed Esek Hopkins of Rhode Island to be commander in chief. He was a brother of Stephen Hopkins, a member of the committee and former governor of Rhode Island. He was fifty-two years old, and his sea life as captain of a merchantman had begun thirty years before. In the French and Indian War he had commanded a privateer. Heading the list of five first lieutenants appointed at this time was John Paul Jones. A month later the committee issued to Hopkins the fleet operations orders. Wind and weather permitting, he was to sail to Chesapeake Bay, there, if the enemy force were not greatly superior to his own, to "search out and attack, take or destroy" all enemy ships found. After executing this assignment, he was to proceed immediately to the southward and overcome such forces as the enemy had in North and South Carolina waters. And then, "having completed your business in the Carolinas you are without delay to proceed northward directly to Rhode Island, and attack, take and destroy all the enemies' naval force that you may find there."

The bold optimism of the committee was magnificent. But the lack of understanding of the limitations of a fleet planned for, but not yet assembled, was indeed naive. Fortunately at the conclusion of these "particular orders," as the committee

[2] For an excellent study of the early organization of the Navy and the first operations, see Paullin's *The Navy of the American Revolution.*

termed them, a loophole was left: in case of unfavorable winds or weather or any unforeseen accident or disaster, Hopkins was to follow his own best judgment.

Throughout January, in a winter of unusual severity, the Delaware River, where lay the nucleus of the fleet, was frozen and the ships could not move. When in February Hopkins got under way and left Philadelphia amid enthusiastic cheers from the crowds assembled on the banks, he proceeded to ignore all orders except the order to follow his own best judgment. He directed the captains of his eight ships on clearing Delaware Capes to sail to an appointed rendezvous off the Bahamas, and from there he proceeded to Nassau in New Providence. He may not have been altogether at fault in what he did. The British had increased their force in the Chesapeake. The resistance he encountered at Nassau was nil, and the capture amounted to eighty-eight cannon, fifteen mortars, and a large quantity of shot and other munitions. For this he was much commended, but the next operation proved his undoing.

As he was returning to Rhode Island, he encountered off Long Island H.M.S. *Glasgow,* 20 guns, commanded by Captain Tryingham Howe. It was at midnight that this stranger entered the squadron. On being hailed, Howe responded with a broadside. Although in the confused night action that continued for three hours he was fighting five Continental ships, during much of the time he dealt with them singly and his fire was much more effective. Finally, when the odds were becoming too heavy, he made his escape. It was again a demonstration of power afforded by organization and training. The American loss was twenty-four killed or wounded, and the British four. This virtually ended Hopkins' naval career, and Congress appointed no further commander in chief.

Arnold's Operations on Lake Champlain

The scene now changes to the inland waterways, in 1776, and to activities which in the grand strategy of the war had an importance beyond that of any other American naval action. Mahan characterizes the struggle for Lake Champlain as "a strife of pygmies for the prize of a continent." [3]

In this Benedict Arnold, who later was to become a traitor, showed himself an officer of outstanding force and ability. Immediately on receiving news of Lexington he had assembled a group of volunteers in New Haven, Connecticut, marched them to Cambridge, and then, with orders issued by the Provincial Congress of Massachusetts, which had given him the rank of colonel, he set out for Lake Champlain, where he joined Ethan Allen in taking Ticonderoga and Crown Point. Late in the autumn, with 1,100 men recruited in Massachusetts, he toiled through Maine and Canada and appeared before Quebec. There he combined with General Montgomery, who led another force; and the American Army, after failing in an assault, laid siege to General Guy Carleton in the famous citadel. Montgomery was killed, and the siege, though it continued for five months, was unsuccessful. Finally, weakened by smallpox and lack of supplies, Arnold's force was compelled to fall back to Crown Point before re-enforcements brought by a British fleet under the command of Captain Charles Douglas.

About this time, July, 1776, Arnold was appointed by General Gates to command the American naval forces on Lake Champlain and Lake George. Fully a year before, Arnold had recognized the advantages afforded by their control. Even at that time he had seized an armed schooner, which enabled him temporarily to occupy the fortifications erected by the British at St. John's, situated at the northern end of Lake Champlain, and to seize the military stores placed there. On his return he urged Congress to insure control of the waterway by building what would prove to be an overwhelming force. To accomplish this he recommended the sending of three hundred carpenters to construct twenty or thirty galleys and gondolas and

---

[3] A. T. Mahan, *Major Operations of the Navies in the War of American Independence*, p. 18. From his excellent chapter on "The Naval Campaign on Lake Champlain," the authors have drawn freely.

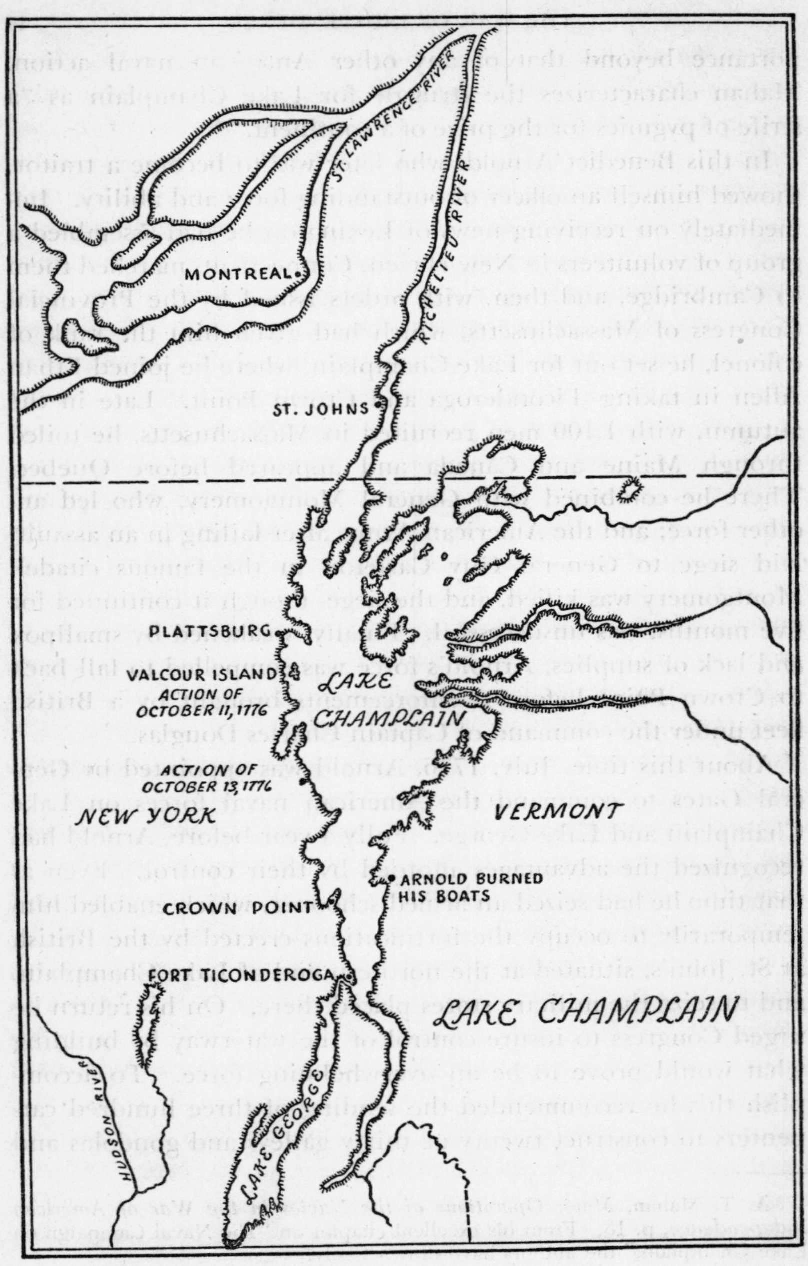
ST. LAWRENCE RIVER
RICHELIEU RIVER
MONTREAL
ST. JOHNS
PLATTSBURG
VALCOUR ISLAND
ACTION OF OCTOBER 11, 1776
LAKE CHAMPLAIN
ACTION OF OCTOBER 13, 1776
NEW YORK
VERMONT
ARNOLD BURNED HIS BOATS
CROWN POINT
FORT TICONDEROGA
LAKE CHAMPLAIN
HUDSON RIVER
LAKE GEORGE

also a 36-gun frigate. Work was begun, but not on the grand scale proposed. Three armed schooners, a sloop, and several galleys and gondolas were eventually built or purchased, but no frigate. Meanwhile, the British in the summer of 1776, drawing on their fleet and transports in the St. Lawrence for men and stores, again showed superior organization. A ship under construction at Quebec was taken apart almost to the keel, and frames and timbers were placed on long boats and floated up the Richelieu River to be reassembled at St. John's. Two fairly large schooners were also brought there, as well as gondolas. Thus, early in October Carleton had outbuilt Arnold and was ready to assert control of Lake Champlain. When the opposing squadrons met in battle, the British could bring forty-two guns to bear against their opponents' thirty-two, and the disproportion was greater than is shown by these figures; for H.M.S. *Inflexible,* armed with eighteen 12-pounders, was of 180 tons burden. She was ship-rigged, with timbers heavy enough for Atlantic storms, stronger indeed than many of the privateers that took prizes in the Caribbean and European waters. With a favorable wind for maneuvering, she should have been able unassisted to clear the lake of opposing craft. She approximated what Arnold had vainly urged Congress to build.

Arnold had swept the lake until the British completed their military preparations; then he sailed southward and decided to meet his enemy in the bay between Valcour Island and the western shore. Well in advance he had made soundings, and he drew up his force so that Carleton in coming up the channel to attack must do so where only a part of his squadron would be effective.

For months Carleton had been waiting impatiently to fight a decisive battle—delayed by the necessity of building and equipping a force that would give him control of the lake and by the difficulty of operating in what to him was indeed wilderness. Perhaps this may explain why on the eleventh of October, as his squadron sailed up the lake or toward the southern end, before a fresh northeast wind, he was carried on by his enthusiasm and neglected to send out scouts to report the position of his enemy. Not until he had passed beyond Valcour Island with its high protecting bluffs did he realize that he had gone too far and must beat back and attack from leeward.

Arnold had drawn up his force in a half-moon formation. On the approach of the British schooner *Carleton,* which had outstripped her companions, he was able to concentrate his fire on her. He used her so hardly that she was reduced to helplessness. Also, he sank a British artillery boat. The *Carleton* at length was ordered to withdraw, but was unable to make sail and had to be towed away by artillery boats sent to her assistance. On the other hand, one of Arnold's schooners, whose commander had not fully grasped his plan of battle, and a gondola were lost to the enemy. At the end of the day, when the *Inflexible* succeeded in approaching to point-blank range where she could bring fresh broadsides to bear on the exhausted American force, she quickly reduced their fire. The British now being certain of victory, and darkness coming on, the *Inflexible* fell back out of range, and the squadron took a position between the south end of the island and the mainland.

Arnold, however, was determined to save all of his small vessels that he could. Aided by a heavy mist and negligence on the part of the British, who failed to station a proper lookout, he slipped past their ships unobserved. He set sail for Crown Point, but the wind proved unfavorable and the injured ships could make only very slow speed. Morning found him at anchor in an inlet far from the desired haven.

Great was the chagrin and anger of Carleton as he discovered the quarry had escaped. He spent the day in a vain search and then returned to Valcour Island, where he learned from scouts that the Americans were at Schuyler's Island, eight miles south. At about this time, Arnold's crippled vessels were again setting out for Crown Point. Throughout the night they were pursued by the British, who overtook them in the morning. A spirited resistance, lasting two hours and a half, followed. Arnold and his second in command, General Waterbury, bringing up the rear, each in a galley, came under the heaviest fire. General Waterbury was killed and his galley was taken. Whereupon Arnold, realizing that his men could not hold out much longer, ran his galley and four gondolas ashore in a small creek, set fire to them, and made his way with the crews through the woods to Crown Point.

Altogether the Americans lost, by capture or burning in the three days' battle, ten out of the fifteen vessels with which they had begun the action and eighty men killed or wounded. The British lost forty men. But the American sacrifice had been worth while. The British, because of the several months' delay imposed upon them in obtaining control of the lake, could not advance until the middle of autumn. Their strategic plan had contemplated that Burgoyne, who was in Canada, should march south and at Albany join Howe, who was to advance up the Hudson. The combined armies could thus sever the northern from the southern colonies. But when all was ready, winter was approaching and the British found it prudent to postpone this operation until the following year. In 1777, when the advance from the north was resumed, Burgoyne, although he succeeded in taking Crown Point and Ticonderoga, failed to have the support of Howe, who had gone to the Chesapeake in a move against Philadelphia. In consequence, he was defeated at Saratoga. This was the turning point of the war, for the success on the part of the colonies induced France to enter the struggle and to give essential aid.

American Operations in European Waters

The sloop *Reprisal,* commanded by Captain Lambert Wickes, was the first of the Continental Navy to arrive in European waters, December, 1776. Wickes had sailed to take Benjamin Franklin to France. On the way over he captured two prizes which he took into Nantes, where they were privately sold. In the February following, he left for a cruise in the Bay of Biscay and returned a few days later with five prizes, one of them the Falmouth packet, which he brought into L'Orient. Because of the loud protests of Lord Stormont, the British ambassador, the French government ordered the *Reprisal* and her prizes to leave within twenty-four hours. But Wickes, urging the necessity of repairs, calmly continued in port and secured the friendly interest of French merchants by selling them the prizes at one-seventh of their value. The American Commissioners in Paris, three months later, thinking that the British protests could be evaded, sent the *Reprisal* out again, this time accompanied by the *Lexington* and the *Dolphin*, with Wickes as commodore. He cruised for a month off the shores of the British Isles and took eighteen prizes.

Wickes had certainly been successful. He "most effectually alarmed England, prevented the great fair at Chester, occasioned insurance to rise, and even deterred the English merchants from shipping goods in English bottoms at any rate; so that in a few weeks forty sail of French ships were loading in the Thames on freight; an instance never before known." [4]

This and the similar activities of Captain Conyngham, recounted later, raised an uproar which became so threatening that the French were forced to take a stronger stand. Whereupon the American Commissioners, yielding to the pressure, issued orders for the *Reprisal* and *Lexington* to proceed to America. On the banks of Newfoundland the *Reprisal* foundered, and the Continental Navy lost in Wickes one of its most gallant captains.

The exploits of Gustavus Conyngham, Irish by birth, parallel those of Wickes. He had been commissioned a captain in the Continental Navy by the American Naval Office in Paris, and was given command of the *Surprise*, a lugger bought in Dunkirk and armed with ten guns. Setting out from that port May 1, 1777, he returned in a few days with two prizes, one of them the British mail packet from Harwich. On this affront

[4] Deane to Robert Morris, August 23, 1777. Wharton, *Diplomatic Correspondence*, II, 380.

Stormont went to the French premier and foreign minister and blustered so vehemently that they gave orders to release the prizes and seize the *Surprise,* throwing the captain and crew into prison. But Conyngham was quickly released and a larger ship, the *Revenge,* was provided for him. Though he was sharply watched by British agents, he sailed in July from Dunkirk, eluded British frigates, sloops of war, and cutters that chased him, and took prizes in the North Sea, Irish Sea, and Atlantic. Two years later on the American coast, he was captured by the British frigate *Galatea* and taken into New York. A prisoner so important was ordered for transfer to the famous Mill Prison, Plymouth. There, in November, 1779, he burrowed his way out, with sixty others or, as he expressed it, "committed treason through His Majesty's earth." Making his way to London, he succeeded in crossing to Holland and then to France.

John Barry, also Irish by birth, who had already achieved success as a privateersman, was given command of the new frigate *Alliance,* 36 guns. Leaving New London in August, 1782, he cruised east and overtook a fleet of Jamaicamen. Capturing nine prizes, he succeeded in bringing four of them into L'Orient. Their rich cargoes of rum and sugar sold for £620,610, an ample return for a short cruise. On March 10, 1783, he engaged the frigate *Sibylle,* 32 guns, the indecisive action of forty-five minutes being the last naval battle of the Revolution.

John Paul Jones's Cruises in American and European Waters

The Scotsman John Paul Jones, though only twenty-eight years old at the beginning of the Revolution, already had a knowledge of naval organization probably beyond that of any other officer in the Continental Navy. He had served several years as a midshipman in the Royal Navy, owing his appointment to the interest of the Duke of Queensbury. Later he had risen in the British merchant marine until he commanded a ship. In the fleet of Esek Hopkins he might at the beginning have had the sloop of war *Providence* or the *Fly,* but as he modestly stated, he realized that he was "imperfect in the duties of a Lieutenant" and preferred to remain in the flagship *Alfred,* where he thought association with the highest officers would rapidly increase his professional knowledge. In this he was doomed to be disappointed.

After Hopkins' fleet had returned from its cruise and the lamentable engagement with the *Glasgow,* Jones was again offered the command of the *Providence,* and this time he accepted. He had now been promoted to captain, and he quickly demonstrated that he deserved the rank. He convoyed some of Washington's troops in the spring of 1776 from Rhode Island to New York, and then sailed on a six-months' cruise against the commerce in the St. Lawrence and about Nova Scotia. The operation was full of daring, for the British ships were heavily convoyed, and twice frigates of size gave him a hot chase. But before his return he had taken sixteen prizes, eight of which he manned and sent in. Setting out again, this time in command of the *Alfred,* he captured with other prizes a large armed vessel having in her cargo a thousand complete uniforms intended for troops of Generals Carleton and Burgoyne in Canada, but destined to bring comfort to Washington's ill-clad army.

The Marine Committee, convinced of Jones's ability, now attempted to give him a proper command. But communications were slow, and the jealousy of Esek Hopkins and others prevented his obtaining it. Jones, who was extremely sensitive, had the mortification of seeing officers junior to him, who had done nothing in comparison, advanced over him. Going to Philadelphia, where Congress was sitting, he applied directly to the Marine Committee.

What the naval establishment especially needed was organization. Jones recognized this and in response to the invitation of the Marine Committee he formulated some essential principles.

The following letter which he wrote to Robert Morris (Chairman of the Marine Committee), February 10, 1777, shows his clear vision:

It would give me much more pleasure could I Join with the other Commanders in Pointing out hints for Useful Rules and Regulations. . . . There are no Officers more immediately wanted in the marine department than Commissioners of Dock Yards to Superintend the Building and Outfit of all Ships of war. . . . The Navy is in a wretched Condition.—It wants a man of Abilities at its head who could bring on a Purgation and Distinguish between the Abilities of a Gentleman and those of a mere Sailor or Boatswain's Mate. . . . Unless some happy expedient can be fallen upon to induce the Seamen to Enter into the Service for a longer term than Twelve Months it will never be possible to bring them under proper Subordination.

And to John Hancock he wrote, April, 1777:

It may also be expedient to establish an Academy at each Dock Yard under proper Masters, who'es duty it should be to instruct the officers of the Fleet when in Port in the Principles and application of the mathematicks, Drawing, Fencing and other manly Arts and Accomplishments. It will be requisite that young Men serve a certain term in Quality of Midshipmen, or Masters mate before they are examined for promotion.

The organization of the Navy was to be of slow growth, and Jones's recommendations, sound though they were, brought no immediate action. The Continental Congress did not establish a code of rules and regulations for the government of the Navy, such as Jones suggested, nor commissioners of dock yards, nor a naval academy. But within three-quarters of a century all of these had come into existence.

Robert Morris, still intent on advancing Jones, now planned to send him to Europe so that he might receive the command of a frigate building in Amsterdam under the direction of Silas Deane, American Commissioner at Paris. But Jones had to wait until the *Ranger,* under construction at Portsmouth, New

Hampshire, should be ready. The jealousy of the Hopkins faction again embarrassed him in securing his complement of officers and men. Those shipped were not of Jones's choosing, and they constantly gave trouble. Further, the frigate building in Amsterdam proved to be a disappointment. The British ambassador at the Hague, hearing of its intended use, applied such pressure upon the Dutch government, then neutral, that Deane sold her to prevent confiscation.

But Jones, going to Paris, met Benjamin Franklin, with whom he formed a lasting friendship. With the latter's encouragement he determined to use what he had and make a cruise in European waters that should surpass the exploits of Wickes and Conyngham. He reached his decision in spite of the known feeling of no small number of his men, who openly said they "had no turn for enterprise." With the first lieutenant, Simpson, they were repeatedly on the verge of mutiny.

Sailing from Brest, April 10, 1778, he took a prize off the Scilly Isles and then proceeded north through St. George's Channel. Nearing Whitehaven, he conceived the bold project of entering the harbor and destroying the shipping. His men not responding to the idea, he called for volunteers and made up a party of thirty-one, who set out at midnight in two boats. He himself led the way with one of the groups into a fort guarding the bay. The sentinels being asleep, he met little or no opposition and spiked the guns in this and in another fort near by. Then he rejoined the officers and men of the other party, who were to set fire to the shipping but who stupidly had done nothing. The sun having risen, crowds began to gather as Jones with his own hands set fire to a large ship which occupied a central position. Holding the onlookers back with his pistol until the flames had reached the rigging, he then took his force off in safety.

At noon the same day, he sailed into Kirkcudbright Bay to St. Mary's Isle and attempted to capture the Earl of Selkirk in his castle—his thought being that so important a hostage would help to persuade the British to agree to the exchange of prisoners, a question on which they had long delayed in reaching a decision. But this, like the earlier project of the day, was unsuccessful. The people at Whitehaven had extinguished the flames when the raiding party withdrew, and the Earl of Selkirk proved not to be at home. But the raids were not without effect. They threw the entire coast into a state of alarm and compelled the British to devote an undue number of ships and men to its defense.

Next, to complete his work, he sailed over to Carrickfergus on the Irish coast opposite with the idea of engaging a sloop of war which he had caught a glimpse of some days earlier when he was passing.

As he approached, he discovered that the sloop, which was the *Drake,* was coming out. He let the *Drake* come up astern and within easy range. Then suddenly he brought the *Ranger* about, almost across the bows of his enemy, and raked her decks with destructive broadsides. Jones wrote:

> The action was warm, close, and obstinate. It lasted an hour and four minutes, when the enemy called for quarter; her fore and main topsail yards being cut away and down on the cap; the topgallant and mizzen gaff both hanging up and down along the mast; the second ensign, which they had hoisted, shot away and hanging in the water; the sails and rigging entirely cut to pieces, her masts and yards all wounded, and her hull very much galled.

The losses in the *Ranger* were two killed and six wounded; in the *Drake* forty-two killed and wounded—among the seriously wounded being the captain and lieutenant, who died later. The *Drake* supposedly was quite the equal of the *Ranger.* Though she was armed with twenty 4-pounders and the *Ranger* with eighteen 6-pounders, the slight disadvantage was balanced by the fact that she was larger and more heavily built. Her greatest handicap was new officers and a raw crew. On the other hand, Jones had men almost on the verge of mutiny. As he said, "Plunder rather than honor was the object of the *Ranger's* officers and crew. . . . I ran every chance of being killed or thrown overboard." The ring leader of the disaffected seamen was the first lieutenant, Thomas Simpson. Only a few days later, so fragrantly did he disobey orders that Jones put him under arrest.

An enthusiastic reception in France awaited Jones on his arrival with the *Ranger* and the *Drake*. The attitude of the American Commissioners, however, was puzzling; Arthur Lee seemed always to side with the enemies of Jones, Lieutenant Simpson and others; John Adams was rather cool; only Franklin, his understanding friend, gave him unfailing support. It was Franklin who helped him to obtain ships, who stimulated him by practical suggestions as they talked over plans for cruises, and who instilled in him confidence of ultimate success. The last was especially important, for Jones, temperamentally impatient and at times violent, made enemies and he found suspicion and jealousy hard to bear. He was magnificent in action, but in the long periods of inaction he was likely to be despondent and at times was close to melancholy. After the capture of the *Drake,* when the French court were making much of him, M. de Sartine, Minister of Marine, promised him a large ship. Consequently, at the urging of Arthur Lee, he consented to the sending home of the *Ranger* in command of Simpson.

But delay and disappointment continued to be his lot. Promises were made good only by new promises and he never received a command such as he merited. He was now to wait fifteen months before he had an opportunity of again putting to sea. Finally, by going to Paris and applying to de Sartine in person, he obtained, not the frigate he was seeking, but a ship of fair size to fly his flag. His new command was the *Duc de Duras,* an East India merchantman, fourteen years old, in wretched condition, which he now proceeded to make over and arm as a frigate. In gratitude to Franklin and his famous *Poor Richard's Almanac,* he named her the *Bonhomme Richard.* He had to scour France to find guns for her. He was promised that guns should be cast, but he was unwilling to wait and took what he found, among them, for his heaviest battery, six 18-pounders that had been condemned. He had like difficulty and ill fortune in obtaining officers and crew, 327 or more in number. Only seventy-nine were Americans, exchanged prisoners; 137 were French marines with two French officers lent by their government; and the rest were a strange assembly of Portuguese, Swedes, Malays, and even English prisoners—certainly unpromising material to mold into a well-disciplined crew. The saving element were the few efficient and loyal Americans (among them Lieutenant Richard Dale, who had escaped from Mill Prison, and Midshipman Fanning), together with the French marines.

In the squadron accompanying the *Bonhomme Richard,* 42 guns, were the *Alliance,* 36 guns, the *Pallas,* 20 guns, and two other small craft, the *Vengeance* and the *Cerf.* The *Alliance* was a well-built American frigate which had lately come over. In grateful recognition of their new ally, the Continental Congress gave command of her to a Frenchman, Pierre Landais. The choice could hardly have been worse. He was insubordinate and always giving trouble. It is strange that his record had not been inquired into before he was commissioned a captain in our Navy. He had been cashiered out of the French Navy. He was always erratic, and later developments showed that mentally he was not quite right. The expense of the cruise was borne by the French government, and though the squadron sailed under the American flag, orders to Jones outlining the cruise were prepared by the French minister of marine.

On August 14, 1779, the squadron sailed from L'Orient and laid its course to southern Ireland, then followed the west coast of Ireland and Scotland to the Orkneys, and finally encircled the British Isles. Various mishaps early occurred. Men in a boat that had been assigned duty in towing took opportunity to desert. Two American officers and twenty men who without waiting for orders took a ship's boat and went in pursuit, became lost in the fog, and were captured by the British. The *Cerf,* which was sent in search of the lost boats, was chased by a superior force and put back to France. The *Alliance,* under

CRUISES OF JOHN PAUL JONES
IN BRITISH WATERS
RANGER
BON HOMME RICHARD
SERAPIS
AFTER SEPTEMBER 25
ALLIANCE
AFTER DECEMBER 27
SCOTLAND
NORTH SEA
LEITH
EDINBURGH
ST. MARY'S ISLE
WHITEHAVEN
CARRICKFERGUS
IRELAND
FLAMBOROUGH
HEAD
TEXEL
ENGLAND
HOLLAND
LONDON
SPANISH
NETHER-
LANDS
ENGLISH CHANNEL
ATLANTIC OCEAN
PARIS
BREST
L'ORIENT
FRANCE
TO SPAIN

the unpredictable Pierre Landais, twice sailed away and was not seen for days. And as the squadron rounding Scotland continued its operations, all of the French captains objected to the protracted cruise and threatened to leave Jones and sail for France. This Jones was powerless to prevent if Landais and the others persisted. According to a concordat he had been obliged to sign just before sailing, although the squadron was supposed to work together, all of the captains had equal rank, and Jones had no assurance that such orders as he gave would be obeyed. Nevetherless, he followed the course which he had laid out, and on September 23, about one o'clock, sighted what he had discussed with Franklin as one of the principal objectives—the rich Baltic fleet. Forty-one sails he counted off Flamborough Head.

The merchant ships recognized their danger and fled, but their escorts, the frigates *Serapis* and *Countess of Scarborough,* held to their course and showed no unwillingness to meet the strangers. The wind was light so that it was not until seven o'clock in the evening that they were within hail. Jones was acutely aware of the dull sailing qualities of the *Richard* and saw that the *Serapis* could easily outdistance her. Thus, since his only chance of victory lay in a combat at close quarters, he made every effort to come as near as possible before the fighting should begin.

The Engagement Between the Bonhomme Richard *and the* Serapis.

On the first exchange of broadsides two of the old condemned 18-pounders of the *Richard,* which were mounted on the gun deck, burst, and the explosion killed nearly every man of their crews and tore a great hole in the side and deck above. The rest of this battery had to be abandoned, and the odds in favor of the *Serapis,* a new 50-gun frigate, fast and agile, as opposed to the 42-gun *Richard,* a worn-out East Indiaman, were now greatly increased. Backing his topsails, Jones then attempted to run under the stern of his enemy and obtain the coveted raking position that enabled a ship to use her broadsides effectively and at the same time expose herself to almost no fire in return. But Captain Richard Pearson, commanding the *Serapis,* took advantage of his speed and himself gained a raking position. Later, as he forged ahead and then reduced speed so that the *Richard* might draw alongside, Jones passed him enveloped in smoke and resorting to a skilful ruse, laid his ship across his opponent's course. Before Pearson was aware of this, the bowsprit of the *Serapis* came over the stern of the *Richard* by the mizzenmast. This was exactly what Jones wanted. Calling for a line he ordered an officer to secure the two ships together, and when the officer fumbled, Jones snatched it from him and lashed the enemy's jibstay to the mizzenmast of the *Richard.* The remainder of the battle was fought with the starboard bow of the *Serapis* against the starboard quarter of the *Richard,* the yards of the two ships interlocked and the muzzles of guns touching the side of the enemy.

When the battle had been in progress an hour, the *Richard* was very nearly a beaten ship. There was the yawning chasm in her starboard quarter already mentioned. Not only were the 18-pounders all silent, but the 12-pounders and 9-pounders on the main deck had been abandoned because of the superior heavy batteries of the British. Yet Jones would not give up, and when the purser in charge of the two 9-pounders on the quarter-deck was wounded, he himself took charge and brought over a third gun from the unengaged side. These were the only guns the Americans now had in action. At this point Lieutenant Dale brought up the force of American and French marines who had been serving the guns below. French marksmen in the tops, being heavily re-enforced, then succeeded, together with the quarter-deck guns, in silencing the British musket men and the gun crews on the forecastle and quarter-deck of the *Serapis,* and gained superiority, at least above.

Before this advantage had been won, the master at arms and the gunner of the *Richard,* dismayed by the fires below as well as by the rising water, were seized with panic. Joined by the carpenter, who had seen one of the pumps shot away, they spread the report that the *Richard* was sinking. Releasing five hundred English prisoners, they began calling for quarter and rushed to surrender. "What scoundrels are those?" cried Jones, and throwing both his pistols at the gunner who had attempted to haul down the flag, he felled him to the deck. Pearson had heard the cry for quarter, and hailed to ask if his enemies had struck.

"I have not yet begun to fight," Jones thundered back, responding to the challenge with a burst of spirit that has fired the Navy through all the years to follow.

Thereupon, Pearson assembled a boarding party to cross over and seize the *Richard.* But as they advanced from under cover, they encountered the fire of the French and American marksmen and then they met a party led by Jones in person. They retreated in disorder.

The British prisoners had for a while been a more serious threat than the boarding party as they swarmed up from below, but Jones forced them back; passing the word that the *Serapis* was sinking, he induced them to man the pumps of the *Richard* in order to save their own lives. One of their number, however, the captain of a merchantman, slipped through a gunport and on to the *Serapis.* Reaching Captain Pearson, he revealed the desperate condition of the *Richard.* Thereupon, Pearson redoubled the fire of his heavy guns, but they now had little effect; since the ships were held together in the same relative position they had occupied for the last two hours, the shot only passed through the holes already opened.

The British in the *Serapis* then experienced a new style of attack. A Yankee sailor climbed from the rigging of the *Richard* to the main yard of the *Serapis,* and dropped a hand grenade down an open hatchway. It happened that loose powder and cartridges brought forward for the guns of the main deck lay exposed there. In the flash that followed twenty officers and seamen of the *Serapis* were blown to pieces.

At this juncture the *Alliance* appeared. Once before, the crazy Landais had joined in the battle but had deliberately fired into the stern of the *Bonhomme Richard*. The bright moon had given no excuse for not recognizing the high poop and distinctive marking of the East Indiaman, and the men of the *Richard,* hailing, implored the *Alliance* not to kill their own countrymen. After this the American frigate sailed away. Now as she returned to the still struggling combatants, she fired grapeshot indiscriminately into both. Apparently the British did not recognize the damage the Frenchman was causing to his ally, for they were seized by panic. Jones, ever alert, noted that their fire was lessening and thereupon quickened his own. At half past ten, after an engagement that had been hotly contested for three hours and a half, the British plainly had all the spirit of fight taken out of them. Pearson himself hauled down the colors, for no one else would venture on deck. The losses had been heavy on each side: in the *Richard,* 116 killed and wounded, in the *Serapis,* 129.

Meanwhile Captain Cottineau, commanding the *Pallas,* had been engaging the *Countess of Scarborough,* and after an hour had captured her. He was about to turn his prize over to Landais and go to the support of Jones when Landais sailed off, as Cottineau supposed, with the same object in mind.

Both the *Bonhomme Richard* and the *Serapis* had been on fire in several places. The flames were now extinguished, but it was soon evident that the *Richard* was a hopeless wreck. The next day, when in spite of makeshift repairs and constant effort at the pumps she had five feet of water in her hold and was continuing to settle, Jones removed his men and prisoners to the *Serapis.* He stayed with his stricken ship to the last. On the second day, as he wrote, "I saw with inexpressible grief the last glimpse of the *Bonhomme Richard.*"

The *Serapis,* which had lost her main and mizzen masts and suffered other injuries, required several days for temporary repairs. The much perturbed British Admiralty sent out several squadrons in pursuit, but Jones eluded them and following instructions given by the French before he left, sailed into the Texel, Holland. The *Serapis* was accompanied by the other prize, *Countess of Scarborough,* as well as the *Alliance* and the *Pallas.* There, notwithstanding the British protests, he remained for twelve weeks. It is not unlikely that the influence of the victory had a part in inducing Holland shortly afterwards to abandon her neutrality and join the coalition against England.

The prizes being turned over to the French, Jones transferred his flag to the *Alliance.* Several British ships lay off the Texel for weeks watching for him. But on December 27 he sailed out, American colors flying, boldly passed a British fleet in the English Channel, and cruised off Spain, taking some small prizes. Then he returned to France, sailing into Groix Roads.

The French, though they had been slow and parsimonious in outfitting Jones, greeted him now as if he were their very own. The son of a humble Scotch gardener was welcomed in some of the most exclusive circles; he was received at court, being given by King Louis an inscribed sword, the medal of Military Merit, and the right to use the title Chevalier; and he was presented to Queen Marie Antoinette at Versailles. When he returned to America he was thanked by Congress and assigned by unanimous vote command of the 74-gun ship of the line *America,* then building at Portsmouth. She was by far the largest and most powerful ship built on this side of the Atlantic in all our early history. But Jones never obtained what was promised. After he had superintended the completion of her building, Congress, having been stirred by the loss of a French ship of the line that ran on the rocks in Boston Harbor, decided to present the *America* to France.

It happened that just at the time of Jones's notable victory with the *Bonhomme Richard* the French were discussing the dispatch to America of a large expeditionary force consisting of an imposing fleet and thousands of troops. Lafayette, who had already served under Washington, had returned to Paris to urge our cause and to assist in preparations, and he had long conversations with Jones. One of the objections to the sending of French troops made by certain French officers was based on the premise that their army and American colonial soldiers, having been opposed to each other in war only one or two decades before, might not get on very well together. Jones had shown to them he could fight at sea, and he made further conquests in Paris by his courtly manners. This was opportune when the sending of troops under Rochambeau and the fleet under de Grasse was being planned. Jones's victory was at least a link in the chain of events that led to Yorktown.

The Battle of Virginia Capes

Washington's great victory at Yorktown could not have been achieved had not the fleet of de Grasse given essential support by driving off the fleet of Graves that sailed to succor Cornwallis. In the naval engagement between the two forces, though in our waters, not an American ship took part.

In 1781 the British under Cornwallis had subdued Georgia and South Carolina, but after a long campaign they were in urgent need of re-enforcements and fresh supplies. When they reached Yorktown, Clinton planned to send them all that was required. The long promised French offensive, however, was now ready. A summons carried by a fast frigate brought de Grasse and his fleet from the West Indies, and Washington and Rochambeau, leaving the unsuspecting Clinton in New York, hurried south, taking boats at the head of Chesapeake Bay. Thus, the supporting fleet sent by Clinton from New York did not arrive until after de Grasse, with twenty-four ships of the line, had come to anchor in Lynnhaven Bay inside the Virginia Capes and had landed soldiers to support Lafayette. Already the latter was opposing Cornwallis a few miles distant at Yorktown. French forces in Newport, Rhode Island, having also been informed, were dispatching a squadron to bring siege equipment.

Graves had only nineteen ships of the line to oppose the

twenty-four ships of de Grasse, but when the latter sailed out he did not hesitate to give battle. When the two fleets were nearly opposite each other, the British admiral wore down to attack. But his van was hard hit, and as the French slightly turned away and maneuvered, his rear never got into action. Although no decision was reached in the first day's fighting, the British suffered the greater losses. For the next five days the two fleets sailed on an easterly course, a few miles apart, maneuvering without fighting. Meanwhile, the Newport squadron had slipped into Chesapeake Bay. Then de Grasse returned to the Virginia Capes, and Graves, admitting the defeat of his purpose, abandoned Cornwallis to his fate and sailed for New York.

Control of the sea for even a brief period thus made possible the great land victory of the American and French armies.

The Part Played by the Navy in the Revolution

What brought success to American arms in the War for Independence? First, the colonies had many sympathizers in England, who believed in the justice of our cause; in consequence, never did the British that actively supported the war represent the entire nation. The raids of our warships and the destruction of commerce, especially in British home waters, created, as already noted, a strong sentiment against war. Second, the colonies had financial, naval, and military aid from France; with almost no preparation on our part for the long war, this aid was absolutely essential. French sea power was vital to secure the victory over Cornwallis, which virtually ended British hopes. And third, we had leaders of the first quality: in our statesmen in Congress, in our army officers, Washington and Greene, and in our naval officers, Jones, Wickes, Conyngham, Barry, Barney, and Manly—leaders of a small group of determined fighters of the finest type. The Navy, though hopelessly outnumbered by its great opponent, had a highly important part. It contributed early to the securing of arms and military supplies. It maintained at all times vital communications by sea, and during a critical period denied them on Lake Champlain to the British. It fostered good relations with France, Holland, and Spain, and assisted in gaining their support.

References

Allen, G. W., *A Naval History of the American Revolution,* 1913.

de Koven, Mrs. Reginald, *The Life and Letters of John Paul Jones,* 2 vols., 1913.

Maclay, E. S., *A History of American Privateers,* 1899.

Mahan, A. T., *Major Operations of the Navies in the War of American Independence,* 1913.

Paullin, C. O., *The Navy of the American Revolution,* 1906.

III

ESTABLISHMENT OF THE NAVY DEPARTMENT. QUASI-WAR WITH FRANCE. TRIPOLITAN WAR

The Beginning of a Permanent Navy

"WHEREAS, THE DEPREDATIONS committed by the Algerine corsairs, on the commerce of the United States, render it necessary that a naval force should be provided for its protection—Be it, therefore, enacted. . . ." This was the preliminary of the "Act to provide a Naval Armament," approved March 27, 1794. It authorized the building of six frigates and was the beginning of the permanent Navy of the United States.

Two years after the treaty with England that ended the Revolution, the last remaining ship of the Continental Navy was sold and converted into a merchantman. Supposedly there was no further need of warships, at least not at this time. And the impoverished central government, such as there was, felt great need of economy. But our commerce, no longer having the protection of the Royal Navy, almost at once had to meet new perils at sea. In 1785, the American schooner *Maria* and the ship *Dauphin* were seized by the Algerian pirates and their crews were held for ransom. The freebooting Dey of Algiers had thus for years filled his coffers by preying on small unprotected ships that were passing, forcing many of the nations to make annual payments if they wished to be immune from his attacks. Our government at once began negotiations to secure the release of our sailors, but the price demanded being exorbitant the negotiations failed and the sailors were held as slaves. The situation was further complicated, in 1793, when Portugal ended her war with the Barbary states, which had prevented the corsairs from operating in the Atlantic. The Straits of Gibraltar then being open, Algerian cruisers boldly began their operations outside. In a month eleven American vessels were captured. Congress suddenly realized that something must be done.

The Navy Department Established

The framers of the Constitution in an authorization that was expressed in language simple and brief but absolutely complete gave Congress power "To provide and maintain a navy." This, one of the provisions that encountered no opposition in the Constitutional Convention, met also with general approval when the great document was sent to the states for ratification. In the congressional act of 1789 establishing the War Department, the Secretary of War was given jurisdiction over the naval as well as the military or land forces. Thus, for a brief period that which has been urged many times in our history was tried —the two Services were under a single administrative head. To be sure, there were no ships, but also there were next to no land forces, and the intention was to build a navy when finances should permit.

When Thomas Jefferson returned from France to become the first Secretary of State, he advocated the fitting out of a naval force to compel Algiers to release our sailors. Though the Federalist Party early was favorable to the idea, the opposition proved so strong as to prevent any action until some years later when the Barbary states were more aggressive.

Then England had entered upon her long war with France and Napoleon. Our neutral commerce was repeatedly attacked by both powers, and the violations kept increasing rather than diminishing. In 1794, however, stress was laid on the depredations of the Barbary pirates, and on the basis of the necessity of finding a means of meeting them, authorization was given to build four 44-gun frigates and two 36's. Joshua Humphreys, of Philadelphia, who later attained great distinction as a ship builder and who was the first to be appointed naval constructor in the Navy, was designated the constructor and master builder of the frigate to be laid down in Philadelphia. His designs were accepted also for the other frigates. Departing from conventional models, he planned that the new frigates should be longer and broader than those of the Royal Navy, but should not rise so high out of the water. Being more stable they could carry as many guns on one deck as some ships of the line were carrying on two. Although they had scantlings almost as heavy as those of a ship of the line, they were fast sailing and could run or fight at will. Humphreys' frigates were the very best of his time.

Diplomatic negotiations, meanwhile, at President Washington's direction, had been continued. In the previous decade, with the softening influence of $10,000 in presents, a treaty had been concluded, in 1786, with the Emperor of Morocco. And now, in 1795, a treaty was obtained from the Dey of Algiers. This, however, cost nearly a million dollars in money and presents because of the Dey's insistence that a large sum be paid to ransom the sailors held in captivity; also the treaty stipulated that the United States should give annually thereafter marine stores to the value of $21,600—not highly satisfactory terms, but regarded at the time as the best that could be secured.

The act authorizing the building of the six frigates had included the stipulation, introduced evidently to placate congressmen opposed to a permanent navy, that "if a peace should take place between the United States and the regency of Algiers, no farther proceeding shall be had under this act." But construction was not altogether abandoned, for Congress now passed a supplementary act providing for the completion of two 44's and one 36.

Any suggestion of a permanent navy had encountered opposition by representatives of the farming sections, especially in western Virginia and North Carolina, as well as in Kentucky. There was always the argument based on expense, also that which regarded a military establishment as a threat to democracy and the opening wedge for a return of monarchy: "In the hands of an ambitious man, armies and navies, instead of affording security and protection, might put our liberties in danger."[1]

But the opposition gave way in the face of an emergency. Thus, Jefferson, who had regularly upheld the agricultural interests of Virginia, admitted, "We are not free to decide this question on principles of theory only." He said that the people were determined "to share in the occupation of the ocean" and he agreed that a display of American force on the sea would "procure us respect in Europe."[2] Alexander Hamilton had for years been advocating a navy. Washington in addressing Congress, December 7, 1796, said:

> To an active external commerce, the protection of a naval force is indispensable. . . . From the best information I have been able to obtain, it would seem as if our trade to the Mediterranean, without a protecting force, will always be insecure, and our citizens exposed to the calamities from which numbers of them have but just been relieved.
>
> These considerations invite the United States to look to the means, and to set about the gradual creation of a Navy.

There was need for the frigates, as many saw, for we had not yet concluded treaties with Tunis and Tripoli. And whereas the friction with Great Britain had been lessened by a treaty negotiated by Jay in 1795, the settlement aroused a feeling of antagonism in the country that Great Britain was at war with, namely France. Our country was supposedly still bound by the alliance made with France in 1778, but the old friendship was seriously threatened by the compromises we made with her enemy. Frankly, some of our statesmen regarded the perpetual obligations imposed upon us by the French alliance as a burden

[1] C. W. Goldsborough, *The United States Naval Chronicle*, I, 61.
[2] H. and M. Sprout, *Rise of American Naval Power*, pp. 17, 18.

Top left, official U.S. Navy photograph; other pictures courtesy U.S. Naval Academy Museum

Top left, BENJAMIN J. STODDERT, FIRST SECRETARY OF THE NAVY. *Top right,* COMMODORE OLIVER HAZARD PERRY. *Center,* COMMODORE STEPHEN DECATUR. *Bottom left,* COMMODORE THOMAS MACDONOUGH. *Bottom right,* COMMODORE DAVID PORTER.

and were ready to renounce them. France helped many of a doubtful mind to reach the same decision by her depredations on our commerce. The Secretary of State reported, June 21, 1797, that French ships had captured in the previous nine months thirty-two American ships, brigs, and schooners, and that their privateers were operating on our very coasts.[3]

The compelling need of action, thus, rather than a study of theory, shaped our history.

On April 30, 1798, the Navy Department was established, and Benjamin Stoddert, of Georgetown, Maryland, was appointed Secretary. The choice was excellent. He had been a successful merchant, and he proved a forceful and competent administrator. With remarkable celerity he somehow succeeded in sending out a highly respectable force, and further, he laid enduring foundations for naval organization and administration. On July 11, 1798, the Marine Corps was formally established, consisting of a major, four captains, sixteen first lieutenants, etc., and 720 privates.

Congress had finally (July 7, 1798) been aroused to the point of declaring that treaties with France were no longer obligatory upon the United States and authorizing our naval officers to seize any armed French vessel found within the jurisdictional limits of the United States or elsewhere on the high seas. Thus the quasi-war with France had its beginning, and no other declaration was thought to be required.

Naval War with France

Even previous to the act of July 7, the frigate *Ganges,* Captain Richard Dale, and the *Delaware,* Captain Stephen Decatur, Sr., had been ordered to cruise between Long Island and south of the Virginia Capes, limiting their operations to the capture of French armed vessels which had committed depredations on our commerce or were hovering near for this purpose. A few days after sailing, the *Delaware* returned

[3] *Naval Chronicle,* I, 78.

to Philadelphia with the French privateer *Le Croyable,* of fourteen guns and seventy men, caught red-handed.

The most amazing activity was now displayed by Congress and Secretary Stoddert. Twenty acts were passed between March 27 and July 16 for strengthening national defense. Thus, provision was made for equipping the three new frigates then completed and for purchasing or constructing twelve other armed vessels of moderate size and ten galleys. The Navy was ready soon for more than merely defensive operations, and before the middle of the summer the Secretary proposed to the President that all ships of the Navy, except one frigate, one sloop of war, and some revenue cutters, reserved for the protection of our coast, should be ordered to the West Indies "to keep up incessant attacks upon the French cruisers on their own ground." The President approving, we had in the winter of 1798 four squadrons comprising twelve ships and sloops of war, a brig, and eight cutters cruising in definitely assigned sections in the West Indies.

The first annual report of the Navy Department, December 29, 1798, shows Secretary Stoddert's vigor and grasp. He asserted that conditions all demanded that our naval force be augmented "to make the most powerful nations desire our friendship—the most unprincipled, respect our neutrality . . . we shall not be easily provoked to carry the war into the country of an enemy; and it well becomes the wisdom of America, to provide a cheap defence, to keep it from our own." Then followed his specific recommendation: the building of "twelve ships of seventy-four guns, as many frigates, and twenty or thirty smaller vessels."

If this recommendation had been carried out and a corresponding increase in personnel had been provided, two wars that were to follow within fourteen years, the war with Tripoli and the War of 1812, would almost certainly have been averted. While unfriendly relations with France were spurring us on, six 74-gun ships of the line were laid down, but work on them was early discontinued and not until the time of the Civil War

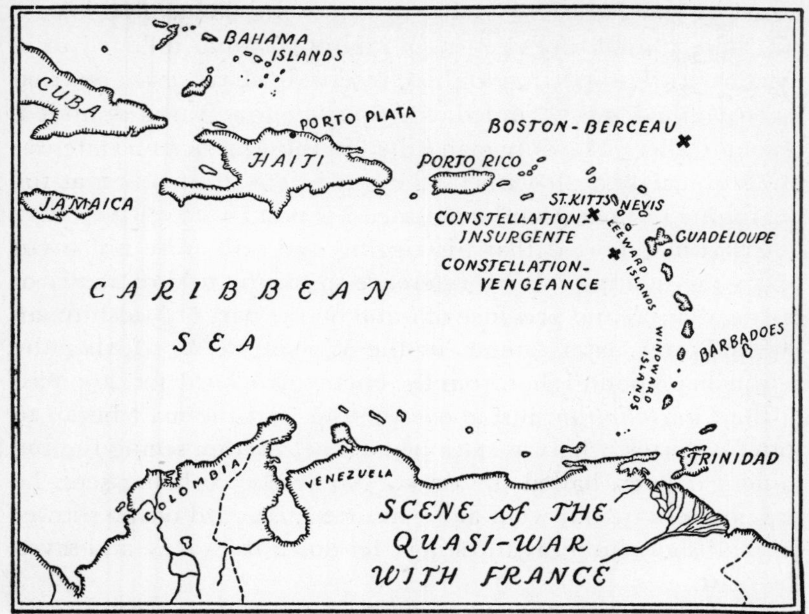

did the Navy reach the strength that the Secretary urged.

The small ships of our Navy occasionally faced heavy odds. Thus on November 20, 1798, the *Retaliation* (previously the *Le Croyable*), commanded by Lieutenant William Bainbridge, while cruising with two other small ships off Guadeloupe, was taken by two heavy French frigates, the *Volontaire,* 44 guns, flagship, and *Insurgente,* 40 guns. Bainbridge, on being taken aboard the *Volontaire* and questioned as to the armament of the American ships that had been with him, greatly exaggerated their strength, and thus saved them from capture by the *Insurgente,* which was ordered by the flagship to abandon the pursuit.

A brilliant victory was gained by the *Constellation,* Captain Thomas Truxtun, when she met the *Insurgente,* February 9, 1799, a few leagues southwest of the island of Nevis. The *Insurgente* mounted 40 guns and had a complement of 409 men; the *Constellation,* though rated as a 36-gun frigate, mounted 38 guns and had a complement of 309 men. In the action, which lasted for one hour and a half, Truxtun outmaneuvered his enemy and, several times getting a raking position, inflicted injuries out of all proportion to those received. The *Insurgente* had seventy killed and wounded; the *Constellation,* three wounded, one mortally. The only man killed in the American frigate was one summarily dealt with by the third lieutenant, when at the beginning of the action he deserted his post.

Truxtun reported that his rigging and sails were much cut up by the fighting. With reference to this he told of an act of great gallantry and presence of mind on the part of Midshipman David Porter, later famous in the War of 1812. During the action an 18-pound shot from the enemy struck the fore topmast of the *Constellation,* just above the cap, and the mast began to totter. Porter, who was stationed in the foretop, seeing the imminent danger, hailed the deck. No assistance being sent, he did not hesitate but went aloft, in utter disregard of the shower of small shot, cut away the slings, let down the yards, and saved the mast.

After the surrender, John Rodgers, first lieutenant of the *Constellation,* with David Porter and eleven men, was sent to take possession of the prize and to superintend the transfer of prisoners to the American frigate. But a heavy wind springing up delayed the completion of the task. When night came on, the wind was blowing hard and separated the ships, leaving Rodgers and his small party to guard 173 prisoners and at the same time to navigate the ship. It was a trying situation. But Rodgers, securing all the small arms, ordered the prisoners into the lower hold and placed a sentinel at each hatchway, armed with a blunderbuss, brace of pistols, and cutlass. For three days and two nights the young officers carried through a vigilant watch and succeeded in taking the ship into St. Kitts, where the *Constellation* was awaiting them.[4]

The second frigate action of the war again brought honor to

[4] Truxtun's report will be found in Knox's *Quasi-War Between the United States and France,* II, 326 ff.

the *Constellation,* even though the final outcome proved disappointing. At dawn on the morning of February 1, 1800, Truxtun made out a large sail west of Guadeloupe, which, as he slowly approached, he discovered to be a French frigate of 54 guns. The wind was light, and as the Frenchman made every effort to get away, the day ended without action. The chase, however, continued, and at eight o'clock the following evening Truxtun got within hail. In response to his demand of surrender, the French ship fired a volley from her stern and quarter guns that cut through the rigging and spars of the *Constellation.* Thereupon Truxtun, directing his men "not to throw away a single charge of powder and shot, but to take good aim, and fire directly into the Hull of the enemy," [5] maneuvered for position and fought on until one in the morning. At this time the fire of the enemy had been completely silenced, and he was sheering off. Truxtun regarded the French frigate as his prize and was trimming his sails to come alongside when the mainmast, every shroud shot away, in spite of efforts to secure it went over the side. An hour was required to clear away the wreckage. During the confusion the French frigate, the *Vengeance,* made her escape. She had an armament of 54 guns and a crew of 480 men —to be compared with the *Constellation's* 38 guns and 310 men. In casualties she had 50 killed and 110 wounded—the *Constellation,* 14 killed and 26 wounded.

In May, 1800, Lieutenant Isaac Hull, in the sloop *Sally,* with ninety seamen and marines who had volunteered for the expedition, sailed into Puerto Plata at midday and captured a fine French privateer protected not only by her own guns but by a fort mounting three heavy cannon. This was done without the loss of a single man killed or wounded. And on October 12, the same year, the *Boston,* Captain Little, took the French corvette *Berceau,* Captain Senes, in an action that lasted two hours, and returned with her to the port of Boston.

A change came in the government at Paris in 1800, the Direc-

---

[5] *Ibid.,* V, 160.

SCENE OF NAVAL OPERATIONS IN THE MEDITERRANEAN

tory being replaced by Napoleon. A treaty was negotiated late in the year, but the embarrassing French alliance was not renewed.

In the struggle of two and a half years' duration, Secretary Stoddert had sent out a force of more than fifty vessels, which in morale and organization was indeed remarkable. The Navy had progressed a long way from the early days of the Revolution. At the same time, we must not forget that France, at war with Great Britain, could not keep the sea with anything like full force in face of the superior power of Great Britain, and sent only frigates and privateers against America. In the conflict she had lost eighty-four vessels, most of them privateers.

War with Tripoli

There was no responsibility left by the Federalists that the victorious Republican Party on assuming power in March, 1801, was less inclined to accept than that of the lusty young Navy. Jefferson thought to reduce it to a minimum and even proposed that a great dock be built at the Washington Navy Yard within which the frigates might be "laid up dry and under cover from the sun." But history brought an ironical about-face. Immediately after Jefferson's inauguration, trouble broke out in the Mediterranean, and theory was again upset by hard facts. The Navy was not to his liking, but the North African pirates were worse.

Yusuf Caramelli, Bashaw of Tripoli, was receiving an annual tribute of $83,000 in money and presents. When, however, he considered what was given to rulers of Algiers, Tunis, and Morocco, he was certain he could make a better bargain. He boldly stated to Mr. Cathcart, the American consul, "Let your government give me a sum of money, and I will be content; but paid I will be, one way or other." Money being slow in reaching him, he cut down the American flagstaff of our consulate, May 14, 1801, and declared war. Months elapsed before news

LIBRARY
FLORIDA STATE COLLEGE FOR WOMEN
TALLAHASSEE, FLORIDA

of this reached Washington, but it happened that about the time of the Bashaw's defiance our government had received reports indicating a hostile attitude on the part of several of the African states and promptly acted by sending to the Mediterranean a "squadron of observation." Commodore Richard Dale was in command, and his flagship, the *President,* was accompanied by the frigates *Philadelphia* and *Essex* and the schooner *Enterprise.* Dale was instructed to protect our commerce, but as he had also been warned that only Congress could declare war he was almost powerless. He attempted to negotiate a peace with the Bashaw of Tripoli, his efforts meeting with no success. The only item of note he had to report was the engagement of the little *Enterprise,* Lieutenant Andrew Sterrett, with the corsair *Tripoli,* lasting three hours. The corsair, notwithstanding her heavier armament, had losses amounting to twenty killed and thirty wounded, and the *Enterprise* not a man even wounded. After compelling her to strike her colors, Sterrett, following instructions, threw her guns and powder overboard, dismantled her of everything but an old sail and spar, and then released her. Truxtun, assigned to the *Chesapeake,* was selected to command the second expedition sent against Tripoli. With his positive, forceful character he could have been relied on to accomplish much. Unfortunately, on being denied a captain for his flagship, he regarded this as a slight, and declined the command. The Jefferson administration construed his withdrawal as equivalent to a resignation, and his naval career thereupon ended.

Thus, the next year (1802), it was Commodore Richard V. Morris who relieved Dale. With the larger squadron which he commanded, it was thought he would soon bring the Bashaw to terms, and he was left very much to follow his own judgment in operations. He sailed from port to port, maintained an irregular and often interrupted blockade, and accomplished so little that he had to face a naval court of inquiry on his return and was dismissed from the Service.

Commodore Preble in Command

Commodore Edward Preble, who sailed in August, 1803, to relieve Morris, did not have as imposing a command as his predecessors; nevertheless, his arrival marked the beginning of a spirited offensive on our part. He had fought in the Revolution, with rank as midshipman and as a lieutenant in the Massachusetts state navy, but he was not widely known in the Service. He was from Maine, had a violent temper, in part due to ill health, and at the beginning of his duty in the Mediterranean was looked upon as a martinet by the young officers under him. But his iron discipline brought results, and if he was severe he was also just. Soon there was mutual regard, and within a year this had developed into warm and loyal affection.

While searching for Tripolitan corsairs, Captain William Bainbridge in the *Philadelphia* spoke a vessel belonging to the Emperor of Morocco. Something arousing his suspicion, he searched her and discovered that she was the American brig *Celia,* whose captain and crew of seven were confined below decks. It happened that for some time Morocco had been on the edge of war. Preble, realizing that she must be dealt with promptly, gathered a considerable force—in which he used certain frigates about to return to America. With this he made a demonstration at the port of Tangier. It had the effect desired. The Emperor announced that it was the governor of Tangier who was responsible for the depredations on our commerce, and publicly disgracing him, renewed the treaty of 1786 without any presents from us.

Loss of the Philadelphia

This success was offset by a sharp reverse. When Preble had gone to Tangier, the *Philadelphia,* which happened to be alone in the blockade of Tripoli, gave chase to a small craft attempting to make the harbor and ran on an uncharted reef, October 31, 1803. Captain Bainbridge made every effort to free her. He laid all sails aback and loosed the topgallant sails; he cast three anchors away from the bows, started the water in the hold, and hove overboard all the guns except a few in the stern, used to defend the ship against Tripolitan gunboats that had begun to fire on her. Finally he cut away the foremast, which in falling carried with it the main topgallant mast. Meanwhile, the gunboats, choosing a position where the guns of the *Philadelphia* could not reach them, became increasingly bold—their attack aided by re-enforcements from the city. At sunset, after a resistance of four hours, the ship was surrendered. Some days later the Tripolitans, employing many small vessels and lighters, got the *Philadelphia* off the rocks, recovered her guns, and in triumph took her into the harbor. The officers and crew they held in captivity for an exorbitant ransom.

Burning of the Philadelphia

The loss of the *Philadelphia* left the *Constitution* as the only American frigate in the Mediterranean, and the fact that three hundred of our officers and seamen were now held as prisoners of the Bashaw complicated the situation. But Preble was resolute in his determination to carry on the war. Bainbridge, who had succeeded in communicating with him through Mr. Nissen, the Danish consul at Tripoli, broached the idea of cutting out or destroying the captured ship at her moorings. Already Preble had thought of this, and had even gone so far as to discuss it with Lieutenant Stephen Decatur, Jr., commander of the *Enterprise,* who volunteered to head an expedition for this purpose. The plan was assisted by the capture of the Tripolitan ketch *Mastico,* which, having a lateen rig, stood a chance of sailing into the harbor without arousing suspicion. When Decatur, assembling the officers and crew of the *Enterprise,* outlined the task and called for volunteers, every officer, man, and boy stepped forward. Five officers and sixty-two men were chosen from the *Enterprise,* and five officers from the *Constitution.* Among the officers were several who later came to distinction: Lieutenant James Lawrence, Midshipman Thomas Macdonough, and Midshipman Charles Morris. A Sicilian pilot, Salvatore Catalano, accompanied them.

Although it was in the middle of winter, the period of storms, preparations were quickly effected, and the *Intrepid* (as the ketch had been renamed) sailed from Syracuse, accompanied by the brig *Siren,* Lieutenant Charles Stewart. The *Siren* was to stand by and cover the retreat. As the expeditionary force in the ketch sighted Tripoli, a gale set in, and for six days they tossed about, wet and most uncomfortable but not at all daunted. Finally, on February 16, 1804, the weather moderated and the evening promised to be favorable.

Directing the *Siren* to keep her distance, Decatur sailed boldly into the harbor. He had timed his approach so as to be concealed by darkness. The plan of attack had been carefully worked out, and one can imagine that Decatur had rehearsed it many times with his force during the days of waiting. United action was to give them command of the frigate, and then the several parties were to go each to an assigned station, receive the combustibles passed to them, and set fire to the ship. Lieutenant Lawrence, with Midshipmen Macdonough and Laws and ten men, was to fire the berth deck and forward storeroom; Lieutenant Bainbridge's squad of about the same size was to fire the wardroom and steerage; Midshipman Morris' was to fire the cockpit and after storeroom; Lieutenant Thorn's was to guard the ketch; and Midshipman Anderson's was to secure all boats alongside the frigate and cut off any of her crew who might attempt to swim ashore.

The evening was still and the light breeze completely died out as the ketch neared the vast hulk visible by the crescent moon. She lay becalmed directly under the guns of the frigate, two hundred yards distant. Here Decatur was hailed by a lookout. But Catalano, standing beside him, answered in such a way as to allay suspicion. Alleging they had lost their anchors in the storm, he requested permission to tie up alongside the frigate. A boat set out from the *Intrepid,* attached a line to the *Philadelphia's* fore chains, and received an after fast from a boat sent by the frigate. On these lines the American sailors, lying concealed on the deck of the ketch, began to haul. Just before the ketch was brought alongside, they were discovered by ten or twelve Tripolitans on the deck above, who raised the cry "Americanos."

A sharp pull brought the ketch up, and Decatur accompanied by Morris sprang to the main chains and climbed up over the rail of the *Philadelphia.* The others quickly following, Decatur with his sword drawn led them, in line abreast, forward from the quarter-deck up the main deck to the forecastle. That they might not sound the alarm to those on shore, they did not fire a shot, but cut down their foe or drove them into the sea.

Within five minutes they had gained possession of the ship. Then passing the combustibles, according to plan, they continued the work. When they withdrew, twenty minutes later, the ship was burning fiercely. So quickly was the work done that Midshipman Morris' squad in the cockpit, the last to receive the combustibles, had scarcely time to effect their escape.

Vigorous pulling on the sweeps carried the *Intrepid* away from the burning ship. The ketch, however, was in a hazardous position. She was within easy range of the Bashaw's castle and of one of his heaviest batteries. Two Tripolitan cruisers were lying within two cable lengths to the southwest, and several gunboats were about the same distance to the southeast. But before the crew of the ketch had gone far, they rested on their oars and gave three cheers "in exultation of their success"—receiving in return a general discharge from the cruisers and land batteries, which finally had waked up. The only shot that struck the ketch was one that passed through her topgallant sail. Decatur's total casualties amounted to one man slightly wounded.

Commodore Preble felt a justifiable pride in the success and on his recommendation Decatur was promoted to captain. Nelson, who was at the time blockading Toulon, is said to have characterized this exploit as "the most bold and daring act of the age."

Attacks on Tripoli

During the spring of 1804, Preble continued as close a blockade of Tripoli as weather would permit. Meanwhile, he had borrowed two mortar boats and six gunboats from the King of the Two Sicilies. With this force to supplement the American squadron, the *Constitution*, five brigs and schooners, and two prizes, he made preparations to bombard the city. The squadron now carried forty-two long guns—those in the *Constitution* and one in each gunboat. These were the only ones that could be used against the heavy batteries of the city. In his entire force, Commodore Preble had 1,060 officers and men, and with them he was attacking a walled city, defended by an army of 25,000 men, forts and batteries mounting 115 guns, and a squadron consisting of a brig, two galleys, and nineteen gunboats.

August 3 was the day of the attack. Most of the fighting was done by the six gunboats, Lieutenant Richard Somers commanding the first division, and Lieutenant Stephen Decatur the second. The account of the action is taken from Preble's report:

> In an instant the enemy's shipping and batteries opened a tremendous fire, which was promptly returned by the whole squadron at grapeshot distance; at the same time, the second division of three boats, led by the gallant Captain Decatur, was advancing with sails and oars to board the eastern division of the enemy, consisting of nine gunboats. Our boats gave the enemy showers of grape and musket balls as they advanced; the Tripolitans, however, soon closed, and the pistol, sabre, pike, and tomahawk were made use of by our brave tars.
>
> Captain Somers, being in a dull sailer, made the best use of his sweeps, but was not able to fetch far enough to windward to engage the same division of the enemy's boats which Captain Decatur fell in with; he, however, gallantly bore down with his single boat on five of the enemy's western division, and engaged within pistol

shot, defeated and drove them within the rocks in a shattered condition and with the loss of a great number of men.

. . . Captain Decatur, in No. 4, after having with distinguished bravery boarded and carried one of the enemy of superior force, took his prize in tow and gallantly bore down to engage a second, which, after a severe and bloody conflict, he also took possession of.

. . . Lieutenant Trippe, of the *Vixen,* in No. 6, ran alongside one of the enemy's large boats, which he boarded with only Midshipman Henly and nine men—his boat falling off before any more could get on board; thus was he left to conquer or to perish, with the odds of thirty-six to eleven. The Turks, however, could not withstand the ardor of this brave officer and his assistants—in a few minutes the decks were cleared and her colors hauled down. . . .

Lieutenant [James] Decatur [6] was the only officer killed, but in him the service has lost a valuable officer. . . . The enemy must have suffered very much in killed and wounded, both among their shipping and on shore. Three of their gunboats were sunk in the harbor, several of them had their decks nearly cleared of men by our shot, and a number of shells burst in the town and batteries, which must have done great execution.

Preble's casualty list, as yet showing almost no losses, rose in the next attack, four days later, when one of the captured Tripolitan gunboats, which had been given a place in the American squadron, blew up and killed or wounded eighteen of her crew. Among the killed were Lieutenant Caldwell and Midshipman Dorsey. Three other attacks followed and Preble pushed ahead so aggressively that those who saw from the inside believed the Bashaw would have been cowed and suing for peace if only Preble had been continued in command. But this was not to be.

The Intrepid *Disaster*

The spirited operations of 1804 were not to end without a reverse. In pursuance of his policy of annoying the enemy by every means in his power, Commodore Preble conceived the

[6] Brother of Stephen Decatur, Jr.

idea of sending in a fireship loaded with explosives that should destroy their shipping and shatter the Bashaw's castle and town. Lieutenant Somers of the *Nautilus,* who had volunteered his services, was given command, and assisted by Lieutenants Wadsworth and Israel he prepared the ketch *Intrepid* for the attack. One hundred barrels of powder and 150 fixed shells were stowed in her, and slow-burning fuses were led to the magazines so that the three officers and ten seamen selected from the *Constitution* and *Nautilus* might make good their retreat in two fast rowing boats when the *Intrepid* had penetrated to the midst of the shipping.

At eight o'clock in the evening of September 4, the *Intrepid* was under sail and stood in for the port with a leading breeze from the east. As she entered the harbor, the officers of the *Argus, Nautilus,* and *Siren,* which had escorted her part way and were to wait for the crew's return, heard several shots from the batteries. Just about the time when they thought that the ketch should have reached her destination, there was a tremendous explosion and then all was profound silence. What had happened was never known, for there were no survivors. It was conjectured that the gallant Somers, Wadsworth, and Israel had fired the magazine with their own hands rather than let ketch and powder fall into the hands of the enemy.

When the war was terminated, the officers of the squadron assigned part of their pay for a monument carved in Italy to memorialize their fallen comrades. This, placed in the Washington Navy Yard and later transferred to the United States Naval Academy, was a tribute to the gallant deeds of Somers, Caldwell, James Decatur, Wadsworth, Israel, and Dorsey.

Termination of the War

Previous to the last attacks, Preble had been informed that he was to be relieved by Commodore Samuel Barron. As the Secretary explained in a letter, the change of command was due solely to the fact that the Department was sending over several additional frigates, and all the captains in the Navy except two were senior to Preble. The question of seniority and the place on the navy list at this time, as often before and since, caused many a heartache, impairing naval efficiency. The change of command occasioned much public criticism. It was indeed unfortunate, for Preble stood head and shoulders above the other commodores in the Mediterranean, those who had preceded and those who followed him.

Barron accomplished next to nothing in the winter of 1804–05. He was suffering at the time from ill health so that it was necessary for him to turn over the command in May, 1805, to Commodore John Rodgers. Meanwhile, two activities were under way, both having the securing of a peace treaty as their object but approaching it by opposite methods.

Eaton, our consul at Tunis, who had seen military service in the Revolution, had broached early the idea of inducing Hamet, a former Bashaw, and brother of the reigning Bashaw, who had deposed him, to head a movement to regain his throne. It happened that Eaton had been sharply critical of the conduct of the war by Barron and James V. Rodgers in 1802, and his proposal was promptly disapproved by them. Returning to America, he received permission from Washington two years later to go ahead. In Egypt he raised a motley army of 1,200 Arabs and freebooters, including the ex-Bashaw and some of his officers, and assisted by three American officers, Lieutenant O'Bannon of the Marines and Midshipmen Mann and Danielson, he drove ahead with remarkable force of will through the Libyan Desert. Reaching the outskirts of Derne, he made contact with the squadron and had the co-operation of the *Nautilus* and *Hornet* in his assault on the fort defending the city. The attack was successful, and he now was confident that he was going to augment greatly his force and challenge the usurping Bashaw, when his project collapsed because of the drive for peace from the opposite quarter.

Colonel Tobias Lear, a former consul to Algiers, came to the

Mediterranean as a passenger in the frigate *President,* accompanying Commodore Barron as he relieved Commodore Preble. Lear had been sent expressly for the purpose of negotiating peace, which rumors indicated was now a possibility. Lear was jealous of Eaton, and of course opposed his plans. Thus Eaton's advance through the desert very probably hastened negotiations for both the parties concerned. At least when Yusuf Caramelli reduced the price of ransom for Bainbridge and the other prisoners from $200,000 to $60,000 and struck out the demand for tribute and further presents, a treaty was quickly agreed to. Disappointment was expressed by younger naval officers that this money should have been paid, but the treaty was much more favorable than any secured hitherto by the European powers.

The Tripolitan War, whatever may be said of its mistakes and irregularities, resulted in several important gains to the youthful Navy. It struck a blow at sanctioned Mediterranean piracy, an evil that leading nations of Europe had tolerated.[7] In consequence it increased American prestige in Europe. Together with the quasi-war with France it gave confidence to the young officers and heightened their morale. There had been passed by Congress, April 22, 1800, at the prompting of Secretary Stoddert, "An Act for the Better Government of the Navy of the United States." [8] It was indeed fortunate that at the time we were not under the spell of French revolutionary ideas that undermined discipline in the French Navy, but patterned our organization after that of the more conservative British Navy. One of the greatest gains of the two wars was the laying of an enduring foundation of naval discipline and training.

---

[7] The amount demanded of the nations as tribute had varied in inverse ratio to their size and the strength of their navies. Great Britain, by paying a small sum, not only secured immunity for her shipping, but used the corsairs to reduce competition from the smaller nations.

[8] The Act is given in full in the *Naval Chronicle,* I, 150–163.

References

Allen, G. W., *Our Navy and the Barbary Corsairs,* 1905.

——, *Our Naval War with France,* 1909.

Goldsborough, C. W. (ed.), *The United States Naval Chronicle,* 1824.

Knox, D. W. (ed.), *Quasi-War Between the United States and France,* 7 vols., 1935–8.

——, *United States Wars with the Barbary Powers,* Vols. I–III, 1939–41.

IV

THE WAR OF 1812: EARLY VICTORIES AT SEA

As the chief neutral carrier, profiting immensely from the increased wartime traffic, yet suffering from the restrictions of both belligerents, it was perhaps inevitable that the United States should be drawn finally into the European conflict which raged through the quarter century up to 1815. On the basis of rights flouted and injuries inflicted—558 ships confiscated by Napoleon in the years 1807–12 and 389 seized by the British in the same period—our nation might have declared war against France with as good cause as against England. But whereas France and the Continent needed our trade, it was Britain that ruled the sea; her restrictions struck home, and were particularly galling to a nation that had fought to win its freedom from overseas control. Besides, Britain, in the phrase of the time, was "tangible," not only to raids on her vast shipping but to attacks on her exposed Canadian frontier.

The Causes of the War

The perennial grievance of impressment, the restraints on our trade, the hopes of halting British traffic with the Indians and opening the way for expansion westward and northward—these were the basic causes that led to war.

Impressment came first in President Madison's war message to Congress in June of 1812. In wartime the British Navy was always shorthanded, while to escape the clutches of the press gang many a British seaman, with or without shift of allegiance, sought a more comfortable and better paid berth in the flourishing American merchant service. These men were hunted out when British officers boarded American vessels for conventional visit and search. Inalienable allegiance—"Once an Englishman, always an Englishman"—was their principle, and little heed was paid to the sound American doctrine that the decks of our merchant ships on the high seas were American territory, where British law did not apply. Furthermore, a hard-bitten British lieutenant, with his eye on a likely foretopman, was not the one to be stopped by legal technicalities or papers, perhaps fraudulent, showing the holder to be an American, naturalized or native-born. It is a question how many Yankee sailors were actually impressed into the British Navy. Some went of their own accord during the depression caused by the Embargo. A British list in 1811 gave the number of Americans in their navy as almost 3,300, and our State Department had a docket of over 6,500 alleged cases when war began.

Anger in the United States became white-hot when, as in the *Chesapeake-Leopard* affair in June, 1807, men were taken from one of our national ships of war. In this instance, the men sought for had joined the *Chesapeake* after deserting from British naval vessels lying at Norfolk, but two of them at least were known to be Americans. When the *Chesapeake,* under Captain James Barron, sailed for the Mediterranean, she was chased and halted well outside the port by H.M.S. *Leopard,* which, upon the *Chesapeake's* refusal to permit search, poured in several broadsides, while the American frigate, unprepared for action and with her decks still cluttered with stores, was able to fire only a single shot with a live coal brought from the galley. After seizing four men, the *Leopard* declined to accept Barron's offer to surrender his ship and went her way. This flagrant offense was later disavowed by the British Government, and after a delay of several years two of the men were returned.[1]

[1] One had died and another had been hanged immediately at the yard-arm. Despite his creditable previous record, Captain Barron was suspended for five

Impressments continued, and when in May, 1811, a flagrant seizure was made by H.M.S. *Guerrière,* just off New York, our naval vessels were ordered to take sharp measures against any violation of our rights. Shortly thereafter, Captain John Rodgers in the frigate *President* sighted a British man-of-war off the Virginia Capes, and in the ensuing darkness, after an unsatisfactory exchange of signals, the two ships opened fire. Before her weak resistance revealed her inferiority, H.M. Sloop *Little Belt,* as she proved to be, was badly damaged, with a loss of thirty-one killed and wounded. In the uncertainty as to who fired the first shot, the affair was dropped diplomatically, but it well illustrated the increasing tension at sea.

Trade difficulties with both England and France had troubled our diplomacy almost constantly since 1793. A most important source of profit for our shipping, aside from our own exports, was the extensive sugar and other traffic from the French West Indies to the home country, which had been largely turned over to American ships at the outset of the Franco-British War. Since the direct voyage from the colonies to France was held illegal by the British under the Rule of 1756—that neutrals in wartime could not take over a trade not open to them in peacetime—our ships adopted the practice of "breaking the voyage" by taking the sugar to American ports, reloading it there for Europe, and securing a new clearance and a "drawback" on duties paid. This re-export trade from French, Spanish, and Dutch colonies, of which we were almost the sole carriers, reached tremendous proportions, amounting in 1806 to $60,000,000, a greater value than that of our similar trade at any time thereafter until the First World War. But the British decision in the important *Essex* Case of 1805 checked the "broken voyage" practice by declaring that in such cases the voyage was not broken but continuous.

---

years for failure to prepare for action. He did not rejoin the Navy during the war, and thereafter his application for active duty was opposed by his colleagues. This led to the Decatur-Barron duel in 1821, in which Decatur was fatally wounded. At the time of his death in 1841, Barron was Commandant of the Philadelphia Navy Yard.

More drastic restrictions developed from the British Order in Council of 1806, which established a limited blockade from Brest to the Elbe River and a strict blockade from the Seine to Ostend. Napoleon later in this year retaliated by the Berlin Decree, declaring the British Isles "blockaded," all trade with them prohibited, and goods of British origin, whatever their subsequent ownership, liable to confiscation. According to later decrees, the ships carrying the goods were also made liable to seizure. England then, in 1807, ordered what amounted to no trade at all except through England, American ships being required to call at British ports, pay duties, and secure trading licenses. Thus caught between the hammer and the anvil of the two belligerents, our commerce was further injured by President Jefferson's efforts at "peaceful coercion" in the Embargo (1807–09) and the Non-Intercourse Acts, which not only ended legal trade, but led to wholesale violations and developed a spirit of lawlessness and disunity which had an ill effect when war came.

Our total export trade fell from $138,000,000 in 1807 to $22,000,000 in 1808. It had risen to about $50,000,000 just before the war, but was down again to less than $7,000,000 in 1814. To realize the importance of this commerce to the nation, it should be noted that in 1810 American shipping in foreign trade was only slightly under a million tons, and our entire merchant tonnage of over two million was about two-fifths that of the British.

Despite their trials, the New England and seaboard shipping interests had profited immensely in neutral trade, and hence bitterly opposed war, which would bring their profits to an end. It was the "War Hawks" from the West and South in Congress who turned the balance in favor of resort to arms. "The conquest of Canada," cried their leader Henry Clay, "is in our power. . . . Is it nothing to extinguish the torch that lights up savage warfare? Is it nothing to acquire the entire fur trade connected with that country?"

Throughout this period, a navy of respectable strength might have safeguarded our interests without recourse to fighting. And if we were resolved on war, we might have timed our entry more opportunely. In 1812 the Continental System was breaking down; England repealed the obnoxious Orders in Council on June 21, three days after war was declared. Before the end of the year, Napoleon was involved in the disasters of the Russian campaign, and by 1814 England was able to spare strong forces for overseas service. Only by our naval success on Lake Champlain and the effectiveness of our commercial warfare at sea, combined with renewed war clouds in Europe, were we able in 1814 to negotiate a peace on fairly even terms.

Opening Operations

There was little or no preparation for war. Despite the call for 50,000 volunteers, the land campaigns were fought largely by levies of raw militia and by the regular army of under 10,000, only about half of which was available on the northern border. A bill to provide new frigates was defeated five months before war began. Jefferson's harbor defense gunboats had been doubled in number in 1807, to a total of over 250, but they were worthless even for defense. The Navy had in commission seven frigates, two large corvettes, and seven or eight smaller sloops of war, brigs, and schooners carrying from 12 to 20 guns. The best of these were the three powerful frigates *Constitution, President,* and *United States,* rated as 44's but carrying upward of 50 guns; the 38-gun frigates *Constellation, Congress,* and *Chesapeake;* the 32-gun *Essex;* and the 18-gun sloops *Hornet* and *Wasp.*

Opposed to this tiny force, the British had nearly seven hundred war vessels in active service, including 124 ships of the line and 116 frigates. At Halifax they had a 60-gun ship and seven frigates, and counting squadrons in the West Indies and elsewhere, they could muster in the western Atlantic a force seven times that of the entire American fleet. Yet the American ships were officered by men, still in early middle age, who had served under Truxtun and Preble in the French and Tripolitan wars, and who, kept on edge by the constant threat of hostilities, had maintained high standards of professional efficiency. It was the Navy in this war that not only lived up to and strengthened its own traditions but sustained the national morale.

Within its limited strength, the task of the Navy in the Atlantic was to harry enemy commerce and do its best to protect our own. Save in dealing with well-guarded convoys, the first purpose could no doubt best be accomplished if our ships avoided battle and dispersed singly over the sea lanes. Yet the method adopted at the outset, that of operating in groups, had the merit that, by forcing the Halifax squadron to remain likewise concentrated, it prevented an early blockading of our ports by single ships and thus facilitated the safe return of homeward-bound vessels and the free exit of privateers.

From New York Commodore John Rodgers, putting to sea on June 21 with the *President, United States, Congress, Hornet,* and *Argus* on a ninety-day cruise, accomplished little save the purposes just named, though he took seven prizes, vainly chased the frigate *Belvidera,* and hunted for a British convoy until close up to the English coast. Captain Philip Broke's squadron, dispatched from Halifax, and including the 60-gun *Africa* and four frigates, was held together to deal with Rodgers; with it occurred the first notable contact of the war.

Chase of the Constitution

This involved the U.S. Frigate *Constitution,* Captain Isaac Hull, which on July 16 off the Jersey coast found herself in proximity to all five ships of the British command. Identities were not fully established till the next morning, when there ensued a chase lasting till the morning of the nineteenth, remarkable both for its duration and for the expert handling of the American ship. In the calms and occasional flaws of wind, the *Constitution* resorted first to towing by boats and then to "kedging," or heaving the ship forward by hawsers attached to a light anchor dropped nearly a mile ahead. By constant repetition of this wearisome labor, the *Constitution* kept beyond effective range till the morning of the eighteenth, when in a fresher breeze she forged slightly ahead. She had picked up her launch and first boat "with so little loss of time or change of sail that the enemy wondered what had happened to them." [2] In a rain squall that evening she gained a mile or more by "letting everything go by the run," to deceive the enemy; but "no sooner had the latter got their sails furled than Captain Hull had his courses and topsails set and the *Constitution* darted forward with great rapidity." Next morning she was clear. This most fortunate escape from five pursuers was made possible by Hull's masterly seamanship and never-say-die spirit. Coupled with the later capture of the *Guerrière,* it placed him, in Theodore Roosevelt's view, "above any single ship captain of the war." [3]

The Constitution *and the* Guerrière

Proceeding to Boston, Hull was at sea again early in August, and was bound southward from the Grand Banks toward Bermuda, when on August 19, about 750 miles east of Boston, he sighted a British frigate. This proved to be the *Guerrière,* 44 guns, detached from Broke's squadron and headed for Halifax, but very eager for an encounter with an American man-of-war. Only a few days before, her captain, Dacres, had written in the log of a merchant vessel a challenge to the effect that he would be happy to meet the *President,* or "any other frigate of equal force to the *President,* off Sandy Hook, for the purpose of having a few minutes' *tête-à-tête."*

From the windward position Hull managed his approach cautiously, yawing from one angle to another to avoid being raked, so that it was three-quarters of an hour later, at 5:55 P.M., when he brought his ship alongside the enemy at half pistol-

---

[2] From the *Autobiography* of the first lieutenant, Charles Morris, which gives a vivid account of the escape. See also *The Naval Monument,* pp. 8–9.

[3] Roosevelt's *Naval War of 1812,* p. 88.

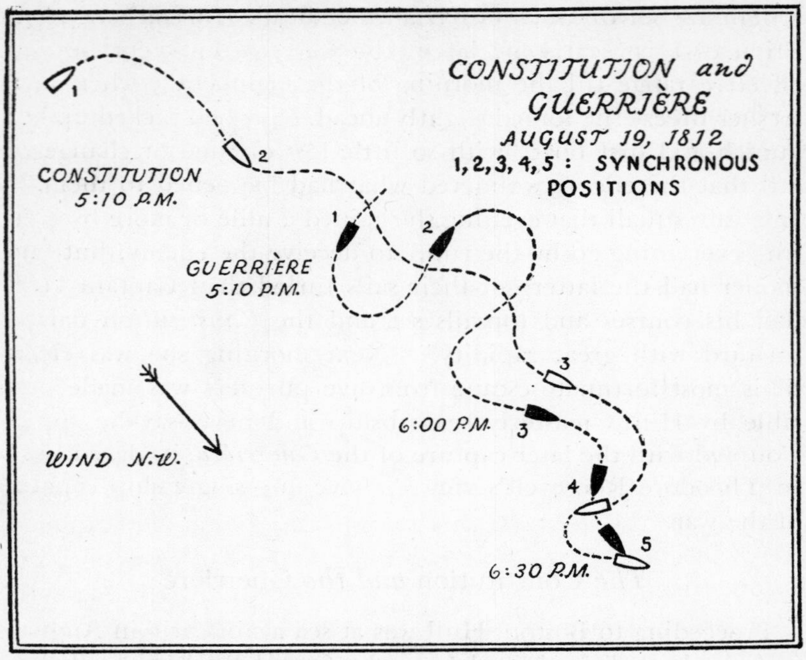

shot range. Though suffering somewhat from the enemy's stern-chasers, the *Constitution* had for some moments held her fire. She now poured in a series of destructive broadsides, slower than the opponent's by almost three to four, but coolly and carefully aimed to injure hull and spars. It was found later that the *Guerrière* had received no less than thirty shots on her engaged side, "five sheets of copper beneath the bends," i.e., below the water line.

After fifteen minutes the *Guerrière's* mizzenmast, hit by a 24-pound shot, went by the board to starboard, acting as a rudder to throw her bow into the wind. The *Constitution* seized this opportunity to pour in two raking broadsides (see diagram, position 4), sweeping the enemy's deck with grapeshot as she passed close under her bow. Shortly afterward, the opponent's bowsprit became fouled in the *Constitution's* mizzen rigging (position 5), and as men assembled for boarding, both sides suffered severely from musket fire in the tops. Captain Dacres was wounded at this time. With the slacking of her forestays as the two ships wrenched apart, both the *Guerrière's* fore and main-masts went down. She was now a beaten ship, and when the *Constitution,* after drawing off for repairs, again approached, the spritsail that had been rigged below the *Guerrière's* bowsprit carried away and her maindeck guns were rolled muzzles under in the trough of the seas.

It was a new experience, after two decades of victories, as the Union Jack was lowered from the stump of the *Guerrière's* mizzenmast. The captured ship was so badly damaged that she was blown up the next day. In this, as in other actions of the war, the surrendered officers were treated with the stately courtesy characteristic of the Service and the period. There is a pleasant record of a meeting between the two commanders years later, when the sturdy, thickset Connecticut skipper commanded our Mediterranean squadron, and the tall, austere Dacres was an admiral at Gibraltar. Upon Hull's arrival at Boston, the word of victory stirred universal exultation, and was a palliative for the very sour coincident news of the surrender of Detroit, by the naval officer's uncle, the aged General William Henry Hull. Congress voted a prize money award of $50,000 to the *Constitution's* officers and men.

At his court martial, Dacres persisted in the view that "fortune" had decided the action. The result was not due to fortune but to the *Constitution's* heavier weight of metal, 736 pounds to 570, combined with better gunnery and seamanship. The superiority in broadside of about ten to seven would not alone account for the greater disparity of losses. The two ships are compared in the following table:

Ship	Guns	Weight of Metal	Crew	Killed	Wounded	Total
Constitution [4]	55	736	468	7	7	14
Guerrière	49	570	263	15	63	78

[4] There is some variation in the figures for weight of broadside, crew, losses, etc. in this and other actions of the war. Roosevelt deducts about 7 per cent from the American weight of broadside, because American shots were lighter than British of the same size.

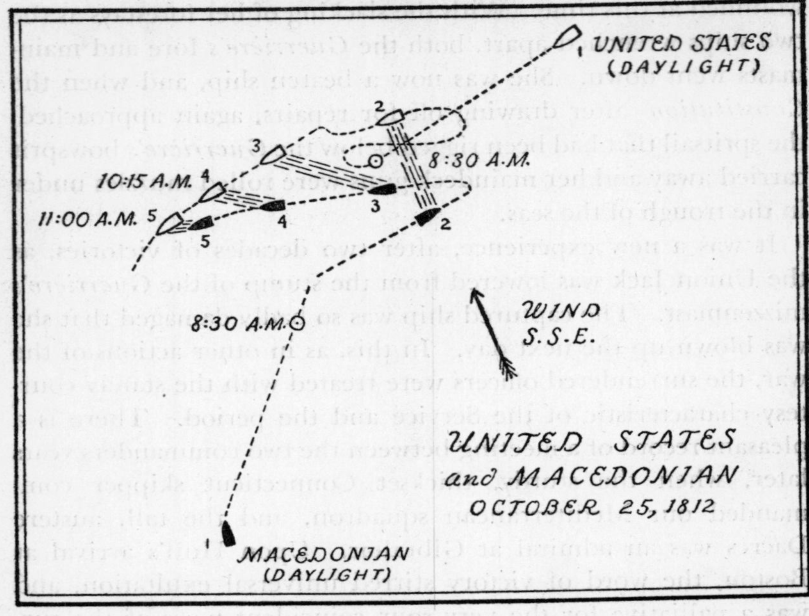

The United States *and the* Macedonian

The return of Rodgers to Boston, soon after Hull, facilitated the dispatch from that port in October of three squadrons, under Rodgers, Stephen Decatur, and William Bainbridge. These, with a few ships operating separately, constituted the bulk of the American fleet. Rodgers' cruise was uneventful; that of Bainbridge will be followed later; Decatur, in the frigate *United States,* after parting company with the brig *Argus,* was soon engaged in the second celebrated frigate encounter of 1812. This was with the *Macedonian,* 38 guns, Captain John Carden, a smaller ship, but fresh from overhaul and possessing a decided advantage in speed. The action occurred on the morning of October 25 near the Canary Isles.

With the weather gage, and no news of the fate of the *Guerrière,* Carden showed no hesitation in joining battle, though his assurance was perhaps increased by a belief that his opponent

Courtesy U.S. Naval Academy Museum

Top, VICTORY OF THE U.S.S. CONSTITUTION OVER H.M.S. JAVA. *Center,* FRIGATE CONSTITUTION BOMBING THE FORTS OF TRIPOLI. Two of the four panels by Gordon Grant in the commodore's cabin of the *Constitution. Bottom,* VICTORY OF THE U.S.S. CONSTITUTION OVER H.M.S. MACEDONIAN. From a painting by Thomas Birch. Engraving in the Beverly R. Robinson Collection, United States Naval Academy Museum.

was the 32-gun *Essex,* reported in the vicinity. The *Essex'* armament was chiefly of short guns, or carronades, which may also explain Carden's error, for which he was criticized in his court martial, in not bringing his ship at once to close range. When he finally sought to do so (positions 3, 4, in the diagram) he had already suffered from the superior fire of Decatur's long 24's. The loss of her mizzen topmast had ended the *Macedonian's* advantage in sailing, and the *United States* was able to keep a position ahead, shifting course from time to time to bring her opponent under a heavy diagonal fire.

Carden and his first lieutenant, Hope, had kept a taut ship, with notorious rigidity of discipline, and before the action had refused to let eight Americans in the crew leave their quarters and go below. With the odds against them, the British now fought with desperate fury, though most of the forward guns were dismounted and rigging and sails shot to ribbons. During a last attempt to close and board, the forebrace was shot away with the effect of throwing the *Macedonian's* head into the wind. Instead of raking the beaten ship, Decatur drew off for temporary repairs. When he returned an hour later, the enemy surrendered, despite Hope's proposal "not to strike but to sink alongside." Though the captured ship had received a hundred shot in her hull, Decatur was able to bring her into New York and refit her for American service.

The table following indicates that, though the *Macedonian* carried as many guns as the *Guerrière,* the American superiority in weight of broadside was somewhat greater than in the earlier action, and the British losses were also greater. In fact the dash-

Ship	Commander	Guns	Weight of Metal	Crew	Casualties
United States	Decatur	54	786	478	12
Macedonian	Carden	49	547	301	104

ing Decatur of Mediterranean days now fought with a mature wariness, preserving his prize from destruction and avoiding injuries to his own ship that might incapacitate her for further cruising. On the other hand, whereas Hull had effected his approach to the *Guerrière* without serious injury, Carden's ship was already beaten when she came to close quarters. The *Macedonian* was an inferior ship, but, as an American officer remarked, she was "just such a ship as the English have achieved all their single ship victories in . . . such a ship as the English prefer to all others, and have, till the *Guerrière's* loss, always thought a match for any single-decked ship afloat."

The American Navy owed many of its finest traditions to the British service, but in seamanship and gunnery it owed much also to American seafaring and to the pioneer skill in handling arms and shooting to kill. In this connection, a British comment on the frigate actions may be cited:

> The Americans would neither approach nor permit us to join in close battle until they had gained some extraordinary advantage from the superior faculties of their long guns in distant cannonade, and from the intrepid, uncircumspect, and often very exposed approach of assailants who had long been accustomed to contemn all maneuvering.[5]

The Constitution-Java *Action*

Sailing from Boston, as already noted, with the *Constitution* and the sloop *Hornet,* Commodore Bainbridge was to have been joined also by the *Essex,* Captain David Porter, but the *Essex* was delayed in fitting out and, after missing Bainbridge at various rendezvous in the South Atlantic, set out on her famous roving cruise beyond Cape Horn.

Off Bahia in December, Bainbridge and Master-Commandant James Lawrence in the *Hornet* for some time blockaded the British sloop *Bonne Citoyenne* with a large amount of specie aboard. In the hope of inducing her commander to accept Lawrence's challenge to a single-ship duel, Bainbridge later left the *Hornet* alone on the blockade, and on December 26, not far off the port, was rewarded by sighting H.M.S. *Java,* another

[5] Lord Howard Douglass in *Naval Gunnery,* quoted by Roosevelt, p. 115.

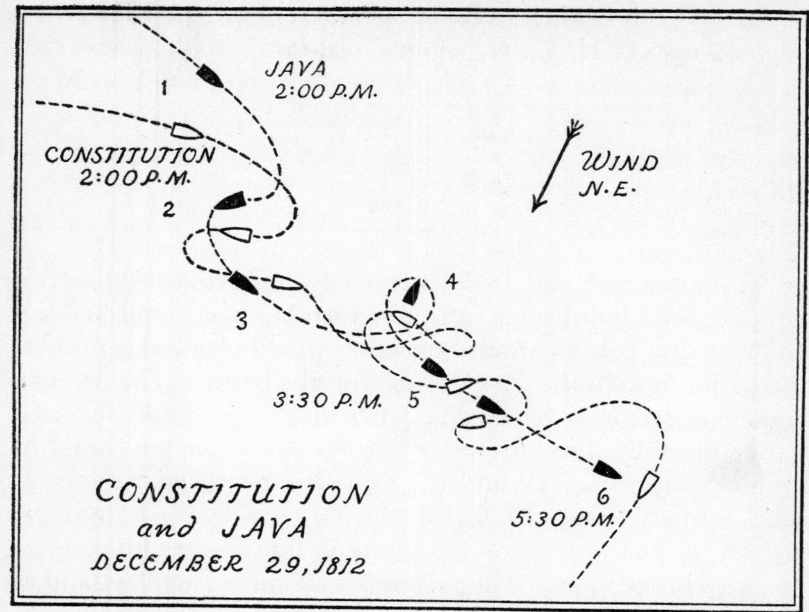

44-gun frigate carrying actually 49 guns, together with an American prize. Since the *Constitution* now carried only 52 guns, and the *Java* possessed an advantage not only in sailing but in quickness of maneuvering, the ships were more equally matched than those of previous frigate encounters.

The ensuing action, as Mahan remarks, was not an artillery duel, as in the engagement with the *Guerrière,* nor one in which a "principal maneuver, by its decisive effect upon the use of artillery, played a part, as was the case with the *United States* and the *Macedonian.* Here it was a combination of the two factors, a succession of evolutions resembling the changes of position, the retreats and advances, of a fencing or boxing match, in which the opponents work round the ring, accompanied by a continual play of the guns, answering to the thrusts and blows of actual encounter."

These maneuvers, indicated in the accompanying diagram, can hardly be followed in full detail. With the *Java* to windward, both ships, when in range, sought a raking position while keeping up a spirited fire. The *Constitution's* wheel was shot

Ship	Commander	Guns	Weight of Metal	Crew	Casualties
Constitution.........	Bainbridge	52	654	475	34
Java..............	Lambert	49	576	426	122

away, so that she had to be steered by relieving tackles, two decks below. Bainbridge suffered a torn hip from a musket shot and a second painful wound from a copper bolt driven into his thigh, but he kept the deck throughout the battle. The decisive maneuver seems to have come when the *Java* caught in stays, as a result of the loss of some of her head sails (see position 4 in the diagram on p. 75), and the *Constitution* raked with great effect. In an attempt to board, the *Java* ran her bow into the quarter of the *Constitution* (position 5), but lost her foremast as the ships broke away. The *Java* was now almost helpless, and at the time of surrender, about 5:30 P.M., three and a half hours after the first shot, she had lost all her spars save the lower mainmast. Her personnel had suffered considerably from musket fire in the tops, from which Captain Lambert of the *Java* received a mortal wound.

In this well-fought action, Commodore Bainbridge fully retrieved the series of misfortunes which had hitherto beset his career. His ship had struck to superior force in the French War, he had been forced to carry tribute to Constantinople for the Dey of Algiers in 1800, and he had lost the *Philadelphia* off Tripoli. "Old Ironsides" redeemed his fame. The *Java* was blown up after the battle, but her wheel, taken for use on the *Constitution,* is still preserved in the United States Naval Academy Museum, together with the captured colors. On her return to Boston, the *Constitution* underwent extensive repairs, and did not get to sea thereafter until December of 1813.

The three frigate victories of the first year, together with two successful sloop actions, not yet mentioned, aroused boundless

American enthusiasm. A hitherto reluctant Congress now voted to build not only six "Humphreys frigates" but four ships of the line. For returning officers and crews there were gifts of swords, medals, and prize money, and countless banquets, toasts, and highflown speeches. In England there was corresponding gloom, with free criticism of naval management. "We shall certainly be very backward," cried the *London Times* on first news of the *Macedonian's* loss, "in believing a second recurrence of such a national disgrace." And again three days later, "In the name of God, what was done with this immense disparity of force?" [6] In truth, the British service had fallen into a state of careless overconfidence. The English historian James, who wrote at the time, speaks of a "neglect to exercise the ships' companies at the guns which prevailed over two-thirds of the British Navy." As will be seen later, the Admiralty, at first placatory and half-hearted in policy, was soon stirred to vigorous and effective measures on the American coast.

To add to the general exultation, James Lawrence in the *Hornet* was back in New York in March with news of the capture of a ship, two brigs, and a schooner, and the defeat of the brig-of-war *Peacock,* of 20 guns, on February 24, 1813, off British Guiana, this last standing out as the most brilliant sloop action of the war. The *Hornet,* after an exchange of broadsides in passing, had got on the enemy's quarter and reduced her to a sinking condition in less than fifteen minutes. The *Peacock* was a notable "spit and polish" ship, with the breechings of her carronades lined with white canvas, but with a crew who had what Roosevelt calls "a marvelous ignorance of gunnery." Moreover, her 24-pounders were no match for the *Hornet's* 32's. After this success, Lawrence, though only thirty-two, was promoted to captain. He was of athletic frame and chivalrous bearing, and one of the most popular officers of the Service. He was now assigned to the *Chesapeake* at Boston with orders for an immediate cruise.

---

[6] *London Times,* December 26, 29. Quoted in Maclay, *History of the Navy,* I, 416.

The Chesapeake *and the* Shannon

For some time the *Shannon,* 38 guns, Captain Philip B. V. Broke, together with the *Tenedos,* had been on watch off Boston. On June 1, 1813, when the *Chesapeake* was lying in the roads, ready for sailing, Broke had sent the *Tenedos* to sea and was penning a courteous challenge inviting Lawrence to a single ship action "whenever it is most convenient to you."

The note was destined never to be delivered, but Lawrence, aside from the fact that he had sharply criticized the captain of the blockaded *Bonne Citoyenne* at Bahia for not coming out to fight, was not the one to disregard the obvious challenge of a single frigate of the *Chesapeake's* strength blocking his exit. Yet his decision was perhaps rash. His officers were new to the ship and to their men, and an unusual number of them were ill or on leave; his ship also was not organized or shaken down by service at sea. Broke, on the other hand, a captain at twenty-five and now thirty-seven, had been in the *Shannon* nearly seven years, and by constant drill had made her a marked ship for expert gunnery. He had held almost daily target practice, and for every gun had cut arcs of circles in the deck with degrees notched for concerted broadside fire. In these circumstances Lawrence, as he approached for action, decided, no doubt wisely, to avoid maneuvers, come alongside his opponent, and fight it out at close quarters.

Thus, while Broke lay under easy sail, awaiting the attack, Lawrence, at 5:50 on the afternoon of June 1, brought his ship along the *Shannon's* weather side, about fifty yards distant, and the guns of each frigate opened fire as they bore. At this point there was a fairly even exchange, but, since the wind cleared the *Chesapeake's* decks of smoke, her officers became a target for the *Shannon's* musketry. The *Chesapeake* also had come up with too much way, and as she forged slowly ahead, she lost some of her forward sails and, by a circumstance frequent in these single ship actions, swung into the wind and lost headway. About this time Lawrence was fatally wounded, and

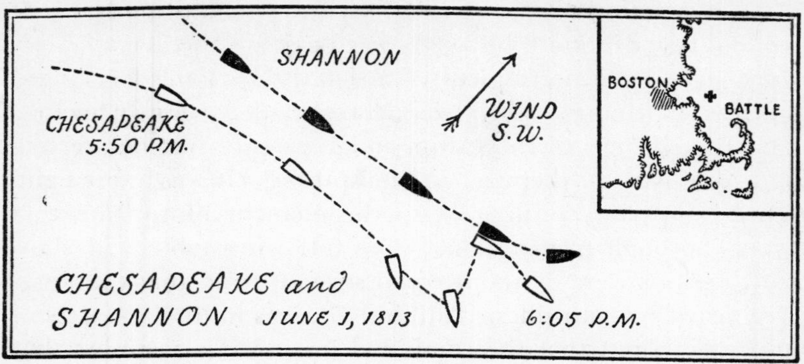

his sailing master was killed. After a raking fire from the *Shannon,* the *Chesapeake's* stern fouled the opposing ship, and both sides prepared to board. In the *Chesapeake* misfortunes now multiplied. In addition to the officers already named, the first lieutenant, the captain of marines, the fourth lieutenant, and the boatswain had all received fatal wounds. The third lieutenant, leading his men on deck, stopped to help his injured commander below. When he attempted to return on deck, the British were ahead of him and had battened down the hatch. There ensued what Broke described as "a desperate but disorderly resistance" from the leaderless men. Some fled below; the forty-four marines on board fought to the last, with a loss of twelve killed and twenty wounded.

The two ships broke apart, but in the final struggle the "Shannons" gained the upper hand. Second Lieutenant Budd of the *Chesapeake,* who had now reached the forecastle, started a short-lived resistance in which he was wounded and thrown to the deck below. At this time Captain Broke also received a sabre cut which incapacitated him in later years. After her surrender, the *Chesapeake* was taken to Halifax. Four days later Lawrence died aboard the *Shannon* en route. In his delirium he had been still in battle and kept repeating the words "Don't give up the ship," an expression which has become a watchword of our Navy.

In the reaction after a series of victories, it was natural that a dozen legends should be seized on to explain the defeat. The *Chesapeake's* men were pictured as landlubbers and foreigners, as drunk, mutinous, and ill led. In reality they were an average crew, though new to their ship, and Lawrence just before sailing had written of them as "in fine spirits." It was a fair fight, won by superior training, with the element of fortune that favors thorough preparation. The following table will show that the ships were of about equal strength, and that the losses were heavy on both sides. Admiral Gleaves in his *Life of Lawrence* points out that the combined losses were only forty-five less than the combined Spanish and British losses at Cape St. Vincent, where forty-two ships were engaged.

Ship	Commander	Guns	Weight of Metal	Crew	Casualties
Chesapeake	Lawrence	50	542	379	148
Shannon	Broke	52	550	330	83

References

See end of Chapter VI.

THE WAR OF 1812: LATER OPERATIONS AT SEA

The Cruise of the Essex

OF ALL THE American commerce destroying cruises made during our second war with England, the most famous was that of the frigate *Essex,* 32 guns, under Captain David Porter. As recounted earlier (p. 74), Porter, in the autumn of 1812, had missed Commodore Bainbridge at appointed meeting places on the South American coast, and thereafter found excellent reasons for sailing into the Pacific on an independent cruise. After a storm-beaten, late-season passage around Cape Horn, the *Essex* reached Valparaiso, Chile, in March of 1813, being the first American man-of-war to show our flag in the Pacific, as she had been first, in 1799, to double the Cape of Good Hope.

A month later Porter was playing havoc with the British whaling industry centered at that time in the Galápagos Islands. Of the twenty enemy whalers reported on the west coast, he had by September captured twelve. To quote his later report to the Secretary:

> I had completely broken up the British navigation in the Pacific. The vessels which had not been captured by me were laid up and dared not venture out. I had afforded the most ample protection to our own vessels, which were, upon my arrival, very numerous and unprotected. The valuable whale fishery there [British] is entirely destroyed, and the actual injury we have done them may be esti-

mated at two and a half million dollars . . . they have supplied me amply with sails, cordage, cables, anchors, provisions, medicines, and stores of every description—and the slops on board have furnished clothing for the seamen. We have in fact lived on the enemy since we have been in that sea; every prize having proved a well-found store ship for me. I have not yet been under the necessity of drawing bills on the Department for any object. . . .

One of the prizes with twenty light guns was taken as an auxiliary and renamed the *Essex Junior.*

Since the *Essex* was in bad need of overhaul, Porter now sailed for the Marquesas Islands, 3,000 miles to westward, where the inhabitants were still in the happy primitive state pictured in Herman Melville's *Typee.* During his stay, from October till early December, Porter took formal possession of the islands, made friends with a shore tribe, and, to protect his base, sent a small force to participate in one of the native wars.

One of his reasons for seeking a safe retreat for overhaul was the report that British ships had been sent in his pursuit. Back at Valparaiso on February 3, he had been in the port less than a week when H.M. Frigate *Phoebe,* accompanied by the sloop of war *Cherub,* sailed into the bay. Porter had wanted a frigate action, but the two enemy ships were more than a match, especially since the *Essex Junior* was too light to stand up against a man-of-war. Furthermore, the British frigate had a decided advantage in long guns. Contrary to the American practice and Porter's own wishes, the main battery of the *Essex* was made up of forty 32-pounder carronades, with only six long 12's; whereas the *Phoebe's* armament, though nominally equal, consisted of thirty long 18-pounders together with sixteen short 32's. In addition, the *Cherub* mounted eighteen 32-pounder carronades and eight of smaller size.[1]

Receiving word from a merchant vessel as he entered the bay that many of the *Essex'* crew were on shore, Captain Hillyar of the *Phoebe* brought his ship close aboard the American frigate

[1] As usual, the sources differ slightly on armament, but in this instance the variation is not significant.

as if bent on attack. The men of the *Essex,* however, had been recalled at the first warning, and were now in complete readiness for action, boarding parties drawn up with cutlasses in hand, and men with slow matches lighted at the guns. Seeing this, Hillyar, who had known Porter in Mediterranean days, hailed courteously, with excuses for his close proximity; and Porter replied in kind, but with the added warning: "You have no business where you are. If you touch a rope-yarn of this ship, I shall board instantly." [2] The *Phoebe's* yards passed clear, and the neutrality of the port was thus preserved.

After six weeks of watchful tension in port, with squabbles of liberty parties ashore and reports of other British ships on their way into the Pacific, Porter resolved to seize the first fair opportunity to put to sea. On March 28, finding his anchors dragging in a flurry of wind from the south, he thought he saw a chance to pass to windward of the British ships near the entrance, and accordingly made sail. But just as escape seemed possible, his maintopmast carried away in a sudden squall, and he was forced to anchor in a near-by cove for repairs.

Though the Essex was still in neutral waters, within pistol shot of the shore, Hillyar was not now to be stopped by technicalities, and engaged, about 4:00 P.M., with the *Cherub* off her enemy's bow and his own ship at the stern, where few of the *Essex'* guns would bear. Under the heavy British fire, springs that had been got out to wind the *Essex* into better position were three times shot away, but she managed to do some damage with three long 12's run out through the stern-ports. After drawing off for a time, the British again engaged heavily at 5:35. Porter now slipped his cable, tried vainly to close with a flying jib as his only available sail, and at last attempted to run ashore, but was foiled again by a shift of wind. By this time flames were leaping through the *Essex'* hatches and close to the magazines. The ship was a wreck and over half her crew were

---

[2] From the *Journal of David Glasgow Farragut.* Farragut, then thirteen, was a midshipman in the *Essex.* He spoke of this period as the "happiest days of my life."

wounded or killed. After a stubborn resistance until every chance was gone, the *Essex'* flag went down. Her losses were fifty-eight killed, sixty-six wounded, and thirty-one missing, as compared with the British casualties of fifteen.

Aside from his violation of neutrality, for which some excuse may be found in the practice of those and later times, Hillyar had conducted his operations skilfully and warily, taking every advantage of his superiority in ships and guns. With corresponding generosity after the battle, he permitted the *Essex Junior* to be used as a cartel ship to convey the Americans to New York as prisoners on parole. On their arrival, there were celebrations and awards for Porter and his men, for it was recognized that the *Essex* had put up a splendid defense against superior force, and that her final loss was more than counterbalanced by the work she had already done. Before her capture, the ship had struck her blow.

The American Coast Blockaded

When the *Essex Junior* reached New York, she found the port closely blockaded by a British squadron. In fact, even before the close of the year 1812, the British Admiralty had been brought to a realization that the war was not to be settled by diplomacy or won by half measures.

As early as July of that year all British ships crossing the Atlantic were strictly required to sail in convoy, and in September His Majesty's naval strength from Newfoundland to the West Indies was united under Admiral Sir John Warren in a single command. By the following February, 1813, the Delaware and the Chesapeake were put under strict blockade, which after March was extended to the chief ports from New York to the Mississippi. To encourage New England disunity, as well as to serve British supply needs, the coast further north was not closed until May, 1814, when the blockade was extended to cover not only ports but "creeks, rivers, inlets . . . and seacoasts" from Maine to the Gulf.

The Burning of Washington

From the summer of 1813 on, British squadrons lay within the Delaware and Chesapeake bays, halting traffic and harrying the coast. There was some scattered fighting with American gunboat flotillas, though these were generally held in check by superior force. "Punitive measures" on a larger scale, intended also as a diversion to hold American troops away from the northern border, were undertaken in the summer of 1814, when the British naval forces in the Chesapeake, now numbering twenty men-of-war under the new British commander, Admiral Cochrane, were joined by General Ross with 2,600 troops. Ascending the Patuxent in August, the British disembarked about 4,000 soldiers and marines and marched upon the capital. At Bladensburg, on the outskirts of Washington, General Wilder had collected, on the twenty-fourth, some five or six thousand American militia (of the fifteen thousand promised him), but the raw "citizen soldiery" fled at almost the first fire—or in fact at the sight of rockets shot in the air. The only effective resistance was offered by about five hundred sailors and marines under Commodore Barney, who had been forced to burn their gunboats and row-galleys in the Patuxent, but now held their ground at Bladensburg until outflanked by far superior numbers.

After burning the Capitol, the White House, and other public buildings, the British returned to the fleet on the twenty-sixth, without meeting further resistance. The Washington Navy Yard, with a frigate and a sloop on the stocks, was burned by the yard authorities. At Baltimore, in September, the defenses at Fort McHenry and elsewhere proved sufficient to ward off attack.

Effect of the Blockade

As a result of the blockade measures on the coast, American foreign trade, except as it was connived in by the British, was brought almost to a standstill in the later years of the war. Prices on imports, such as sugar, tea, and spices, went sky-high. Interference with coastal traffic was also injurious, since land transit was slow and difficult over the wretched roads of the time. From Philadelphia to South Carolina four wagonloads of dry goods took forty-six days; freight from Philadelphia to Boston took seventeen. In consequence, there was wide variation of prices in different areas; flour quoted at $6.00 a barrel in Baltimore cost $11.87 in Boston.[3] Along the seaboard, commerce was stagnant, and hitherto busy harbors were like forests with the masts of idle ships.

In these later years, American naval operations in the Atlantic were also much restricted, for even ports not subject to commercial blockade were sharply watched to prevent the exit of ships of war and privateers. After a vain effort to escape to sea in May, 1813, both the frigate *United States* and the refitted *Macedonian* were afterward dismantled above New London, and the crew of the latter ship was sent to the Great Lakes. The *Constellation* remained bottled up at Norfolk throughout the war, and from the end of 1813, the *Congress* and the *President* were shut in, the first at Portsmouth, N.H., and the second at New York.

Capture of the Cyane *and the* Levant

Of the later frigate actions, perhaps the most notable was that of the *Constitution* with the light frigate *Cyane,* 32 guns, and the sloop *Levant,* 20 guns. After months in port, the *Constitution,* under Captain Charles Stewart, had slipped through the Boston blockade in December, 1814,[4] and at the time of the encounter, February 20, was about two hundred miles northeast of Madeira. Though the combined broadsides of her two opponents were somewhat superior, the *Constitution* had a marked advantage in her long guns, heavier structure, and unified control. Captain Stewart maneuvered cleverly to rake both British ships, without suffering much injury to his own. The *Cyane* surrendered after three-quarters of an hour, at 6:50 P.M., and the sloop, after a plucky resistance, was taken three hours later. The *Levant* was afterward recaptured, but

[3] Figures cited in Mahan, *Sea Power in . . . the War of 1812,* II, 17, 184.

[4] Though the peace treaty was signed at Ghent on December 24, 1814, the news did not reach America until February, shortly before the ratification of the treaty on February 17. Hostilities actually continued for some time after the ratification, owing to the slow transmission of news.

despite a general alarm and pursuit, the *Constitution* sailed safely into Boston with her larger prize.

Loss of the President

At New York the *President,* now commanded by Stephen Decatur, had been held idle for nearly a year. With plans in view for a cruise to the East Indies, in company with the sloops *Hornet* and *Peacock* (a new vessel named in honor of Lawrence's capture), Decatur pushed out through the Narrows on the night of January 14, 1815, in a howling northwester. His ship grounded heavily on the bar, and, when set free two hours later by the tide, had suffered injuries which cut down her speed.

Next morning she was sighted off Long Island by the blockading squadron, a razee of 56 guns and three frigates. Foremost in the ensuing chase was the *Endymion,* 40 guns, which at sundown was well in range and doing much damage with her bow guns. Decatur turned on her and succeeded finally in dismantling her; but the delay enabled the rest to close in, and at 11 P.M. the *President* surrendered without further fire. In his report Decatur noted "one-fifth of my crew killed and wounded, my ship crippled, and a more than fourfold force opposed." In truth, as Admiral Cochrane remarked later, the *President* was "completely mobbed." Decatur, though he had not put up a last-ditch defense, remained a popular idol, and the court of inquiry, called after his parole from Bermuda, had only words of praise.

Sloop Actions

Not knowing of the *President's* capture, the two sloops escaped eight days later, and near the lonely island of Tristan da Cunha, west of the Cape of Good Hope, the *Hornet,* Captain Biddle, captured the brig *Penquin,* 19 guns, on March 23, in the last action of the war. With nearly equal broadsides, the continuing excellence of American gunnery was shown in the action, in which the *Penquin* was rendered "a perfect wreck" while the *Hornet* was not struck by a single shot in her hull.

In fact, throughout the war the clean-lined American sloops rendered excellent service, having a light draft that facilitated escape from port, and speed, gunpower, and maneuverability that suited them for both fighting and raiding. In eight sloop and brig actions of the war, seven were American victories, and most of these were with ships comparable in size, if not in other fighting qualities.

Of these actions, two were fought by the *Hornet*—the one with the *Penquin* just mentioned and the earlier engagement resulting in the capture of the British brig *Peacock* (see page 77). The *Hornet's* sister-ship *Wasp,* 18 guns, under Master-Commandant Jacob Jones, had contributed one of the first much acclaimed victories of the year 1812 by her capture of the brig *Frolic,* of about equal strength, in a hot gunnery contest on October 18 near Bermuda. In the heavy sea running, the American fire was surprisingly accurate; when the *Frolic* was boarded she was found to be unmanageable and not twenty of her crew were left uninjured. Yet her stiff resistance was not in vain, for before the *Wasp* could make off with her prize they were both captured by a British ship of the line. In 1814 a new *Wasp,* with twenty 32-pounder carronades and two long guns, under Master-Commandant Johnstone Blakely, won two sharp actions in the English Channel with the brigs *Reindeer* and *Avon*. Driven off from her second prize by other British ships, the *Wasp* was later lost at sea. She was spoken in October, south of the Madeiras, but there was no further trace of ship or crew.

In the three remaining encounters, the single American defeat was that of the brig-of-war *Argus,* which in the summer of 1813, carrying the commerce warfare into the Channel and Irish Sea, had captured or destroyed nineteen merchantmen in a month's time. She was taken by the brig *Pelican,* heavier in armament, in an action in which the American commander,

W. H. Allen, and his first lieutenant were wounded, and their vessel later became unmanageable. In the next engagement, between the *Enterprise* and the *Boxer,* fought in September of the same year off the Maine coast, both contestants were 14-gun brigs, but the winning ship, the American *Enterprise,* though newly at sea, had a slight advantage in weight of metal and number of men.

To complete the record of these single-decker battles, the *Peacock,* of similar design and armament to the second *Wasp,* won a fifteen-minute gunnery duel with the brig *Epervier,* 18 guns, in April, 1814, off the Florida coast. After using speed and deception later to escape two British frigates, Master-Commandant Warrington of the *Peacock* brought his prize safely into Savannah, with $120,000 of specie found on board, and was soon off again for a cruise in the Bay of Biscay.

Like the frigate encounters, these eight sloop and brig contests were little more than pinpricks in their effect on British naval superiority, and, though vastly stimulating to American morale and self-esteem, they should be regarded as incidental to the more significant work of the American cruisers in commerce warfare.

Privateers

In such operations, the major contribution was made by the big fleet of American privateers. Their work was of the utmost strategic value, and, though it has sometimes been underestimated in order to stress the importance of a regular navy, it is difficult to see how, in that day, it could have been accomplished by vessels under direct government control. Of the twenty-two ships in the naval service, eighteen were employed in commerce destroying and took a total of 165 prizes. Of the privateers, there were 526 registered, but only about two hundred actually got to sea and operated successfully, accounting for a total of 1,344 British ships captured or destroyed. In the later months of the war, when the privateers were larger, faster, and more heavily armed, and extended their cruises more widely over the trade routes, the number of captures greatly increased. During the last eighteen months they totaled 1,054, or an average of nearly two a day, a rate of loss to the enemy that was severely felt then, as it would be in later times.

With their speed and lighter draft, the privateers, like the sloops, could run the blockade more readily than the heavy frigates, and they could dispose of their prizes in either neutral or friendly ports. Their profits were the salvation of sailors made idle and shipowners brought near to bankruptcy because of the blockade. Their exploits, if not strictly a part of naval history, make a lively story of their own. Typical of the more successful privateers was the *Chasseur* of Baltimore, with sixteen 12-pounder carronades, which captured thirty prizes in all, and capped her career by boarding and taking the schooner *St. Lawrence,* a 15-gun man-of-war. The American skipper was lured into this affair by the enemy's ruse of covering most of their gun-ports, and he apologized later for "having sought a contest with a King's ship, knowing that is not our object." The *Yankee,* of Bristol, R.I., took forty prizes, the value of which, with their cargoes, was put at $3,000,000. Another famous raider was the *Kemp* of Baltimore, which off the Carolina coast encountered a frigate with eight ships in convoy. Decoying the frigate away in the darkness, she ran back to the convoy next day, boarded six of the merchant ships, and managed to get away with four.

When profit or necessity prompted, the privateersmen would fight "like pirates"—their not too remotely distant kin. The *General Armstrong,* 14 guns, while anchored at Fayal in the Azores in September, 1814, repulsed repeatd attacks by boat crews from three enemy men-of-war, and inflicted a loss of about 210 killed and 140 wounded before her captain, Samuel Reid, decided to sink his brig and escape ashore with his men. The British ships, carrying troops and artillery for the Louisiana campaign, spent a week or more in refitting and replacing losses —a delay which greatly aided Jackson's preparations at New Orleans.

Spread over the shipping lanes and sailing boldly into British home waters, the privateers and government cruisers inflicted injuries to British trade comparable, on a lesser scale, to those of the submarines in later wars. Commerce suffered not only from actual losses but from the delays incident to the convoy system. Insurance rates doubled and tripled; from England to Ireland they went up from 15 shillings 9 pence per cent to 5 guineas. "At a time when we are at peace with all the world," protested the merchants of Glasgow, . . . "it is equally distressing and mortifying that our ships cannot traverse with safety our own channels, that insurance cannot be effected but at an excessive premium, and that a horde of American cruisers should be allowed, unheeded, unmolested, unresisted, to take, burn, or sink our own vessels in our own inlets, and almost in sight of our own harbors." Coupled with the threat of renewed war on the Continent, these trade injuries created a strong British sentiment for peace on reasonable terms.

References

See end of Chapter VI.

VI
THE WAR ON THE LAKES

BECAUSE OF THE immense superiority of the British Navy, American naval strategy on the sea front during the War of 1812 was of necessity largely defensive, and limited in its later stages to the effective commerce warfare of the sloops and privateers. Far different was the situation on the Great Lakes, along our northern border. Here the two nations, starting the war with the most limited equipment in ships and base facilities, were on practically equal terms. Furthermore, it should have been clear that control of this all-important line of water communications was essential to the success of any military operations on the Canadian frontier.

With their preoccupations in Europe, the strategy of the British in Canada was primarily defensive up to the last year of the war, and on this line of water transport they were solely dependent for the holding of upper Canada and for all military operations in the west. The strong arm of the British fleet reached only to Montreal. Beyond this point, all ship fittings, anchors, cables, guns, munitions, and military supplies of every kind had to be carried in boats up the rapids of the St. Lawrence, through the intervening smooth water, and thence to Kingston, a distance of some 150 miles. From Kingston, supplies destined for the upper lake region were shipped by vessels to the head of Lake Ontario and portaged around Niagara Falls. In these circumstances, it was said that an anchor or a cannon, by the time it reached Lake Erie from a British dockyard, had cost in transit the worth of its weight in silver. Yet the British had this advantage: the Canadian side of the frontier had been longer settled and was better supplied with men and shipping facilities—for the chief settlements were along the St. Lawrence and the Great Lakes, which had been used by the French and British as a main route of western travel for 150 years—whereas the American side had not been opened up for any extensive settlement until after the Jay Treaty of 1794.

For the Americans, in view of the almost impassable roads of the period, the lake communications were of no less vital importance, both for operations on the Niagara frontier and in the area around Detroit. To reach the lakes, American communications were also chiefly by water. From New York the route ran up the Hudson and Mohawk rivers, thence by short portage to Oneida Lake, and down the Oswego River to Lake Ontario. Another route from points further south lay over the Cumberland Trail to Pittsburgh, then up the Allegheny River, and over sixteen miles of fair road to the new naval base at Erie (Presqu'isle). Over these wilderness trails and waterways passed the troops and seamen, the gangs of shipwrights and riggers, the artillery and munitions of all varieties, for the building, equipping, and manning of our lake squadrons. Only the timber for construction was available in unlimited quantities on the shores.

A joint board of strategy, had it existed in that time, might well have seen, as was remarked later by Admiral Mahan, that the proper point of attack on the lake line of communications was not at Detroit, which was like starting to cut a tree down from the top, but rather at some point much further down the trunk, such as Kingston or Montreal. Kingston was probably preferable, since it was equally accessible to American forces, and could not be supported directly by the British fleet. In either case, the severing of the line would have meant an end, sooner or later, to all resistance in the regions beyond. Yet, as often happens, the actual decision was guided by other than strictly strategic considerations. War sentiment was

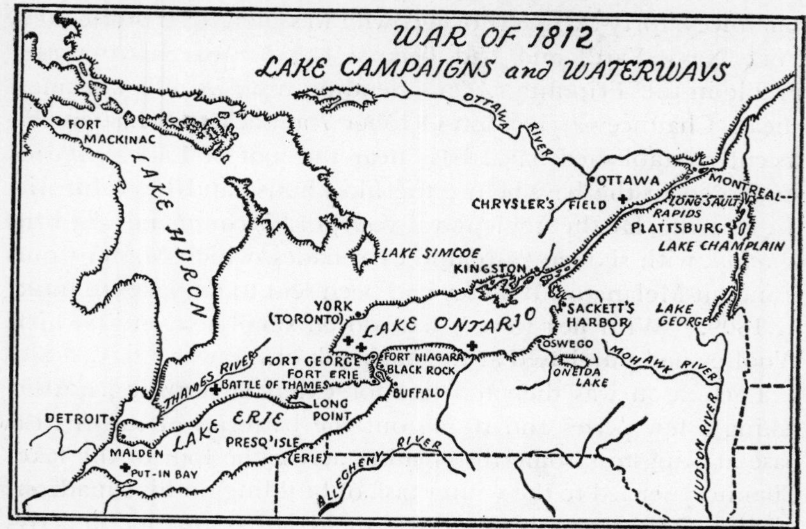

strongest in the West, whereas in the eastern border states it was lukewarm or even opposed. In the West, forces were available for invasion, and it was here that General Hull made the first brief advance beyond the border, issuing a magniloquent proclamation which offered the Canadians a choice between "peace, liberty, and security," on the one hand, and on the other, "mere slavery and destruction." It was in the West also that Brock, the able British general, in a vigorous offensive-defensive calculated to win support from the Indians, gained his first success by capturing Fort Mackinac, at the head of Lake Huron, before the little garrison knew that war had been declared, and on August 16 achieved the surrender of Detroit without striking a blow.

Operations on Lake Ontario

The news of these disasters aroused Washington to the importance of lake control. To the general naval command on the Great Lakes, President Madison appointed Captain Isaac

Chauncey, forty-two years of age, who was then head of the New York Navy Yard, and had been a capable executive under Preble in the Tripolitan War. Sending supplies and workmen ahead, Chauncey arrived on October 7 at Sackett's Harbor, the recently established naval base near the foot of Lake Ontario. Anchored in the bay, before the blockhouse and log cabins in the clearing, lay the single naval vessel of his command, the brig *Oneida,* with sixteen 24-pound carronades, which Master-Commandant Melancton Woolsey had been sent to the lakes to build in 1809.[1] With her were a half dozen small schooners which Woolsey had purchased at the outbreak of the war.

The season was then too late for extended cruising. After taking a few prizes and trying out the batteries of the British base at Kingston, some thirty miles across the foot of the lake, Chauncey settled to the winter task of building up his squadron, turning the little settlement into the hive of construction activity which it continued to be throughout the war. Two single-decked ships, the *Madison,* to carry twenty-four short 32's, and the *General Pike,* to carry fifteen long 24's, were laid down and finished by the next spring.

Across the lake, the British were also busy with construction work, for two ships were built, one at York (Toronto) and one at Kingston, to add to the considerable force of armed government vessels in service when the war began. In May of 1813, Captain Sir James Lucas Yeo, with twenty-eight officers and 450 British seamen, arrived to take over the lake command. In keeping with the general British strategy in Canada, his orders from the Admiralty imposed a strictly defensive policy: he was to do his best to keep communications open, yet avoid decisive action except on the most favorable terms.

Upon Chauncey, however, no such caution was imposed; the American aims in the north justified the risks of a vigorous

[1] He was accompanied by Midshipman J. Fenimore Cooper, who resigned in 1811, but in his brief naval service increased his knowledge of both sea life and life on the frontier.

aggressive, designed to clear the lake of enemy forces and definitely establish American control. That such results were unfortunately never realized must be attributed partly to Chauncey's own defects in military leadership, partly to the lack of any sound strategic direction from above, and partly to the contrarieties, not to say imbecilities, of some of the army commanders with whom he had to deal. Though Lake Ontario remained a principal theater of naval operations, its control fluctuated throughout the war. There was shipbuilding on a grand scale; there was much movement and skilful maneuvering of large squadrons; but later-day interest has turned to other waters, where more resolute, aggressive officers won decisive victory and enduring fame.

In the spring of 1813, Chauncey had one of his ships, the *Madison,* finished ahead of the British. With the army forces available, Kingston at this time might have been successfully attacked; but in view of exaggerated reports of its strength, the leaders adopted the second-best step of a joint attack on the little village of York (Toronto), then the seat of government of upper Canada. Here, after a spirited action [2] in which the ships and seamen aided in reducing the shore defenses, the 24-gun ship under construction was burned on the stocks, a brig was captured in the harbor, and stores were destroyed which had been intended for the British squadron on Lake Erie. Thereafter, the fleet joined in successful operations against Fort George on the Niagara River, but it was soon called back by a threat of Yeo against Sackett's Harbor.

Later in the summer the two squadrons were in contact three times in August and September, on the first occasion for a period of four days. It so happened that in these encounters Chauncey had a decided superiority in long guns, many of which were mounted in ten small schooners, top-heavy, cranky,

[2] General Pike, for whom Chauncey's second ship was named, was killed in the attack. A British royal ensign, said to be the only one ever captured, was taken from the government house, and has since been preserved at the United States Naval Academy.

and slow. His advantage thus lay in light breezes at long range, whereas Yeo's sturdier ships and carronades were better in blowing weather and at close quarters. In view of the tempers and policies of the two commanders, the results were as might be foreseen. When one was ready to fight, the other was ready to withdraw. On the night following the first contact (August 7), two of Chauncey's schooners foundered in a sudden gale, and three days later two other American schooners were cut off and captured, while Chauncey's only maneuver to save them was to "edge away," as he said, in hope the enemy would follow. In the final engagement, September 28, called by the Americans the "Burlington Races," the British flagship *Wolfe* was badly mauled by the *Pike's* long guns, but managed to speed away before the wind.

In the autumn of this year (1813) an army of about 11,000 was gathered at Sackett's Harbor under that "tarnished warrior" General Wilkinson, who since the Revolution had led an unsavory career in and out of the Army. With this force available, Commodore Chauncey now very properly advocated a joint operation against Kingston, which was near at hand, and where the troops could be given effective fleet support. For no conceivable reason other than sheer wilfulness, or a desire to avoid action altogether, Wilkinson chose instead a late season advance down the river toward Montreal. He was checked in a minor engagement near the Long Sault Rapids (at Chrysler's Field) and his army was disbanded after spending a miserable winter in camp on the northern border. Thus a golden opportunity was frittered away.

That Chauncey's own attitude toward joint action was not wholly above criticism is suggested by his response to a far abler general, Jacob Brown, who in the next year appealed for Chauncey's co-operation on the Niagara frontier. "For God's sake," Brown wrote, "let me see you. Sir James [Yeo] will not fight." To this the Commodore replied stiffly, "We are intended to seek and fight the enemy's fleet, and I shall not be diverted from my efforts by any sinister attempt to render us subordinate to, or an appendage of, the army." [3]

During 1814 the two squadrons on Ontario were scarcely in contact at all. With his new construction finished first, Yeo controlled the lake up to July, raiding Oswego and blockading Sackett's Harbor. Then Chauncey got two new frigates out on August 1 and blockaded Kingston until the middle of October, when he beat a quick retreat upon the completion of the enemy's monster ship-of-the-line *St. Lawrence,* mounting 112 guns. The building rivalry was still at its height when peace came. Two three-deckers were on the stocks on the American side, and one of them, the *New Orleans,* though never launched, was carried on our navy list until after the Civil War. There was never a happier clause in a peace settlement than that which after this war limited armed vessels on the Great Lakes to a few small revenue cutters, each mounting a single gun.[4]

Victory on Lake Erie

Operations on Lake Erie were a very different story. Dispatched by Chauncey to start naval preparations on this lake, Master-Commandant Jesse D. Elliott arrived at Buffalo in September of 1812, purchased five or six little schooners, and began altering and equipping them at his temporary base at Black Rock, on the Niagara River. On October 8 he learned of the arrival at Fort Erie, across the river, of two British armed brigs, the *Caledonia* and *Detroit,* the latter being a former United States Army vessel with six 6-pounders, captured by the British at the time of Hull's surrender. With commendable initiative, Elliott that very night gathered about fifty sailors and seventy-

[3] Quoted in Roosevelt's *Naval War of 1812,* p. 364. As Roosevelt remarks, the so-called "sinister attempt" was simply an effort to have Chauncey "cooperate intelligently in a really well-concerted scheme of invasion."

[4] The Rush-Bagot Agreement of 1817 limited each side to a single 100-ton vessel armed with one 18-pounder on Lake Ontario, another of similar size on Lake Champlain, and two on the upper lakes.

five soldier volunteers for a cutting-out expedition, surprised and captured both vessels, and succeeded in getting the *Caledonia,* with a rich cargo of furs, to the American side. The *Detroit* stranded on Squaw Island and had to be burned after removal of her guns. Thus at Black Rock was gathered the nucleus of a squadron, though it was an almost fatal objection to Elliott's choice of base that its exit to Lake Erie was against a 4-knot current and in range of the guns of the Canadian fort on the opposite shore.

Meanwhile, by arrangements made directly from Washington, work was also begun on the construction of two 20-gun brigs at Erie, Pa., then called Presqu'isle. In February, 1813, Master-Commandant Oliver Hazard Perry, who had been in charge of gunboats at Newport, R.I., but now sought more active service on the lakes, was appointed, subordinate to Chauncey, to take over the Lake Erie command.

It must be realized that in this new assignment Perry, like his senior on Lake Ontario, had to fill a double or multiple role. He did not step aboard a squadron ready for action, but had to build his ships from oak and chestnut still in the forest, settle labor troubles and organize militia to defend his base, secure provision of innumerable material needs from sources hundreds of miles distant, assemble his flotilla, and struggle with his superiors for an adequate force of officers and men. The task was one calling for both optimism and ceaseless drive. With a superiority of perhaps three to two, Perry's final victory was creditable; but even more creditable was the energy which built up this superior force and brought it into action. Here indeed was illustrated Thomas Carlyle's theory that "all noble work is at first impossible," but may be accomplished by courage and indomitable will.

For the youthful commodore of twenty-seven, the spring months were filled with activity. He was early in Pittsburgh hastening the delivery of ship-fittings and guns, then at Buffalo seeking more workers, and in May he headed a force of seamen in the attack on Fort George. This last also served his special purpose, for it necessitated the British evacuation of Fort Erie, and enabled him with the aid of ox teams and two hundred soldiers to warp the *Caledonia* and four schooners up from Black Rock to the lake, where they slipped past an enemy squadron to reach Presqu'isle.

As thus united, the American force at Erie was made up of the two new brigs *Lawrence* (flagship) and *Niagara,* each mounting eighteen carronades and two long 24's, the brig *Caledonia* with two long 24's and a short 32, and six small schooners each armed with one or two heavy long guns. They were ready for sailing by mid-July, but, as the lake level had gone down in the meantime, there remained the big task of getting the brigs across the four- or five-foot bar at the harbor mouth, while the British squadron, now under Captain Robert Barclay, a thirty-two-year-old veteran of Trafalgar, lay just outside, ready to interfere. However, perhaps overestimating his opponent's difficulties, Barclay lifted the blockade temporarily on August 2—according to a report, to attend a dinner across the lake—a false move which quite possibly cost him the campaign. When he returned, on August 4, he found that Perry had all his smaller craft and one brig outside.[5] Lined up for action, even with the brig's guns still dismounted, the force looked too imposing for Barclay to tackle. Instead, he made off for his base at Malden, at the head of the lake, to hasten the completion of his new ship *Detroit,* which was still without her guns.

The value of an American naval force on the lake was now quickly made evident. From his temporary station at Put-in-Bay in the Bass Islands, Perry could completely cut off all British traffic up the lake to Malden. By September the British base was so destitute of supplies that, according to Barclay's later report, "there was not a day's flour in store, and the crews of the squadron were on half allowance," while the Indians with

[5] To lighten each brig over the bar, her guns were taken off and two big scows or pontoons, called "camels," were filled with water until they just floated and then placed on each side, with timbers passed athwartships through the gunports of the brig and resting on the scows. When the scows were pumped out, they lifted the brig sufficiently to enable her to scrape across to deep water.

LIBRARY
FLORIDA STATE COLLEGE FOR WOMEN
TALLAHASSEE, FLORIDA

their squaws and papooses infesting the camp—and swelling its population to about 14,000—were wantonly killing cattle and clamoring for food. Despite incomplete preparations Barclay was now forced to fight for lake mastery.

The British squadron consisted of the new ship *Detroit* with an assortment of 19 guns, 17 of them long, mostly taken from fortifications on shore; the *Queen Charlotte,* also ship-rigged, with 17 guns; the brigs *Hunter,* 10, and *Lady Prevost,* 13; and the smaller schooner *Chippewa* and sloop *Little Belt.* As indicated in the table following, the American superiority of nine ships to six gave an advantage not so much in tonnage and men—the latter were a mixture of regular navy seamen, soldiers, and lake sailors on both sides—as in weight of broadside, especially at close range. The superiority in long guns was nearly as three to two and in carronades about two to one.

	Number of Ships[6]	Tonnage	Men	Broadside (total lbs.)	Broadside (long guns)
American . . .	9	1671	532	896	288
British	6	1460	440	459	195

With this comfortable margin of strength, Perry had still the task of keeping his ships of diverse type united, and bringing them into vigorous, effective action. It was the problem, as yet rare in American experience, of a squadron engagement, even though the total armament on both sides was hardly that of a single ship of the line.

At dawn of September 10, 1813, the lookout at the masthead of the *Lawrence* sighted the British flotilla coming out of Malden with a light southwest wind, which shifted later to the southeast, giving the Americans the weather gage. Perry's plan of battle, outlined to his captains the night before, has a special interest in view of the controversies that arose after the engagement, especially over the handling of the *Niagara* under Perry's

[6] The figures are taken from Roosevelt's *Naval War of 1812,* pp. 260–261. They are based on careful study of divergent sources, and give a fair approximation.

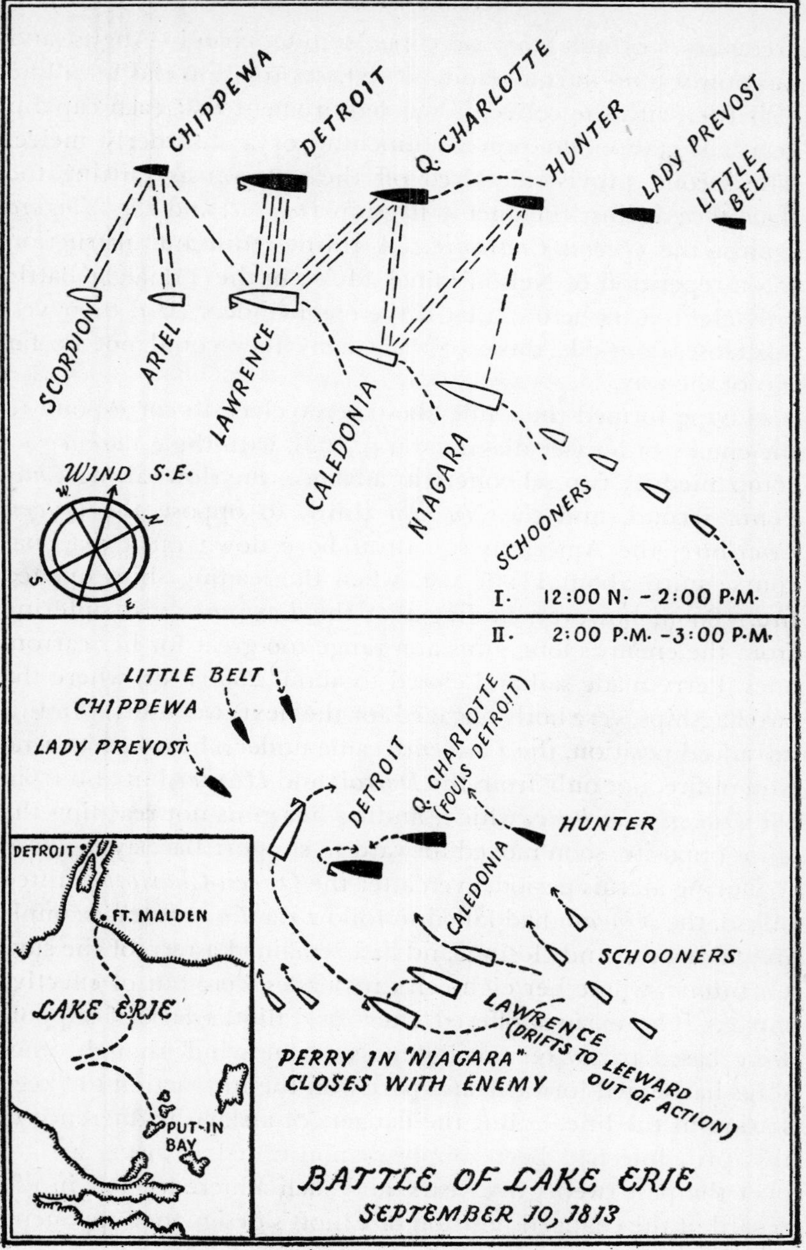

BATTLE OF LAKE ERIE
SEPTEMBER 10, 1813

predecessor Elliott, who had come from Ontario in August and was now second in command. The first provision was for a line of battle, with the conventional requirement that each captain keep his station, to prevent flinching or a disorderly melee. The second provision paired off the antagonists, pitting the *Lawrence* against the enemy flagship *Detroit,* and the *Niagara* against the *Queen Charlotte.* A third significant instruction was a repetition of Nelson's final advice in the Trafalgar battle only eight years before, that if the commanders "laid their vessels close alongside those of the enemy they could not be far out of the way."

Having formed their line about ten o'clock to correspond to the enemy order (see diagram on p. 103), with the *Lawrence* accompanied by two schooners in advance, the slow-sailing *Caledonia* second, and the *Niagara* third, to oppose the *Queen Charlotte,* the American squadron bore down on a diagonal course until about 11:45 A.M. when the leading ships opened fire. Soon, however, finding that the *Lawrence* was suffering from the enemy's long guns at a range too great for her carronades, Perry made sail and closed to about 250 yards, where the two flagships were hotly engaged for the next two hours. In this advanced position, the *Lawrence* came under a heavy concentration of fire, not only from the *Detroit* and *Hunter* but also from the *Queen Charlotte,* which, finding her guns not reaching the ships opposite, soon moved forward to support Barclay.

During all this period, even after the *Queen Charlotte* shifted ahead, the *Niagara* had failed to follow the *Lawrence's* example in making sail and closing, and had remained astern of the slow *Caledonia,* where her eighteen carronades were out of effective range. The excuses offered later for Elliott's lack of support were based partly on the lightness of the wind, though other ships had edged forward, and partly on the instruction to "keep station in the line." But the dangers of a slavish adherence to this principle had been amply demonstrated in naval actions over the past twenty-five years, and such adherence was in disregard of the changed position of Elliott's designated opponent, the concentration on the flagship, and the third instruction to "put their ships close alongside." Whatever the motives involved, whether pique or a kind of obstinate inertia, the fact is now generally accepted that whereas the *Niagara* just before the action was within hailing distance of the *Lawrence,* she had been allowed to drop astern and, in Mahan's words, "for two hours remained at such a distance as to render useless all her battery except her two long guns."

Even though Perry's advance might be considered precipitate, leaving little time for the rear ships to close up, it assured decisive action, avoided delay, and set an example which he had every right to expect the ships astern to imitate. Aside from her dull sailing, the *Caledonia's* position had adequate excuse in her light merchant-ship construction and her armament of long guns. Shortly after two o'clock, when the breeze freshened, this ship, on orders from Elliott, forged ahead into close action, but while the *Niagara* also made sail and moved forward, her course was to windward of the *Caledonia* and the flagship.

Meanwhile, the *Lawrence* had been reduced almost to a wreck, with but one gun of her starboard broadside still firing and more than half her crew killed or wounded. Leaving the national colors flying, Perry at this point took his fighting flag, "Don't Give Up The Ship," and with four sailors made his famous boat passage to the *Niagara.* Once aboard, he sent Elliott to bring up the schooners in the rear, and took his fresh ship against the enemy van. During the two hours' action, the British leading ships, though admirably handled, had been reduced almost to the condition of the *Lawrence.* In a desperate effort to bring fresh broadsides to bear on the new opponent, the *Detroit* and *Queen Charlotte* now fell foul, and in this position were raked repeatedly by the *Niagara* and by the smaller American vessels which had closed in. The battle was thus decided. The *Detroit* and the three ships near her surrendered about 3:00 P.M., while the *Chippewa* and *Little Belt* were later overtaken in an effort to get away.

To receive the surrender, Perry returned to his flagship, whose blood-stained and wreckage-strewn decks still evidenced the struggle she had come through. For a few moments her flag had been lowered, but it had been raised again when the tide of battle turned. Of the 123 American casualties, over two-thirds—twenty-two killed and sixty-one wounded—were suffered on the flagship. The British losses were 135. Perry's laconic message to General Harrison summed up the action: "We have met the enemy and they are ours; two ships, two brigs, one sloop and one schooner."

In its larger results, the victory led at once to the British evacuation of Detroit and of all American territory in that area, while the danger of Indian ravages was ended soon afterward by the death of their leader Tecumseh in the American victory of the Thames. There was no longer any serious question of setting up an independent Indian state, under British influence, in territory south of the lakes. The security of the West was won.

The Battle of Lake Champlain

Up to 1814, owing to the concentration of effort in the West and the indifference in the eastern area toward "Mr. Madison's War," the Lake Champlain line of water communications had played little part in the conflict. Together with the Richelieu River and the Hudson, the lake formed a vital avenue for invasion northward or southward, but so little significance was attached to operations there that it was not even included under Chauncey's general command. In 1813 the Americans had an advantage on Champlain of three small schooners to one, but in September two of these, the *Eagle* and the *Growler,* were caught in narrow waters and captured when they ventured too close to the British base at Ile aux Noix.

In the next year, however, the lake assumed a new importance when the British, with veteran troops made available by the interim of peace in Europe, adopted plans for more aggressive operations overseas. One of these operations, aiming at control of the Mississippi outlet, was slower in getting under way and was ended by Jackson's victory at New Orleans, two weeks after the peace treaty was signed. The other was an invasion southward via Lake Champlain, and was intended to establish a firm foothold on American soil which would strengthen British claims to territorial concessions on the northeastern frontier. Upon the Duke of Wellington's refusal of the Canadian command, largely on the ground that control of water communications was essential and not assured, the direction of operations fell to Sir George Prevost, Governor General of Canada, an officer of good past record but overcautious and seemingly disinclined toward aggressive action. Under him, in August of 1814, a force of about 12,000 men, largely British regulars, was assembled on the Lake Champlain border. To oppose him, there were fewer than 3,000 men under General Macomb, for by one of those singularly fatuous moves frequent in our land operations in the war, 4,000 men had been sent westward from Champlain to Sackett's Harbor on the very eve of the British advance.

In this advance, naval control of the lake was a prime essential, both for transport of supplies and for protection of the flank and rear. In anticipation of the naval conflict, construction work had been pushed busily on both sides for months before. At Ile aux Noix the British were building a powerful frigate, the *Confiance,* whose twenty-seven long 24's and ten carronades would make her apparently superior to any two American vessels opposed. Supporting her were the *Linnet,* with sixteen long 12's, and the two captured American schooners, now renamed the *Finch* and the *Chubb,* together with a flotilla of about a dozen row-galleys, each with one or two guns mounted in the bow. The force was manned and equipped largely from the fleet at Quebec, and on September 2 Captain George Downie, R.N., arrived to take command.

Opposing him on the American side was Master-Commandant Thomas Macdonough, thirty years of age, pious and serious of temperament, energetic of action, who as a youth had boarded the *Philadelphia* with Decatur at Tripoli. By concentrated efforts through the winter, Macdonough had most of his vessels ready at the end of May and could range the lake freely, transporting supplies and establishing a base at Plattsburg on the New York side. His flotilla was made up of the ship-rigged *Saratoga,* 26 guns, the brig *Eagle,* 20, the *Ticonderoga,* 17, converted from a steamboat, the little sloop *Preble,* 7, and ten row-galleys. While the British were favored by the concentration of strength in the *Confiance,* the two squadrons, as shown by the following table, were otherwise about equally matched:

	Number of Ships	Men	Number of Guns	Weight of Broadside	Long Guns
American .	14	882	86	1194	480
British. . .	16	937	92	1192	660

For the Americans, an advantage which proved decisive lay in Macdonough's thorough preparations and his well-chosen defensive position, which he utilized with the utmost skill. In this respect an interesting comparison or contrast may be made with the battle of the Nile, fifteen years earlier, with which the Champlain action has some points of similarity. At the Nile, the French fleet of fifteen ships was also in a selected defensive position, with supposed protection by shoals and shore batteries; yet it was caught unready and overwhelmed by Nelson's thirteen ships in a swift concentration on the van and center which ended in the loss of every French ship but two. At Champlain the British attack lacked these vital factors of speed and surprise.

For the British advance southward up the lake a fair north wind was almost essential. With such a wind, Macdonough's position in Plattsburg Bay (as shown in the diagram) was so chosen that the enemy would have great difficulty, under the lee of Cumberland Head, in working their ships up to or around the head of his line. He was beyond effective range of the batteries on shore, if they were captured by Prevost's superior land forces, and his rear was supported by the galleys and

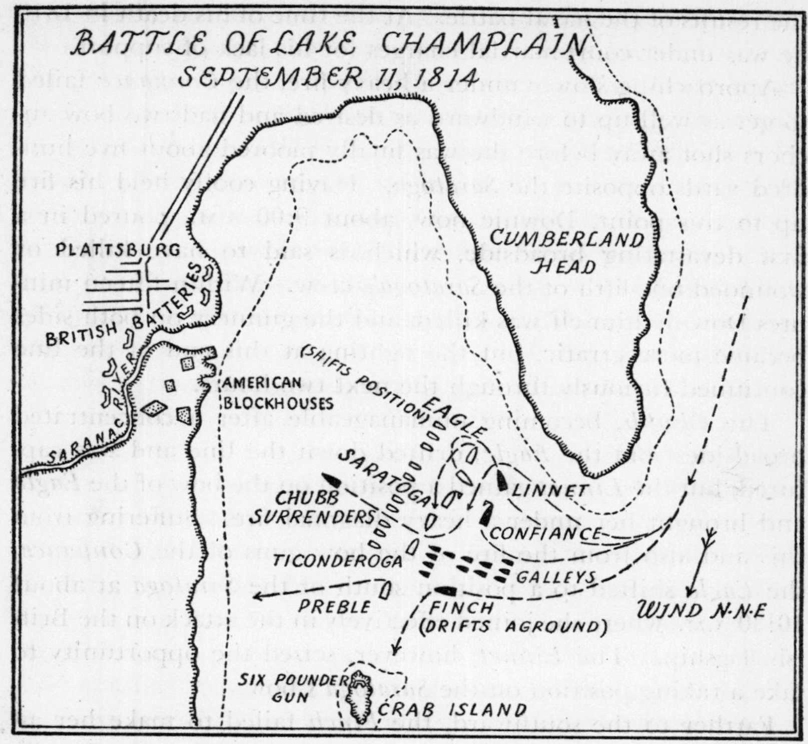

a battery on Crab Island. A most useful preliminary measure, as shown in the event, was the mooring of his ships with springs and spare anchors, so that if needful they could be winded to bring fresh broadsides to bear.

Downie, on the other hand, was new to his command and was hurried into action by Sir George Prevost's importunate demands and implied criticism of any naval delay. As he approached Plattsburg on the morning of September 11, shipwrights were still busy on the *Confiance* until two hours before the action, and the British sailors aboard had hardly fired the guns. Downie had expected Prevost to seize and utilize the batteries on shore, but Prevost, after advancing to the Saranac River, which runs through the village, had sat down to await the results of the naval battle. At the time of his death in 1816 he was under court-martial charges for his lack of support.

Approaching slowly under a heavy fire, the *Confiance* failed to get as well up to windward as desired and had two bow anchors shot away before she was finally moored about five hundred yards opposite the *Saratoga.* Having coolly held his fire up to this point, Downie now, about 9:00 A.M., poured in a first devastating broadside, which is said to have killed or wounded one-fifth of the *Saratoga's* crew. Within fifteen minutes Downie himself was killed, and the gunnery on both sides became more erratic, but the fighting at this end of the line continued furiously through the next two hours.

The *Chubb,* becoming unmanageable after a concentrated broadside from the *Eagle,* drifted down the line and was captured, but the *Linnet* gained a position on the bow of the *Eagle* and brought her under a heavy diagonal fire. Suffering from this and also from the fire of the bow guns of the *Confiance,* the *Eagle* shifted to a position south of the *Saratoga* at about 10:30 A.M., where she joined effectively in the attack on the British flagship. The *Linnet,* however, seized the opportunity to take a raking position on the *Saratoga's* bow.

Farther to the southward, the *Finch* failed to make her assigned station and drifted on the Crab Island shoals. On the American side also the little *Preble,* armed only with 9-pounders, was forced to take refuge under the shore batteries, leaving the *Ticonderoga,* without much support from the light American galleys, to meet the thrice-repeated assaults of the British gunboats. Ably directed from the taffrail by her commander Lieutenant Stephen Cassin, the *Ticonderoga* beat off these attacks with volleys of canister and grape, though some of the boats got close alongside.

Meantime the action between the leading ships was continuing fiercely, in fixed positions, calm water, and at almost point-blank range. It was found later that the *Saratoga* was struck by round shot about fifty-five times, while the *Confiance* received 105 hits in her hull. The British flagship had to be heeled over to starboard to prevent her sinking, and shortly before eleven o'clock she had not more than four guns on her engaged side capable of fire. With his own starboard battery in even worse case, Macdonough now found his preparations for winding ship of the utmost value, for they enabled him to reverse his position and bring his fresh port broadside into play. The *Confiance* attempted to do the same, but could be swung only partly around and was thus brought under a heavy raking fire. The battle was now decided. In a few minutes the *Confiance* surrendered, and fifteen minutes later the *Linnet,* which throughout the action had been most ably handled by her commander, Captain Pring, was also forced to strike her colors. Macdonough's first message after the battle was characteristic: "The Almighty has been pleased to grant us a signal victory on Lake Champlain in the capture of one frigate, one brig, and two sloops of the enemy."

The losses, heavy on both sides, and especially on the flagships, amounted to about two hundred for the Americans and three hundred for the British, in addition to nearly four hundred British captured. For his well-considered preparations and hard-fought victory against experienced forces of at least equal strength, Macdonough stands, in Roosevelt's opinion, as "down to the time of our Civil War . . . the greatest figure in our naval history."

Strategically, the victory was of the highest importance. Sir George Prevost quickly withdrew his forces across the frontier. When the news reached the peace commissions, already in session at Ghent, Belgium, there was no longer any serious British insistence on territorial concessions, a neutral Indian state in the Northwest, or exclusive control of the Great Lakes. The peace treaty was signed December 25. In it there was no mention of impressment or trade restrictions, for with the prospect of European peace they were no longer pressing issues. Provision was made for a boundary commission to fix the frontier as far west as the Lake of the Woods.

Despite all the border fighting on land, the War of 1812 has always been considered as primarily a naval war. The mismanaged land operations, the rigors of the blockade, and the raids on our capital and coastal towns have passed into the background, while popular memory has treasured the single ship actions and the two decisive squadron victories on Erie and Champlain. In the war the Navy won well-merited popularity, and contributed not a little toward the stronger feeling of patriotism and national unity which followed the war.

References

Cooper, J. F., *The History of the Navy of the United States of America,* 1846. Of special value for this period.

James, William, *Naval Occurrences of the Late War Between Great Britain and the United States of America,* 1817. Intensely pro-British.

Mahan, A. T., *Sea Power in its Relation to the War of 1812,* 2 vols., 1902.

Roosevelt, Theodore, *The Naval War of 1812,* 1880.

Niles' Weekly Register (Baltimore), *The Naval Chronicle* (London), and *The Naval Monument* (1816) contain official reports and contemporary material.

PROTECTION OF COMMERCE AND NATIONAL INTERESTS VII

DURING THE RELATIVELY peaceful period between the War of 1812 and the Civil War, interest in the Navy was maintained and our naval forces were kept occupied by a range of activities perhaps even more varied than those of later times. A chief motive for continued naval strength in these years was our flourishing merchant marine, which, along with our foreign trade, expanded greatly and culminated in the heyday of the clipper ships, from about 1845 to 1860. From a low point of $7,000,000 in 1814, our exports quickly climbed to over $90,000,000 in 1818, and by 1860 had risen to about $400,000,000, with a total foreign trade of $762,000,000. Throughout the period, from 60 to 90 per cent of this trade was carried in American bottoms, and from 1850 to 1860 our merchant marine, nearly equal in size to England's, constituted about one-third of the world's total.

Fast Black Ball and Swallowtail sailing packets were long-time favorites in the Atlantic passenger traffic. Swift clipper ships—the *Flying Fish, Flying Cloud, Sovereign of the Seas, Great Republic, Westward Ho!, Glory of the Seas,* and others of names renowned in maritime annals—cut the Atlantic crossing to thirteen or fourteen days, and reduced the long swing around Cape Horn to the gold of California to a matter of three-months' time. Thence, crossing to China for return cargoes, the clippers with their long, sharp lines, clouds of canvas, and expert Yankee skippers, had a vital speed advantage in the oriental trade over the lumbering British East Indiamen of that era. The wooden sailing ship finally gave way to iron hulls and steam propulsion, but in its day the American clipper stood supreme.

After 1815, as indeed before, this trade called for immediate and continued protection, from the Barbary pirates of the Mediterranean, from the corsairs of the Caribbean, from interference afloat and ashore in the Far East. For this purpose our naval ships were as a rule scattered, singly or in small squadrons, over the seven seas, in the East and West Indies, in the Mediterranean, on the African coast, on the Brazilian coast, and in the Pacific. There were squadrons in all these areas, but there was no regularly constituted Home Squadron until 1841. Since British interests and British naval strength in general supported our Monroe Doctrine against Old World aggression in the Western Hemisphere, American naval policy took little thought of an organized fleet, trained in fleet tactics for the defense of home waters. Rather, this was left to shore defenses or improvised "floating batteries." In time of war our Navy was for commerce destroying. And in time of peace its great mission was to "show the flag" in the backward trade areas and far distant ports of the world.

Commerce Protection in the Mediterranean

Scarcely was the ink dry on the peace treaty with Britain when, in March, 1815, Congress declared war on Algiers. Our grievances were long-standing. Since 1795 we had paid Algiers annual tribute. Yet in 1812, on British assurances that the little American fleet would be "swept off the seas in six-months' time," the Dey had broken treaty pledges, turned loose his cruisers on American shipping, and in particular had seized the American brig *Edwin* and held her crew as slaves.

With the frigates *Guerrière, Macedonian,*[1] and *Constella-*

[1] The *Macedonian* was the former British frigate; the *Guerrière* was a new frigate named for Hull's prize of 1812.

tion, and smaller units, Commodore Decatur sailed through Gibraltar in June. In answer to his hope of catching some of the Algerian cruisers still at sea, the frigate *Mashuda* was sighted on the seventeenth off Cape de Gat, Spain. With the support of other vessels, the *Guerrière* made short work of her, rendering her almost helpless by two broadsides at close quarters, while the little brig *Epervier* prevented her escape by hanging to a raking position under her stern. Two days later the Dey's sloop *Estido* was driven ashore. Having aboard nearly four hundred prisoners from the two ships, Decatur next appeared off the harbor of Algiers, threatening to capture any vessel coming in, and thus giving to his proposals for a treaty the kind of backing the Dey could best understand. The treaty, providing for the release of the *Edwin's* crew, satisfactory damages, and an end of tribute, was to be signed within forty-eight hours. As usual, the Dey tried to hold matters up, but he signed the treaty quickly when he saw Decatur clearing for action against an Algerian ship approaching the port.

Moving on to Tunis and Tripoli, which had allowed England to recover prizes captured by American cruisers and sent into their ports, Decatur settled on similar terms, securing payments of $46,000 damages from Tunis and $25,000 from Tripoli. "Why," complained the Bey of Tripoli, who remembered Decatur from his exploits of twelve years earlier, "why do they send wild young men to treat for peace with old powers?" In September Commodore Bainbridge joined at Gibraltar with a second squadron, including the new ship of the line *Independence.* Though the work was already done, the show of force was a useful manifestation of the new maritime power overseas.

At the time of Decatur's first arrival in the Mediterranean, the Algerians had twelve vessels of 360 guns to Decatur's armament of 210 guns. His firm, vigorous methods prevented a costly and perhaps indecisive campaign. A further curb on the Barbary pirates resulted from a British expedition against them in the next year, in which, incidentally, the British lost seven hundred killed and wounded.

Suppression of Piracy in the West Indies

The suppression of piracy in the West Indies was less quickly accomplished. It had grown out of the widespread privateering and buccaneering of the Napoleonic and earlier wars, and received a new impetus after 1810 when many of the Latin-American states were in revolt against Spain. Letters of marque were easily procured, and with or without them, these "Brethren of the Coast" plied their bloody trade. Scarcely a peaceful trader could get through the Caribbean without an attack. Master-Commandant Patterson, in charge of our naval base at New Orleans, cleaned out the pirate nest of the LaFitte brothers at Barataria, La., in 1814, but had inadequate force to operate farther at sea. After 1815 the rapid growth of the New Orleans export trade and increased commerce and contacts with Latin America made the extirpation of the pirates doubly necessary.

It was on a diplomatic mission to Venezuela, attempting to check the issue of privateering papers, that Commodore Oliver H. Perry met his death from yellow fever in 1819. Naval forces under Commodore James Biddle in 1821–22, and under Commodore David Porter in 1823–24, operated effectively against the pirate craft. In addition to numerous small schooners, Porter put into action a steam ex-ferryboat, the *Seagull,* and our first "mosquito flotilla" of row-barges, aptly named the *Mosquito, Gnat, Midge, Sandfly,* and *Gallinipper.* With these he cleared out pirate vessels and hideouts from San Domingo to the Isle of Pines. Altogether about sixty-five pirate craft were captured, and the scourge was practically ended by 1825.

Porter's excellent service was halted at the close of 1824 by his recall following the once much-discussed Fajardo Affair. This grew out of the arrest by Spanish officials and temporary imprisonment of an American lieutenant who had been sent ashore at Fajardo, Puerto Rico, to confer with the local authorities over the recovery of stolen American goods. On learning of the arrest, Porter called for apologies, and noting some preparations for defense, he soon landed a force, spiked the shore battery, and marched to the town, where the *alcalde* met him with the required amends. Though the Spanish government made no formal complaint, the authorities in Washington, for political or other motives, saw fit to recall the Commodore and summon a court of inquiry, which led to his suspension for six months. In natural resentment, Porter resigned and for several years had command of naval forces in Mexico, then at war with Spain. Later President Jackson made him Minister to Turkey, where he died in 1843.

Checking the Slave Trade

Somewhat akin to the anti-piracy campaign were the cruises on the African coast for suppression of the slave trade, which had been forbidden to American vessels in 1808 and had been declared piracy by act of Congress in 1819. Thereafter American and British cruisers off Africa put some check on the traffic, but convictions were difficult in the courts of either country unless the slavers were caught red-handed, with the slaves actually on board. A case in point was that of the slaver *Brilliante,* which was said to have escaped seizure in 1831 by fastening six hundred blacks to the anchor cable, suspending it clear, and then letting go the anchor when British cruisers closed in.

It must be admitted also that the instructions given to American cruisers were often more concerned with illegal search of American vessels than with halting the slave trade. By the Webster-Ashburton Treaty of 1842 the United States agreed to co-operate with the British by maintaining an African Squadron of at least eighty guns, but the trade still flourished, with American capital and fast American clippers involved, down to the time of the Civil War.

Mutiny on the Somers

It was on a return voyage from the African coast in 1842 that the little brig of war *Somers,* Commander Alexander Slidell

Mackenzie, was the scene of the only approach to mutiny in the history of our Navy—an affair which, though it can be merely touched on here, involved problems of shipboard psychology adequate for a Conrad novel. The source of trouble was a young acting midshipman named Philip Spencer, son of the Secretary of War, who had apparently been put in the Navy as a last resort for discipline. With a half-crazed dream of seizing the ship and converting her to piracy, Spencer approached a score or more of the crew, and made a list, with English words in Greek script, of those regarded as "certain" or "doubtful." When this was revealed to Mackenzie, he arrested Spencer and two other alleged leaders, and some days later a court of ship's officers declared them guilty of "attempted mutiny." Possibly overestimating the seriousness of the affair, and certainly realizing keenly the difficulty and risk of holding dangerous prisoners in the crowded little brig, the commander had them hanged next day at the yard-arm. When the brig reached New York, Mackenzie's report aroused nation-wide controversy, and though he was exonerated by a naval court, the affair injuriously affected his later service career. It had the effect also of emphasizing the need of more careful selection and training of naval personnel.

The Founding of the Naval Academy

The *Somers* affair was among the influences that led to the establishment of a naval academy. Though the need of such a school had become increasingly evident, it had been opposed by anti-military sentiment in Congress and by older naval officers, who laughed at the idea of "training sailors ashore." The historian George Bancroft, President Polk's able Secretary of the Navy, achieved its adoption by first securing its approval by committees of older and younger officers, then obtaining from the Army the use of old Fort Severn at Annapolis, and finally putting a number of the corps of naval schoolmasters on half pay to provide funds. Thus the school was opened in the

Top left, courtesy U.S. Naval Academy Museum

Top left, SECRETARY OF THE NAVY GEORGE BANCROFT. From a painting by Gustav Richter. *Bottom left,* COMMODORE ANDREW H. FOOTE. From a photograph. *Right,* COMMODORE MATTHEW GALBRAITH PERRY. From a photograph.

autumn of 1845 with fifty students, seven instructors, and a rigid disciplinarian, Commander Franklin Buchanan, as its first Superintendent. Congressional approval and appropriations were soon forthcoming. Until 1851, when the regular four-year course was instituted, most midshipmen came for a year at the Academy after previous service at sea. The Academy increased naval esprit de corps and encouraged higher officer attainments in professional fields. Its value was fully demonstrated when its early graduates, such as Mahan, Sampson, and Dewey, attained prominence in the Spanish-American War.

The Navy in the Mexican War

Though with little or no opposition afloat, the Navy played an important part in the hostilities with Mexico, 1846–48, by securing sea communications, landing troops and supplies, and maintaining in all seasons an effective blockade of the Mexican east coast. It was the chief instrument also in establishing control over the vast new empire of California.

Considerably before the war, in fear of similar action by the British, a United States naval force in 1842 had actually seized the California capital at Monterey and held it for a day or two. In 1846, when news of the war (declared May 13) was certain, Commodore Sloat of the Pacific Squadron was in a position to act promptly by again occupying Monterey on July 7, and ordering Commander Montgomery to take similar steps two days later at San Francisco. Succeeding soon afterward to the command of the squadron, Commodore Robert F. Stockton took possession of other ports, and with a force of about five hundred seamen, marines, and soldiers under Major Frémont marched upon and occupied Los Angeles. The little garrison left in this town was later driven out by the Mexicans, but, with the aid of a few soldiers from General Kearny's troops, which had pushed west from Santa Fe, Stockton was able to recapture it in December. In the following January he negotiated a treaty with the Mexicans which placed all California under American control. The Navy had thus provided most of the regular government force needed to bring under the flag this new sea front on the Pacific, within a few years to become the El Dorado of the forty-niners.

On the east coast of Mexico, the "Home Squadron" under Commodore Conner was at first engaged chiefly in blockade duty and in operations against coastal towns, in which it was hampered both by lack of light draft vessels and by the over-cautious policy of its commander. On March 21, 1847, Conner was succeeded by Matthew Calbraith Perry, his former second-in-command. Meantime, when army plans had been changed in favor of a landing at Vera Cruz and a direct march on Mexico City, the Navy assumed the difficult task of putting ashore General Scott's forces of about 12,000 men. On March 8, 1847, the troops were shifted from the transports to naval vessels, and were then carried ashore in sixty-five specially constructed boats, while gunboats and light craft covered the beach. The movement, under the direction of Commander French Forrest, was well planned and rapidly executed; without opposition, over 10,000 troops were landed in about five hours.

In the subsequent siege and capture of Vera Cruz, vital aid was afforded by a naval battery of six heavy shell guns, put ashore and operated by naval crews. In its two days' service the battery fired about 1,300 rounds and opened a wide breach in the walls. On March 22 and 23 a light draft flotilla under Commander Tattnall also attacked the fortifications from the seaward side. With the steamers *Spitfire* and *Vixen,* towing five gunboats, Tattnall ran up within eighty yards of the Castle of San Juan and remained there amid a furious but ill-directed cannonade. According to David D. Porter, first lieutenant in the *Spitfire,* Tattnall kept firing away at this point-blank range for a half hour or more, until Perry sent a boat with peremptory orders for his retreat.

Negotiations for the surrender of Vera Cruz began on March 26, and Scott, marching inland, ended his successful campaign by entering Mexico City in the following September. In the meantime, with increased light forces, Commodore Perry carried out successful operations against Alvaredo, Tuxpan, and Tabasco, though most of the marines in his fleet had been sent inland with the Army. Throughout the war the Navy suffered far less from enemy action than from the hardships of the climate, the sudden "northers" that swept down on the coast in winter, and the spring and summer plague of yellow fever.

The Navy and Diplomacy

During this period, in view of the very limited consular and diplomatic service, naval officers in distant waters frequently had to deal with situations that called for diplomacy, as well as a show or use of force. Whatever the measures needed, the officers usually handled these situations with good judgment and skill. Typical among such naval activities may be mentioned Captain James Biddle's Pacific cruise in the sloop *Ontario,* in which he raised the flag at the mouth of the Columbia River in August, 1818, to claim the Oregon country, and on the outward and return voyages gave protection to American commerce and whalers threatened by warfare between Chile and Peru. Typical also were O. H. Perry's mission to Venezuela in 1819, already mentioned; the visit of Commodore Rodgers' squadron to Turkey in 1825, which resulted in a commercial treaty; and the cruise of Captain Geisinger in the *Peacock,* 1832–33, with Mr. Edward Roberts as diplomatic agent, which opened relations with Siam and other small Asiatic states. Commanding our squadron on the China station in 1842, in the aftermath of the British "opium war," Commodore Lawrence Kearny, by fair yet firm dealing, gained the good will of the Chinese authorities at Canton and secured a promise of "most favored nation" treatment, which would assure equal concessions to those obtained by the British. This paved the way for our first treaty with China, negotiated by Cushing in the next year.

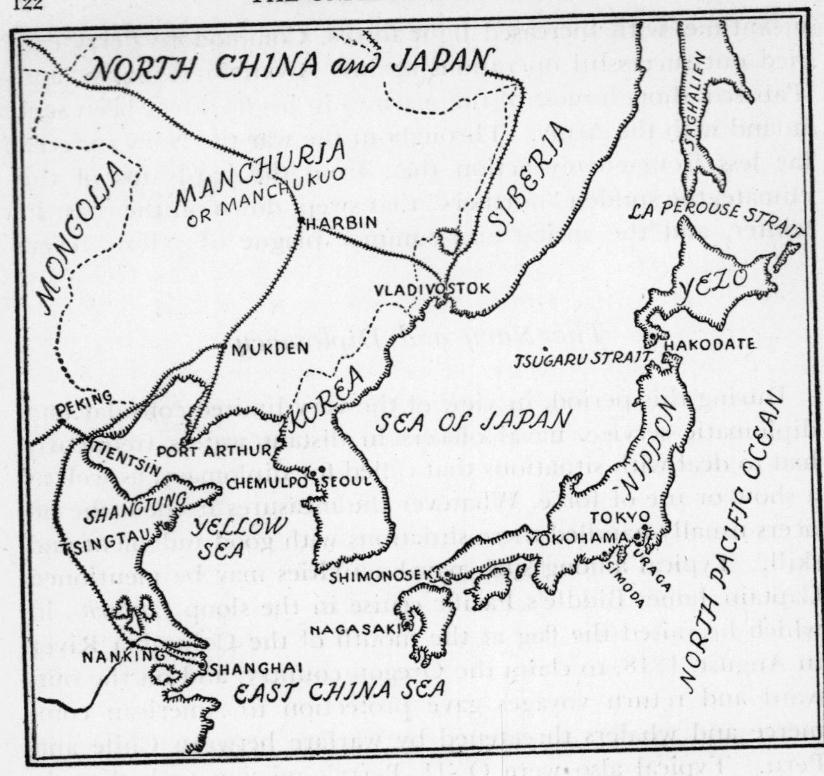

The Opening of Japan

The most celebrated of these diplomatic missions was that of Commodore Matthew Calbraith Perry to Japan. The need for more cordial relations with the island empire had been emphasized by the extension of our whale fisheries into far eastern waters and by our rapidly increasing trade with the Orient. Since the early seventeenth century, save for a few privileges granted the Dutch at Nagasaki, Japan had held herself isolated from the outside world. Now, as President Filmore's letter to the Emperor pointedly stated, the Commodore was sent "with a powerful squadron," to arrange for the friendly treatment of shipwrecked seamen, seek a station for coal and supplies, and if possible open Japanese ports to our trade.

Perry's plans for the expedition were in some measure guided by earlier contacts, notably the futile visit of Commodore Biddle at Uraga in 1846, and that of Commander Glynn in the *Preble* at Nagasaki in 1849, when by vigorous action he had secured the release of fifteen imprisoned whalers. Profiting by their experience, Perry made thorough preparations to insure success, purchasing Dutch charts of eastern waters at a cost of $30,000, and reading all available literature on Japan. His policy was to combine a show of force with courteous yet stiff and ceremonious bearing, by which he should appear not as a humble trader but as the dignified representative of a powerful nation overseas.

Of the approach of Perry's squadron to their waters the Japanese had some forewarning as a result of its earlier visits in the Loochoo and Bonin Islands. Hence there were measures of preparation, as well as much agitation when, on July 8, 1852, the big side-wheelers *Mississippi* and *Susquehanna,* towing the *Plymouth* and *Saratoga,* dropped anchor in Yedo Bay, only twenty-seven miles below the capital.

Thronging small boats were forcibly fended away. The Vice Governor of Uraga, when he came aboard, was permitted to parley only with a lieutenant; and the Governor when he appeared was met by a committee of captains. It was only upon arrangements for the receipt of his proposals by a direct representative of the Emperor that the great Commodore himself, the "Lord of the Forbidden Interior," would consent to be revealed.

The pomp and pageantry of this first appearance were calculated to strike the oriental mind. The big "black ships" were moved in so that their guns bore on the pavilion where the President's messages were to be transferred. The fifteen boats, each with a carronade in the bow, halted midway to the beach, as a salute of thirteen heavy guns announced that the

Commodore was about to enter his barge. In the procession ashore were one hundred marines, two hundred seamen, and two brass bands. The Commodore, with the officers of his staff in full dress, was flanked by two immense negroes, "armed to the teeth," as a bodyguard. Immediately ahead of him, two ship's boys bore the gold mounted rosewood box containing the precious documents, inscribed on vellum. The box itself was lined with blue velvet and closed by seals of solid gold.

After the solemn ceremony of delivering the messages to the two imperial princes designated to receive them, Perry gave assurances that he would be back for an answer, "probably with a larger squadron," in the next spring. His sailing was delayed until the seventeenth for further soundings in the bay. Hastened in his return by fears that the French and Russians were trying to forestall him, Perry was back in February with five additional vessels, and this time he anchored much nearer to Tokyo. Meantime the Japanese policy had been decided. Resistance would be futile; Japan would sign the treaty, and as soon as possible master the arts and skills, the ships and weapons, of the barbarians.

Further processions and ceremonies accompanied the negotiation and signing of the treaty. There were dinners overflowing with champagne, Madeira, and punch; there were celebrations and presentation of gifts—rich brocades, lacquer work, and carved ornaments, in exchange for sewing machines, tools, telegraph instruments, a miniature railway on which dignified mandarins spun around "at the rate of twenty miles an hour with robes whirling in the wind," and other products of Western progress.

The chief provisions of the treaty, signed March 31, were for friendly treatment of shipwrecked seamen and the opening for trade of two ports, Hakodate and Simoda. It was the entering wedge, and other nations soon secured arrangements on similar terms. For the role of august ambassador, the gruff Commodore had shown himself not ill suited. By his leading part in breaking down the barriers of Japan he had won for his nation an immediate reward of friendship and prestige, with more distant significance then unforeseen.

Exploring and Scientific Expeditions

It was typical of the scientific interest of the time that Perry's mission to Japan was accompanied by a large corps of botanists, naturalists, and ethnologists, the results of whose researches were published, along with the narrative of the cruise, in three huge volumes. The decades from 1840 to 1860 saw a whole series of these naval exploring and scientific cruises, of which the Wilkes Expedition into the Antarctic and Pacific (1838–42) is perhaps the best known. With the sloops *Vincennes* and *Peacock,* the brig *Porpoise,* and two small schooners, Wilkes spent several months in antarctic waters, chiefly in January and February of 1839, meeting hardships and dangers for which the ships and crews were most inadequately prepared. Yet, under the driving energy of their young commander the ships skirted the southern ice barriers and confirmed the existence of an antarctic continent for about 1,600 miles. They also surveyed some 280 islands in the Pacific and conducted surveys and explorations on the Oregon coast, where the *Peacock* was wrecked, without loss of life, at the mouth of the Columbia River.

Other expeditions included that of Lieutenant William F. Lynch, in 1848, which in two metal boats made the difficult two-hundred-mile descent of the Jordan River from the Sea of Galilee to the Dead Sea; the first American arctic expedition under Lieutenant De Haven, in 1850–51, in which the two vessels spent a winter adrift in the ice floes west of Greenland; and the expedition of the *Water-Witch,* Lieutenant T. J. Page, in 1854–55, for the exploration of the Parana, a branch of the La Plata River. The unprovoked firing on the *Water-Witch* by Paraguayan batteries led to the sending to South America of a large force of eighteen vessels under Commodore Shubrick, which secured apologies from Paraguay and a new treaty of commerce.

Naval Progress

Amid these varied activities it was a primary task of the officer personnel to keep the Navy abreast of the rapid technological progress which was now altering the whole character of naval warfare. The mid-century decades were in fact marked by notable forward steps in the shift from sail to steam, from wood to iron and steel, from shot to shell, and from muzzle-loading, smooth-bore cannon to rifled breech-loaders.

Fulton's curious experiment the *Demologos,* or "Voice of the People," completed in 1815, may be regarded as the first successful application of steam to naval propulsion. The *Demologos,* or *Fulton* as she was later named, had two hulls with a paddle wheel between, and a heavy connecting deck above on which was mounted a battery of thirty 32-pounders. Though unseaworthy and limited to less than six knots' speed, the *Fulton* in calm weather might have done much injury to a blockading fleet of sail. She was destroyed by an explosion in 1829.

The next American experiment in a "steam battery," the *Fulton II,* of 1837, had somewhat similar defects. But to her first commander, Captain M. C. Perry, an advocate of steam propulsion who had observed developments abroad, she suggested many improvements which were embodied in the two paddle-wheelers *Mississippi* and *Missouri,* completed in 1842. The *Mississippi* was a big ship for her time, of over 3,000 tons, with two 10-inch and eight 8-inch shell guns. The *Missouri* was burned in 1843, but the *Mississippi* proved highly useful in the Mexican War, sailed with Perry to Japan, and served effectively until she was grounded and destroyed at Port Hudson in 1863. After this no naval vessels, save a few sloops, were built exclusively for sail, though many an old-timer shared Secretary of the Navy James K. Paulding's regret at seeing "the grand old ships supplanted by these new and ugly sea monsters."

Contemporary with the *Mississippi* was the first screw-propelled naval vessel, the U.S.S. *Princeton,* largely a product of the enthusiasm of Captain Robert F. Stockton, U.S.N., who had met the Swedish inventor John Ericsson in England and had induced him to come to America and apply his genius to naval construction. As proved in the *Princeton,* the great advantage of the screw propeller over paddle wheels was that not only the screw but the engine and boiler could be placed below the water line, and thus protected from enemy fire. The *Princeton* was also one of the first American naval vessels with an iron hull; she burned hard coal, had forced draft and telescoping smokestack, and mounted twelve heavy guns [2] on the center line, available for fire on either broadside.

Chief expert in the development of American naval ordnance was Lieutenant John H. Dahlgren, who in the 1850's greatly increased the strength of guns by improved methods of founding and by the curve of pressures, which made the gun heavier at the breech than at the muzzle. Smooth-bore "Dahlgren guns" of from 9- to 15-inch bore were the chief ordnance of the Union Navy in the Civil War. Rifling of naval guns had been practiced since about 1830, but the increased accuracy thus obtained was not regarded as of much importance at the "decisive ranges" of that day.

In the Crimean War, 1853–56, both the British and the French had noted the superiority of steam battlecraft, the disastrous splintering effect of shells on wooden hulls, and the need of iron construction and armor. But in these respects American naval progress was relatively slow up to the outbreak of the Civil War. Of the forty-two ships in commission at that time, the only ones that could be accounted of much practical value were twenty-three serviceable vessels propelled by steam.

---

[2] The explosion of one of these guns, a big 12-inch cannon of Stockton's own design called the "Peacemaker," was a serious setback to ordnance experimentation. Occurring in the Potomac in 1849 during a demonstration of the *Princeton's* armament, the accident killed the Secretary of the Navy, the Secretary of State, and several other notables.

References

Allen, G. W., *Our Navy and the West Indies Pirates,* 1929.
Baxter, J. P., *The Introduction of the Ironclad Warship,* 1933.
Benjamin, Park, *The United States Naval Academy,* 1900.
Griffis, W. F., *Matthew Galbraith Perry,* 1887.
Paullin, C. O., *Diplomatic Negotiations of American Naval Officers,* 1912.

THE WAR FOR THE UNION: A DIVIDED NATION

Economic Conditions

THE REPORT OF the Census of 1860 recorded the vast internal expansion of the United States. The industrial revolution had come to America; and in a decade, manufactures and inventions, as well as mining, farm products, and population, had increased by leaps and bounds. Cotton goods manufactured in New England showed a total for 1860 of $80,-310,535, an increase in ten years of 83.4 per cent; those manufactured in the middle states, of $26,272,111, an increase of 77.7 per cent. Boots and shoes and leather had reached a total production of $152,640,651, an increase of over 67 per cent, the greatest increase being in New England and the Western states.

A similar story is told of the increase of agricultural implements, sewing machines, flour, cotton, tobacco, mine products (especially gold), and petroleum.[1]

Further, there was a revolution in transportation, for railroads had increased in mileage, 1850 to 1860, nearly 300 per cent.

These changes had promoted growth of population—that of the 15 slave-holding states having reached a total of 8,039,000

[1] Messrs. Bowditch and Drake of New Haven in August, 1859, had commenced operations for oil in Pennsylvania; boring to a depth of 71 feet, they had struck a "fountain" that yielded 400 gallons daily. In that year 325 barrels were marketed; three years later the wells were producing nearly one thousand times as much in a week.

white people, an increase of 27.33 per cent; and that of the nineteen free states and territories with the District of Columbia, a total of 18,936,579 white people, an increase of 41.24 per cent. The latter had been greatly influenced by immigration.

In this industrial progress the Southern states had not shared equally. South Carolina in 1860 for the most part still held in her economic and social life to the standards of 1810, and thus was entirely out of step with the new order. When her people saw their own products in textiles, flour, and leather goods actually decreasing, in contrast with the amazing development in other states, their white population only slightly increasing—thus relatively smaller—and recognized the wide chasm between their own patriarchal society associated with slave labor and the busy, machine-based social order of the North, where everyone prided himself on being a worker of some kind, they thought to protect themselves and stay the inevitable by withdrawing from the Union. Other Southern states shared in their feeling of apprehension and reached a like decision. Thus, it is to be noted that every state convention deciding for secession contained some reference to the disregard or invasion of their property rights.

Weakness of American Nationalism

Although the root of the trouble was chiefly economic, and for years economic differences had promoted divergent political ideas and party conflicts, states near the line of cleavage, Virginia, Maryland, Kentucky, and Tennessee, were not so plainly affected as the cotton states by profit and loss considerations. In these and also in Illinois, Ohio, Indiana, New York, and Massachusetts, principles of government and questions relating to the origin of the republic became the important issue.

In all states the controversy on slavery aroused passion on the part of a minority and provoked endless discussion. Among the anti- and pro-slavery advocates there were high-minded idealists and out-and-out fanatics. Their intense feeling must have had influence. But neutral observers, as in England, in their simplification of the issue saw a conflict between champions of two opposite ideas of government, defenders of sectional liberty or state rights, and defenders of the Federal Union. Both were terribly in earnest.

Comparatively few prominent men on either side had realized what was coming—this although sharp political differences had existed between large sections of the North and the South for thirty years. There was no extensive preparation until a few months or weeks previous to hostilities. Lincoln's election in November, 1860, decided matters for South Carolina, and she seceded in December. Other states having followed, seven joined, on the eighth of February, 1861, in establishing the Confederate States of America. Ominous activities soon were reported in all parts of the South, but the Administration in Washington continued in a state of lethargy.

This has often been explained as due to the machinations of the preponderating number of Southerners and Southern sympathizers that were to be found in every executive office and even in the President's Cabinet. As a matter of fact, the great majority in both the North and the South had been apathetic. Many well-informed public speakers and writers like James Russell Lowell clung to the idea that a compromise could be effected, and that the seceded states would then return to their allegiance. On the other hand, General Winfield Scott, in command of the United States Army, gave as his solution of the problem, "Wayward sisters, depart in peace." This sentiment was concurred in by Horace Greeley of the *New York Tribune* and fervently desired by a large number of abolitionists, who for years had been advocates of a complete and permanent separation of the Free states from the Slave states.

Thus, the weakness of American nationalism early in 1861 was evident, just as it had been in 1812. The large mass of people, North and South, did not know where they stood. Voicing the views of only a minority, was Lincoln, the President-Elect, who affirmed that although the new administration might yield on many contested points relating to rights of slave-owners, it would uphold without the slightest wavering the preservation of the Union.

Public affairs continued to drift until the firing on Fort Sumter, April 12, 1861. Suddenly, indecision was ended. Hundreds of thousands saw the issue clarified and took sides, some almost overnight reversing their previous positions.

Not only had statesmen and publicists in general been blind to the coming of the "inevitable conflict," but they were slow to recognize its magnitude when fighting had begun. This will explain at least in part the pressure early put on the Federal Army to march on Richmond and to expose itself to defeat at Bull Run. Signal as was that disaster, however, it tended to stimulate the champions of the national cause. The Northerners were taught to respect their foe, and began to see more plainly what lay before them. On the other hand, their adversaries, at least many of them, fell into the error of magnifying and grossly overestimating their own prowess.

The Navy Unprepared

Like other branches, the Navy was unprepared and disorganized—both in personnel and in ships. On the fourteenth of January, previous to the final act of secession, Lieutenant Haralton had addressed an appeal to "Southern Officers of the U.S. Navy," to resign and accept a commission from the states, and he urged, "Bring with you every ship and man you can, that we may use them against the oppressors of our liberties." It is significant, however, that only about one-fifth of all the officers and midshipmen in the Navy and Marine Corps resigned. The acting midshipmen, under instruction at the Naval Academy, occasioned the greatest loss, only twenty-two from the Southern states continuing in the national Service and 106 leaving to support their states. But even with these included, the final count showed 350 Southerners who remained in the Service as against 321 who resigned.[2] Long association under the Flag proved to be a strong bond. Further, it is significant that not one officer took his ship with him to his new allegiance. Indeed, the fact that many Southern officers waited until their resignations could be acted on and their relief designated was so marked that the historian Channing regards the acceptance of their resignations as one of the worst blunders made by the Navy Department; he gives it as his opinion that if the officers had been held to the fulfillment of the oath sworn to by each, Buchanan, Catesby Jones, and dozens of others would have given loyal service to the Union, and the Confederacy would have been denied its outstanding naval leaders.

The United States Navy, in March, 1861, had forty-two vessels in commission, and of these, as remarked on a previous page, only twenty-three which were propelled by steam could be regarded as efficient. The Home Squadron consisted of twelve vessels, and on the day of Lincoln's inauguration but four were in Northern ports. The retiring Secretary of the Navy, Toucey of Connecticut, a Southern sympathizer, was popularly blamed for this, as well as for the bad state of repair of most of the ships. But we must remember that beginning with 1857 the country had passed through one of its periodic depressions and Congress had not listened to the recommendations of the Secretary of the Navy but had cut the annual appropriation to the lowest figure; also that in not assembling the available ships at Northern ports Toucey was but carrying out the general policy of President Buchanan.

Although critics have flayed the National Administration for the failure to adopt aggressive measures in the spring of 1861, it is safe to say they would have been equally severe if the opposite policy had been followed. Hostilities would have begun several weeks or months earlier, and the consequences might not have been favorable to the Union cause. It is certain that in Kentucky the legislature, even in May, very nearly voted for

[2] J. T. Scharf, *History of the Confederate States Navy*, pp. 32, 33.

secession, a majority of one inducing the state to adopt a policy of neutrality. In the weeks that followed, her people were impressed by the calmness and discretion of Lincoln and his willingness to respect their neutrality. And many of them turned from the Confederates, first because of the haste with which the Southern sympathizers left the Union, and later because of their presumption in assuming that Kentucky belonged to them. When the Confederates made a distinct trespass on her neutrality, Kentucky abandoned the middle course, and in September adopted a policy of complete allegiance to the Federal Government.[3]

Preparations for Conflict

When the die had been cast, there was certainly no feebleness on the part of the new Secretary, Gideon Welles. Ships were recalled from squadrons in Brazil, the Mediterranean, West Africa, the East Indies, and the Pacific. Even with the utmost expedition, however, time was required; the Mediterranean Squadron did not return till midsummer, and the Africa Squadron not until autumn. Every navy yard in the North meanwhile hummed with intense activity. Seventy-six vessels of the old Navy that previously had been dismantled and placed in ordinary were, in 1861, repaired and put in commission. Eight sloops of war were laid down in navy yards, and twenty-three "ninety-day gunboats" and twelve paddle-wheel steamers (for the shallow rivers) were contracted for with private firms. Besides these, 136 merchant ships that could be armed and used for blockade or for other purposes were purchased. Their acquisition by United States agents in New York, Baltimore, Halifax, and elsewhere served a double purpose. It provided an important addition to the Federal force. And it forestalled the efforts of Confederate agents sent to procure vessels to use as privateers and blockade runners. To man the growing fleets, the Navy Department correspond-

[3] N. S. Shaler, *Kentucky*, pp. 231–256.

ingly increased the number of seamen, from 7,600, March 4, 1861, to 22,000, December 2, 1861.

As we look back three-quarters of a century, seemingly the odds in this great struggle preponderately favored the North. It had a population of 19,000,000 against 9,000,000; and the 19,000,000 had iron works and steel mills, shoe factories, cotton and woolen mills, gun factories and munition plants, merchant vessels and naval vessels—the latter giving command of the sea. They had wealth and free communication with the countries of Europe, such as was essential for commerce and the increase of wealth. All this was largely denied the opposite side. But the 9,000,000 of the South were fighting on interior lines. And whereas the soldiers of the North contended for the preservation of the Union, which at the beginning was for some little more than an abstract principle, the soldiers of the South fought for their homes and liberties, their personal danger arousing them to extreme resistance.

Numbers were against the South, but it might be recalled that the Thirteen Colonies, against much greater odds, had gained their independence. The Colonies, however, had their resolute and resourceful seamen, their Arnold, Jones, Barry, Conyngham, Wickes, and also their hundreds of privateer captains. These seasoned fighters, eluding the superior forces of the Royal Navy, seized supply and munition ships, defeated scattered units, and materially assisted in gaining the recognition and support of France. The fact that at the beginning of the war the North had the nucleus of a navy, capable of rapid expansion, and the South had no navy at all was of the utmost significance.

Early in the summer of 1861 the Navy Department outlined its mission, comprised in three lines of operations: (1) Blockade of the Southern ports along a coast line of more than 3,000 miles, including the naval occupation and defense of the Potomac. (2) Organization of combined naval and military expeditions against strongholds on the Southern coast; and cooperation in similar expeditions on the Mississippi and its tributaries, including operations of the Army to cut off Confederate supplies coming to the east from the west. (3) Pursuit of Confederate cruisers and privateers.

On account of the great distances involved and the fact that naval vessels would be called upon to engage in a type of warfare in which they fought against heavy odds—as when they attacked forts and earthworks in harbors and rivers—the Department recognized they had undertaken a highly difficult program.

The Confederate Navy Department, on the other hand, decided that their proper counteroffensive was to prey on American commerce, to assist in maintaining the intercommunications of their armed forces and supply trains, and to break the blockade and allow foreign aid to enter. Being without a fleet, they planned to obtain ships by conversion and by purchase, believing that if they could themselves build or have built for them by contract even a few ships that were superior because of armor and rifled guns they might successfully challenge the naval supremacy of the North.

The head of the United States Navy, Secretary Gideon Welles, was one of Lincoln's excellent appointments. He had previously had experience in public life as a newspaper editor, holder of several state offices, and chief of the Bureau of Provisions and Clothing, Navy Department. His patriarchal beard critics found a subject of amusement, but his administrative ability, as they were obliged to admit, was of the highest order. "He seldom forgot a face, a name, or a personality. He was an uncanny judge of men." Furthermore, he was fortunate in having as the Assistant Secretary, Gustavus V. Fox. Mr. Fox, after eighteen years' service in the Navy, had resigned as lieutenant (1856) to enter business. The office to which he was appointed was newly created to bring harmony in the various bureaus of the Department. He was the professional adviser, and he brought technical skill and understanding to the planning of operations and the removing of superannuated and inefficient officers. There had previously been no age for retirement. Thus, at the beginning of the war, the commandant of the Norfolk Navy Yard was sixty-eight, the commandant of Pensacola sixty-seven, and a captain still in command at sea was nearly seventy. To fill vacancies that were created by retirement and to officer the ships lately added, the Department made rapid promotions. Upper classes at the Naval Academy were sent to sea and midshipmen became lieutenants before they reached the age of nineteen. Also volunteer officers were called for, and 7,500 were commissioned during the war. But the Navy did not suffer as did the Army from political appointments, and there was no rear admiral or commodore who gained his first acquaintance with the sea as commanding officer of a fleet.

Foreign Relations

The strength of a country engaged in war is determined not only by the united support at home but by the continued friendly relations with neutral powers. In the Civil War the Federal Government, though at first conspicuously lacking in united national feeling, was fortunate in its international relations.

William H. Seward, Lincoln's Secretary of State, in the early months of 1861 realized the sad disunity and thought to remedy this by a foreign war. He seriously presented to the President the fantastic idea of engaging the United States in a conflict with one or several of the leading powers of Europe, in the face of which South and North would drop all differences and rally to the common defense. But Lincoln's wisdom asserted itself, and an international imbroglio was averted. As seen later, European intervention was cherished by the South as their trump card. For four years this was their hope and expectation, and through it they were confident of ultimate success.

England and France did not believe the North would win the war, but impressed by Seward's firm tone and the consistent blockade maintained by the Navy, they adhered to a neutral course and refused entry into their ports of prizes taken by either belligerent. This policy caused hardship especially to the Confederates, for it prevented them from profiting by privateering. Jefferson Davis remarked that the neutral nations of Europe, instead of acting in a way hostile to the North, "pursued a policy which, nominally impartial, was practically most favorable to our enemies and most detrimental to us." [4]

Statesmen of the South confidently expected that if all else should fail, King Cotton would decide the issue in their behalf. Four million workers in England, as well as 600,000 in France, were directly or indirectly dependent on cotton for their livelihood. Economists urged that to cut off the supply would mean disruption of all industries and widespread unemployment—a national disaster that could not be tolerated. But "King Cotton proved a feeble Monarch because of his very opulence." [5] Crops had been unusually large previous to the war and that of 1860 had already been marketed. There being an oversupply in England, merchants welcomed a chance to dispose of the stock on hand, especially when prices began to rise. In time the demand for American cotton became less insistent. Egypt and India were developing their fields. Further, old King Cotton had found a rival in young and lusty King Corn. There were several bad grain harvests in Europe, and the nations that had seriously considered raising the blockade were unwilling to face the prospect of war and the loss of shipments of wheat at a time when wheat was most essential.

North and South were so nearly equal in strength it is easy to see that the added weight of a European power thrown into the balance might have changed the destinies of America. But the growing Navy of the North was a factor that soon had to be reckoned with, and our ships were a strong argument against intervention. Further, not merely the larger number of men

---

[4] Jefferson Davis, *A Short History of the Confederate States of America*, p. 319.

[5] S. F. Bemis, *A Diplomatic History of the United States*, p. 372.

in the field and aboard ship counted as the war went on. The Confederate states were weak in the organization of their government, and leaders in state and military affairs did not work well together. On the other hand, the Federal Government, which at first had suffered from flabbiness and irresolution arising out of a divided purpose, unwillingness to give wholehearted support, placing of personal ease and financial security before national interests, before long gave evidence of a new patriotism. The Navy, like the Army, reflecting this, developed a unity and efficiency the country had never known before. For some years previous there had been the question of whether the United States of America was more than a geographical term. The Union became a reality when millions rose to sacrifice everything for it, even life itself.

References

Adams, E. C., *Great Britain and the Civil War,* 2 vols., 1925.
Channing, Edward, *History of the United States,* Vol. VI, 1926.
Morison, S. E. and Commager, H. S., *The Growth of the American Republic,* 2 vols., 1937.
Reports of the Secretary of the Navy, 1860–61.
Scharf, J. T., *History of the Confederate States Navy,* 1887.

ESTABLISHING THE BLOCKADE

IX

Significance of the Blockade

In the grand strategic plan, the Navy and the Army were to crush all armed resistance wherever it appeared. On the sea, the Navy's own peculiar element, the engagements were destined to be few in number, for the reason that the Confederacy, though it had a Navy Department, never developed a sea-going fleet and seldom had more than a few scattered ships.

The Navy was to play, however, a part of vital significance in joint operations with the Army, and to accomplish what was of still greater importance in its work of breaking down communications of the enemy, internally between their own forces and externally between them and the foreign powers. The latter were ever ready to furnish munitions and supplies of all kinds when there was gold, cotton, tobacco or any other commodity to secure in exchange. Military equipment and manufactured articles were absolutely essential to the South for the successful prosecution of the war, and great assistance was expected from abroad. It was because of the blockade that commerce for the South became increasingly difficult. Of the several lines of naval operations planned by the North, the blockade was the first to be tried, in 1861, and it was unrivaled in the magnitude and consistency with which it was maintained throughout the four years that followed.

Control of the Potomac

It will be recalled that Secretary Welles, as he announced what the Navy plans included, grouped the "naval occupation of the Potomac" with the blockade of the Southern ports. Commonly, the blockade thereafter was described as beginning with Washington and extending to the Rio Grande. This would seem to be as great a mistake in terms, as it would be to speak of the blockade of the upper Mississippi. There is a difference between the occupation of hostile territory, denying to an enemy the advantage of moving men and supplies at will, and the sealing of a frontier, prohibiting ingress and egress to both enemy and neutral traders—which is the function of a blockade. But however occupation of the Potomac should be classified, the fact remains that it was a matter of utmost importance that the river on which the national capital is situated should continue open for Federal operations to Chesapeake Bay and the sea.

This was to be the work of the Potomac Flotilla, under Commander J. H. Ward. On May 31, 1861, Ward attempted to destroy batteries erected by Confederates at Aquia Creek. He found it easy to silence three which had been placed at the railroad terminus, but others back on the heights proved more formidable. They were above the elevation of his guns, and their volleys, sprinkling the water nearer and nearer, soon reached the ship and made his position untenable. Next day, when the Confederates had returned to their position in the lower battery with fresh guns placed there, the work of the gunboats had all to be done again. There developed a kind of guerrilla warfare which might be expected to break out at any point. In this, a month later, Commander Ward, who was protecting a party sent ashore to clear a wood and himself sighting a gun, met his death. As Secretary Welles observed, "It was clearly foreseen by the department that without the active co-operation of the Army it would be impossible to prevent the navigation of the river from being obstructed by batteries on the Virginia side." The Navy, however, continued to maintain a constant patrol, and by this enabled vessels to steam up and down until the fifteenth of October. Then the river was virtually closed. Not until the following spring did operations of the Army of the Potomac compel the Confederates to abandon their posts on the Potomac in order to strengthen the lines about Richmond.

Announcement, Organization, and Operation of the Blockade

In diplomatic communications with European nations, Washington long held to the view that the war was but an insurrection. Any country may at will decide to close certain of its ports, and logically this might have seemed to be the proper procedure for the Administration in dealing with a strictly domestic situation. But if Washington had followed this course, the Federal forces could have proceeded only against offenders caught entering or leaving a closed port.

The other course open to the Administration was the establishment of a blockade, which gave the right of stopping, searching, and seizing any suspected vessel on the high seas, whether near a blockaded port or not—provided her papers showed that she was bound for or had cleared from a blockaded port. Blockade, however, is commonly regarded as a war measure, applied only to the ports or boundaries of a belligerent. The Administration, in issuing two announcements of blockade in April, 1861, which were sent to all foreign powers, showed that it was concerned not so much with theory as with practical measures.

The proclamation of April 19 announced the intention of blockading the Southern coast, South Carolina to Texas; that of April 27 extended this by including Virginia and North Carolina. According to the Declaration of Paris, 1856, "A blockade in order to be binding, must be effective—that is to say, it must be maintained by a force sufficient really to prevent access to the enemy coast line"—or as commonly interpreted, by a force sufficient to make it hazardous to attempt to enter or leave the prohibited territory. Now, on the day of the first proclamation, the Navy had available but three ships that could be assigned to this duty—a number hardly sufficient to blockade even one Southern port. But the Administration had definite plans, and by giving due notice had determined to institute a blockade that should be legal and binding, and later to extend it without loss of time. A proclamation of blockade had commonly defined certain areas to which it applied, when the blockading ships were in position to make it effective. But Lincoln's proclamation was rather a declaration of intention, and the blockaded coast was extended without additional notice. It read as follows:

> Now therefore, I, Abraham Lincoln, President of the United States . . . have further deemed it advisable to set on foot a blockade of the ports within the States aforesaid, in pursuance of the laws of the United States and of the Law of Nations in such case provided. For this purpose a competent force will be posted so as to prevent entrance and exit of vessels from the ports aforesaid. If, therefore, with a view to violate such blockade, a vessel shall approach or shall attempt to leave any of the said ports, she will be duly warned by the commander of one of the blockading vessels, who will endorse on her register the fact and date of such warning, and if the same vessel shall again attempt to enter or leave the blockaded port, she will be captured, and sent to the nearest convenient port for such proceedings against her and her cargo as prize, as may be deemed advisable.

At the outset, Washington did not look upon the blockade as a highly formidable task. It contemplated the closing of four or five ports on the Atlantic coast and as many more on the Gulf, with a patrol of vessels cruising up and down the coast between. European countries, on the other hand, were of the opinion that it would prove impossible, and they did not protest, for they thought the war would be of short duration. The project grew until it extended over a coast line of 3,000 miles with 185 ports or openings, and the National Government found it a gigantic undertaking.

The blockade actually began with Hampton Roads, and this was its most important point. The *Niagara* when she returned from Japan, April 24, was dispatched to cruise off Charleston. The *Brooklyn* and *Powhatan* were ordered to the Gulf. As previously stated, construction of warships was begun and everything afloat that could be purchased or chartered was pressed into service, including screw steamers, side-wheelers, tugs, ferryboats, and even sailing vessels. During the war 418 vessels, 313 of them steamers, were thus acquired—most of them for the blockade.[1] To man these ships the Navy procured officers and men chiefly by drawing on the merchant marine, the "sea-militia" of the Navy.

Early the European merchants trading with the Confederates hit on the idea of shipping to the Southern ports, not directly, but through intermediate neutral ports. This was to lessen the length of voyage during which there was risk of capture. To ship a cargo to Nassau, Bermuda, or Havana, and then to transship it to a Southern port, reduced that part of the voyage during which there was danger of capture from 3,500 or 4,500 miles to one-seventh of the distance. The three Southern ports on the Atlantic through which most shipping entered were Wilmington, Charleston, and Savannah. Nassau was nearest to Savannah, being five hundred miles distant; Bermuda to Wilmington, being 674 miles distant; Havana was conveniently situated with relation to Mobile and New Orleans, as well as the harbors or inlets of Florida and Texas. Matamoros was only across the river from Brownsville, Texas. The National Government, however, did not long permit this commerce through the neutral ports of the West Indies, for its lawyers announced the doctrine of "the broken voyage," judging the cargo by the ultimate destination. Thus it might be seized even though it was consigned to a neutral port. The

[1] J. R. Soley, *The Blockade and the Cruisers,* pp. 17, 18.

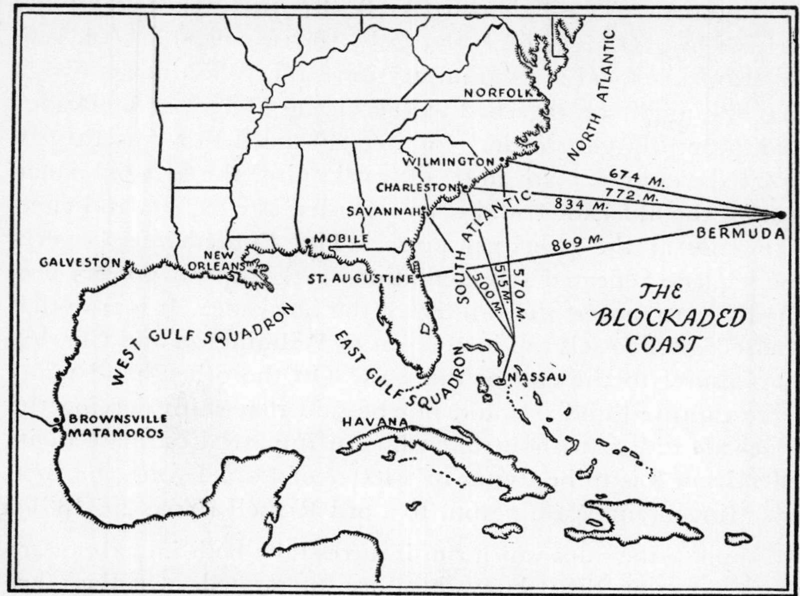

action was protested, but it was finally recognized as regular and in accordance with international law.

When the blockade was established at Hampton Roads, Commodore Pendergrast had command. As it was extended, Commodore Stringham took over the Atlantic blockade as far as Key West, and Commodore Mervine, the Gulf blockade. Afterwards Cape Canaveral, Florida, was the point that divided the two, and the Gulf blockade was further divided into the East Gulf, extending to Pensacola, and the West Gulf lying beyond. Farragut commanded the West Gulf Blockading Squadron from February, 1862, to the latter part of 1864.

Although no time had been lost, the Government was nevertheless careful during the first month not to disregard the rights of neutrals. According to instructions issued by the Department, officers of ships after they had published the notification of blockade were to allow a reasonable number of days, not less than fifteen, for neutral vessels to depart with or without cargoes. A case that attracted attention was that of the British brig *Herald,* captured July 16, two days out of Wilmington and two hundred miles from land. Washington feared that she might be regarded as the victim of "paper blockade" and promptly gave orders for her release. Nor was this an isolated example. Not until six weeks after the first proclamation of the blockade could it be regarded as effective, and effective only at the principal ports. The Confederate Government made repeated representations to European powers urging them to protest the validity of the blockade. It is true that small coastal vessels ran in and out of Wilmington and Charleston, almost to the end of the war. On the other hand many were captured and it could not be said that ships defying the blockade did so without hazard. An impartial estimate of its effectiveness is to be found in a letter of Lord Lyons, the British Minister in Washington, to Lord Russell (Nov. 29, 1861):

> I suppose the ships which run it successfully both in and out are more numerous than those which are intercepted. On the other hand it is very far from being a mere Paper Blockade. A great many vessels are captured; it is a most serious interruption to Trade; and if it were as ineffective as Mr. Jefferson Davis says in his Message, he would not be so very anxious to get rid of it.

The statement of Lyons was made when the blockade had been in operation for six months. It became more strict as the war continued, and after the second year the only ships that stood a fair chance of eluding it were those especially designed for this purpose, of unusual speed and low freeboard, and painted so as to be not readily discernible in the dusk of evening or on a cloudy day. During the war 1,149 prizes were brought in, 210 being steamers; and 355 vessels were burned, sunk, or driven ashore, 85 of them steamers; making a total of 1,504 vessels of all classes.[2]

The blockade runners developed a technique that was daring and often brilliant. They would select a time in the dark of

[2] Soley, *op. cit.*, p. 44.

the moon and approach their port when night was descending. Since a ship especially built for the purpose showed above deck but two short masts and a smokestack, with the lead-colored hull invisible at 100 yards, the chances of her slipping past were more than even. Wilkinson, one of the most successful runners, wrote that the *Lee* while under his command had run the blockade twenty-one times and carried abroad between 6,000 and 7,000 bales of cotton selling for about $2,000,000 in gold and brought to the Confederacy equally valuable cargoes. Captain Roberts, an Englishman who engaged in the traffic, says that a captain received for a round trip £1,000, a chief engineer £500, and each of the crew about £50. Before leaving England he inquired of a Southern lady what was needed most. On being told that it was "corsages," he determined on a private business venture; buying in Glasgow 1,000 pairs at one shilling, one penny each, he sold the whole stock on reaching port to a dealer for twelve shillings each, making a profit of nearly 1,100 per cent; and he disposed of a quantity of tooth brushes in Richmond for seven times what they had cost. He made twelve successful trips through the blockade in 1863–64. On one of these, when approaching Wilmington, he heard firing ahead and guessed that the blockaders were chasing a runner. Soon he made out a ship hurrying on to help her companions to capture or destroy the contraband. Deeming the rear of the squadron a position of greatest safety, he followed the cruiser he had sighted for several miles, and when the firing ceased and his guide turned out to sea, he stopped his engines. The pilot could not make out the entrance to the river but was sure that the ship was close to shore. An hour before dawn she ran aground and soon was discovered by two blockaders, who began firing on her. By frantic effort, Roberts lightened his ship and succeeded in getting her afloat. Then, when the guns of Fort Fisher compelled the cruisers to move farther out, he entered the river.

The enforcement of the blockade, month after month in all kinds of weather, was hard work. While for those running the blockade there was a short period of intense action, for those who were enforcing the blockade vigilance was required that seemed never ending and they had constantly to be on the alert.

Supply ships visited the blockaders at regular intervals and were enthusiastically welcomed, not only for the replenishment of the larder, but for letters, newspapers, and the brief contact with the rest of the world. This duty, especially off some of the smaller ports of the Gulf, where perhaps for months at a time no blockade runner ever appeared to give the excitement of a chase, was deadly monotonous. Within a week officers and men were talked out; isolation told terribly on their nerves; and many ceased to be on speaking terms with most of their shipmates.

Not infrequently Confederates on shore attempted to harass the blockaders and by a sudden attack destroy the ships and raise the blockade. In the sounds of North Carolina during the spring of 1864, as will be narrated later, the ironclad ram *Albemarle,* which had been built in the Roanoke River, sank the *Southfield,* and for two hours and a half gave battle to the whole Federal flotilla there. She continued to be a threat until the following October when she was torpedoed by Cushing. Off Charleston, in 1863, two ironclad rams captured the *Mercedita* and engaged her companions in the blockading squadron. Coming out of Savannah, the improvised ironclad *Atlanta,* which earlier had been the blockade runner *Fingal,* boldly attacked two Union monitors in Wassaw Sound, but was captured after an action that lasted fifteen minutes. At Galveston, in January, 1863, a force of river boats descended upon the Federal blockading squadron, took the *Harriet Lane,* induced the blowing up of the *Westfield,* which had run aground, and compelled the other ships to seek safety in flight. On the basis of this success, the Confederate general commanding in Texas proclaimed that the blockade was broken. But he delayed too long in making the announcement; before the proclamation was issued Farragut had a new squadron off the city.

Antedating all those attempts just mentioned, there was another effort to break the blockade, which for a brief period gave Confederates wild dreams of naval supremacy and filled the Federalists with deep apprehension. This and events leading up to it occurred at Hampton Roads.

The Loss of the Norfolk Navy Yard

It was the fate of the Navy, as of the Army, early in the war to meet a signal reverse that proved the weakness of its organization. The loss of the Norfolk Navy Yard, occurring several weeks before the defeat of the Army at Bull Run, in fact only eight days after hostilities had commenced, represents the greatest disaster sustained by the Navy during all the four years of fighting. It was even more far-reaching than that at Pearl Harbor, eighty years later. Nor was the humiliation lessened by the realization, which a few days brought, of how unnecessary was the costly sacrifice. In resistance to the threatening forces in the vicinity, not a single life was given, not a gun fired. The Union had ships with powerful batteries that could have dominated the yard, and military forces of strength at Fortress Monroe, which could have been brought to the defense of the yard in less than twenty-four hours. The affair was an outstanding example of the weakness, indecision, and fear of provoking hostile action that prevailed early in 1861.

The Government had rightly considered Virginia to be of greatest importance and to the last hoped that she might be saved for the Union. In accordance with the policy of giving no offense to doubtful states, General Winfield Scott had opposed sending troops to Norfolk. Commodore C. S. McCauley, commanding the Navy Yard there, was sixty-eight years old, and imbued with the spirit of extreme caution. Although of undoubted patriotism, he was alarmed by the resignation of officer after officer following Virginia's secession. Dejected and feeling that the Union cause had been utterly deserted, he exaggerated the force that he was told was just outside the gates, as well as the weakness of the yard. Chief Engineer Isherwood and Commander James Alden had been sent from Washington to take out the frigate *Merrimack*. But McCauley, influenced by reports of obstructions placed in the channel and of hostile action that would immediately attend any effort to move the Union ships, gave orders when the *Merrimack* was ready to put to sea that her fires be drawn. Thereupon, Isherwood and Alden, finding they could do nothing, at once returned to Washington to report the situation to the Navy Department.

Recognizing the imminent danger, Secretary Welles dispatched Commodore Paulding with an improvised force on the *Pawnee* to take over the Navy Yard. He arrived on the morning of April 20, only to become a victim of the evil spell that had come over the yard. He accepted what he was told—he had come just too late. McCauley had begun the destruction of the government property and had scuttled all but one of the ships of any value. Commodore Paulding, with 1,000 men under his command, could probably have held the yard for weeks. But he, like McCauley, exaggerated the hostile forces surrounding it; and since the work of destruction had begun, he saw no other course but to carry it through and prevent what might be used for war purposes from falling into Confederate hands. All the Federal officers seemed to suffer from hysteria and even the work of destruction was hurried and ineffective. As the Union forces withdrew, crowds waiting outside the gates rushed in. They extinguished the fires that had been set, and saved the dry dock, which had been mined, before the fuse set off the charge. Later the Confederates recovered the heavy guns and shells that had been thrown into the river, and raised and rebuilt the frigate *Merrimack* that had been set on fire and scuttled.[3]

In the capture of the yard the Confederates gained over 3,000 pieces of ordnance, among them 300 Dahlgren guns of

---

[3] Reports of Captain Arthur Sinclair and Major General W. B. Taliaferro of the Confederate Army, included in *Naval War Records,* IV, 306–309.

the latest type. With these and what they had taken at the Pensacola Navy Yard they were able to arm their fortifications on the coasts and rivers at a time when gun factories in the South had only been projected and munitions from Europe had scarcely been contracted for.

The Federal Government lost, besides the steam frigate *Merrimack,* the sloops of war *Germantown* and *Plymouth,* the brig *Dolphin* (all ready for sea), and the older ships *Pennsylvania, United States, Columbus, Delaware, Raritan,* and *Columbia,* with an unfinished ship of the line *New York.* However, as Admiral Porter later observed, "great as was . . . the loss of our ships, it was much less than the loss of our guns."[4]

A Race in Shipbuilding

In the vast theater of operations, 1861 to 1865, the waters absolutely essential for the Union Navy to control were Hampton Roads and the mouth of the Chesapeake. Here the blockade began and here the flagship of the North Atlantic Blockading Squadron made its station. Furthermore, for the Army, it was the key to offensive and defensive operations in eastern Virginia and along the Potomac and Rappahannock and the Chesapeake; that is, it was the key to operations threatening either Richmond or Washington. McClellan's advance on Richmond in the spring of 1862 was about to begin. With the assurance of strong Union control at Fortress Monroe and of the waters on which the fort looked, he planned to use the rivers. The challenge that came from the initial success of the Confederate ironclad *Virginia,* about to be related, was a serious setback. Had this success been repeated, the movement of Union troops would have been interrupted and the Peninsular Campaign would not have taken place.

Napoleon had taught the world that great land battles may be fought on the map, the issues being decided before the

[4] Porter, *Naval History of the Civil War,* p. 33.

armies exchange a shot. The engagement at Hampton Roads demonstrated that sea battles may be fought in the shipyard. A new type of fighting craft was to be a decisive factor in future engagements, and the result of the first great battle in which the new ships were tried was determined in a large degree by the opposing yards at Norfolk and Brooklyn. It began with a race to determine which belligerent could place its champion first in the fighting zone.

The hard-fought battle of Hampton Roads and all the anxious uncertainty that preceded and followed it were direct consequences of the abandonment of the Norfolk Navy Yard. The *Merrimack, Germantown, Plymouth,* and *Dolphin* had been set on fire and scuttled. Water having extinguished the flames as the ships sank, their hulls were not injured to a great extent and their batteries suffered not at all. The *Merrimack, Germantown,* and *Plymouth* were raised, but because of lack of equipment and facilities the work of rebuilding and fitting-out was concentrated on the *Merrimack,* which had been one of the latest and strongest steam frigates in the Navy of the 1850's.

The Confederate States possessed an important asset in their Secretary of the Navy S. R. Mallory. In earlier years as chairman of the Senate Committee of Naval Affairs, he had gained extensive knowledge of fighting ships. He knew of the latest developments in the navies of Great Britain and France, and realizing the impossibility of building so as to match the Union Navy, ship for ship, he decided to improvise and produce a new type, superior to any then existing. His idea was expressed in the following: "Such a vessel at this time could traverse the entire coast of the United States, prevent all blockades, and encounter with a fair prospect of success their entire Navy." [5]

The *Merrimack,* on being raised, furnished for his new ship the hull, boilers, and engine. Lieutenant John M. Brooke and

[5] Letter to Honorable C. M. Conrad, May 10, 1861. Quoted in *Naval War Records,* Series II, II, 69.

Naval Constructor John L. Porter produced plans for converting her into an ironclad. Upon their adoption, Porter was directed to proceed with the constructor's duties at Norfolk. Brooke was to superintend the manufacture of the armor and the additional guns required for her battery at the Tredegar Iron Works, Richmond. And Chief Engineer William P. Williamson was to attend to the machinery. On the twenty-third of June, 1861, these three officers met Mr. Mallory and began the work.

In Washington, however, delay was inevitable. First, Congress met in extra session and voted an appropriation. Then a special board of naval officers was appointed to make the recommendation. As they knew little about ironclads, the officers of the board felt it necessary to study the whole situation and cautiously feel their way. Thus it was not until the fourth of October that the Department was ready to complete the contract for John Ericsson's strange craft the *Monitor*. In this novel race, where the difference of a single day might spell victory or defeat, the South had the advantage of the earlier beginning, amounting to nearly three months. On the other hand, the North had the advantage of skilled workmen to draw upon and a shipyard fully equipped.

The *Monitor* had hull, engines, and mechanical devices that were unfamiliar in design and introduced countless problems. Workmen, however, caught the spirit of the contest and pressed on in eight-hour shifts, three shifts a day. It certainly was an achievement that three months after building had begun she should be ready for launching, January 30, 1862. Of course she was still far from completion. Machinery, guns, and general equipment had to be installed, and this seemed only the beginning of what was required. Almost daily, reports had been received of the progress made on the *Virginia* (as the Confederates had renamed the *Merrimack*), and the Navy Department apprised the builders in Brooklyn of the necessity of completing their ship at the earliest possible moment. At the end, without even a trial run at sea, the *Monitor* steamed out of New York and headed south (March 6), attended by the tug *Seth Low,* which was detailed to tow her.

So hazardous, according to general opinion, was duty in this strange craft that the Department did not attempt to furnish a complement by ordering officers and men, but allowed Lieutenant John L. Worden, who had been given command, to call for volunteers, selected from the receiving ship *North Carolina* and the frigate *Sabine.* That the peril had not been greatly exaggerated was shown on the second day out when the *Monitor* ran into a gale, which increased in violence through the afternoon and evening. Water poured in, about the turret, through the hawse pipe, and even down the blowers and smokestack. The engine stopped, the pumps were useless, and the engineers, overcome by gas, had to be dragged out to avoid asphyxiation. Twice during those anxious hours the strange vessel was near to foundering. But by heroic perseverance, Worden and his men succeeded in weathering the storm. Holding determiningly to their task, on Saturday afternoon, a little more than two days after they had left New York, they sighted the capes at the entrance to the Chesapeake. Grateful for their deliverance, they were ready to enjoy the rest which they had earned after their fierce struggle with the elements. But as they crept into the bay, they could make out a ship burning in the distance—the *Congress,* victim of the *Virginia*—and soon they learned the story of the serious disaster wrought by the Southern champion in a brief half day. The *Virginia,* winning the shipbuilding race of seven and a half months by one day, had begun the battle of Hampton Roads with a brilliant success. Night had interrupted the fighting, but, as both sides knew, it was sure to be continued in the morning. There could be no rest for the officers and crew of the *Monitor.* Only by accepting the challenge and meeting the ironclad that had already sunk two ships in the presence of the Union Fleet could the other ships be saved. One of the critical moments of the war had come.

Development in Guns and Ships

Although nearly half a century had elapsed between the War of 1812 and the Civil War, no great conflict with the exception of the Crimean War (1853–56) had occurred. This explains why in America as well as in Europe many of the guns and fighting craft belonging to the beginning of the period were still in use at the close. The Dahlgren gun, as stated on p. 127, was the best of the smooth-bores. Because of the "curve of pressures," being heavy at the breech and light at the muzzle and of unusual strength for its weight, this gun was unusually well adapted for naval vessels. The Dahlgren, like all smooth-bore guns, was muzzle-loading. It was not until 1875 or 1880 that breech-loading rifles gained general acceptance. Rifle guns had been tried in Russia as early as 1836, but it remained for much later years to demonstrate their superiority in penetrating power, range, and accuracy.

As told in a previous chapter, the first steamships were side-wheelers and a few of this type were in the main fighting line in the 1860's. But the stronger and less vulnerable craft were the steam frigates such as the *Merrimack* and the *Hartford*, which had screw propellers. Several old-time sailing ships, though they were obsolete, still retained a place in the fleet. The superiority of the steamship was evident, for it could maneuver, like the Greek and Roman galleys, even against wind and tide. On long cruises, however, the steam vessel was expected to depend on sail power and to use steam merely as an auxiliary.

The ironclad had already found its way into the French and British navies. Three French floating batteries, armored with 4 ½-inch plates, had been tried with signal success in the attack on Kinburn in the Crimean War, and after the war Napoleon III had ordered the construction of four armor-plated steam frigates, which were in commission in 1861. England had promptly followed with five of similar type. Although these ships had never been tried in war, their general structural features were well known in naval circles. And thus it was that Secretary Mallory, seeing that the only hope for the Confederacy to meet their enemy on even terms lay in the early adoption of the ironclad and the torpedo, had at once made plans for both.

Battle of Hampton Roads: Engagement of the Virginia *and the Union Fleet*

The frigate *Congress,* 50 guns, and the sloop of war *Cumberland,* 24 guns, had for some time been lying off Newport News, to give a semblance of blockade of the James River and especially to prevent the escape of the *Jamestown* and *Yorktown.* These were two steamers of the Old Dominion Steamship Company that had been seized at Richmond and armed. The sailing ships could serve only as floating batteries and as such could not effectually blockade the river. They might give some protection to transports and supply ships in the vicinity of Newport News and Fortress Monroe, but they themselves were in a hazardous position. Shore batteries near by and the heavy steam frigates *Roanoke* and *Minnesota* six or eight miles away might be expected to give support. But when the trial came the support was inadequate.[6]

At noon on March 8, 1862, lookouts in the Union Fleet reported a ship, the like of which had never been seen before, coming from the direction of Norfolk. She slowly steamed down the Elizabeth River, and on reaching Sewell's Point turned toward Newport News. She was attended by two

---

[6] The Navy Department was not altogether blind to the weakness of the position of the sailing ships at Hampton Roads, as is shown by a telegram sent from Secretary Welles to Captain John Marston (the senior naval officer in the squadron) March 7, 1862: "Send the *St. Lawrence, Congress,* and *Cumberland* into the Potomac River. Let the disposition of the remainder of the vessels at Hampton Roads be made according to your best judgment after consultation with General Wool." The order was, however, countermanded by telegraph the following day: "The Assistant Secretary will be at Old Point by the Baltimore boat of this eve. Do not move the ships until further orders, which he will carry." *Naval War Records,* VI, 687.

Top, courtesy U.S. Naval Institute; *bottom,* courtesy U.S. Naval Academy Museum

Top, ENGAGEMENT BETWEEN THE MONITOR AND THE VIRGINIA. From a contemporary engraving. *Bottom,* SURRENDER OF THE CONFEDERATE RAM TENNESSEE AT MOBILE BAY. From a painting by Xanthus Smith.

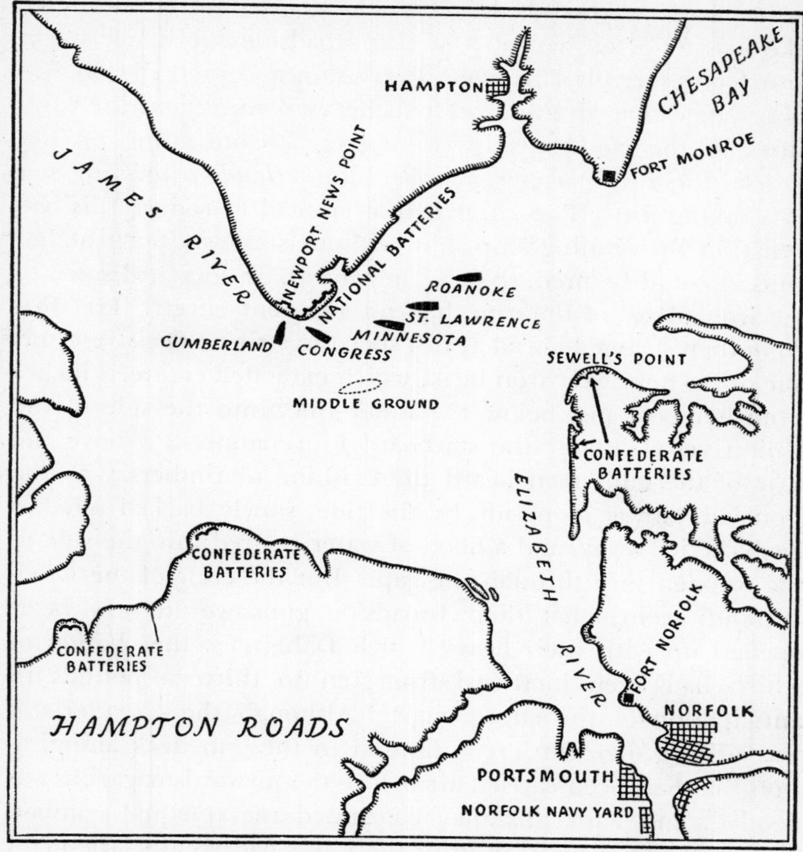

armed steamers. From the reports of her building which had reached the Union forces, they were quick to identify her. She presented a strange sight: an iron covered casemate, 178 feet long, was superimposed amidships upon the hull, sloping at an angle of 35 degrees and rising nine feet from the decks, which were awash. As described by an eyewitness, she looked "like a house submerged to the eaves, borne onward by a flood." [7]

As the *Virginia,* commanded by Flag Officer Franklin Buchanan, passed the *Congress,* on the latter's starboard side, she

[7] Stiles, *Military Essays and Recollections.*

received a heavy broadside. The shot glanced off her casemate like hailstones on a roof, but the broadside she delivered in return was terribly effective. Every shot and shell she fired at close range that afternoon caused heavy damage and the casualties in the wooden ships were large. Continuing on her course, the *Virginia* engaged the *Cumberland,* subjecting her to a raking fire. The latter had attempted to relieve this bad situation by winding ship, but without success. Such of her guns as could be fired, though they may have loosened some of the iron plates of the ram, had no apparent effect. The *Virginia* then steamed ahead at full speed to strike a decisive blow. She drove her heavy iron beak, which extended eighteen inches from her bow just below the water line, into the side of the Union vessel, under the starboard fore-channels. Above the roar of the guns men heard the crashing of timbers. As the ironclad, swung alongside by the tide, slowly backed off, her beak carried away, and a flood of water poured into the side of the wooden ship through the gap. But the crew of the *Cumberland,* seeing that their broadside guns would now bear, opened up with their heavy 9-inch Dahlgrens, the charges of which had been increased from ten to thirteen pounds in anticipation of the engagement. Although the *Cumberland* was sinking, her gun crews hoisted to the gun deck ammunition that had been carried aft before the forward magazine was flooded, and with this they continued the unequal combat. In fact, they did not stop until the water had risen to the main hatchway and the ship had canted to port. Orders were given to abandon ship, but the determined fighters insisted on firing one gun more before they left.

Commander Radford, the captain of the *Cumberland,* that morning happened to be aboard the *Roanoke,* six miles distant, a member of a court of inquiry. On the appearance of the *Virginia,* he went ashore and rode on horseback to Newport News. Though he arrived too late to take part in the engagement, he had the consolation of seeing his colors still flying. The *Cumberland* was resting on bottom, the water coming only to the tops. The executive officer, Lieutenant George U. Morris, officers, and crew had fought a good fight and given their utmost. The casualty list was large; when a muster was made the following day, only 251 responded out of a complement of 376. Their resistance, however, had not been in vain. They had detained, for several priceless minutes, the *Virginia* in her first flush of victory, when she was to all intents and purposes invincible, undoubtedly saving from destruction one or more of the large wooden ships that had been struggling through the shallow water and mud to get into the battle. Furthermore, although none of the Union shot penetrated the ironclad, a volley given by the *Cumberland* when the two ships were close alongside shattered the muzzles of two guns of the *Virginia,* reducing her armament from ten heavy guns to eight. During the day's fighting the casualties in the *Virginia* amounted to two men killed and eight wounded, nearly all occurring at the time of her fight with the *Cumberland.* Her armor was "somewhat damaged; the anchors and all flag-staffs shot away and smoke-stack and steam pipe were riddled." [8]

When Lieutenant Joseph B. Smith, commanding the *Congress,* had seen the fate of the *Cumberland,* he attempted to save his ship by setting jib and topsail and running ashore with the assistance of the tug *Zouave.* But he was unsuccessful. The *Virginia,* moving cautiously because of her deep draught, secured a position 150 yards distant, from which she could rake her enemy fore and aft. In reply the *Congress* could bring only two guns in her stern to bear, and they were soon disabled. Meanwhile, one of the Confederate steamers was firing from a position on the starboard quarter. The combat lasted an hour. Lieutenant Smith having been killed, Lieutenant Austin Pendergrast sought to end the further sacrifice of life by hauling down his colors. Two Confederate steamers were then sent by Buchanan to receive the surrender and burn the ship. But batteries from shore opening upon them drove them off. Whereupon the *Virginia* resumed her fire, and following this

[8] *Naval War Records,* VII, 42.

with hot shot and incendiary shells made certain the destruction of the Union frigate.

While all this was taking place, the two steam frigates *Roanoke* and *Minnesota* and the sailing frigate *St. Lawrence* had been struggling forward to engage their enemy. But neither their own sail and steam nor the assistance of tugs could bring them to the desired position. The *Minnesota,* the only one that arrived within gunshot, grounded at a point a mile and a half distant. That nearness, however, almost spelled disaster to her.

Aboard the *Virginia,* Lieutenant Catesby R. Jones was now in command, Buchanan having been wounded by a musket ball fired from shore. Jones, after making certain that the *Congress* was doomed, thought next to attack the *Minnesota.* But the pilots, realizing that the ironclad drew twenty-two feet, refused to advance to a position nearer than one mile. At this range, the fire of the gun crew was not accurate and only one shot hit its target. Also ineffective was the fire of the 10-inch pivot gun of the *Minnesota* in reply. But the *Jamestown* and the *Patrick Henry,* Confederate steamers armed with rifled guns, taking positions off her bow and stern, caused damage until a heavy gun was brought to bear and drove them off. Then the fighting slowed down, but continued until seven o'clock, when the pilots of the *Virginia* warned Jones that on account of the ebb tide he must withdraw or be grounded. It was decided that enough had been done for one day and orders were given for the ram and her consorts to return to Sewell's Point.

At once telegrams flashed to Richmond, Washington, and all centers far and near. In the South there was wild exultation. A great naval victory had been gained and the blockade was broken. In the North there was corresponding gloom. Secretary Welles in his *Diary* tells of being called to the White House, Sunday morning, the ninth. The Cabinet was soon assembled. Its members were all excited, and Secretary Stanton was almost frantic:

The *Merrimack* [*Virginia*], he said, would destroy every vessel in the service, could lay every city on the coast under contribution, could take Fortress Monroe; McClellan's mistaken purpose to advance by the Peninsula must be abandoned, and Burnside would inevitably be captured. Likely the first movement of the *Merrimack* would be to come up the Potomac and disperse Congress, destroy the Capitol and public buildings; or she might go to New York and Boston and destroy those cities, or levy from them contributions sufficient to carry on the War.[9]

This was hysteria, but it sounds much like what in our century has been heard after a striking success gained for the first time by submarine, airplane, tank, or gas units.

From reports received by the Navy during the construction of the *Virginia,* Secretary Welles knew of her limitations, which would prevent her operating beyond Chesapeake Bay, and he was one of the few officials in Washington who continued calm. He put his confidence in the *Monitor,* news of whose arrival in Hampton Roads was hourly expected. Had he known how near she had lately come to foundering, his optimism might have been less resolute.

Battle of Hampton Roads: Engagement of the Monitor *and the* Virginia

The narrowness of the margin by which the Confederates had won the race in shipbuilding, bears out Nelson's dictum: "Time is everything; five minutes may spell the difference between victory and defeat."

The night following the first day's fighting at Hampton Roads permitted little rest for the Federal fleet. Captain Van Brunt of the *Minnesota* labored from ten o'clock until four to haul his ship off the mud bank. All hands pulled on the hawsers that had been led out, and steam tugs added their power, but without success. Captain Marston of the *Roanoke,* the senior officer, realized that his own ship could do little.

[9] *Op. cit.,* I, 63.

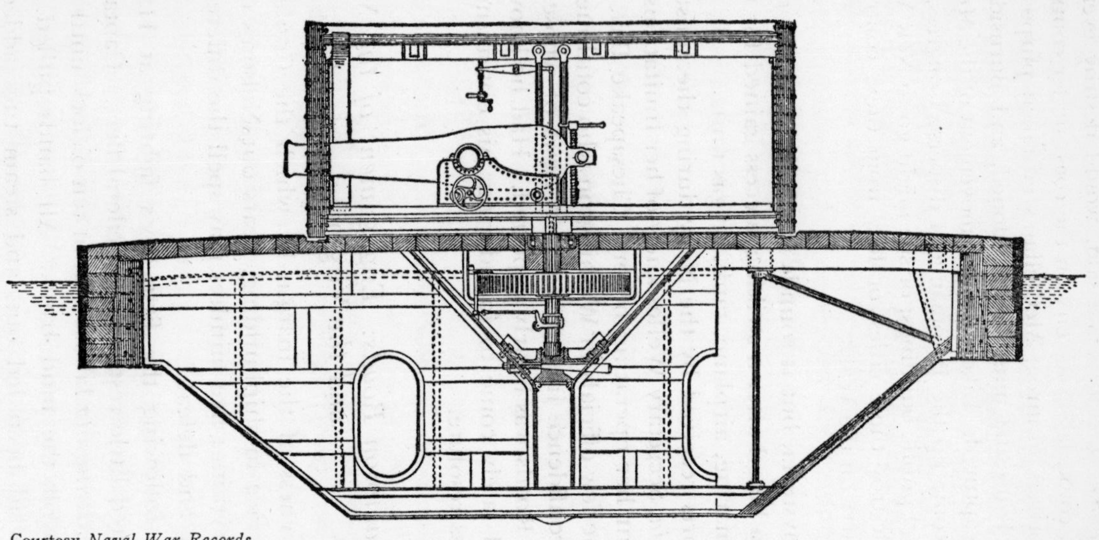

Courtesy *Naval War Records*

TRANSVERSE SECTION THROUGH TURRET OF ORIGINAL *Monitor*.

Although he knew that orders from the Navy Department, issued when the *Monitor* was steaming out of New York harbor, directed that she should proceed to Washington, he took the responsibility of changing them and instructed Worden to remain in Hampton Roads. On board the *Monitor* the night was spent in last moment preparations for the supreme test all knew would follow. At about two o'clock she drew up to the *Minnesota* and, dropping anchor, waited for the dawn.

In the *Virginia* there had been similar activity, and shifts were kept busy in making adjustments and minor repairs. Before the sun was up she got under way, and after steaming toward the Rip Raps, approached the *Minnesota* by the course she had followed the day before.

The *Minnesota* opened the battle when her stern guns bore and the *Virginia* replied with one of her destructive shells. Then the *Monitor* appeared and boldly advanced toward the enemy. If the first glimpse of the strange Confederate ironclad had brought bewilderment, this effect was equaled by the novel Union ship, repeatedly characterized as a "cheese box on a raft." What impressed all onlookers was the disproportionate size of the two contestants: the *Virginia,* 3,500 tons burden, the *Monitor,* 776; the length of the raised iron casemate of the former being almost equal to that of the entire hull of the *Monitor,* 172 feet, which included 50 feet of overhang at bow and stern.

Worden, withholding his fire, approached at low speed, and finally stopped his engines that he might slowly drift by. When he was broad on the *Virginia's* beam, his two guns in the revolving turret belched forth. But the shot, though they went true to the mark, did not penetrate. In return, the broadsides given by the *Virginia,* according to Captain Van Brunt, had "no more effect, apparently, than so many pebblestones thrown by a child." A slight casualty in the *Monitor* was that suffered by Acting-Master Stoddard. He had been in charge of the machinery rotating the turret. Leaning against the inside iron walls as a shell struck the outside, he was stunned by the sharp concussion. Fire continued from each ship, the crews handling their guns with the utmost speed. The two guns of the *Monitor* were fired every seven or eight minutes; such of the eight guns of the *Virginia* as bore were fired much more often.

Both ships were slow and hard to handle. The *Monitor* had a speed of six knots,[10] which was probably more than that of her opponent, whose machinery, even during the last of her days in the Union Navy, had been condemned. The *Monitor* did not steer well, but she had a draught of only ten and one-half feet to the other's twenty-two and being much shorter had a great advantage in maneuvering. Thus Worden came about, and, thinking to disable the screw or rudder of the *Virginia,* crossed under her stern. His move was well planned, for the rudder was one of the least protected parts of the ram and a heavy impact would have wrought havoc. But Worden was not bold enough, and missed by a few feet. Passing along the ram's port side he again fired as he passed.

Lieutenant Jones, commanding the *Virginia,* convinced that his fire on the Monitor was bringing no result, then renewed the attack on the *Minnesota.* Van Brunt brought an entire broadside to bear, the shot idly bouncing off. But a single shell from the *Virginia's* rifled bow gun "passed through the chief engineer's stateroom, through the engineer's mess room, amidships, and burst in the boatswain's room, tearing four rooms all into one in its passage, exploding two charges of powder, which set the ship on fire." [11] A second shell exploded the boiler of the tug *Dragon,* which was standing by. After firing a third shell, the ram was again threatened by the *Monitor.* She then attempted to change her position, but in doing so grounded. Had the *Monitor* been more aggressive, she now might have attacked at will and chosen her position under the

---

[10] Report of Lieutenant William N. Jeffers, commanding officer of the *Monitor,* May 22, 1862, *Naval War Records,* VII, 412.

[11] Van Brunt's report, *Naval War Records,* VII, 11.

most advantageous terms. But her tactics at this time, as throughout, were governed by caution, and her role was defensive. In a few minutes the *Virginia* was free. Jones thereupon put on all power and making for the *Monitor* attempted to run her down. But Worden put his helm hard to starboard and received only a glancing blow. The sole injury inflicted was to the *Virginia,* for the blow opened up the bow and caused a leak in the temporary repairs made where the iron beak had been.

The *Monitor* had been fighting for two hours. The enemy having been diverted from the *Minnesota,* Worden ran into shoal water to replenish ammunition in the turret—an awkward procedure which required that the turret be stopped at the point where the opening was directly above the hoist. When this was done, he returned to renew the engagement.

Up to this point, the fire of the *Virginia* had not been any too well directed. The larger number of missiles had passed over the low hull of the *Monitor,* and such as struck the turret scarred the outside but did nothing more. Now the gunners concentrated on the small pilot house. A shell, striking this, fractured one of the iron logs that formed its protecting wall and raised the iron cover, which was merely laid on, set in a groove. Worden, who from this station had been looking out between the slits to direct the battle, was burnt by the exploding powder and his face and eyes were cut by the slivers of iron driven through. Blinded and bleeding, he gave orders to put the helm to starboard, and sending for the executive officer, Lieutenant S. D. Greene, who had been stationed in the turret, turned over the command to him.

The quartermaster with Worden had been stunned. For some minutes, no one being at the wheel, the little craft pursued an irregular course, away from the enemy. When Greene brought her about to resume the engagement, he found that the *Virginia* was headed toward Norfolk. He fired two shots at the retiring foe, but the challenge, if this was what he meant it to be, was ignored. The battle of the ironclads was ended.

As we read the story of Hampton Roads, we can give only highest praise to the courage and stamina evidenced by both sides during the two days' engagement. But the same cannot be said of that essential part of any battle or campaign—the period of preparation. Not infrequently success or failure is so plainly due to the latter that the actual meeting of the armed forces may be regarded as but the concluding phase of the combat. The *Roanoke, Minnesota, St. Lawrence, Congress,* and *Cumberland* had been in Hampton Roads for months. Their officers knew the *Merrimack* was being rebuilt and might appear at any time as an ironclad, of whose prowess the Confederates openly boasted. Why had they not studied out a plan for fleet action the moment the monster entered the roads? Why had they not made soundings and acquainted themselves thoroughly with the confined waters so as to avoid the danger of grounding? Why in their fire did they not seek out the vulnerable points to aim at and repeatedly strike? It should be noted that only the *Cumberland* gave an especially good account of herself in the first day's battle, and for this there had been frequent drill at the guns in the winter of 1861–62. If the ships, at the first warning of the impending action, could have taken their place according to a prearranged and definite plan so that the ram would have been opposed to the combined fleet, as at Mobile Bay, and not to each ship singly, the battle would have been different. And constant pounding might have revealed the *Virginia's* weak protection where casemate and hull joined at the water line. This defect was recognized by the officers of the *Virginia,* as shown in the letter of Jones written to Brooke on the fifth of March:

> Our draft will be a foot less than was first intended, yet I was this morning ordered not to put any more ballast in—fear of the bottom. The eaves of the roof will not be more than six inches immersed, which in smooth water would not be enough; a slight ripple would leave it bare except the one-inch iron that extends some feet below. We are least protected where we most need it,

and may receive a shot that would sink us; a thirty-two pounder would do it.[12]

The handling of the *Virginia* on the first day reflects the experience and ability of the officer in command. Buchanan, though he brought his ship out at noon, proceeded so directly to attack that he had all the advantage of surprise. He struck at the innermost end of his enemy's line, at the right flank, and dealing with the units one at a time proceeded with deliberation and great thoroughness to annihilate them. The pilots were cautious and acted as a check upon the eager officer. But they knew the waters and were intent on keeping the *Virginia* from grounding. Her crew were green and the gunners showed the lack of training, giving evidence of fatigue in the latter part of the day. They had in the *Minnesota* a fixed target, but the range of a mile was too much for them and they hit her only once. Thus they lost the opportunity of destroying her Saturday evening. Next morning, when they were fresh, their marksmanship at the same distance was better, and they hit the frigate repeatedly whenever they were permitted to concentrate on her.

In the second day of the battle the two ironclads, powerful though they were, according to standards of 1862, showed their limitations. Each was much better in defensive than in offensive operations. The turret of the *Monitor* was hard to control and in the early part of the battle the men had to fire "on the fly" as the guns bore. Thus it was difficult to operate, for the gunners in the revolving turret, losing all sense of direction, knew of the outside world only what they saw through narrow cracks along the side of the guns. In the smoke of battle they were in danger of firing on their own pilot house, which was in the forward part of the ship. They fired altogether forty-one solid cast-iron shot. If these had been aimed at the same spot of the armor or had struck a vulnerable point under the knuckle, they might have been effective.

The handling of both ships in this, the second day's conflict,

[12] *Southern Historical Society Papers,* XIX, 31.

was characterized by studied caution. Worden, as previously stated, made an attempt to ram the *Virginia.* Had he been more resolute in his endeavor, it is improbable that he would have missed the ship, and he certainly could quickly have found another opportunity. Evidently he was not sure that the *Monitor* might not suffer as much as the *Virginia* and he was playing safe. On the other hand, had the *Virginia* continued the fight just a little longer she would have caused Van Brunt to set fire to and abandon the *Minnesota.* In his official report Van Brunt stated that when he saw the *Monitor* retreat to shallow water after the injury to the pilot house, and learned that his own solid shot had nearly all been expended, he decided that on the *Virginia's* returning to attack his ship he must destroy her.

It was a surprise to both Unionists and Confederates that Jones should have withdrawn when he did. In answer to the sharp criticism of the South he defended his action as follows:

> We had run into the *Monitor,* causing us to leak, and had received a shot from her which came near disabling the machinery, but continued to fight her until she was driven into shoal water. The *Minnesota* appeared so badly damaged that we did not believe that she could ever move again. The pilots refused to place us any nearer to her (they had once run us aground). About twelve the pilots declared if we did not go up to Norfolk then, that we could not do so until the next day.[13]

Lieutenant Davidson of the *Virginia,* in a letter, throws additional light on this question: "Our officers and men were completely broken down by two days' and a night's continuous work with the heaviest rifled ordnance in the world." [14]

It should be borne in mind that it was the executive officer Lieutenant Jones and not Flag Officer Buchanan who, during the second day, was in command. A junior officer, conscious of a suddenly imposed responsibility, is likely to be governed by

---

[13] *Naval War Records,* VII, 59.
[14] *Ibid.,* VII, 61.

caution. Like Worden and Greene, Jones had strongly fixed in his mind how vital it was to save his ship for the future service that would be required of her. "Old Buch," who was impetuous and fiery, if he had continued in command might have run the *Virginia* hard aground and even have lost her, but it is certain he would have given the *Monitor* a much sterner fight.

In the battle, although the *Virginia* was somewhat the more aggressive and compelled her adversary to seek safety in temporary retreat to shallow water, the *Monitor,* on the other hand, held the field at the conclusion and saved the *Minnesota* as well as the other Union ships from destruction. The engagement is commonly regarded as a drawn battle. If, however, later results are considered, the advantage lay with the North. The blockade was not broken, and the *Virginia* had been checked in her career.

Subsequent History of the Virginia *and the* Monitor

Both North and South expected a further engagement to follow and each studied means of overcoming the champion of the other. But increasing caution governed the movements of the two ships and neither was willing to give battle except under terms affording a distinct advantage. Thus they never met again. Because of the advance of the Union Army, Norfolk and Portsmouth were evacuated May 10. Immediately the Confederates had to meet the problem of what they should do with the *Virginia.* They planned to take her up the James River to Richmond to assist in its defense. But Commodore Tattnall, then in command, being convinced that it would be impossible to accomplish this on account of her draught, set fire to her and destroyed her.

Four days later the *Monitor* took a minor part in the bombardment of Drewry's Bluff, seven miles below Richmond, with the *Galena, Aroostook, Naugatuck,* and *Port Royal.* The ironclad *Galena* was pierced by plunging shot eighteen times, and suffered thirteen men killed and eleven wounded. The *Monitor* was struck three times, but not injured. The end of the gallant little craft came in the following December. She had left for Charleston, South Carolina, in tow of the *Rhode Island.* When she had passed Cape Hatteras Shoals she struck a gale. Had the *Rhode Island* not held to her course but early come about and run before the wind, the *Monitor* might have been saved. From eight o'clock to midnight, the evening of the thirtieth, Commander J. P. Bankhead and his men made a heroic fight against the heavy sea which broke over the deck and, pouring through the crevices, made the engines work with increasing difficulty. About midnight boats of the *Rhode Island* began taking off the shipwrecked crew. Four officers and twelve men of the *Monitor* were lost. Soon after Commander Bankhead had reached the *Rhode Island,* the red light in the *Monitor* disappeared. The *Monitor* had fought her final battle and succumbed, not to the shot and shell of the Confederates, but to the world enemy and friend, the sea.

Far-Reaching Influence of the Battle of Hampton Roads

The two-day engagement demonstrated the power of the ironclads and was critically studied by the navies of the world. Crude as these first ships of their type were, they introduced elements of naval construction in use even to the present day: the turret, armor plate, protective deck, rifled guns, all heavy guns, etc. No engagement since the time of Nelson was more significant in the development of naval science. France and England had already begun building armored ships, but their superiority had never been tested in battle. Hampton Roads furnished the demonstration.

Charles Francis Adams, the American Minister to England, wrote home on April 3:

> The late naval action in Hampton Roads has made a great sensation, and is regarded as likely to work a complete change in the policy of this country [England] in fortifications and the Naval

Marine. You will not fail to observe the notice already taken of it in Parliament. The opinion on the military and naval efficiency of the United States has undergone an astonishing change within the last month.[15]

Dayton, the Minister to France, similarly wrote from Paris:

The change in the conditions of things at home has produced a change, if possible, more striking abroad. There is little more said just now as to the validity of our blockade, or the propriety of an early recognition of the South. The fight between the *Monitor* and the *Merrimack* has turned the attention of these maritime governments, and of England more especially, in another direction.

And Rear Admiral P. H. Colomb of the Royal Navy, a keen student of naval warfare, wrote in the London *Times* (December, 1894): "In the American Civil War, the deciding battle was between the *Monitor* and the *Merrimack;* and no one can doubt that . . . if the *Merrimack* had gained the victory there would scarcely now be the United States of America. The fate of that Nation was decided then and there." What would have happened if destiny had taken the other road is a matter of conjecture, but the United States Navy on the eighth and ninth of March fought hard and rendered a great national service.

References

Baxter, J. P., *Introduction of the Ironclad Warship,* 1933.
Church, W. C., *The Life of John Ericsson,* 2 vols., 1891.
Lewis, C. L., *Admiral Franklin Buchanan,* 1929.
Official Records of the Union and Confederate Navies in the War of the Rebellion, Vol. VII, 1898.
Selfridge, T. O., Jr., *Memoirs,* 1924.

[15] This and two comments following are quoted by Rear Admiral S. B. Luce, *Military Historical Society of Massachusetts,* XII, 150–152.

EARLY COMBINED OPERATIONS OF THE ARMY AND THE NAVY

Capture of Forts Hatteras and Clark

THE NAVY DEPARTMENT, anticipating the need of naval stations on the southern coast, as well as harbors that might serve as bases for combined military and naval operations, had appointed a board to make an investigation. This board consisted of Captain Samuel F. Du Pont and Commander Charles H. Davis of the Navy, Major John G. Barnard of the Army, and Professor Alexander D. Bache of the Coast Survey. In accordance with their recommendation, two combined naval and military expeditions were early organized.

The first was to Hatteras Inlet on the coast of North Carolina, from whence "piratical" operations had begun to annoy the Union shipping. On August 26, 1861, a force of fourteen vessels under Flag Officer Silas H. Stringham and 860 troops of the Army under Major General Benjamin F. Butler sailed from Hampton Roads. Two days later, at ten o'clock in the morning, two of the largest ships engaged Fort Clark. A third passed inside and opened fire. "These vessels," reported Stringham, "continued passing and repassing the fort until it was abandoned by the enemy." The maneuver was effective, for, on account of the frequent change of range, the shot of the fort fell short or passed over the ships. By noon Fort Clark was seen to be abandoned, the garrison escaping to Fort Hatteras. In the afternoon the ships engaged Fort Hatteras and the following morning compelled its surrender. Here were captured 615 officers and men, including Samuel Barron, "Flag Officer, Confederate States Navy, commanding naval defenses of Virginia and North Carolina." In the ships not a man was killed or wounded. The forts commanded the entrance to Pamlico Sound, and their capture ended the commerce raiding in this vicinity. The victory, coming soon after the debacle at Bull Run, was timely in maintaining the morale of the North.

Capture of Port Royal

The easy success achieved at Hatteras Inlet was due not only to the strength of the attack but also to its promptness—the assault being made before the Confederates had perfected the defenses, as they had at Fort Fisher. The same was true in the second operation, against Port Royal. This expedition was directed by Captain Samuel F. Du Pont, who had lately been appointed flag officer and given command of the South Atlantic Blockading Squadron. As chairman of the board ordered in June, he was thoroughly informed of the coast line. He sailed from Hampton Roads with a fleet, including army transports (forces under command of Brigadier General Thomas W. Sherman), of fifty vessels. The utmost secrecy had supposedly been taken. Sealed orders, not to be opened unless the ships of the fleet were separated, were given to the several ships, and twenty-five coal vessels under convoy were dispatched the day previous to rendezvous off Savannah to hide their true objective—but all in vain. The Confederates had full information before the fleet cleared Lynnhaven. Off Hatteras, the fleet ran into a storm, which increased almost to the proportions of a hurricane. The ships were widely scattered, and when the *Wabash,* flagship, neared her destination, only one sail was in sight. But on the weather's moderating, steamers and ships began to appear, each with reports of near disaster. One ship, recently purchased, had been saved only by throwing her battery overboard. Another, with a battalion of marines, was with difficulty kept afloat until the marines had been removed. The living cargo of another transport in a sinking condition was also saved. It was with great relief that Du Pont anchored off the bar of Port Royal, twenty-five vessels in company, and others already on the horizon.

The bar of Port Royal lies ten miles out from the low sandy shores. Buoys marking the channel had been removed, but their absence was soon corrected. Commander Davis, the fleet captain, and Mr. Boutelle of the Coast Survey sounded out the channel and buoyed it. Many of the shallow-draft vessels, including the gunboats, had already entered, and at high tide the next morning the *Wabash* and the heavier ships crossed the bar and anchored four or five miles from the earthworks.

Two forts, two and five-eighths miles apart, guarded the entrance: Fort Beauregard on Bay Point, to the north, mounting twenty guns, and Fort Walker on Hilton Head to the south, mounting twenty-three guns.

The Army, in preparation for the joint operation, had embarked at Annapolis 13,000 troops under General Sherman. But the decks of their transports being flooded by the storm, most of the means for disembarkation had been carried away. As they came into the bay, the troops discovered that before they could land they would have to be ferried five or six miles. Prompt action, with no delay in beginning the attack, Du Pont regarded as essential. The original plan, therefore, was changed, and it was decided that the fleet unaided should give battle.

Summoning his captains to the flagship, Du Pont discussed his plan. Analyzing the situation, he emphasized the superiority of Fort Walker, which was to receive chief attention, and pointed out its weakness on the northern flank. A small enemy squadron under Commodore Tattnall might also have to be reckoned with.[1] Taking advantage of the flood tide of the morning, the ships were to advance,

[1] He had already twice attacked the Union forces: when the gunboats and lighter transports first had crossed the bar, and next morning as the larger ships were about to follow. After the battle he assisted the Confederate Army in their retreat.

> . . . a main squadron ranged in a line ahead, and a flanking squadron, which was to be thrown off on the northern section of the harbor to engage the enemy's flotilla and prevent them raking the rear ships of the main line when it turned to the southward, or cutting off a disabled vessel. . . . The plan of attack was to pass up midway between Forts Walker and Beauregard, receiving and returning the fire of both, to a certain distance about two and one-half miles north of the latter. At that point the line was to turn to the south, round by the west, and close in with Fort Walker, encountering it on its weakest flank, and at the same time enfilading, in nearly a direct line, its two water faces.[2]

While standing to the southward, the vessels of the line would be head to the tide, under control, but their speed diminished. Abreast the fort, they were still further to slow down, passing the batteries in slow succession so as to avoid becoming a fixed mark for the enemy's fire. On reaching the extremity of Hilton Head, the column was to turn to the east and north and repeat the maneuver, except that the ships were to pass nearer to Fort Walker. The main squadron was to consist of nine vessels, headed by the frigates *Wabash* and *Susquehanna;* the flanking squadron of five vessels, all gunboats, was headed by the *Bienville.*

This plan, simple in outline, was well adapted to the situation; its excellence was proved on its being followed without modification. At eight o'clock the next morning, November 7, the signal was made to get under way. Slowly advancing until each unit had reached its assigned position, the fleet proceeded on its course. At 9:26 A.M. the forts recognized the challenge: a gun was fired from Fort Walker and another from Fort Beauregard; the fire was promptly returned by the leading ships, and the battle had begun. At ten o'clock the column turned southward and soon the order was given for closer formation. The ships passed Fort Walker about 800 yards distant.

As had been foreseen, Commodore Tattnall's squadron of

---

[2] Report of Du Pont given in *Naval War Records,* XII, 262.

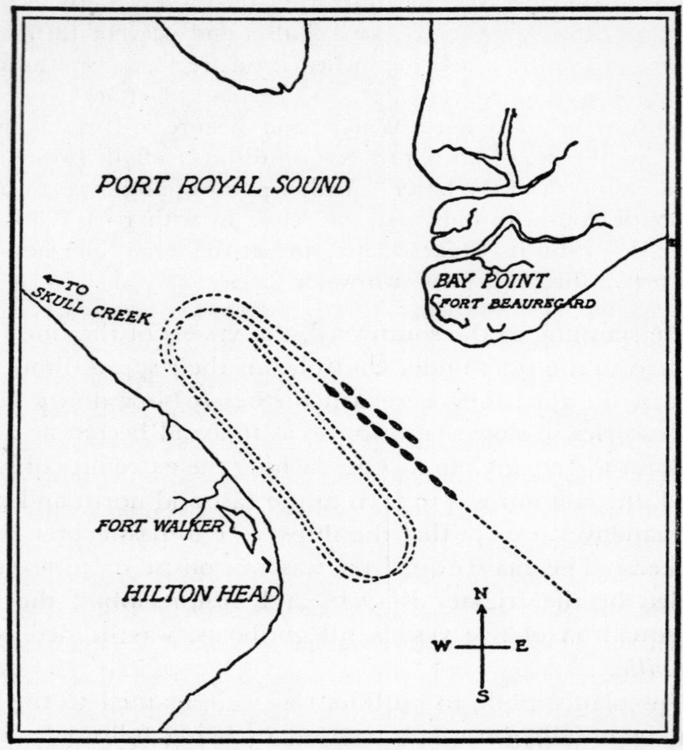

BATTLE OF PORT ROYAL

seven steamers attempted to harass the rear of the Union Fleet. But the flanking squadron of five gunboats drove them off into Skull Creek and then took a position north of the earthworks of Fort Walker, where from their enfilading position they reduced the fire from the fort while the main squadron was passing. As the main squadron, after completing the ellipse, passed Fort Walker a second time, it approached to within 600 yards and thus changed the range. The enemy fire had already weakened, and as the fleet passed a third time, it ceased entirely. Commander John Rodgers was sent ashore with a flag of truce. Finding the fort deserted, at 2:20 P.M. he hoisted the Union colors.

The *Pocohontas,* Commander Percival Drayton, had been delayed by the storm so that it did not enter Port Royal until the battle was in progress. Promptly taking its place in the column at about twelve o'clock, it engaged both forts in passing. Family divisions in this war were not infrequent: Commander Drayton was here fighting against his brother Brigadier General Thomas F. Drayton of the Confederate Army, commanding the forts. They were of South Carolina stock.

When the fate of Fort Walker had been decided, Captain Du Pont dispatched some ships to the other stronghold, to reconnoiter and to prevent Confederate steamers from carrying away either persons or property. Near sundown the Union forces discovered that the flag over Fort Beauregard was no longer flying, and next morning they took possession of the works. Both forts were then formally turned over to the Army for occupation.

Port Royal was the most important Union success of 1861, and Du Pont's attack as a naval action is praiseworthy in every particular: (1) His reconnaissance furnished a clear estimate of the situation and his analysis of the strength and weakness of Fort Walker was most accurate. He knew that the Confederates had prepared their defense on the two sides toward the sea and were without defense on the north toward Port Royal Sound. He might have found Tattnall's squadron annoying if he had not held his own flanking squadron in readiness to drive it off. He had taken the flood tide also into consideration and used it to hasten or delay maneuvers as desired. (2) He cleverly decided on an elliptical course for the main squadron and by constantly changing the range bewildered the gunners in the forts and minimized the losses of the fleet. (3) He took advantage of surprise, losing no time before he struck the decisive blow.

If the campaign is studied as a joint operation, however, there is criticism that deserves consideration. If the troops had been landed before beginning the action, the advantage might well have justified the delay. The troops having taken a strategic position on shore could easily have captured the defenders of the forts and, pushing forward rapidly toward Charleston and Savannah, have taken important works which immediately after the battle were defenseless. Had the action been planned as a campaign and not as a single battle, much of the costly effort of the next three years required for the taking of these cities would have been unnecessary. This is suggested in an unofficial report or letter, written three weeks after the battle by Commander Percival Drayton to Captain H. A. Wise, Chief of the Bureau of Ordnance.

> I have just returned from a scout up the St. Helena Sound and the adjacent rivers, and have been so impressed with its wonderful importance that I am in hopes of seeing it at once occupied. It is only inferior to this place in a slight difference of depth, in everything else, including nearness to Charleston, decidedly superior. I found every place deserted, except by the negroes, and took possession of three forts, any one of which might have given us a great deal of trouble had they been occupied. . . . That the demoralization can only be compared to that after Bull Run throughout the whole lower country is undoubted, and I am satisfied that during the first week we could better have moved with 6,000 men than now with 40,000; the golden opportunity is passed, and as we won't go in search of them they are coming to us.[3]

The official report of Brigadier General Thomas F. Drayton, C. S. Army, commanding the forts, shows not only how inadequate had been the preparations for defense but also how impossible it was greatly to improve them within a few days. Fort Walker was manned by two companies of South Carolina Militia and seven companies of South Carolina Volunteers—whose training, we can imagine, had been the slightest. Furthermore, many of the guns, because of lack of protection or lack of proper handling and ammunition, proved to be useless. General Drayton writes:

[3] *Naval War Records,* XII, 273.

The 32-pounder on the right flank was shattered very early by a round shot, and on the north flank, for want of a carriage, no gun had been mounted. After the fourth fire the X-inch columbiad bounded over the timber and became useless. The 24-pounder rifled cannon was choked while ramming down a shell and lay idle during nearly the whole engagement. The shells for the IX-inch Dahlgren were also too large. The fourth shell to be rammed home could not be driven below the trunnions, and was then at great risk discharged.[4]

In overcoming this rather pathetic defense the Union losses amounted to eight killed and twenty-three wounded.

Interesting as related to what followed this battle is the part played by General Robert E. Lee. He reached Charleston early in November to assume command of the department of South Carolina, Georgia, and Florida. Seeing that the islands could not be held, he quickly withdrew troops and supplies to an interior line where the power of the Navy could not be employed. He realized the desperate situation and superintended in person the erection of defenses to check the expected march on Savannah and Charleston.

The Trent *Affair*

On the same day the Union flag was raised over Fort Beauregard there occurred an event which at first was hailed as a great achievement on the part of the Navy, but which soon aroused dark forebodings.

The Confederate government had already sought to win the support of European nations, but though its representatives were given a friendly reception, in England from the prime minister and many of her leading statesmen and in France from the emperor and the ministry, they were treated officially only as private citizens. Thereupon, President Davis resolved on sending commissioners of highest standing and ability, James

[4] *Ibid.*, 302.

M. Mason of Virginia and John Slidell of Louisiana, both United States senators at the time their states seceded.

Eluding the blockade, the commissioners reached Cuba, and at Havana took passage on the British mail steamer *Trent,* Havana to St. Thomas, on their way to England. Meanwhile, Captain Wilkes of the U.S.S. *San Jacinto,* returning from a cruise off the coast of Africa, heard of their movements, which after their arrival in Cuba were not kept secret. Taking a position in the old Bahama Channel, he intercepted the *Trent* as she was passing and removed with a show of force the two Southern emissaries and their secretaries. Then he allowed the steamer to go on her way.

In a year marked by indecision on the part of the North, the bold and positive action of Captain Wilkes aroused greatest enthusiasm. The public press lauded him and Congress thanked him in a joint resolution.[5] But the British responded with an equally excited outburst of public feeling. They looked upon the proceeding as a violation of international law and as a wanton insult. Most of their statesmen thought that war was inevitable, and the government, ordering the fleet to be in readiness, began preparations for sending troops and supplies to Halifax. The Atlantic cable, fortunately, was not in operation and the time required for the exchange of communications by mail gave opportunity for calmer minds on both sides to prevail. The British parliamentarians Bright and Cobden, staunch friends of the North, wrote urging America to disavow the act. Their letters were read by Sumner, who attended an anxious Cabinet meeting on Christmas day. A satisfactory reply had already been formulated by Seward, and it was decided that the commissioners should be given up.

Much in international law has been written concerning the incident. It is conceded that Captain Wilkes had the right to stop the *Trent* and search her for contraband; further, that he had the right to take her as a prize if he had found anything

---

[5] E. D. Adams, *Great Britain and the Civil War,* I, 220. For Wilkes's report see *Naval War Records,* I, 130, 131.

that had been defined as such. But neither the commissioners nor their dispatches, which were nonmilitary, came under this category. Whether courts would have regarded the slight resistance to search offered by the captain of the *Trent* as sufficient ground to justify the seizure and condemnation of the ship is a question. It is certain that international law did not countenance Wilkes's removing four passengers and then granting permission to the ship to resume her voyage.[6]

Capture of Roanoke Island

After the loss of Hatteras Inlet, the Confederates had set to work to fortify Roanoke Island, the key to Albemarle Sound and the greater part of the inland waters of the North Carolina coast. The Union forces saw they could not ignore this if they would maintain an efficient blockade. General Burnside with 12,000 troops embarked at Annapolis early in January, 1862; and Rear Admiral L. M. Goldsborough with a large naval force, consisting of converted steamers, ferryboats, and tugs, met him at Hatteras Inlet on the thirteenth of that month. Opposed to them, the Confederates had a force of several thousand troops on Roanoke Island and the adjacent mainland.

In February when all was ready the naval force, in a battle of two days, forced the passage through the marshes at the southern end of the island and supported the landing of the Army. Quickly overcoming the resistance of the opposing gunboats, it co-operated with the Army in taking the enemy forts and batteries.

Then, losing no time, the Union ships pursued the Confederate gunboats to Elizabeth City, capturing one and destroying three, besides an armed schooner. In the next month, the Navy extended the victory by assisting the troops to capture Newbern, where a large supply of munitions and naval stores were taken.

---

[6] T. L. Harris, *The Trent Affair*, p. 264.

As a result of this expedition, no ports or inlets along the entire North Carolina coast were left to the Confederates except Wilmington.

Early Operations on the Mississippi

It will be recalled that one of the major lines of operations planned by the Navy Department was co-operation with the Army in the occupation of the Mississippi and surrounding country. The North recognized that the free use of this vast river was absolutely indispensable for commerce in peace times and deemed it equally important for military operations in war. Considerable numbers of men and much needed stores of food were being forwarded from the states west of the river to the armies in Virginia. For the North the gaining of its control and cutting off of this source of supply to the enemy was essential to the successful prosecution of the war. The magnitude of the Mississippi River project is indicated by the distance involved: from Cairo to the mouth of the river, 480 miles in a line due north and south, but 1,097 miles by the stream. Its banks, for the most part low, were on the left side occasionally crowned with high bluffs, well suited for batteries that might deliver a destructive plunging fire upon boats that attempted to steal past. The bluffs beginning with Columbus, twenty-one miles downstream from Cairo, appeared again at New Madrid, Memphis, Vicksburg, and Baton Rouge.[7]

Operations on the Mississippi and its tributaries were from the beginning characterized by efficiency. On May 16, 1861, Commander John Rodgers was ordered, under the direction of the War Department, to begin construction of an inland navy. In Cincinnati he purchased three river steamers. Though they had no iron plating, he strengthened their resistive powers by raising perpendicular oak bulwarks, five inches thick, proof against musketry, and by dropping boilers into the hold and lowering steam pipes. They were taken to Cairo on August 12,

[7] Mahan, *Gulf and Inland Waters*, pp. 9–11.

ready for service. Further, he let a contract with James B. Eads of St. Louis to construct seven gunboats, 175 feet long and 50 feet wide, with one large paddle wheel placed amidships well forward of the stern, protected by the sides and the casemate.

As it was expected that these steamers would fight bows on, the forward end of the casemate had iron plating two and a half inches thick, which was superimposed on oak, twenty-four inches thick. There was also the protection of two and a half inches of iron abreast the boilers and engines. The sides, like the front and rear casemates, sloped at an angle of about 35 degrees. When the vessels had their guns in place and were equipped with coal and stores, the casemate deck came nearly to the water, and they drew from six to seven feet.[8] These gunboats, with a converted heavy snagboat—the largest, strongest, and slowest of all—constituted the chief strength of the river fleet throughout the war.

Early in September Captain Andrew H. Foote had relieved Commander Rodgers. In the preceding months embarrassment had arisen for the reason that direction of affairs relating to the western rivers all came under the War Department, and orders relating to the equipping and operating of ships had frequently to be referred to army officers, they being the senior officers present. When Captain Foote was assigned to this duty, he was made a flag officer. He then ranked with a major general in the Army; and no one but the commander in chief of the department being senior to him, he was virtually in control. Not until July, 1862, were the Mississippi gunboats transferred to the Navy Department.

The first important service carried out by the wooden gunboats was on November 7, 1861. Union troops, 3,000 in number, under Grant, their transports convoyed by the *Tyler* and the *Lexington,* landed at Belmont, Missouri, opposite Columbus, where the Confederates were assembled in considerable

---

[8] *Ibid.,* pp. 12–14; Eads, *Recollections of Foote and the Gunboats,* in *Battles and Leaders of the Civil War,* I, 339.

numbers. Engaging the troops encountered there, Grant's force slowly drove them back to their camp and then forced them to give way and run for the protection of the river bank. At this point, the lately recruited Northern troops, who had thus far fought well, became demoralized, the hastily evacuated camp offering too great a temptation for looting. The victors were now in grave danger of being captured by the superior Confederate forces sent across from Columbus, and advancing toward the transports. Grant, seeing this, ordered his men to cut their way through and re-embark. At this juncture, the *Tyler* and the *Lexington* opened upon the Confederates with grape, canister, and five-second shell and drove them back with loss. Thus they permitted the harassed troops to complete their embarkation and the transports to withdraw. When the affair was thought to have been successfully terminated and the transports were proceeding up the river, General McClernand discovered that some of his troops had been left behind. Immediately the gunboats put back, picked up the missing men and took forty prisoners.

Grant had planned the attack as a military diversion, to prevent the Confederates from detaching troops from Columbus; and, further, he sought to give confidence to his own command, such as would be gained by a daring raid. A reverse for him at this time might have been fatal. He was still Grant the unknown. Though a West Point graduate, he had for years been out of the Army, and after several unsuccessful business ventures he had but lately returned to the Service. The gunboats thus had an essential part in giving him his start, and prepared the way for the military victories at Fort Donelson, Vicksburg, and Richmond.

These early attempts at combined military and naval operations each had its lesson, but it was reserved until the years following to gain all that might be accomplished by full co-ordination and a carefully elaborated plan. The Norfolk Navy Yard might have been saved if only the Navy had held on a little longer or the services of the Army at Fortress Monroe had been secured earlier. On the Potomac, the Navy found the dislodging and driving back of the enemy from their hastily prepared fortifications fairly easy, but without the Army to hold what was gained, had constantly to repeat the task. In the attacks at Hatteras Inlet and Port Royal the Army was present and ready to give substantial support if resistance of the enemy had required it. The Navy unaided was sufficient to gain the immediate objective. The Army, however, was essential to hold what had been gained. Had the troops been better organized and the combined forces more aggressive they could have pushed far into North Carolina, South Carolina, and Georgia and brought panic into those states. The Union forces failed to take full advantage of the opportunity that was offered, and to achieve in 1861 what strategically would have been of greatest value in the prosecution of the war. Roanoke Island furnishes an example of what could be accomplished by use of the entire force provided for a joint operation. The Confederates had ample warning of the impending attack. There was no surprise. But they were handicapped by the lack of engineers and heavy guns and other munitions. The Union forces planned their attack so as to be practically irresistible, advanced into adjacent territory, and suffered almost nothing in losses.

References

Battles and Leaders of the Civil War, Vol. I, 1887.
Mahan, A. T., *Gulf and Inland Waters,* 1883.
Official Dispatches and Letters of Rear Admiral DuPont, 1883.
Official Records of the Union and Confederate Navies in the War of the Rebellion, Vol. XII, 1901.

XI OPERATIONS ON THE WESTERN RIVERS

The Mississippi Gunboats: A New Type

THE WAR IN the West for the control of the Mississippi River system and for maintaining the Union cause in the states which it penetrated was at the beginning directed wholly by the War Department. But the Army, as has been told, early requested that for handling the boats essential for military operations naval officers and men be assigned. Credit is due to the Army for taking the initiative. This should not be lost sight of even though it must be added that for efficient organization the Navy soon had to have the direction of its own personnel and assume full responsibility for operations.

In April, 1861, James Buchanan Eads of St. Louis had been summoned to Washington by Lincoln to give advice on the best methods for utilizing the western rivers for attack and defense. Eads was an engineer of outstanding ability and he had an intimate acquaintance with the Mississippi River system. It was he who planned the Mississippi River gunboats earlier described. He skilfully distributed the work of construction between St. Louis, Cincinnati, Louisville, Pittsburgh, and other cities; consequently, although all shipyards and engineering companies were badly demoralized, he would have had the seven ironclads promised ready for service in sixty-five days—

as specified in the contract—had not the Government caused delay by changes in design and slowness in payments. Success came to the Union cause from his ability to devise an entirely new type of fighting craft that met the special conditions. Each gunboat, though drawing only six or seven feet of water, mounted thirteen guns. It was a strong floating fortress, well adapted to the service demanded of it, and a distinct innovation in naval warfare.

Early in January, 1862, Grant received orders issued by McClellan to make a reconnaissance in western Kentucky, which was especially planned to prevent Confederates from sending re-enforcements to Bowling Green, near which General Buell and General Thomas were operating. The Confederate line of defense at this time extended from west to east along the southern border of Kentucky, with strong positions at Columbus on the Mississippi, Fort Henry on the Tennessee, Fort Donelson on the Cumberland, Bowling Green at a junction of railroads leading from Nashville and Memphis to Louisville, and Mill Spring in eastern Kentucky near the Cumberland Mountains (see map, p. 188).

The reconnaissance marked the beginning of the most successful military campaign in the first twelve months of the war, and the Navy operating with the Army had an essential part in it. The Confederates were prevented from sending re-enforcements and General Thomas was victorious at Mill Spring. Of greater consequence, Grant returned to Cairo convinced that with the force available he could take Fort Henry and also Fort Donelson, and drive the enemy out of Kentucky. The plan was presented by Grant in person to his departmental commander, General Halleck, but it received only an abrupt disapproval. When, however, three weeks later he renewed this suggestion by telegram and Flag Officer Foote, who was to operate the gunboats serving with him, sent a similar dispatch, permission was given. On the day following, February 2, the expedition set out.

Capture of Fort Henry

There not being enough boats or men to move all the 17,000 troops that Grant required, he loaded the boats with half that force, and when they were landed nine miles below Fort Henry, he hurried the boats back to Cairo to bring up the rest. On the sixth of February at eleven o'clock, Army and Navy were to advance in a concerted attack on the fort.

Fort Henry, on the east bank of the Tennessee River, had a garrison of 3,200 men and was defended by seventeen heavy guns. Its strength would have been augmented by Fort Heiman on the west bank of the river directly opposite—if only the latter had been garrisoned and properly equipped. Eleven miles to the east was Fort Donelson, with a force of Confederates numbering 15,000 or more. It was the common expectation that Donelson, being near, would send heavy re-enforcements when an attack began. For the Union forces prompt action was imperative.

The plan for a simultaneous attack by Union troops and gunboats proved, at the last moment, impossible of execution. In consequence of heavy rains, the river was high and the country inundated. Wallowing in the water and not finding the roads that led through the forest, the Union troops were delayed. Although influencing the decision, they took no part in the fighting.

Foote advanced on the fort with four river ironclads, followed by three wooden gunboats, opening fire at twelve-thirty when he was 1,700 yards distant. The fort replied with eleven heavy guns that bore, and their fire seems to have been fairly accurate. The *Cincinnati,* flagship, was struck by thirty-one shots (more than struck all the others combined), but the armored casemate gave protection, as is shown by the losses, one killed and nine wounded. The squadron continued to advance until they were within six hundred yards of the fort—all except the *Essex*. In the latter part of the action, she had her boiler exploded by a shot, and the current carried her astern and out of the battle.

In the Confederate works there was trouble such as was experienced at Port Royal. The gunners seem not to have understood the handling of a rifled cannon, for after a few discharges the one they were using burst, killing three men and disabling several others. The premature discharge of a 42-pounder caused further casualties. A 10-inch Columbiad became silent when the priming wire jammed and was broken in the vent. After fighting for an hour and a quarter, the small force still remaining in the fort was discouraged and exhausted. General Tilghman, in command, lowered his flag and sent the adjutant general and the captain of engineers in a boat to Flag Officer Foote to arrange for surrender.

The cavalry of the Union forces appeared on the scene about this time, but served only to harass the rear of the Confederates retreating to Fort Donelson. The delay of the Union Army, however, made no difference in the immediate result. As learned later, Tilghman acknowledged defeat several hours before a gun was fired. Scouts having informed him of the position and strength of the opposing forces, he evacuated Fort Heiman; and convinced of the futility of protracted resistance, he gave orders for the garrison of Fort Henry to withdraw and march to Fort Donelson, retaining less than one hundred men in addition to his staff to man the batteries and cover the retreat.

Capture of Fort Donelson

No less commendable than the handling of the Union forces at Fort Henry was the prompt following up by them of the advantage gained. Lieutenant S. L. Phelps, with the gunboats *Conestoga, Tyler,* and *Lexington,* was ordered to proceed up the Tennessee River to seize or destroy Confederate gunboats, steamers, and military stores, and Commander Walke was dispatched with the *Carondelet* to destroy the bridge of the Memphis and Bowling Green Railroad where it crossed the river. Neither force encountering serious opposition, these tasks were speedily accomplished. In four days Phelps returned, after having gone to Muscle Shoals, Alabama, as far as the river was navigable. He had forced the Confederates to burn six of their transport steamers, loaded with military supplies; and had captured two other steamers and the half finished gunboat *Eastport,* which he brought back loaded with 250,000 feet of lumber. She was later completed and taken into the Federal Navy.

Meanwhile Grant was pushing preparations for an attack on Fort Donelson. For this the gunboats were not ready. Damages inflicted in the battle of Fort Henry had not been repaired. As Foote wrote to Secretary Welles:

I go reluctantly, as we are very short of men, and transferring men from vessel to vessel, as we have to do, is having a very demoralizing effect upon them. . . . I must go, as General Halleck wishes it. If we could wait ten days, and I had men, I would go with eight mortar boats and six armored boats and conquer.

Fort Donelson, surmounting a bluff one hundred feet above the Cumberland River, had been well fortified. Protecting it from approach by the river were two strong water batteries, excavated in the side of the slope. It was these the gunboats had to fight. The fort, according to Grant's later statement, was held by 21,000 men—the Confederates reported their number as nearly a third less. Believing that it would be reenforced rapidly, Grant advanced from Fort Henry when his immediate force was only 15,000. His comment was, "I felt that 15,000 men on the eighth would be more effective than 50,000 a month later." Thus he had asked Foote that gunboats at Cairo should proceed up the Cumberland, not even waiting for those that had gone to Florence to return.

At ten o'clock in the morning of the thirteenth the *Carondelet,* Commander Walke, at Grant's direction, opened fire on the battery from behind a point that afforded partial shelter and for six hours dropped shells into the fort, not causing any great damage, but serving to divert the attention of the enemy while the Army brought into position the last of their batteries. In return she received the enemy's fire, and a 128-pound solid shot, piercing the port casemate forward, burst the steam heater and wounded half a dozen of the crew.

At three o'clock in the afternoon of the following day, Foote, with the ironclads *St. Louis, Louisville, Carondelet,* and *Pittsburg,* and the wooden gunboats *Tyler* and *Conestoga,* advanced against the water batteries. The order of attack was similar to that employed at Fort Henry; the ironclads steaming forward, the heavy bow casemates toward the batteries, and the wooden gunboats bringing up the rear. The fleet reserved their fire until they were within a mile of the batteries. As they opened fire they moved forward rapidly until they were within six hundred yards of the enemy, then continued slowly until they had decreased this to four hundred yards.

The fighting was spirited on both sides. The Confederates had held their fire until the gunboats were within fairly close range, and then, at a signal, fired every gun simultaneously. They had an advantage in their elevated position which made their heavy shot doubly effective and protected their own gunners. The Union gunboats were repeatedly hit, the flagship *St. Louis* receiving fifty-nine shots, and the others about half that number each. Foote nevertheless continued the fight, and on observing that the fire of the enemy was slackening and that some of the men were running from their guns, he had the confident expectation of capturing the batteries. But about this time, the action having lasted an hour and a quarter, the wheel of the flagship and the tiller ropes of the *Louisville* were disabled by shots. Relieving tackles not being sufficient to steer the ships in the swift current, the disabled vessels were carried down the river and out of the action. The other two ironclads had been badly damaged between wind and water, and when the Confederates returned to their guns they were forced to withdraw.[1]

The gunboats had made a gallant fight. Mahan gives as his opinion, "Notwithstanding its failure, the tenacity and fighting qualities of the fleet were more markedly proved in this action than in the victory at Henry."

In the original plan, after the gunboats had silenced the water batteries they were to run past the fort and secure a position above, to assist the Army in pushing a force through to the river and completing the investment. In this they failed, but undoubtedly the fight they made helped to tire out the enemy. Foote, though wounded, was still in command of his force. He recommended to Grant that the troops entrench while he took the gunboats off for necessary repairs, which he

---

[1] Foote's report will be found in *Army War Records,* VII, 122–124.

estimated would take ten days. But the enemy prevented any such delay. Before Grant returned from his interview with Foote, they had made an attempt to cut through the Union lines and escape, but they were driven back. Although Generals Floyd, Pillow, and Forrest that night succeeded in slipping out with 4,000 troops, the main part of the Army, numbering about 15,000, surrendered unconditionally the following morning.[2]

Pittsburg Landing

The Navy's further notable service in co-operation with Grant in 1862 was at Pittsburg Landing—in the battle of Shiloh, on the Tennessee River. The Confederate forces under General A. S. Johnston were concentrated at Corinth, Mississippi. As both sides knew, the conflict would be joined somewhere in this vicinity. While the Union forces were being slowly collected, Johnston suddenly took the offensive, and on the sixth of April made a surprise attack on Grant's command at Pittsburg Landing. The Confederates pressed forward with an abandon that gave no thought to losses, and with superiority in numbers seemed to be on the point of gaining a great victory. The Union front was forced back, and an entire division of 2,000 men was captured. Many of Grant's officers and men were inexperienced, but in spite of heavy losses they continued their stubborn resistance. In the afternoon, two of the wooden gunboats, the *Tyler,* Lieutenant William Gwin, and the *Lexington,* Lieutenant J. W. Shirk, which had been operating in the river as part of Grant's force, found their opportunity to render important service. The Confederates had been making a furious drive to turn the left wing of the Union Army and reach the river, and seemed about to seize the Landing and the Union transports. The little *Tyler* at 2:50 P.M. joined the battle, and within less than an hour had silenced the enemy batteries at this point. Later, accompanied by the *Lexington,*

[2] Grant, *Memoirs,* I, 294–315.

she steamed a short distance up the river, and the two gunboats succeeded in stopping the fire of other Confederate batteries. Thus the battle was waged, first one side and then the other having the advantage. At the end of the day the Confederates had reached a point close to the river where, because of a deep ravine, practically no Union troops except the Union artillerists and a small supporting infantry force were stationed. This was at 5:35 P.M. But the Union gunboats supporting the artillery delivered an effective fire that outmatched the opposing batteries and drove them back. Throughout the night, first the *Tyler* and then the *Lexington* threw a shell at regular intervals, every ten or fifteen minutes, that searched the Confederate right wing and disturbed the sleep of the exhausted troops.[3]

Union re-enforcements had also arrived, General Buell having come up late in the afternoon with 20,000 troops. On the other side the Confederates sustained a great loss when their leader, General Johnston, was killed. The Union Army, now decidedly superior in numbers, on the following morning made a strong counterattack, and carried all before them. The battle of Shiloh was one of the most hotly contested engagements of the war, and, in the opinion of Grant, decisive. In his report he commented on the important assistance given by the little wooden gunboats.

Capture of Island No. 10

The sound strategy of the campaign on the Tennessee and Cumberland rivers was already bringing results. The Confederate line was pierced at the center when Forts Henry and Donelson were taken and the wings were isolated. First, Bowling Green, the railroad center, was abandoned, leaving wide open the avenue to Nashville, where rich stores had been accumulated; and about two weeks after the surrender of Donelson, Columbus, grandiosely referred to as "the Gibraltar of the

[3] Report of Lieutenant Gwin, *Naval War Records,* XXII, 762–4; General Grant's report, *ibid.,* 765–6.

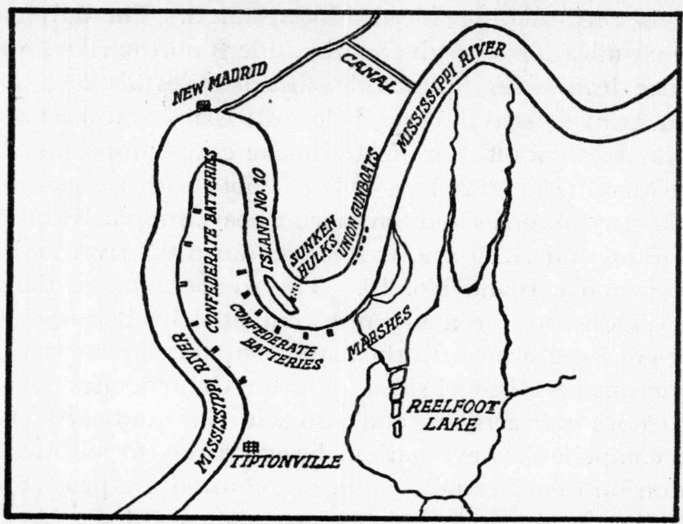

ISLAND NO. 10

West," was also evacuated. The latter operation was cleverly masked, and not until two days previous to its completion did the Union forces discover what was taking place. By this move General Leonidas Polk, in command, transferred a considerable amount of guns and military stores to Island No. 10 in the Mississippi, where the Confederates made their next stand.

This island, fifty-five miles from Cairo, and taking its name from its numerical position in the series of islands south of that city, presented a strong defense. Situated between Missouri and Tennessee just below the Kentucky boundary where the winding river made a deep "S" in reverse (∼), it lay at the bottom of the loop to the right. Its armed force consisted of fifty or more heavy guns, besides a floating battery and several Confederate gunboats. Supported also by fortifications at New Madrid, a town at the top of the loop to the left, these defenses controlled the river. The strength of the Confederate position was further augmented by impassable swamps on the Tennessee side. But its isolation was also its weakness. The only means of communication with the South, aside from the river, was by the road leading to Tiptonville, fifteen miles distant. If the Union Army crossed the river below the island and reached this road it could cut off supplies and make escape impossible.

On March 15, 1862, Flag Officer Foote with a squadron of six ironclad gunboats and ten mortar boats, supported by Colonel Buford and 1,200 troops, steamed down the river and took position above Island No. 10. The co-operation of the gunboats had already been urgently requested by Brigadier General John Pope, who with the main army was threatening New Madrid on the Missouri side. This the Confederates defended with troops and artillery and also with six gunboats. When Pope compelled its evacuation, he was ready to advance to a position on the river below, but he required the protection of the Union gunboats that the Army might cross the river and complete the encirclement of the island fortress.

On the sixteenth Union mortar boats began shelling the batteries of the island and the Tennessee shore and also the floating battery. Next day Foote, continuing the bombardment, attempted to advance that he might make the guns of the ironclads more effective. But he saw that the rapid current would sweep a steamer that had been disabled, not as at Fort Henry and Donelson out of range and to a point of safety, but right under the guns of the enemy and to certain destruction. The risk made him cautious and he did not come nearer than 2,000 yards. A rifled gun of the *St. Louis* burst, killing or wounding fifteen—probably more than the losses inflicted on the Confederates by all the gunboats combined. Pope's request for gunboats to run the batteries did not meet with a favorable response. In a council of war the gunboat captains decided that the project was too hazardous to justify the undertaking. The only dissenting opinion was that of Commander Henry Walke of the *Carondelet,* who favored its trial. Meanwhile, the Army had cut a canal through a bayou, giving an approach for light army transports to New Madrid from the river above without passing the island. This made Pope more insistent in urging that a gunboat should run the batteries and protect the Army as it crossed to the Tennessee side—where the shore was guarded by Confederate light batteries and gunboats.

An important preliminary to further operations was a small Army-Navy boat expedition which at midnight slipped down to Battery No. 1 on the Tennessee shore, spiked six guns, and returned without the loss of a man. Two days later the Union gunboats shelling the floating battery cut it loose from its moorings. Whereupon the current carried it two or three miles down the river before it could be secured.

Commander Walke had volunteered to run the batteries in the *Carondelet,* and permission having been granted him, he set out on the night of April 4 at about ten o'clock. Every preparation had been made to protect the pilot house and all vulnerable parts of the ship. Lights had been concealed, and men had been warned not to speak above a whisper, and only as duty demanded it. The hour chosen was when the moon would set. It happened that a violent thunderstorm burst as the gunboat got under way and continued for the next two hours. Walke had a gauntlet of nearly fifty guns to run. He trusted that he might slip past at least several of the batteries unobserved. But as he approached the first, a smokestack catching fire gave full notice of the project, and when the flames were extinguished the frequent flashes of lightning revealed the gunboat's progress. The *Carondelet* was greeted by a furious bombardment, but in the wild excitement, the storm adding to the confusion, the Confederates aimed their guns badly and their shot passed over the gunboat. Shortly after midnight she joined Pope's force at New Madrid. The exploit was one of the most daring and dramatic of the war, and great credit was due Commander Walke for its success. To the surprise of all, the *Carondelet* suffered no casualty; indeed she was not struck once.

Two nights later, the gunboat *Pittsburg,* also in a thunderstorm, duplicated the achievement of the *Carondelet.* General

Pope, secure from attack by the Confederate gunboats, then began crossing the river. About the same time, the Confederates undertook the evacuation of Island No. 10. The few hundred men left under General Buford surrendered the island to Foote. The main Confederate force, however, had begun their retreat too late. Intercepted by Pope on their way to Tiptonville, they were all captured, 5,000 or 6,000 in number.

Further Progress Down the Mississippi

"Had not General Pope's army been withdrawn, we have every reason for believing that a plan we had adopted would have insured the fall of Fort Pillow in four days, and enabled us to have moved on Memphis in two days afterward." This comment of Foote to Secretary Welles shows his disappointment on the change of plans eleven days after the taking of Island No. 10. The combined forces had advanced to a point below the northern boundary of Arkansas and the capture of Fort Pillow, thirty miles distant, seemed a fairly easy task. But the Confederate army at Corinth under Beauregard, having been strengthened, was again threatening the Union forces opposed to them. In consequence, General Halleck ordered Pope with 20,000 troops to join him at Pittsburg Landing, leaving only 1,200 men and Foote's gunboats to proceed against Fort Pillow. Until the situation was remedied, the utmost the Union forces could do was to maintain their position.

Early in May, Flag Officer Foote, in consequence of the wound received at Fort Donelson, was obliged to turn over his command. He was succeeded by his old friend, Captain Charles H. Davis, a highly capable officer who had already demonstrated his ability as fleet captain under Du Pont and as a member of the ironclad board.

Meanwhile, Confederate gunboats at Fort Pillow and below frequently attempted a surprise attack on the Union ships. And soon a new type of fighting ship which already had gained a signal success at Hampton Roads received its trial on the Mississippi—the ram. It was used by both the Confederate and the Union forces.

Charles Ellet, Jr., a civil engineer, who had done outstanding work in bridge building and flood control, visited Europe during the Crimean War and urged Russia to employ "ram-boats" for the relief of Sebastopol. Disappointed on gaining nothing more than a hearing, he returned home and offered his idea to successive secretaries of the Navy. Finally, when the *Virginia* sank the *Cumberland,* the power of the ram was demonstrated. Almost immediately (March, 1862), Ellet was authorized by Secretary of War Stanton to prepare a ram fleet—its object to gain control of the Mississippi. With great dispatch he remodeled nine river boats, and then joined Davis' squadron above Fort Pillow.

Ellet was an engineer, and his plan of operations had the familiar characteristics of the amateur, the spirited but untrained fighter. He desired no commission, and he wished to have no officers or seamen aboard his craft, but to rely solely on volunteers. Yielding, however, to Stanton, he became less of an irregular by accepting the commission of colonel and tolerating in each boat an officer and armed guard of soldiers. But the rams went through their first battles without a single cannon on board.

The boats he built were side-wheelers and stern-wheel towboats "with strong machinery and great power . . . hurriedly strengthened and braced to maintain a severe headlong blow."

Early on the morning of June 6, the Confederate gunboats, also converted into rams, left the protection of the batteries of Memphis and advanced against the Union Fleet, which they thought to catch unawares.

At this very time, Ellet, eager to fight but far from being prepared, was steaming down the river with his rams to join Davis. As the *Queen of the West* (his flagship) came abreast Davis' squadron, which was at anchor, a shot fell near by. Though mist hid the enemy, Ellet felt certain that his dream of years was now to be realized. His rams would fight, and he was to lead them in battle. He did not take time to report to the commander in chief, but headed downstream at full speed, waving his hat and shouting to his brother, Lieutenant Colonel A. W. Ellet, who commanded the ram *Monarch,* to follow him. The *Queen of the West* engaged the *General Lovell,* the leading Confederate ram, and striking her amidships cut so deep that she was held by the sinking craft. Whereupon the *General Beauregard,* taking advantage of the situation, charged upon the *Queen* and smashing her port paddle wheel rendered her helpless so that she had to make for the Arkansas bank.

The *Monarch* had singled out the *General Price* as her antagonist and the two met in head-on collision. The *Monarch* had the better of this encounter and then she eluded the *General Beauregard* and the *General Bragg,* which were charging down upon her from opposite quarters. In consequence they did not succeed in ramming their enemy but crashed into one another.

About this time, Captain Davis' gunboats joined the combat, and their heavy guns decided the battle. Seven Confederate rams were sunk or beached and only the two remaining made their escape. Although Davis did not support Ellet's claim that the rams had done most of the fighting and had sunk or put out of action five of the seven victims, he highly commended in his report the work of the Union rams.

It was not long before the officers of these strange fighting craft recognized the danger they were subjected to by guerrilla bands infesting the river banks and applied to the Secretary of War for brass field pieces; and in time the volunteers and irregulars gave way to regulars with training and organization, who proved more efficient. But there was no denial that even in the beginning the rams, operating in the confined waters of the rivers and the sounds, were often highly successful.

References

Crandall, W. D., and Newell, I. D., *History of the Ram Fleet. . . . The Ellets and Their Men,* 1907.

Dictionary of American Biography, for articles on J. B. Eads and Charles Ellet.

Grant, U. S., *Personal Memoirs,* 2 vols., 1885–6.

Hoppin, J. M., *Life of Andrew Hull Foote,* 1874.

Official Records of the Union and Confederate Navies in the War of the Rebellion, Vol. XXII, 1908.

OPERATIONS ON THE LOWER MISSISSIPPI

XII

Plans for the Capture of New Orleans

WITH THE SINGLE exception of Richmond, the capture of no other city was so important as that of New Orleans. In 1860, it was the largest city of the South and the sixth city of the whole country, its population of 168,675 being greater than that of St. Louis, 50 per cent larger than that of Chicago, and only slightly less than that of Boston. It was, in comparison with the other principal Southern ports, including Norfolk, Portsmouth, Wilmington, Charleston, Savannah, Mobile, and Galveston, greater than all combined.[1] Nearly one-third of its people represented the growth during the decade previous to the war, caused in large part by the increasing volume of trade in cotton, beef, and tobacco. Commanding the commerce brought down the Mississippi, it had become one of the great export centers of the world. It was also of consequence to the armies fighting in Virginia and Tennessee, who depended in part on the supplies brought to them from the West beyond the Mississippi. Indeed, its importance to the Confederate cause is not likely to be exaggerated.

In the series of Union combined operations, the taking of this city was a project in which the Navy bore the principal part. For, during the first year, the Army concentrated on the

[1] Eighth Census, 1860.

defense of Washington, the campaigns against Richmond, and the holding of Kentucky, Missouri, and other border states. In the early planning, military strategists had conceived of the war in the West, that is on the Mississippi and its tributaries, as a strictly military operation, directed by army officers. In accordance with this view, not until they had taken the territory to the north could they advance down the river and attack New Orleans. For such an operation they estimated an army of 50,000 would be required, and because of the demands elsewhere troops were not available.

The Navy, on the other hand, looked upon New Orleans as a seaport and felt certain that it was open to attack from the sea.

The campaign had its inception at a conference in Washington, November 15, 1861. Secretary Welles had brought the project to the attention of the President, who called a meeting at the home of General McClellan. In addition to those mentioned, also present were Assistant Secretary Fox, who had taken many a ship from the Gulf to New Orleans, and Commander David D. Porter, who had recently returned from blockade duty off the mouth of the Mississippi. McClellan, who at this time was entrusted with the direction of the Northern armies, was certain that troops required for a joint attack could not be furnished. But when he was informed that 10,000 soldiers, chiefly for holding the city after capture, were all that the naval plan called for, his objection vanished. He had the engineer's conviction that the two strong forts defending the city from the south must be reduced by siege operations. But Fox and Porter were confident that warships coming from the Gulf might deal with them. The enthusiasm and confidence of the Navy prevailed. The project was approved, and all agreed that strictest secrecy should be maintained.

Next the council discussed who should command the expedition. Porter did not have sufficient rank himself to be eligible, but he suggested his foster brother, Captain David Glasgow Farragut. The question of Farragut's loyalty was at once raised, for he was born in Tennessee and both his first and second wives were from Virginia. Fox had Farragut also in mind for the undertaking, and he called attention to the clear sense of duty and quick decision Farragut had shown in the preceding April. When Virginia seceded, Farragut, who with his wife and son had been making his home in Norfolk, immediately took steamer to Baltimore, proceeded to New York, and offered his services under the Flag.

Porter was instructed to sound him out. Soon Farragut was ordered to Washington where the full plan was put before him. Welles and Fox now felt doubly sure of the correctness of their judgment as they witnessed his enthusiasm and heard his confident assertion that he could carry the operation through to a successful termination with even fewer ships than were promised.

His son tells of an "abrupt and mysterious" note, written by Farragut from Washington, December 21, 1861: "Keep your lips closed, and burn my letters; for perfect silence is to be observed—the first injunction of the Secretary. I am to have a flag in the Gulf, and the rest depends upon myself." The last words were fundamentally characteristic of Farragut and reveal a quality that brought success.

People later wondered that an officer could have seen so much active service and be so little known. He had been appointed midshipman when he was nine years, five months old. He had accompanied his foster father, Captain David Porter, to sea when he was ten, and in the War of 1812, being ordered to the *Essex,* had a full experience of cruising and fighting when he was eleven and twelve. He had helped to exterminate the West Indian pirates, and had sought to take an active part in the Mexican War but the opportunity was denied him. Thus he had gone forward, quietly doing the duty assigned, and had reached the age of sixty, not widely known. But his shipmates always held him in high regard.

Two forts, Jackson and St. Philip, situated about twenty miles above the Passes of the Mississippi, formed the chief defense of New Orleans from the south. Armed with 109 cannon and rebuilt and strengthened a few years previous, they made the river, as commonly believed, impassable. Progress was further denied by a log barrier stretched across the river under the guns of Fort Jackson, carrying two-and-a-half-inch iron cables, the middle section of the barrier being filled with eight heavy schooners, anchored in position and joined by chains. A Confederate flotilla of fifteen gunboats, two of them ironclad rams, lay between the ports and New Orleans; other ironclads were in the process of being built.

The Confederates, with their efficient spy system in Washington and elsewhere, ordinarily had full information of Northern plans of campaign. But in this instance, either the service did not function, or the defenders of the city were overconfident of the strength of their defenses. They were certain that if any attack was attempted it would come from the north. The threat was so remote they felt no concern. Their sense of security was evidenced by the withdrawal of some of the gunboats assembled there. These were ordered to Memphis.

On the Union side, as well as the Confederate, there was the realization that the capture of New Orleans would be an undertaking of the first magnitude.

Porter, an officer of unusual energy and resourcefulness, always had some novel idea to propose at a council table. At the first meeting to discuss the expedition, he had suggested that a flotilla of mortar schooners should accompany the attacking squadron and reduce the forts. This at once won the approval of McClellan, a thoroughgoing engineer, who tended to exaggerate the strength of works that engineers had prepared. Early it was decided that Porter should command the mortar schooners, and he received the necessary orders for their purchase and equipment. Farragut as a matter of course accepted this auxiliary force, but if he had been consulted in advance he would probably have expressed the opinion that the mortars were unnecessary and of doubtful value.

Farragut's Preparations

We would have to turn back to the battle of the Nile or the Trafalgar campaign, exemplifying the genius of Nelson, for a comparison with the clear estimate of the situation and strategic insight displayed by Farragut in the preparations for his attack.

First, he did not disclose his plans and warn his enemy, as was done in so many campaigns in the Civil War and as did the British and French in a somewhat similar situation years later at Gallipoli. He assembled his squadron in the late winter of 1862 at Ship Island, 100 miles from the Passes in the Gulf. But it was not until the spring that he had ships, troops, and mortar schooners at hand or on their way. Day after day was spent in dragging the deeper draught ships over the bars and through the mud before the entrance to the river, the Passes. Indeed to take the *Pensacola* into the deep water inside was two weeks' work.

Thus, although Farragut had arrived at the mouth of the Mississippi in the latter part of February, it was not until April 7 that he had in the river the bulk of his fleet. This, not counting the schooners of the mortar flotilla and the *Portsmouth* operating with them, consisted of seven steam sloops of war, one large side-wheeler, and nine gunboats—seventeen vessels carrying 154 guns. His flagship, the *Hartford,* was a sloop of war with auxiliary steam power giving a speed of eight knots. She was comparatively new, having sailed on her first cruise to China in 1859. Farragut believed in mounting a gun whereever a place could be found, and his ship carried twenty-two 9-inch Dahlgrens—a heavy armament for that time.

To show the care Farragut gave to the preparations aboard his ships, the following is quoted from his general order:

> Make arrangements, if possible, to mount one or two guns on the poop and topgallant forecastle; in other words, be prepared to use as many guns as possible ahead and astern, to protect yourself

against the enemy's gunboats and batteries, bearing in mind that you will always have to ride to the current, and can only avail yourself of the sheer of the helm to point a broadside gun more than three points forward of the beam.

Have a kedge in the mizzen chains (or at any convenient place) on the quarter, with a hawser bent and leading through the stern chock, ready for any emergency, also grapnels in the boats ready to hook on to, and to tow off fire ships. Trim your vessel a few inches by the head, so that if she touches the bottom she will not swing head down the river. . . .

Have light Jacob ladders made to throw over the side for the use of the carpenters in stopping shotholes, who are to be supplied with pieces of inch board lined with felt, and ordinary nails, and see that the ports are marked in accordance with the Ordnance Instructions on the berth deck, to show the locality of the shothole. Have many tubs of water about the deck, both for the purpose of extinguishing fire and for drinking.[2]

On April 16, Farragut, having advanced his fleet to within three miles of the forts, ordered Porter to begin his bombardment when he was ready. Two days later the mortars opened up, dropping a large shell every ten minutes. At once the forts made a spirited response. But as the schooners were moored close to the river bank they were screened by the woods and their mastheads were camouflaged by branches tied to the tops. In consequence the enemy was slow in discovering the position of the schooners and obtaining a correct range. On the other hand, the mortars seem to have been fairly accurate. Early they set fire to the citadel and wooden buildings in Fort Jackson. The gunners were driven into their casemates and their fire slackened. Nevertheless, resistance in the forts continued the next day and before long it looked as if the defenders were becoming somewhat inured to the bombardment.

After three days, Farragut, convinced that the forts could not be reduced by the mortars, decided to bring the ships into ac-

[2] *Naval War Records,* XVIII, 48.

tion. On the night of the twentieth he sent his fleet captain, Henry H. Bell, with two gunboats to destroy the chain barrier. Greeted by a lively fire from the guns of Fort Jackson, crews of the gunboats realized they had embarked on a hazardous undertaking. They planted some heavy charges in the obstruction, but the charges were useless, for the electric connections parted and failed to explode the powder. Finally, however, they succeeded in forcing an opening in the barrier sufficient for a ship to pass, and they returned without loss.

Earlier the same day Farragut had called the commanding officers of the several ships to the flagship, not to consult them on what should be done, but to acquaint them with the plan which he had decided to follow. He showed them charts of the river and explained to each the position of his vessel. Three methods of attack had been considered: (1) running past the forts at night or in a fog and advancing on New Orleans; (2) attacking the forts with the fleet and mortar boats and capturing the defenses before going farther; and (3) making a joint attack on the forts with the troops and the ships of the fleet and the mortar flotilla. Porter, who could not be present at the council, had written that he favored the third. It was a combination of the first two that Farragut had decided to use. The fleet was to steam past the forts firing as their guns bore. When the ships were above the forts, a force should be furnished to protect the troops when the latter were brought through the bayou from the Gulf; and then both should move up the river.

During the afternoon immediately preceding the attack Farragut visited each ship to make sure that the officers understood the orders and had everything in readiness. They were all imbued with the need of preparation, and each had made his own arrangements to protect boiler and machinery from enemy fire, using piles of hammocks, coal, bags of ashes, bags of sand, and other articles. As the fight was to begin in the dark before dawn, certain captains had whitewashed the decks to make essential gear visible.

The mortar boats had been given their test, and now there

was to be no delay. Captain Bell has transmitted to us one of the fundamental principles his commander in chief emphasized at this time, "He believed in celerity."

Passing the Forts

Two red lights displayed from the flagship at five minutes before two on the morning of April 24, 1862, gave the signal for the ships to get under way. According to plan, they were to advance in two columns, one well to the right to attack Fort St. Philip, and the other to the left to attack Fort Jackson. Just before the attack, Farragut had taken the precaution of sending a gunboat to explore the breach in the barrier and satisfied himself that the Confederates had done nothing to repair it. But it was so narrow that he decided to change the fleet formation. In passing the barrier, the column to the right, which was the First Division, was to precede the column to the left, the Second and Third Divisions. The First Division, comprising three sloops of war, one side-wheeler, and four gunboats, was commanded by Captain Bailey; the Second Division, three sloops of war, was commanded by Flag Officer Farragut; and the Third Division, one sloop of war and five gunboats, was commanded by Captain Bell. The change made the fleet less compact, but gave the ships a better chance of passing the barrier without becoming entangled in the obstruction or fouling one of their own number.

The attack had been most carefully studied out and the first step toward victory had already been taken. A grim fight, nevertheless, was to follow.

According to orders, the three divisions moved in succession through the barrier, and as they came opposite the forts they opened with all the guns that bore. They were supported as they moved on by the mortar schooners and the *Portsmouth,* which, remaining below, took part in the battle with a heavy bombardment.

Running past the forts proved an ordeal of fire, and many

challenges had to be met. The current being strong and some of the anchors being deeply imbedded in the soft river bottom, not until half past three did the First Division, led by Captain Bailey in the *Cayuga,* pass the barrier. The forts, no appreciable number of their guns having been destroyed by the mortars, promptly began a heavy cannonade. The gunboat *Cayuga,* not able to do much in opposition, sped along. But the *Pensacola* and the heavy ships that followed reduced speed to return the fire. Although darkness and the heavy pall of smoke that enveloped the forts made their fire inaccurate, the same conditions made the steering of the ships uncertain and difficult. Fire rafts came drifting down, and one, pushed by a tug, fouled the *Hartford.* To make matters worse, the flagship, seeking to avoid the raft, ran aground. In a few moments flames were licking the paint on the port beam and rose halfway to the main and mizzen tops. It was a critical situation, but calm judgment on the part of the officers and efficient organization of the crew saved them. A part of the crew, going to fire quarters, soon had the flames under control; the gunners had already put a shot through the boiler of the tug; and as the ship, by Farragut's order, was backed with all speed, the force of the propeller threw the raft and the tug on shore and drew the ship off the mud bank into deep water. Watson, the flag lieutenant, relates that Farragut, who during the battle had his station forward to observe the conflict, stood at the rail during this period of extreme danger, coolly giving orders, watching the ship slowly turn, and occasionally referring to a small compass he had on his watch chain.

It was fortunate for the *Hartford* that none of the enemy rams attacked her when she lay helpless. Only a few minutes later, the *Manassas,* looking like a monstrous turtle, came lumbering down, her speed accelerated by the current. She made for the *Pensacola,* but the latter avoided her by a quick turn of the helm. Continuing on her course, she struck the *Mississippi* but failed to give more than a glancing blow, which did little harm. Later, running across the current, she rammed the *Brooklyn* at the starboard gangway. It was only the "chain armor" (chains hung over the sides to protect the engine), according to the report of her executive officer, that saved the ship. The stem of the *Manassas* had cut between two frames, crushing the outer and inner planking. She fired her one gun, a 32-pounder, when ten feet away, and the shot, entering five feet above the water line, lodged in the sandbags placed to protect the steam drum. As was evident, the precautions devised by Farragut and his officers to safeguard the ships had a vital significance. In importance to the Navy, the *Brooklyn* ranked next to the *Hartford*.

After daybreak the *Manassas* was still in the battle, though her one gun had been put out of action by the shock of ramming the *Brooklyn*. When the *Mississippi* returned to attack her, she was run ashore and abandoned by her crew.

The gunners in the forts, though they had been driven to shelter by the heavy fire of the fleet, resumed their stations when the *Hartford, Brooklyn,* and *Richmond* had passed, and they concentrated their fire on the gunboats that brought up the rear. The *Kennebec* was delayed by fouling one of the schooners in the barrier. The *Itasca* received a shot in her boiler that rendered her helpless. The *Winona,* following astern, became entangled in the logs and moorings of the hulks in the barrier. Day was breaking, and the Confederate gunners, able now to correct their aim, showered missiles on each gunboat as it appeared. Thus, these last three gunboats were forced to abandon the project of running the forts. Withdrawing to safety, they joined Porter's division below.

Meanwhile, the gunboats *Cayuga* and *Varuna,* which had sped along while the main fleet was giving battle to the forts, found the Confederate River Defense Fleet and other enemy ships awaiting them, and for twenty minutes, being outnumbered, had a spirited engagement all of their own. In this the *Varuna* was rammed by two Confederate steamers, and her commander, finding that she was sinking, ran her ashore. The Confederate ships, however, as they met the heavier ships of the Union Fleet, were hopelessly outclassed. Of a combined force of thirteen, only two escaped by taking refuge under Fort Jackson. One of these was the *Louisiana,* an ironclad armed with sixteen guns and reputed to be of superpower. But as she was still under construction, her engines not yet running, she took no part in the battle beyond that of a floating battery. Only her bow and starboard broadside guns (six altogether) could be brought to bear.

The Confederate forces afloat suffered in not being under a unified command. The three captains who had been formerly in the United States Navy handled their ships effectively, but the Mississippi River Defense Squadron, their captains drawn from the merchant service, and jealously maintaining their independence, were a negligible force. Had Farragut delayed his attack a few months, affording the Confederates time to complete the *Louisiana* and organize the river force, he might have sustained much greater loss.

The Capture of New Orleans

Farragut now had thirteen vessels above the forts. Leaving the gunboats *Wissahickon* and *Kineo* to guard the landing of the army forces under General Butler, should the troops come by way of Quarantine Bayou, he steamed next morning to New Orleans.

Five miles below the city, at the English Turn, which took its name from the repulse of the British in 1815, he was fired on by batteries, but he quickly silenced them and approached the city. Farragut reported:

> All the morning I had seen abundant evidence of the panic which had seized the people of New Orleans. Cotton-loaded ships on fire came floating down, and working implements of every kind, such as are used in shipyards. The destruction of property was awful. . . . The levee of New Orleans was one scene of desolation; ships, steamers, cotton, coal, etc., were all in one common blaze, and our ingenuity was much taxed to avoid the floating conflagration. . . .
>
> We now passed up to the city and anchored immediately in front

of it, and I sent Captain Bailey on shore to demand the surrender of it from the authorities, to which the mayor replied that the city was under martial law, and that he had no authority. General Lovell, who was present, stated that he should deliver up nothing but, in order to free the city from embarrassment, he would restore the city authorities and retire with his troops, which he did.[3]

Farragut had undisputed control of the Mississippi in this vicinity and looked now upon New Orleans, which lay defenseless under his guns; but he had perplexing problems still to meet. The people of the city were in a defiant mood and any ill-advised act was sure to result in an outbreak. He had sent messengers to both Butler and Porter after he had passed the forts, but he could not expect the arrival of troops for several days. Though his guns might punish a hostile demonstration, they would include women and children among the victims. The desire was not to subjugate New Orleans but to bring it back to normal activities. To accomplish the latter, a considerable force of troops was essential. By insistence and tact Farragut made no little progress, even before the coming of the troops. The national colors were raised over the mint and the custom house, and the Louisiana flag lowered on the city hall. The marine guard ordered to do this marched through the excited populace without resorting to force.

On the morning of the twenty-ninth Captain Bailey brought news of the surrender of Forts Jackson and St. Philip. They might have held out for some weeks. For although Farragut was in a position to prevent supplies reaching them from New Orleans, they commanded the southern approach, and the situation might easily become critical for the Union Fleet in the midst of a hostile country. A part of the soldiers in the forts were foreigners and their mutiny hastened the surrender.

Farragut, on arrival at New Orleans, unlike the many who pray when confronted by peril but forget to express gratitude when the crisis is over, proclaimed by general order the hour of eleven o'clock, April 26, "for all officers and crews of the fleet

[3] *Op. cit.*, 158.

to return thanks to Almighty God for His great goodness and mercy."

Operations Above New Orleans

If in 1861 the advisers of the President, as they planned operations on the Mississippi, had not appreciated the part the Navy was prepared to play, the following year they went to the opposite extreme. Ships could be called upon for anything. The Navy Department's order to Farragut instructed him after taking New Orleans to proceed as follows: "If the Mississippi expedition from Cairo shall not have descended the river, you will take advantage of the panic to push a strong force up the river to take all their defenses in the rear. You will also reduce the fortifications which defend Mobile Bay and turn them over to the army to hold.[4]

At the time of the capture of New Orleans, Davis' fleet was 900 miles from the mouth of the Mississippi, and nearly a month and a half was required before it could pass Memphis. But Farragut did all in his power to carry out orders. An advance squadron took Baton Rouge and Natchez, and called upon impregnable Vicksburg to surrender—the last treating the demand with ridicule and contempt. This, however, did not satisfy the Department, and when a report appeared in the New York papers that the fleet was returning to New Orleans, a fast steamer was sent from Hampton Roads to carry very positive orders, signed by Assistant Secretary Fox: "It is of paramount importance that you go up and clear the river with the utmost expedition. Mobile, Pensacola, and in fact, the whole coast sinks into insignificance compared with this."

Farragut realized, as the Administration in Washington could not, the difficulties involved in the program laid down. Coal and provisions were slow in reaching ships as they went farther and farther up the river. Gunboats were in need of repairs. The river was falling, and when Farragut had run

[4] *Ibid.*, 8.

past the batteries at Vicksburg with several of his larger ships, he was apprehensive lest delay should prevent his bringing them down again. Large numbers of the crew in his fleet and in Davis' above Vicksburg were ill. Davis reported that in his flagship one out of every four was sick or incapacitated and in the *Carondelet* one out of every two. Only 1,500 troops under Brigadier General Thomas Williams were available to hold what the Navy might seize, and the country being hostile and a Confederate army of 30,000 being in Vicksburg or vicinity, the work of the ships was certain to be futile.

Yet Farragut, so far as he was able, carried out his instructions. He ran past the batteries of Vicksburg, employing the general plan used with success at New Orleans. For two days Porter bombarded the forts with his mortars. Then Farragut, his fleet being formed in two columns, with gunboats and lighter vessels to port so as to protect them from the shore batteries, attempted the passage. At two o'clock on the morning of June 28 he weighed anchor and at four he was engaging the works. Farragut reported:

> The *Hartford* fired slowly and deliberately and with fine effect—far surpassing my expectations in reaching the summit batteries. The rebels were soon silenced by the combined efforts of the fleet and of the flotilla [the mortar boats] and at times did not reply at all for several minutes, and then again at times replied with but a single gun. . . .
>
> The Department will perceive, from this report, that the forts can be *passed* and *we have done it,* and *can do it again as often as may be required of us.* It will not, however, be an easy matter for us to do more than silence the batteries for a time, as long as the enemy has a large force behind the hills to prevent our landing and holding the place.[5]

Farragut, having accomplished this task with seven ships, met a division of Davis' fleet commanded by Lieutenant Colonel Ellet and anchored above the city. The *Brooklyn,* the *Katahdin,* and the *Kennebec,* which had brought up the rear of his

[5] *Ibid.,* 609, 610.

two columns, delayed too long in engaging the batteries, and becoming separated from the rest of the fleet, were forced by the heavy fire to retire below the town.

While the Union ships were lying at their anchorage, off the mouth of the Yazoo, fires banked so as to save the limited coal supply, they had an unexpected and disappointing encounter with the Confederate ironclad *Arkansas.* This was a ram the South had been building at Memphis and had taken up the Yazoo to carry on to completion. She was protected by an iron casemate, and to provide this the Confederates had scoured the country for miles—their chief source of material being worn-out railroad tracks which they salvaged.

Farragut, hearing vague reports indicating that the ram was nearing completion, sent Colonel Ellet with one of his rams and two gunboats up the Yazoo River on a reconnoitering expedition. When Ellet had gone only six miles up the river, he met the *Arkansas* on her way down. In the running battle that ensued, the light Union ironclad *Carondelet* clung to her adversary but got rather the worst of it. The unarmored *Tyler* gave such assistance as she could to her consort and then fled down the river. Ellet's ram *Queen of the West* had already preceded her in order to give the alarm to the fleet. The warning, however, was almost simultaneous with the appearance of the monster. Since none of Farragut's ships had steam up, they could not maneuver or follow; but they trained their guns as they bore. To Farragut's mortification, the ironclad succeeded in running the gauntlet and anchored under the forts at Vicksburg—a threat to all of the ships below. That very evening Farragut took his ships past the forts and down the river, hoping to destroy the *Arkansas* on the way, but the Confederates had shifted her position under cover of darkness and she escaped. Other attacks followed without success. It was not until some weeks later, when she lumbered out to support the Confederate troops attacking Baton Rouge, that she met her end. Her machinery, never wholly satisfactory, broke down. While she lay helpless against the river bank, the Union ironclad *Essex* came in sight. The Confederates, accepting the inevitable, then set fire to their craft.

In July the Department, finally recognizing the real situation, gave orders that Farragut should take his fleet down the river again. With difficulty he got his ships back to New Orleans. Having now destroyed the *Arkansas* and having extricated his ships from a dangerous position, he experienced great relief.

Results of Farragut's Campaign

There was no naval engagement of the war that had a greater international importance than the capture of New Orleans. It gave courage to the supporters of the Union cause not only in America but in England and France. Northern prestige, after the defeat of Bull Run and the slowness and repeated reverses of operations directed against Richmond, had reached a low point and few neutral observers entertained the belief that the Union would be victorious. Louis Napoleon's pro-Southern leanings were not disguised. Had it not been for the successes in the west, beginning with Fort Henry and continuing to New Orleans, France, even without the co-operation of Great Britain, would have recognized the Confederacy. Industrial conditions in France in the spring of 1862 were bad, worse than at any time previous in ten years. The distress being ascribed to the blockade, Napoleon was seriously considering breaking the blockade and opening New Orleans and the Mississippi to commerce. He had been deterred by the realization that this act might cause war with the United States. New York, Philadelphia, and Baltimore, the chief depots of wheat and beef, would be closed in event of hostilities. If the choice had to be made, wheat and beef were even more important than cotton. Napoleon had hesitated, and after Farragut's victory Seward was so quick in proclaiming that New Orleans was open to commerce as to preclude any immediate action in behalf of the South. Farragut in his New Orleans campaign gained a brilliant victory for the Navy and rendered outstanding service to the North.

References

Farragut, Loyall, *The Life of David Glasgow Farragut,* 1879.

Mahan, A. T., *Admiral Farragut,* 1897.

——, *The Gulf and Inland Waters,* 1883.

Official Records of the Union and Confederate Navies in the War of the Rebellion, Vol. XVIII.

West, R. S., *The Second Admiral; A Life of David Dixon Porter,* 1937.

FURTHER OPERATIONS ON THE SOUTHERN RIVERS AND GULF

XIII

THE COMMAND OF THE Mississippi River Squadron above Vicksburg, which had worn out Foote and Davis, was in October, 1862, transferred to Porter. Meanwhile Farragut, continuing the work of the West Gulf Blockading Squadron, took port after port with little or no resistance, and on October 15 reported that Galveston, Corpus Christi, and Sabine Pass were now in the possession of the fleet. Two months later only Mobile remained to the Confederates. But on the first day of January, 1863, the blockaders met a sharp reverse when, as narrated in a previous chapter, Galveston was taken by the Confederates in a surprise attack.

Passing the Batteries at Port Hudson

Until the close of the war, Texas continued to be an unfailing source of supplies for the Confederate armies in the east. Early in 1863 cattle, sheep, corn, and munitions (brought in through Matamoros) were being shipped down the Red River and across the Mississippi between Vicksburg and Port Hudson. Porter had attempted to gain at least local control by sending two ironclads, the *Queen of the West* and the *Indianola,* past Vicksburg to the river below, but they had been captured. Whereupon, Farragut saw it was for him to close the traffic by sending up some of his heavy ships from New Orleans. Port Hudson, which ranked next to Vicksburg in strength because of its high commanding position at a 90-degree turn in the river, had during recent months been fortified with nineteen heavy guns, many of them rifled, and a large number of field pieces. To pass them while going upstream and making the turn was for ships a formidable task.

General Banks, who had succeeded Butler in the command at New Orleans, was asked to make a diversion by attacking the batteries in the rear. But he delayed, and the fleet was compelled to act alone.

Farragut assigned for this project seven ships not especially fitted for blockade duty because of slow speed. On the port side of each of three heavy ships was lashed a lighter ship, the latter thus being protected from the enemy fire to starboard and prepared to give assistance if her consort should receive injury to her engine or run aground. The heavy side-wheeler *Mississippi,* which came at the rear, operated singly without companion. The passage was attempted on the night of March 14, 1863. In the course of his preparation, to be found in the general order to the squadron, Farragut enunciated what has since become a well-known maxim of the Service, "The best protection against the enemy's fire is a well-directed fire from our own guns."

It was the right angle turn, with the strong current and treacherous sand bar extending far toward the batteries opposite, that was the cause of disaster. The Confederates had given alarm and lighted a great bonfire when Farragut, leading with the *Hartford* and *Albatross,* was passing the lower batteries. Smoke from the fire of the ships as well as of the forts made it hard to train guns accurately, and still more difficult to navigate the ships and follow the channel. At the turn, the *Hartford,* suddenly feeling the sweep of the current, grounded; but with the *Albatross* backing her engines, and her own going ahead hard, she was soon free. Farragut's precaution of placing the pilot in the mizzen top, connected with the deck by a speaking tube, enabled the flagship, even with the heavy pall of smoke, to keep the channel for the most part.

The *Richmond,* coming next, received a plunging shot in the steam pipe, upsetting both safety valves. She was helpless, and when her consort, the *Genessee,* proved unable to push ahead with her against the current, the two retired.

The *Monongahela* ran on the shoal at the turn, and the impact broke the lashing which held her companion. After utmost effort she freed herself, but then the crank pin became heated and the engine stopped. Unmanageable, she drifted downstream.

The *Mississippi,* similarly lost in the smoke, grounded heavily on the shoal close to the turn. For thirty-five minutes her officers and crew labored to get her off. Meanwhile, the Confederate batteries were repeatedly hulling her. Deeming the situation hopeless, the commanding officer set fire to her and abandoned the ship.

Only two ships out of seven had succeeded in passing the batteries, four having been driven back and one destroyed. From Port Hudson to Vicksburg was two hundred miles. Seven strong ships might have maintained an effective patrol; two could not. But the project was not an entire failure. As the *Hartford* and *Albatross* steamed slowly up the Mississippi, they took occasion to destroy quantities of stores which had been accumulated on the levees. When they appeared off the Red River, they closed it as completely as if they had been ten, and even when they moved on they made its further use hazardous. At Grand Gulf Farragut communicated with Grant, who had begun the final campaign against Vicksburg and had brought his army below on the west bank. Indirectly, Farragut gave support to Porter in the important combined operation, which was nearing its climax.

The Campaign Against Vicksburg

After the capture of New Orleans, had the necessary troops been available, the Union forces might have occupied Vicksburg, which then was not heavily fortified, and Grand Gulf and Port Hudson as well. But when the Confederates had lost their control of the river to the north, they erected batteries for the defense of the places just mentioned and bent every effort to strengthen their general position. The high bluffs on the east bank gave them a great advantage. The region being near to the state capital, Jackson, the home of Jefferson Davis, there was a sentimental as well as an economic reason for holding it against attack.

Halleck had done little after the battle of Shiloh to drive the Confederates from western Tennessee and Mississippi, and on the capture of Memphis he turned over to Grant the problem of completing the work and gaining the entire control of the river. The latter attempted to advance from the army base at Corinth to Vicksburg, with the idea of striking in the rear from Jackson. But his supplies, brought by the Navy to Memphis, had from this point to be forwarded by a long line, which was cut by the Confederates. In consequence, the Union forces had to fall back. Next, Grant attempted to gain a flanking position by attacking Haynes's Bluff on the Yazoo to the north of Vicksburg. This movement was directed by General Sherman with the support of Porter, who about this time had been promoted from commander to rear admiral. Again he was unsuccessful. As an interlude in this campaign, Porter, supporting 32,000 troops under the command of McClernand and Sherman, led the way up the Arkansas River—the combined forces consisting of fifty naval vessels and transports. Their objective was Arkansas Post, a base for several regiments of Texas cavalry. This was an easy success, and the Navy received the surrender before the Army had begun their final attack.

Little progress, however, had been made toward the capture of Vicksburg—so strongly defended by nature as to be referred to as the "Gibraltar of the West." The city was situated on a hairpin bend of the river on steep bluffs two hundred feet high, and its batteries made navigation extremely hazardous. The vast Yazoo Delta, stretching almost to Memphis, made it impossible for an army to follow the east bank, and the west bank was impassable when inundated during the winter months. But Grant had already decided that a detour by the south and west furnished the best approach. He waited only until conditions should be favorable. For the operations planned, the co-operation of the gunboats was essential. And in this, the most brilliant of Grant's campaigns, the Navy carried through its part with marked efficiency. Referring to the Vicksburg campaign, Mahan remarks that never in all the history of combined movements was there more hearty co-operation than that between the Army and the Navy under the leadership of Grant and Porter.

With the coming of spring, the level of the river fell and the back waters receded. Grant at once started McClernand's division toward New Carthage, thirty miles below Vicksburg on the Louisiana side. For the troops to cross the river a large force of gunboats was required. Accordingly, on the night of April 16–17, the running of the batteries at Vicksburg was attempted. Seven ironclads had been made ready, their engines given additional protection by bulwarks of coal and logs to guard them against plunging shot and by coal barges lashed to their starboard sides. Three army transports loaded with stores and forage for the horses also accompanied them. They planned, if possible, to steal past, but they were early detected. Houses set on fire by the Confederates, tar barrels, and a calcium beacon quickly illuminated the whole river. The current twisted gunboats and transports around, and several of the coal barges had to be cut loose before the gunboats could come again on their course. One of the transports piled high with cotton, a "cotton-clad," was set on fire by the shells and lost. All the others steamed or drifted down the river and next morning joined the Army at New Carthage. It was one of the most spectacular exploits of the war. In spite of the terrific fire, the expeditionary force lost not a single man killed and only a dozen wounded.

With the main army, Grant then marched down the west bank, and sent by night six more transports with stores past the batteries, five of them getting through. His plan was to cross at Grand Gulf. Since batteries had been placed there by the Confederates, they had first to be reduced. This task was given to Porter. He made a spirited attack, but the batteries on land proved superior to those afloat. After an engagement of four hours and a half, the losses and injuries sustained by the gunboats convinced Grant that another plan must be tried. At Bruinsburg, a few miles farther south, he crossed without opposition, the gunboats protecting the transports and also ferrying the troops.

While this operation was proceeding, Sherman to the north of Vicksburg was simulating an attack on Haynes's Bluff, in which Fleet Captain Breese participated with such gunboats as were available. Union troops were seen to be landing in large numbers, and General Pemberton, completely deceived, hurried forward his reserves from Vicksburg and made no effort to block Grant's advance, which he regarded as a ruse. By the time he was undeceived, Grant with 30,000 men had gained the long desired position on high land on the east bank of the river. Threatening Grand Gulf from the rear, he compelled its evacuation. Then adopting a bold measure, he cast loose from supply trains and, living on the country, advanced on Jackson, where he defeated General Joseph Johnston. Sherman, having accomplished the end sought in his strategem, then crossed to the west bank, marched down to Grand Gulf, ferried to the east bank, and soon really was attacking Haynes's Bluff, this time from the south.

In nineteen days Grant had marched 180 miles and fought five victorious battles. Interposing his army between Johnston and Pemberton he defeated them with what at the beginning was an inferior force. In the latter part of May, he had Pemberton securely locked in Vicksburg, where no aid could reach him.

During this period Porter and the Federal gunboats were continuously active. After ferrying Grant across the river, Porter made a dash up the Red River, and took Fort De Russy, destroying a large accumulation of stores—sugar, molasses, bacon, rum, and salt. Then, returning quickly to Vicksburg, he was in time to assist Sherman in destroying the fortifications surrounding Haynes's Bluff. Taking advantage of the demoralization that had spread through the surrounding country, Porter then pushed fifty miles up the Yazoo River to Yazoo City and destroyed sawmills, machine shops, and two ironclads that were building, as well as general stores intended for Vicksburg.

The Army, after two unsuccessful attempts to take Vicksburg by storm, settled down to a grim siege that lasted a month and a half. In this the Navy also took part. The gunboats were constantly on watch to prevent supplies from being sent into the city. The mortar boats were called upon to shell the fortifications and supply depots, and kept up a steady fire night and day. Though, as Grant was told later, the number of people whom the mortars killed was surprisingly small, the fire served to wear down the defenders' morale and thus hastened the end.

On the fourth of July, 1863, Pemberton and 30,000 men laid down their arms. On the same day, news flashed through the country of the victory at Gettysburg. As millions remarked, it was indeed a National day. About the same time the moral aspect of the conflict had been further emphasized in the minds of many supporters of the Union cause, American and British. Lincoln had issued the Emancipation Proclamation, which became effective just as Grant was beginning his long campaign. With the great victories won at Vicksburg and Gettysburg the war had reached a turning point.

Five days after the fall of Vicksburg, Port Hudson was surrendered. Then the whole length of the Mississippi was open to commerce. Guerrilla bands might fire on passing steamers, but the last forts had been captured and the Confederacy had been cut in two. Vicksburg was a great military and naval success and the outstanding economic victory of the war.

In the spring and summer of 1864 occurred two more joint operations. The Red River Expedition, undertaken by Gen-

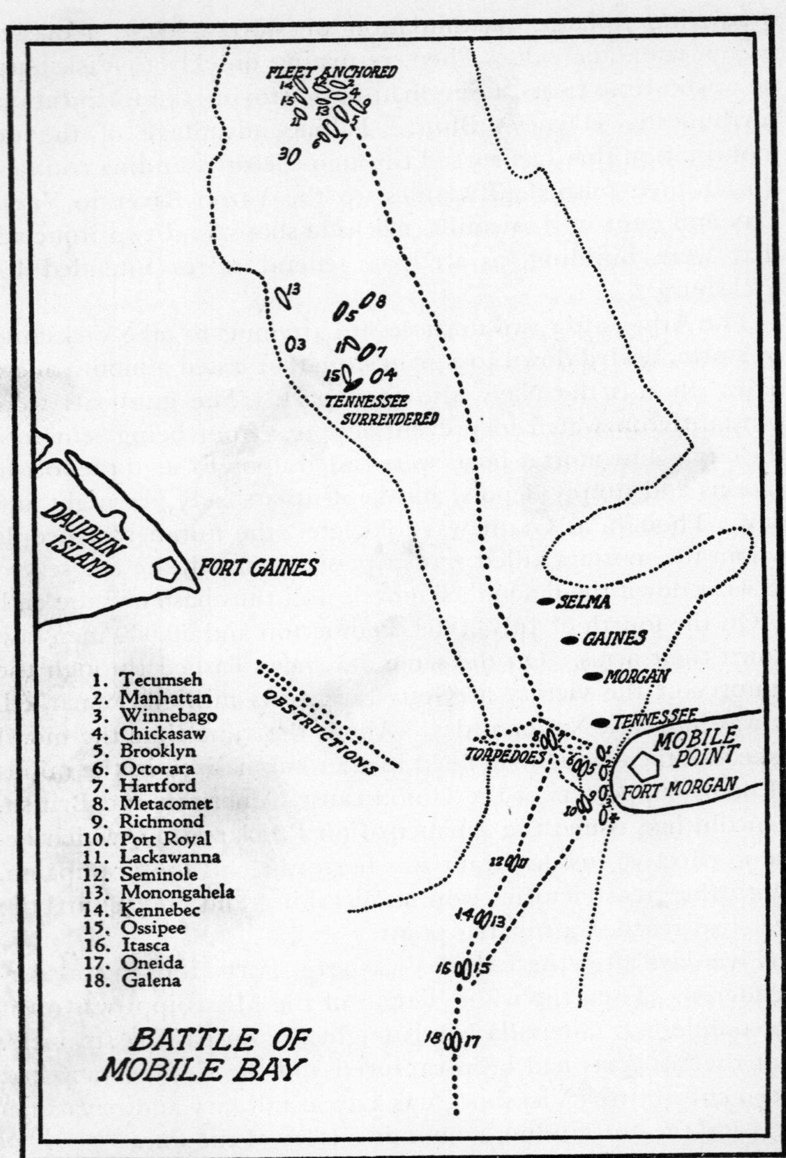
FLEET ANCHORED
TENNESSEE SURRENDERED
DAUPHIN ISLAND
FORT GAINES
OBSTRUCTIONS
SELMA
GAINES
MORGAN
TENNESSEE
TORPEDOES
MOBILE POINT
FORT MORGAN
1. Tecumseh
2. Manhattan
3. Winnebago
4. Chickasaw
5. Brooklyn
6. Octorara
7. Hartford
8. Metacomet
9. Richmond
10. Port Royal
11. Lackawanna
12. Seminole
13. Monongahela
14. Kennebec
15. Ossipee
16. Itasca
17. Oneida
18. Galena
BATTLE OF
MOBILE BAY

eral Banks and Admiral Porter at the prompting of Secretary Seward, was planned not only to extend commerce in Louisiana and gain a foothold in eastern Texas, but also to dampen the ardor of Napoleon III in his Mexican schemes. Banks was not a trained soldier and he was handicapped by receiving orders from superiors far from the field of action. At critical times he failed to support Porter, and everything went wrong. Shreveport, which was to have been the goal of their operations, was not taken, and speculators did not obtain the cotton they expected. On the Army's meeting two defeats, a general retreat was ordered. The river in April and May was unprecedentedly low. Consequently, the large river ironclad *Eastport* had to be abandoned and set on fire. Indeed, the other members of the river squadron might also have been lost if extreme efforts, including the raising of the level of the river by a temporary dam, had not been used.

Battle of Mobile Bay

This sad fiasco was in marked contrast with Farragut's expedition against the forts at the entrance of Mobile Bay, culminating in the famous battle of August 5, 1864.

Here there was splendid co-operation between the two Services. The initial fighting fell to the Navy, but the Army, standing ready to follow up the Navy's success, lost not the slightest time in continuing the operation against the forts. The engagement affords another excellent example of Farragut's genius in planning. He looked forward to the meeting with the forces of the enemy with a marvelously clear and correct understanding of what would be the situation. Yet on the occurrence of an unforeseen disaster his highly finished plan did not prevent his making a quick change to meet the new conditions. The battle shows Farragut's outstanding ability as a tactician as well as a strategist. No other naval engagement in American history brings us closer to the commanding officer. It reveals not only his relations with his brothers in arms but the inner working of his spirit. As a revelation of a great leader it can thus be compared with the Trafalgar campaign, which affords the final and most intimate approach to Nelson. It was the climax of a long and unusually varied naval career that had begun fifty-three years before.

The operation against the forts commanding the entrance to Mobile Bay, as Farragut thought, should have been undertaken immediately after the capture of New Orleans—that is, two years earlier. It was essential for the completion of the Gulf blockade, which was the task assigned him. At that time Fort Morgan and its two supporting forts had little of the strength later developed, and Farragut's seagoing ships, which, as we have seen, labored under grave difficulties when they advanced several hundred miles up the Mississippi, would have had no trouble in reducing them. A much earlier attack was favored also by Grant. And if the decision had rested with him, he would have assigned a military force for this project instead of for the futile Red River undertaking. When finally Farragut was free to proceed, Fort Morgan was singly more powerful in its batteries than the combined forts below New Orleans, and it was supported not only by two neighboring forts, but by a unified naval force. This force promised soon to be the nearest to a strong fleet the Confederates ever possessed: the ironclad ram *Tennessee* and three gunboats, all armed with rifled guns, under Admiral Buchanan, the fearless and aggressive officer trained in the National Navy who had destroyed the *Cumberland* and *Congress* at Hampton Roads. He was determined he would accomplish now what he had attempted in the earlier engagement, the breaking of the blockade. In addition to this force, three ironclads of lesser size and strength, at various stages of completion, were building in the bay near Mobile. The Confederates, circulating wildly optimistic reports, were convinced that a naval victory would soon be theirs.

By the information brought by refugees and deserters, Farragut had kept posted on the progress made by the Confederates in strengthening their military and naval defense, and he regretted every day of delay. In January, 1864, he had written to the Department that if his force could be strengthened by even one ironclad he would destroy the whole enemy flotilla, and with 5,000 troops he would occupy the forts. In his fight with the ram *Arkansas* he had seen how great was the power of resistance of vessels of her type. He knew that the *Tennessee* was reported to draw only fourteen feet. As he wrote, unless he had an ironclad to engage her, she might lie on the flats where he could not follow and work havoc with her rifled guns. He had great confidence in the fighting powers of his wooden ships where they could be maneuvered, but it was necessary that they should be able to come to close quarters so as to run down their enemy or pour in a broadside.

In the end, two large single-turreted seagoing monitors were sent, the *Tecumseh* and the *Manhattan,* and two Mississippi River monitors, the *Winnebago* and the *Chickasaw,* together with 2,000 troops under General Granger. Although Farragut had been making every effort to end postponement and assemble this force, not until the evening of August 4 did the last unit, the *Tecumseh,* arrive. The following morning he made the attack.

Farragut was keenly alive to the underlying causes of the reverses which the Union had suffered—the lack of unified feeling, the mercenary spirit of many at home, the unnecessary delays in building ships and furnishing supplies, the incompetence of leaders—and his letters in the period previous to the battle show the depression all this occasioned him. He was fully aware too of the magnitude of what lay immediately before him. Before the battle of New Orleans he had written, "As to being prepared for defeat, I certainly am not. Any man who is prepared for defeat would be half defeated before he commenced. I hope for success; shall do all in my power to secure it, and trust to God for the rest." [1] The evening before the present engagement he wrote to his wife: "I am going into

[1] L. Farragut, *Life of David Glasgow Farragut,* p. 218.

Mobile Bay in the morning, if God is my leader, as I hope He is, and in Him I place my trust. . . . Your devoted and affectionate husband, who never for one moment forgot his love, duty, or fidelity to you, his devoted and best of wives. . . ."[2]

As he was writing this, the *Tecumseh,* though she had reached Pensacola, had not yet come to where the fleet lay. But the Army had landed on Dauphin Island the night before and was ready according to schedule to begin the attack on Fort Gaines, one of the minor defenses, three miles west of Morgan. Farragut had made his plan of battle weeks before, assigning the position of each ship. As events later showed, it was unfortunate that he could not have assembled his captains and made sure that each understood what was to be his part. It was the latest arrival, Captain Craven of the *Tecumseh,* who by a too free interpretation of the general order for the attack which Farragut had issued lost his ship and very nearly caused the turning back of the entire fleet.

Farragut had outlined his plan in a letter to Commodore Palmer, three weeks before:

> I propose to go in according to program—fourteen vessels, two and two, as at Port Hudson; low steam; flood tide in the morning; with a light southwest wind; ironclads on the eastern side, to attack the *Tennessee,* and gunboats to attack rebel gunboats as soon as past the forts. Ships run up into deep water, seven vessels outside to assist the Army in landing on the beach and to flank the enemy.

With this should be considered what was included in General Order No. 11, July 29, 1864:

> There are certain black buoys placed by the enemy across the channel from the piles on the west side of the channel toward Fort Morgan. It being understood that there are torpedoes and other obstructions between the buoys, the vessels will take care to pass to the eastward of the easternmost buoy, which is clear of all obstructions.

---

[2] *Ibid.,* pp. 405, 406.

Early in the morning of August 5, two hours before dawn, after a night of broken slumber, the Admiral called his servant and inquired about the wind. The slight breeze from the southwest was precisely what he wanted, for it would carry the smoke from the guns of the ships upon the batteries at Fort Morgan. This and the flood tide, assured for this morning, had been specified in his original plan.

Signals were given to the ships to take their place in the battle line, in each case the heavier ship on the starboard side where her guns as they bore might be trained on Fort Morgan. It was about half past five, while Farragut was sipping a cup of tea on the quarter deck of the *Hartford,* that he turned to the captain of the ship and remarked, "Well, Drayton, we might as well get under way." Almost at once the expected signal was flashed through the fleet.

Farragut thought that the *Hartford* with the *Metacomet* should lead the column of wooden ships. But at the last moment he yielded to the wish of his captains and let the *Brooklyn,* commanded by Captain James Alden, accompanied by the *Octorara,* precede him. His officers had urged that the flagship ought not to be too much exposed, and stressed the advantage possessed by the *Brooklyn,* which "had four chase guns and an ingenious arrangement for picking up torpedoes." After the battle, Farragut remarked that in yielding he had made a mistake. The four Union ironclads, being slower than the wooden vessels, were ordered to get under way in advance, and on passing Fort Morgan to go inside the main column and abreast the four leaders. As the channel made almost a right angle turn before reaching the entrance to the bay, the wooden ships in approaching could use only their bow chasers. The monitors, which could fire from any position, were to engage the land batteries and the Confederate ships and thus protect the wooden vessels until their guns could be properly trained.

Everything had been arranged, and comparatively little time was required for the ships with their consorts to take their positions. The *Tecumseh* opened the battle at thirteen minutes before seven by firing on Morgan. A few minutes later the fort opened on the *Brooklyn,* which promptly replied.

Union officers felt that everything was favorable and that all was proceeding according to plan. About this time, however, their chief foe, the *Tennessee,* which had been lying athwart the channel under the guns of the fort, was seen to be slowly steaming toward the west.

The crew of the *Tecumseh* were all eagerness to engage her, and the commanding officer, Commander T. A. Craven, after his first shot was holding his fire in readiness. As he neared the buoy which he was to pass to eastward he remarked to the pilot, "It is impossible that the admiral means us to go inside that buoy," adding that if he did so he might not be able to turn ship later to follow the channel to the west. The movements of the *Tennessee* then wholly occupied him and he headed directly for her, although the change of course threw him right across the path of the advancing Union ships. Suddenly a muffled explosion was heard; the bow of the *Tecumseh* rose out of the water and then quickly sank. In less than thirty seconds the monitor had disappeared beneath the surface, and all of her large complement were carried under except a dozen picked up by a boat of the *Metacomet* and eleven others who saved themselves.

Captain Alden in the *Brooklyn,* a near spectator, appalled by the disaster, stopped and backed his engines, and this threw him athwart the channel, blocking the way. The *Hartford,* following after, at Farragut's order stopped but did not back; the captains of the later ships, not knowing what had happened, were still advancing. Alden, notwithstanding Farragut's order to go forward, was lost in indecision. As he afterwards reported, he saw black objects, believed to be torpedo buoys, almost under his bows, and the lookout reported shoal water. Meanwhile the gunners in the fort, seeing the confusion, opened with redoubled fury, and the Union column was now in danger of losing all semblance of formation and order.

It was the most critical moment of all Farragut's naval career.

From his position in the rigging of the *Hartford* he had witnessed the sinking of one ship, and he was faced with the prospect of seeing all turned back with the destruction of many of his fleet. The battle was near to being lost. What had been the ruling habit of his life now guided him as he prayed: "O God, who created man and gave him reason, direct me what to do. Shall I go on?" "And it seemed," said the Admiral, "as if in answer a voice commanded, 'Go on!' "[3]

There was but one way to do this—turn sharp to port, pass under the sterns of the two ships ahead, and cross the line of torpedoes. It involved great peril, but Farragut had made his decision.

At this time, the monitor *Winnebago* was drawing abreast and then ahead of the column. Her commanding officer, Commander Thomas H. Stevens, could be seen calmly pacing up and down on her exposed deck. Following her was the *Chickasaw;* and her captain, Lieutenant Commander George H. Perkins, twenty-eight years old, was equally indifferent to danger. Referring to the latter, an officer aboard the flagship describes the scene, "As he passed the *Hartford* he was on top of the turret, waving his hat and dancing about with delight and excitement." Like Nelson's captains at Trafalgar, Stevens and Perkins were going into battle with the gusto and zest of boys in a football game. It was either victory or death—and death was not decreed for them.

When the *Hartford* passed the *Brooklyn,* there came the warning cry "Torpedoes ahead!" "Damn the torpedoes!" shouted the Admiral, intent only on his high mission. "Four bells! Captain Drayton, go ahead! Jouett, full speed!"

The flagship and her consort steamed directly across the line of torpedoes. The other ships followed them, and the confused column straightened out as by magic. No more torpedoes exploded. Farragut had previously sent his flag lieutenant, J. C. Watson, to make nightly reconnaissances and learn what he could. The information brought had been meager, but Far-

[3] Mahan, *Admiral Farragut,* p. 277.

ragut thought it probable that since the torpedoes had been for some time in the water they might be innocuous. This proved to be very nearly correct.

The *Tennessee,* when the Union flagship had passed the fort, bore down with the intention of ramming. But because of her slow speed, she was eluded by her opponent. With a like absence of results, she attacked in turn the *Brooklyn* and *Richmond,* which fled past. But the *Monongahela,* which had been fitted out with a sharp iron cutwater, was eager to come to grips and made directly for her. The Union ship succeeded in striking a glancing blow, but this did no more harm than the broadsides discharged by the several ships in passing.

Three Confederate gunboats had accompanied the *Tennessee.* During the early part of the engagement they had put up a spirited fight, but they were forced to flee when the Union ships were in the bay. The *Selma* was captured by the *Metacomet.* The *Gaines* was driven to the beach in flames. The *Morgan* escaped to the protection of the fort, and under cover of night slipped past the fleet and found refuge in Mobile.

When injuries in the Union fleet were reported, it was discovered that the ships had suffered more damage from the rifled guns of the gunboats raking them as they advanced toward the entrance than from the batteries of Fort Morgan. Only the *Oneida* had been severely hit by the fort, a shell piercing her starboard boiler. This of course delayed her, but the other boiler, which was not injured, and her consort, the *Galena,* took her through.

At 8:45 Farragut had all fourteen wooden ships with which he had started and three of the four monitors in the wide pocket four miles above the fort. Some had already come to anchor, and the men, in high spirits, were getting out the mess gear. Farragut, however, was turning over in his mind the threat of the formidable foe they had just engaged. Taking advantage of the shallow draft of the *Tennessee,* Buchanan might select a position on the flats and harass the fleet with his rifled guns. Or he might steam outside, disperse the blockading ships remaining there, and compel Farragut to abandon the joint operation against the forts and follow. Quick and resourceful, Farragut had already decided on his course of action. When night came, he would take the monitors and attack the ram. He "believed in celerity," but now it was his enemy that relieved him of any delay. For the lookout on his ship reported that the ram had left the protection of the fort. She was seen to be advancing alone, heading for the *Hartford* to give battle to the Union flagship and the whole fleet. The impetuous Buchanan had abandoned strategy and discretion, and was about to risk all in a trial of strength.

Quickly, word was passed to the heavier wooden ships to attack the *Tennessee,* not only with their guns, but bows on at full speed. The monitors received more general orders, but they too were to advance against their foe.

The *Monongahela* was the first to strike her. The impact carried away her own iron prow and cutwater, but did the foe no perceptible injury. Next, the *Lackawanna,* coming at full speed, rammed her at the after end of the casemate. Her own stem was crushed in, but the only effect on the *Tennessee* was to cause a heavy list. The *Hartford* was the third vessel to engage her, but as the ram turned to meet her she gave only a glancing blow. While scraping past, she also discharged her heavy broadside.

The *Hartford* and the *Lackawanna* then both drew off that they might again assault the floating fortress. As they were coming about, however, the *Lackawanna* crashed into her own flagship just forward of the mizzenmast, breaking two ports into one, dismounting a Dahlgren gun, and cutting a great gash that reached within two feet of the water. Farragut climbed over the side to see the extent of the damage. "Immediately," says Captain Drayton, "there was a general cry all round, 'Get the admiral out of the ship!' and the whole interest of everyone near was that he should be in a place of safety." But Farragut had no thought of leaving his ship, and gave orders to renew the attack.

Meanwhile, the monitors were using their guns at close range. The *Manhattan* could fire only one gun—the other had been disabled—but with this she planted a heavy 15-inch shot that penetrated the armor and woodwork of the *Tennessee's* casemate and was held only by the netting inside. The *Winnebago* too was having difficulty, the machinery for revolving her turrets having broken down. But she aimed her guns, the only way possible, by pointing the ship. The little double-turreted *Chickasaw,* commanded by the boyish Perkins, put up a brilliant and most effective fight. She secured a position under the stern of the *Tennessee,* and as the Confederate pilot said later stuck "like a leech."

Aboard the *Tennessee* Admiral Buchanan, during most of the engagement, was superintending the handling of the guns. After the encounter with the *Hartford* he received the report that his ship was leaking rapidly. Thereupon he sent word to Commander J. D. Johnston in the pilot house to steer for Fort Morgan. But the wheel chains, which by a mistake in construction lay exposed on deck, in the searching fire had carried away. The smokestack had been riddled, and the defective draft made it increasingly difficult to keep up steam. A port cover which had been struck by the 11-inch shot of the *Chickasaw* then jammed. Another shot fired by the monitor in the same place killed a machinist who was attempting to remove a pin bolt, mortally wounded one of the gunners, and broke Admiral Buchanan's leg. Port after port was now sealed by the guns pounding her. Indeed, during the last half hour of the engagement the ram could not fire a gun. Johnston discovered that the relieving tackles had been shot away and the tiller unshipped from the rudder head. The ram was utterly helpless. The only course left was surrender.

The battle ended at ten o'clock, having lasted for three hours and a quarter with a half-hour's intermission. The losses had been large: in the fleet 52 killed and 170 wounded—of this number 25 were killed in the *Hartford*. In addition there were 113 drowned in the sinking of the *Tecumseh*. The losses in the

Confederate fleet were small in comparison: 10 killed and 16 wounded.

Farragut, giving no thought to fatigue, lost no time in going ahead to complete the victory. A few hours later on the same day he sent the *Chickasaw* to shell Fort Powell, which was evacuated that night. Next day the same monitor attacked Fort Gaines, and co-operating with the Army compelled it to capitulate on the seventh. Then Farragut took the fleet, including the monitors and the captured *Tennessee,* against Fort Morgan, and the Army opened on it with their heavy siege guns. The defenders withstood the bombardment for one day and then surrendered.

Here Farragut halted. He estimated that to take the city of Mobile would require 20,000 or 30,000 men, and to hold it also a considerable number—and troops were not available. He had accomplished his avowed purpose in completing another large section of the blockade.

From a strictly military point of view, in the grand strategy of the war, the battle of Mobile Bay cannot be compared with that of New Orleans or of Vicksburg. But on the political front it was of great importance. The Union cause in 1864 was passing through another crisis. Grant, who had been campaigning against Lee in Virginia, after meeting enormous losses at the Wilderness and Cold Harbor had settled down to a warfare of position, much like the slow-going trench warfare of later years. Meanwhile the Confederate cavalry leader General Early had met with signal success in the Shenandoah and on the eleventh of July he had reached Fort Stevens, only five miles from the capital. Lincoln deemed it necessary to call for a half million more volunteers.

The situation was generally regarded as bad. This had an index in the value of greenbacks, which fell to their lowest point, 33 cents to a dollar in gold. War had now been waged for more than three years, and in the opinion of many professed loyalists, the Union could never be restored. The country was tired of war. A national election was about to take place, and the feeling of millions was reflected in the pacifist movement that in the Republican Party weakened and divided its members and in the Democratic Party secured a peace plank in the party platform. The re-election of Lincoln even many of his friends despaired of, and if he failed of re-election the presumption was the Union could not be saved.

Farragut's victory at Mobile Bay was thus most timely. News of this and of Sherman's march through Georgia and capture of Atlanta was the occasion of a proclamation of national thanksgiving and prayer issued by the President to be observed on the fourth of September "in all places of public worship in the United States."[4] As Seward remarked, "Sherman and Farragut have knocked the bottom out of the Chicago [Democratic] nominations." Soon Sheridan had also gained his victory at Winchester and Fisher Hill. People realized that the war had taken on a new vigor. The election took place in November, and Lincoln received 212 electoral votes and his opponents, 21. "In spite of burdensome taxation, weariness of war, and mourning in every household, they had decided on this election day of 1864 to finish the work they had begun."[5]

Farragut Our First Admiral

A few months before Appomattox, Farragut saw further service on the James River. He had earlier been offered command of the expedition against Fort Fisher. The communication came about two weeks after the battle of Mobile Bay. He realized, however, that he was unequal to the task. As he wrote to the Department, he had been on duty in the Gulf for five out of the last six years, excepting two comparatively brief

[4] "The signal success that Divine Providence has recently vouchsafed to the operations of the United States fleet in the harbor of Mobile and the reduction of Fort Powell, Fort Gaines, and Fort Morgan and the glorious achievements of the army under Major General Sherman in the State of Georgia, resulting in the capture of the city of Atlanta, call for devout acknowledgment to the Supreme Being, in whose hands are the destinies of nations."

[5] Rhodes, *History of the United States,* IV, 539.

Bottom, official U.S. Navy photograph

Top, THE SINKING OF THE ALABAMA BY THE KEARSARGE. From a painting by Xanthus Smith in the collection of President Franklin D. Roosevelt. *Bottom,* ADMIRALS DUPONT, FARRAGUT, AND PORTER.

periods spent at home. He was physically worn out and required rest. The rank of Admiral was created for him by act of Congress, July, 1866—an honor of greatest distinction, for the first time conferred upon an officer of the Navy.

In his keen understanding of strategy and his marvelous ability in action he stands in his time without an equal. He was intent on securing victory but still more on winning the war. The campaigns he projected had a large end in view. He planned so discriminately and worked out details with such patience and care that he was near to victory before a gun had been fired. At the inception of a campaign he seemed almost slow, but when all was ready he struck fast and hard. He believed in celerity, yet the well-studied plan did not prevent his making a change in the middle of a fight when something went wrong. In his great battles fought when he was sixty-one years old or more he was decidedly a conservative. He preferred to use the type of gun and ship he had known all his life. But at New Orleans he gave Porter opportunity to try his mortars to the limit before he passed the forts, and at Mobile he waited many months for ironclad monitors, which he recognized would be essential to cope with ironclad rams. The opportunity of gaining an education such as schools afford was denied him, but he was a clear thinker, and he has given the Navy more trenchant utterances epitomizing naval science than any other officer of our Service.

In the battles that came at the summit of his career, he was fighting not only against ships but against forts, and he realized that though ships might pass the forts, it required an attack from the rear, the cutting off of supplies, the co-operation of an adequate military force, to accomplish their destruction. To appreciate his grasp of strategy, one should read by way of contrast the story of Gallipoli in the First World War. The situation there was not altogether unlike that which faced Farragut at New Orleans. One cannot help thinking that had Farragut been in command of the Allied forces in the Mediterranean, holding to his strict rule of not striking till he was ready and of not advancing until the co-operating military forces were at hand, he would have succeeded in forcing the Dardanelles.

The secret of his success, the heart of it all, was his inner strength, his deep moral character. He was religious, and religion for him had an essential place in daily life and in relation to others. He was keenly alive to the part the Navy should take in national affairs, and the responsibility involved. He was approachable, and officers and men who served under him felt the close personal relationship such as characterized Nelson and his associates. It was a matter of pride and confidence later for an officer to say that he had served under Farragut. An outstanding tribute paid him was that expressed by Dewey in the Spanish-American War, who on the critical evening of his entrance into Manila Bay, when everything was strange and uncertain, reverted to the decisive action of his great leader thirty-six years before. On the earlier occasion, Dewey, as executive officer of the *Mississippi,* had been in the fleet of Farragut when the ships passed the forts below New Orleans. At Manila Bay Dewey asked the question, "What would Farragut do?" The assurance that again he was following his leader gave him guidance and strength.

References

Alden, C. S., *George Hamilton Perkins, Commodore, U.S.N.; His Life and Letters,* 1914.

Farragut, Loyall, *The Life of David Glasgow Farragut,* 1879.

Grant, U. S., *Personal Memoirs,* 2 vols., 1885–6.

Mahan, A. T., *Admiral Farragut,* 1897.

Official Records of the Union and Confederate Navies in the War of the Rebellion, Vol. XXI, 1906.

West, R. S., *The Second Admiral; A Life of David Dixon Porter,* 1937.

DECLINE OF THE MERCHANT MARINE. THE CONFEDERATE CRUISERS XIV

The Decline Previous to 1861

IN THE PERIOD 1815 to 1858 the American merchant marine had flourished, and its general growth and individual exploits had aroused a national enthusiasm such as has been seen neither before nor since. This was the time when Europe was drawing heavily on America for foodstuffs and raw materials, and our shipyards were building better ships than those of any other nation. The ships flying our flag paid higher wages to the crews; and they could afford to, for the crews, which usually were more efficient, could be smaller in number, and faster ships made more frequent voyages. The competition was sharp, and among the factors that entered into it were the new types of ships that were introduced and the government support in subsidies that made possible bold ventures on the part of ship companies.

The new is constantly challenging the old. During the years 1831 to 1845, it was the wooden steamship that made the bid for supremacy; and from 1845 to 1861, it was the iron steamship. Our builders held stubbornly to the old, and trusted that by the excellence of their wooden sailing ships they might still carry the ocean freight. Not only could these leave behind any other sailing ships, but they repeatedly outdistanced the early steamships when the wind was favorable. Thus the clipper ship *Sovereign of the Seas,* at a time when the fastest ocean steamship could make only 13 or 14 miles an hour, sailed 362 miles in 24 hours, or 15 miles an hour, and the *Flying Cloud* sailed 374 miles in one day. But the wind was not always favorable, and the advantages of the steamship, so evident to the later generation, slowly asserted themselves. When ships changed from wood to iron, our builders did not keep abreast with new ideas, and they lost the strategic position that was theirs when they were close to where the principal building material, lumber, was produced. In contrast to the liberal grants paid by the British government to the Cunard Line and others lately formed, the aid through mail subsidies paid by the United States to American lines was decidedly reduced in the latter part of the fifties, even though these lines were making a losing fight for existence. In the merchant marine, North and South found a zone of conflict, and opposing interests clashed some years before their armies fought over the fields of Virginia and Kentucky. In earlier years, all parts of the country had joined in legislation to promote a newly established steamship company, the Collins Line, that promised ships of the best type for the trans-Atlantic trade—ships that at the prevailing rates could be operated only at a loss. But as the sectional feeling became intensified, senators from the South and Southwest observed that these ships were sailing from Northern ports and that the cargoes carried enriched Northern merchants in a greater degree than Southern. Their enthusiasm for American shipping thereupon changed to indifference or thinly disguised hostility.

Thus, although American production and foreign commerce greatly increased in the period we have considered, tonnage carried in American bottoms decreased; in 1831, 86.5 per cent of the combined exports and imports were carried in American ships; in 1846, 81 per cent; in 1860, 66.5 per cent. Then came war, in which American commerce was very directly concerned, and the decline which, in the beginning, was due merely to economic conditions was greatly accelerated. In 1864 the combined exports and imports carried in American ships was only 27.5 per cent.

This last sudden decline was caused mainly by the Confederate cruisers. It occurred in successive steps: (1) Confederate cruisers preyed on American shipping: (2) shipowners, faced by rising rates of insurance, increased transportation charges; (3) neutral ships sailing on the same routes gained in the competition and obtained the cargoes; (4) American ships were sold and sailed under foreign flags; (5) American shipyards built only a much reduced number of new vessels; (6) American capital, being more profitably employed in farming, mining, railway transportation, and manufacturing, was diverted to these channels.

The Savannah, Sumter, *and* Florida

In 1861 the United States among the maritime powers was second only to Great Britain. As nine-tenths of the shipping was of the loyal states, this was exposed to commerce raiding, and there was next to no shipping on the part of the South that was liable to attack in return.

Early, President Davis had announced his intention of issuing letters of marque and reprisal. Whereupon, President Lincoln had proclaimed that any Southerners caught preying upon American merchantmen would be charged with the crime of piracy. Notwithstanding the warning, the Charleston pilot boat *Savannah* sallied forth in quest of prizes. Her career of adventure was brief. In three days she was captured by a brig of the blockading force. Other small craft had similar experiences. Then followed sharply contested trials in court and long discussions in the public journals to decide whether the captives should be executed as pirates. From the South came the threat of retaliation, and from the North, what had more weight, the opinion of certain loyal jurists who argued that the offense of making war upon the Federal Government by a few dozen men on the sea was no more treasonable than making war by hundreds of thousands on land. The less severe course finally was adopted, and sailors as well as soldiers on being captured were treated as prisoners of war.

The *Sumter* was the first regularly commissioned naval vessel to get out and attack Northern shipping. Raphael Semmes, a former officer of the United States Navy, was her captain. She was a converted merchant steamer, fitted out at New Orleans. Slipping past the *Brooklyn,* blockading off the Passes, she began her cruise in the Caribbean and in a short time had taken seventeen prizes—two ransomed, seven later released in Cuban ports, and two recaptured. The six that she burned with their cargoes were the real losses. When she was discovered at Gibraltar by Union cruisers and closely blockaded, her officers realized that her career was ended. She was surveyed and sold.

The *Florida* was of English origin. Built at Liverpool, 1861–62, she sailed to Nassau, and then, lying off an uninhabited island of the Bahamas, took on her batteries and ammunition and was placed in commission. Her active career began in January, 1863, when she left Mobile. Her commanding officer, Maffitt, said his "instructions were brief and to the point, leaving much to the discretion, but more to the torch."

He quickly began his work by capturing and burning three small vessels. In a five months' cruise from east of New York to south of Bahia, he took and destroyed fourteen prizes. Off Brazil, one of the prizes was the brig *Clarence.* He armed this ship, and put Lieutenant Read in command. Read operated with great daring between Chesapeake Bay and Portland. He took sixteen prizes, twice changing his flag to stronger ships and destroying the old. Running into Portland, he led a party of men in boats, and surprising the revenue-cutter *Caleb Cushing* took possession of her. But that was going too far. Next morning he was captured by steamers sent out from Portland.

The *Florida* continued her work of destruction, and after being docked and thoroughly repaired in Brest, for three months raided the shipping on our own coast. In the harbor of Bahia she was captured by the *Wachusett,* which sailed off with her as a prize. This seizure in a neutral port was a plain violation of international law, but the not oversensitive American public were for the most part well satisfied with the action, not unmindful of the negligence of West Indian and South American nations in the observance of their duties. For they had repeatedly furnished the cruisers with fuel and general supplies, besides permitting long stays in their harbors. The *Florida* was taken to Hampton Roads where she was sunk in a collision with an army transport. The United States disavowed the act of the offending captain of the *Wachusett* and subjected him to a court martial.

The Alabama

The most successful cruiser of the war was laid down according to contract at Lairds, Birkenhead, England, and was known during her building, 1861–62, as No. 290. She was a wooden ship, bark rigged, having also auxiliary steam power and a propeller that could be disconnected and raised in fifteen minutes and lowered in even shorter time. She had beautiful lines, and being built for speed, was splendidly adapted to her appointed activity. For more than a month before her completion, the vigilant United States minister, Charles Francis Adams, brought evidences of her intended mission to the attention of the British Foreign Office, beginning with the deposition of a seaman who had been urged to ship in her and serve under the Confederacy. But action on Mr. Adams's warnings encountered many delays, and the Queen's law officers did not make their report until the twenty-ninth of July. On that day the ship had left for a short run or trial trip—never to return. After a brief stay in one of the out-of-the-way English harbors, she sailed for the Azores. There she was met by a bark from

London, which brought battery, ammunition, stores, and coal; and by a steamer from Liverpool, which had as passengers Captain Raphael Semmes and the remainder of her officers and crew.

She was placed in commission on the twenty-fourth of August, 1862, and immediately began cruising against American commerce in the sea lanes of the North Atlantic, going as far north as the Banks, and then slowly making her way to the Caribbean. In two months she had taken and burned twenty prizes. In Martinique she met, according to arrangement, the *Agrippina,* which came with coal for her. And she came near to meeting the U.S.S. *San Jacinto,* which, observing neutrality laws, lay off the harbor, with the hope that she might intercept her. The *Alabama,* however, took advantage of a dark night and slipped out. Making another capture, she then headed for Galveston. Here, not revealing her identity but suggesting by her suspicious actions that she might be a blockade runner, she lured away from the Union blockading squadron the *Hatteras,* a fragile iron side-wheeler, tolerably adapted to her earlier work, that of carrying passengers on the Delaware, but possessing little of the character of a warship beyond being armed with eight light guns and having a spirited captain and crew. The *Hatteras* made all the resistance she was capable of, but, being hopelessly outclassed, was in thirteen minutes shot to pieces and sinking. Semmes' further itinerary took him to Jamaica; to a cruising station near the equator at the crossroads of the East Indian and Pacific trade, where he spent two months and took eight prizes; to Fernando de Noronha, where he coaled in the harbor and took two prizes; to the coast of Brazil, spending two months and taking ten prizes; to the Cape of Good Hope; and then to the East, where he cruised for six months and took seven prizes.

Meanwhile the Federal Government had made systematic efforts to check the growing menace to commerce and had sent warships to catch the raiders. Thus, a flying squadron was fitted out in the fall of 1862 to cruise in the West Indies. Captain Wilkes, in command, had altogether sixteen ships for the task. Several times they crossed the paths of the *Alabama* but never near enough to sight her. The swift steamer *Vanderbilt,* sent out with a roving commission, went to the equator, coast of Brazil, and then to the Cape of Good Hope. At the Cape she missed the *Alabama* by only a few days. Semmes, hearing that pursuers were in the vicinity, at once had laid his course to the East, going to the China Sea. There his depredations came as a complete surprise and paralyzed American commerce. The United States sloop of war *Wyoming,* cruising near the Straits of Sunda to protect commerce, got within one hundred miles of the *Alabama,* but like all the other patrols, never caught up with her. Semmes had shrewdly estimated the time that was likely to elapse before the news of his depredations in a definite locality would reach Washington and be transmitted to ships on a foreign station, and shifted to a new scene before his pursuers appeared. His bold entrance, however, into the much frequented harbor of Cherbourg, where he planned to have his ship docked and given an extensive overhaul, proved his undoing.

A telegram immediately sent by the American minister, William L. Dayton, was handed to Captain John A. Winslow of the United States sloop of war *Kearsarge,* which was lying in Flushing. In no time Winslow had cleared the harbor and was steaming down the English Channel. In order that he might be entirely free in his movements and not held by the restrictions imposed by a neutral power, he did not enter the harbor of Cherbourg but cruised back and forth before the entrance.

France had declined to give Semmes the permission he requested for docking his ship in the government yard. Those aboard the *Kearsarge* had been anxious lest their enemy might make a prolonged stay in the harbor or escape under cover of night. But their fears were relieved by a communication that soon came from Semmes. He begged that the Union ship should not depart, for he intended to come out and fight.

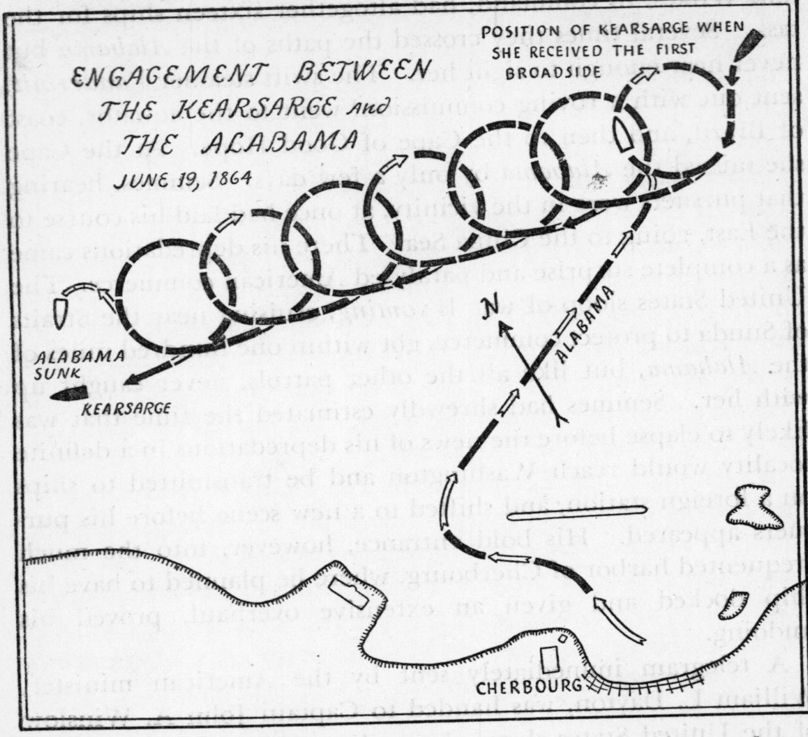

On Sunday morning, June 19, 1864, between nine and ten o'clock, the *Alabama* was seen to be heading out. Captain Winslow, who had been maintaining his watch three miles off the eastern entrance, then slowly led the way out to sea, steaming to a position about seven miles from land before he turned to engage his enemy. He wanted to make sure that the action should take place outside of neutral waters, also that the Confederate cruiser, if disabled, should not have the chance of escaping to refuge in the harbor. The French officials, to guard their neutrality from violation, had ordered their ironclad *Couronne* to accompany the *Alabama* until she was three miles out. A British yacht, the *Deerhound,* which followed well in the rear, and the crowds of people who lined the heights on the shore, were interested observers.

At 10:50 A.M. the *Kearsarge* had come about and was heading for her enemy. In response, the *Alabama* reduced speed and sheered so that her starboard guns might be trained. Seven minutes later, when the ships were still a mile apart, the Confederate cruiser opened fire. Her first broadside was ineffective, and her second and third were but little better, the only damage inflicted being in the rigging of her opponent. When the range had been reduced to nine hundred yards, Winslow realized that the raking position of the *Alabama* might afford opportunity for real injury. So he turned his helm to port, and presenting the starboard battery of the *Kearsarge* to the starboard battery of the *Alabama* opened fire. The two ships began to circle around a common center, and before the end of the battle had made seven complete revolutions.

Rarely has there been a single-ship action in which the two antagonists were more evenly matched. In tonnage they were almost precisely the same, approximately 1,000. The *Kearsarge* had a heavier weight of projectile; but as the *Alabama* had eight guns to the other's seven and fought seven guns on an exposed side to the other's five, the superiority in gun power was not certain at the beginning. The *Alabama* should have had the advantage in fighting at long range, for she had a rifled 100-pounder, one 8-inch shell gun, and six long 32-pounders. On the other hand, the *Kearsarge* could fight more effectively at short range, for she was equipped with two 11-inch Dahlgren smoothbores, four short 32-pounders, and one 30-pounder rifle. It was at close quarters that the crushing power of the heavy Dahlgrens and the 32-pounders would be most felt. This helps to explain the maneuvering. At the beginning, the *Kearsarge* attempted to run in under the stern of the *Alabama,* and the latter avoided this by sheering and keeping her broadside still toward her foe. The *Kearsarge,* slightly superior in speed, succeeded in decreasing the distance so that at the end of the conflict she was only five hundred yards distant.

A long period of commerce raiding is usually demoralizing to a warship. This was noticeable in the relative effectiveness of the gunfire of the two ships. The crew of the *Alabama* had had little practice in firing at a target. A considerable number of them were British; some were said to have served in men-of-war and others in the naval reserve. A few had joined the ship only the night before. The crew of the *Kearsarge* had been given consistent training and were of American nationality. The fire of the *Alabama* was rapid, but wild, especially at the beginning; that of the *Kearsarge,* deliberate and accurate throughout. The gunners of the latter had been cautioned not to fire without direct aim and to point their heavy guns close to the water line. Thus the 370 shot and shell of the Confederates caused little injury in comparison with the 173 shot and shell of the Federals. A shell lodged in the stern post of the *Kearsarge,* but failed to explode. The comment of the Confederates, expressed later, was that the failure of the percussion cap to function cost them the battle. But as the projectile was fired near the end of the engagement, their conclusion is to be regarded as hardly more than a speculation. The thirteen or fourteen shot and shell that struck the hull of the *Kearsarge* did practically no damage. Semmes in his report of the battle attributed the immunity enjoyed by his opponent to the spare chain which had been stopped up and down over the outside of the hull of the *Kearsarge,* covering the vital parts amidships. This was a protective device suggested by the executive officer, Thornton, who had seen it used by Farragut at New Orleans.

The losses suffered by the two opponents, which at the beginning seemed to be so nearly equal in power, were highly disproportionate. Only three men of the *Kearsarge* were wounded and but one of them fatally. In contrast, the heavy Dahlgrens of the Union ship did terrible execution on board the *Alabama.* The after pivot gun of the *Kearsarge* was especially effective. One shell killed or wounded eighteen men and disabled a gun. Another exploded in the coal bunkers and blocked up the engine room. Others opened up large holes in the sides of the vessel. Captain Semmes, as he was completing the seventh circle in the maneuvers, realized that the day was going against him, and ordering the fore-trysail and two jibs set, sought to escape to neutral waters. But he was too late. The engine room was already flooded. The ship was sinking rapidly by the stern. At this point the *Kearsarge,* steaming across her bow to a raking position, had the enemy at her mercy. The flag of the Confederate was struck, but some of her gunners, evidently not receiving the word, continued their fire. Whereupon, the *Kearsarge* again trained her guns on the sinking craft. After three or four shots, however, Winslow, noting that a white flag displayed over the stern of the *Alabama* was still flying, gave orders to stop firing. Shortly after this he received a boat dispatched from the *Alabama* asking for succor.

Only small assistance could be furnished, for several boats of the *Kearsarge* had been damaged in the fighting. But as the yacht *Deerhound* drew near, Captain Winslow hailed, asking the British to assist in the work of rescue. Many of the Confederate officers and men were already in the water clinging to spars or wreckage. Thus it happened that the *Deerhound* picked up Captain Semmes and the executive officer, Lieutenant Kell, as well as forty others. Then, edging away, she made for Southampton. Three other officers and six seamen, picked up by a French pilot boat, similarly made their escape.

Winslow had expected that the *Deerhound* would turn over the fugitives to him as prisoners, and indignation was expressed generally in Federal circles that the British should not have done so. But Professor James Soley, one-time Assistant Secretary of the Navy, after careful study expressed an entirely different opinion, averring that the British were quite within their rights. He held that if the officers of the yacht on their own motion had interfered to pick up survivors to save them from drowning or from capture, they would have connected themselves "inexcusably with belligerent operations." But, on the other hand, when they had been requested to assist, and in consequence had a group of survivors aboard a British ship, it was their duty to treat them as on English soil and to make sure of their safety and protection.

Further Building

The exploits of the Confederate cruisers were a part of the large plan of operations formulated in Richmond in 1861. In June of that year, Captain James D. Bulloch (a former lieutenant in the United States Navy and uncle of President Theodore Roosevelt) had been sent to London. Funds were forwarded to him. He was the officer who had contracted for the construction of the *Florida* and the *Alabama*. His program called for the building of many other vessels. Secretary Mallory had directed that he take steps for the building also of ironclads, and he contracted with Lairds for two double-turreted armored ironclads of 1,800 tons each, armed with four 9-inch rifles. Learning that measures might be taken to prevent the delivery of the ships, he arranged that Messrs. Bravay, bankers of Paris, should be the purchaser, who were to make the pretense of ordering them for the Viceroy of Egypt, transferring them at sea to the Confederacy. Mr. Adams, the American minister, early obtained evidence of their intended use, which he put before Earl Russell of the Foreign Office and followed with repeated protests of growing seriousness. The second ironclad had been launched, and still the Foreign Office was doubtful that the evidence was sufficient for legal proceedings and had taken no action. This was in September, 1863, when the maintenance of the Union blockade was of the first importance. Two ironclads of such superior force might conceivably destroy or drive away the blockaders at any point of their choosing. It was a critical moment in our foreign relations, and recognizing this, Mr. Adams issued what was scarcely less than an ultimatum: "It would be superfluous in me to point out to your lordship that this is war." Even as Mr. Adams' communication was being penned, Earl Russell, realizing the seriousness of the American representations and impressed by the Union successes at Gettysburg and Vicksburg, had given orders to cancel the contracts. The ironclads were taken over by the British government and eventually were commissioned in the Royal Navy.

Four steam corvettes and two ironclad rams were ordered in 1863 by Captain Bulloch and Mr. Slidell in France. Although at this time, as earlier, the French government was disposed to render assistance to the Confederacy, the protests of the American Embassy had their effect. The guarantees given to Bulloch and Slidell were revoked and the six ships were sold. One of the rams acquired by Denmark in her brief war with Prussia was transferred to the Confederacy in January, 1865. She received her officers and supplies off Quiberon and was commissioned in the Confederate Navy as the *Stonewall.* Springing a leak, she put in at Corunna and later proceeded to Ferrol. There she was closely watched by the *Niagara* and the *Sacramento.* Although she finally reached Nassau and Havana, the war was then ended. Taking no prizes, she was a total loss to the Confederacy.

The Shenandoah

Of the several other craft secured by the Confederate agents, only one had anything like the success of the *Sumter, Florida,* and *Alabama,* and that was the *Shenandoah,* originally named the *Sea King* and designed for the East Indian trade. She was a full-rigged ship with auxiliary steam power, of 790 tons, built on the Clyde. She was fast, and often sailed 320 miles in twenty-four hours. Clearing from London for Bombay early in October, 1864, she sailed to Funchal, Madeira. At Desertas, an uninhabited island, she met a blockade runner, the *Laurel,* coming from London, which brought supplies and Confederate officers. There she was placed in commission, Lieutenant James I. Waddell taking command. After cruising for three months in the Atlantic and taking several prizes, he sailed to Melbourne, where he laid his ship up for repairs, besides taking on board three hundred tons of coal sent from Liverpool. Then, sailing north and timing his approach to agree with the appearance of the American whalers in the neighborhood of Bering Strait, he virtually wiped out the whaling industry in that region. Between June 21 and 28 he destroyed or ransomed twenty-one ships.[1] But it was a useless operation, for it came two and a half months after the surrender at Appomattox. News of the downfall of the Confederacy was finally given to him by a British merchantman. Dismounting the guns and slightly altering the appearance of his ship by whitewashing the funnels, he then sailed for Liverpool and turned her over to the British government.

The Alabama *Claims*

In each step taken for securing Confederate cruisers, Bulloch had employed learned counsel. It is still a debatable question if there was a breach of neutrality on the part of the British in building the *Florida* and the *Alabama,* which, it will be recalled, became ships of war only on being armed, equipped, and placed in commission, long after they had left English waters. Their later visits to British ports for supplies and overhaul were another question. Certainly, the stay of the *Shenandoah* in Melbourne was not justified by international law. London may not have been immediately involved, but responsibility inevitably rested on the home government.

After the Civil War was ended, leading Englishmen realized that their government had blundered in handling American affairs. They saw how disastrous for themselves might be the precedent they had helped to establish—the right of a neutral country to fit out cruisers and assist in their operation for a belligerent. The commerce of the mistress of the seas might suffer from such an interpretation of international law.

A Joint High Commission consisting of five American and five British representatives met in Washington in the spring of

[1] Scharf, *History of the Confederate States Navy.*

1871 and framed a treaty that arranged for the settlement of the *Alabama* Claims, the San Juan Islands boundary dispute in the northwest, and the fisheries question in the northeast. The validity of neutral rights was incorporated in the treaty. This prepared the way for the arbitration held in Geneva to decide the *Alabama* Claims. The United States was awarded $15,500,-000 in gold for the depredations of the *Florida, Alabama,* and their consorts, and also of the *Shenandoah* after she had left Melbourne. This ended the ill feeling between Great Britain and the United States, giving strength and protection to the maritime interests of the former. Her gain was out of all proportion to the amount she was called on to pay.

The Strategic Value of the Confederate Cruisers

The work of the commerce destroyers of the Confederate Navy was well planned. It was a successful operation undertaken by a belligerent that entered into war with no fighting ships. Raiders flung themselves across the shipping lanes in the North and South Atlantic and in the Indian Ocean, audaciously appeared at the very entrance to Northern ports, and visited the fishing and whaling grounds in the Atlantic and Pacific. The *Alabama* captured no less than sixty-nine vessels; other cruisers were also highly successful, and it is estimated that the cruisers altogether took 261 Northern craft. The direct losses to the Union in ships and cargoes may have reached a total of $25,000,000. The indirect losses went far beyond this figure, for the menace caused insurance rates to be doubled, induced merchants to ship under foreign flags, and besides checking new construction brought about the transfer of American vessels to firms of other nations, so that our tonnage engaged in foreign trade was cut in half. A thousand vessels were transferred to the British alone.[2]

Further, the menace brought the merchants and city officials in the Federal ports to a condition verging on panic. They

[2] C. Day, *History of Commerce of the United States,* pp. 221, 222.

implored the Navy Department to grant them protection and pressed Secretary Welles to send ships that should hunt down the raiders even to the neglect of the blockade. If the Secretary had not been adamant in holding to this all-important operation of the Navy, the result would have been most detrimental. The work of the raiders, however, was indirect and in the end had no effect on the progress of the war. That is, no Union warship worthy of the name was taken or destroyed, it being the policy of the Confederate cruisers to avoid combat. In this they were undoubtedly right. The Union, with her expanding Navy, could afford to take the chance of occasionally losing a ship; the Confederacy with her few scattered vessels had no replacements, and the destruction of a single cruiser meant the curtailment or end of operations in some designated area. Although the fear inspired was undoubtedly worse than the actual captures, the commerce raiders constituted a serious challenge. And American foreign shipping, instead of increasing in volume with the enlarged foreign interests, rapidly diminished. The blockade, however, was maintained, and the war in time was brought to a successful conclusion.

References

Ellicott, J. M., *The Life of John Ancrum Winslow,* 1902.

Kell, J. M., "Cruise and Combats of the Alabama," *Battles and Leaders of the Civil War,* IV, 600–614.

Official Records of the Union and Confederate Navies in the War of the Rebellion, Vol. III, 1896.

Scharf, J. T., *History of the Confederate States Navy,* 1887.

Semmes, Raphael, *Memoirs of Service Afloat,* 1869.

Sinclair, Arthur, *Two Years on the Alabama,* 1896.

TIGHTENING THE BLOCKADE

IN DESCRIBING THE Navy's greatest operation during the war, the blockade of the Southern ports, personal narratives dwell more often on its failure than on its success. The skill displayed by the blockade runners, the daring and quickness of the officers and crews making it possible to take cargoes in and out of the most closely guarded ports, are material for a good story. In comparison, the long watches and the repeatedly unsuccessful chases of the ships on blockade seem drab. In truth, the Union blockade was never entirely effective. But has there been any widely extended blockade in modern times of which the same criticism could not be made? The Navy held to it with no respite until the last Confederate troops had surrendered or had been disbanded, for the Government realized that it was exerting a great influence on the progress of the war.

The Albemarle *Attempts to Raise the Blockade (North Atlantic Blockade)*

The widely scattered blockaders were constantly threatened by ships and troops, secretly organized in some of the rivers or harbors, that came out to deliver a surprise attack. The most serious attempt to break the North Atlantic Blockade, after that by the *Virginia* at Hampton Roads, was the one made by the *Albemarle* at Plymouth, North Carolina. The *Albemarle* was an ironclad ram, designed by John L. Porter, who, previous to his resignation in 1861, was a naval constructor in the United States Navy, and who was then made Chief Constructor in the Confederate States Navy. In general features she resembled the *Virginia,* which Porter had helped to design; though she was not so large and not nearly the equal in gun power, she had the advantage of shallow draught—only eight feet—which adapted her to fighting in the inland waterways. News of her building at Edward's Ferry in the Roanoke River came to Lieutenant Commander Flusser, in charge of the Union ships in the vicinity, and information of the Confederates' military preparations to attack Plymouth was received by the Union Army in that city. But neither Army nor Navy had the force at hand to ward off the threat.

Doing what they could, Flusser and his companions had placed obstructions in the river above Plymouth—torpedoes, sunken vessels, and piles, which should have afforded considerable defense. A spring freshet, however, made it possible for the ram to slip over the obstructions and under cover of night to steam past the outlying Union batteries. Operations began with an attack by the Confederates on Plymouth (April 17, 1864). Though they considerably outnumbered the defenders, they were driven back. The Federal troops had been assisted by the fire of the gunboat *Southfield* stationed above the town and of the *Miami* stationed below. Aware that the *Albemarle* was preparing to come down the river to take part in the battle, Flusser had placed two smaller craft, the *Whitehead* and *Ceres,* to serve as patrols. Therefore he had a brief warning when the ram was discovered to be steaming toward Plymouth. He realized that his two largest gunboats, though carrying a formidable battery (each armed with a 100-pound rifled Parrott and five or six 9-inch Dahlgrens), were weak in defense. But he conceived the novel idea of a bow attack upon his enemy, with his two boats connected by heavy chains and held apart by spars. If he could catch the ram in this trap, he might hammer away until he had destroyed her. The evident weakness of the strategem was that his boats being thus harnessed had little maneuverability.

Lieutenant J. W. Cooke, in command of the *Albemarle,* handled his craft well. After passing the batteries at Plymouth, he kept steadily on, under the shadow of the woods lining the bank, and he followed closely after the *Ceres,* which had given the alarm. When he neared the gunboats, he advanced from the shore with every bit of speed the clumsy *Albemarle* was capable of. Easily avoiding the trap which had been set for a craft coming down the main channel, he made for the starboard bow of the *Southfield.* Although subjected to a heavy fire from the Union gunboats, he kept on, his gunports closed, and in attack depended solely on his ram.

The ram penetrated the fragile *Southfield* as far as the fire-room, and she sank in three minutes. On the other hand, the assailant for a while was threatened with a similar fate; for the sinking craft, holding her fast, dragged her down until the water was entering her ports. But as the gunboat reached bottom, she turned partly over and released her grip. Meanwhile, Flusser, on the deck of the *Miami,* had trained his large guns, loaded with shell, on the *Albemarle.* The only damage that resulted was aboard the *Miami.* Fragments of shell bounding back killed the gallant Flusser.

The *Miami* and the two gunboats accompanying her then discontinued the action and steamed out into the sound. Next day Plymouth surrendered, and the *Albemarle* was afforded a safe refuge.

Plainly, what had occurred was but a preliminary to further attack, and the blockading force took immediate steps to meet it. The large double-enders *Sassacus, Mattabesett,* and *Wyalusing* were sent to Albemarle Sound under the command of Captain Melancton Smith. They were in time to encounter the *Albemarle* when two weeks later she came out, accompanied by a steamer carrying troops and an army transport loaded with provisions and coal. They met her ten miles from the mouth of the Roanoke and opened fire on her at 150 yards' distance. The *Sassacus* then tried ramming and struck the ram amidships, just abaft her beam. The blow made the *Albemarle* careen, but caused no perceptible damage. In return she fired her 100-pound Brooke rifle and sent a shot through the boiler of the *Sassacus,* the steam scalding many of the crew. The honors of the day were, however, about even. The *Sassacus,* rendered helpless, drifted out of the action; on the other hand, the Confederate store vessel was captured, and the *Albemarle,* after being severely pounded, withdrew to Plymouth.

Her career came to an end the following October. The Union Navy had no shallow draft monitor to send against her, but Lieutenant W. B. Cushing, who had already carried through several daredevil exploits, set out one stormy evening in a specially constructed launch, equipped with a spar torpedo, to accomplish her destruction. With fourteen officers and men in his launch and thirteen in a cutter which was towed, he steamed quietly under the lee of the bank and passed without a challenge the guard stationed on the wreck of the *Southfield.* Keeping on, he reached a position opposite the ram, which was lying at a wharf in Plymouth, before a sentry gave the alarm. Casting off the cutter, he thought to make a bold dash, but discovered that the ram was protected by a boom of logs, thirty feet out, which surrounded her. It was a time for quick action. Backing the launch off, he then drove at full speed for the barrier and succeeded in forcing the bow up on the logs to a position where he could bring the spar under the overhang of the ram. As the launch had neared the barrier, her crew fired the howitzer in the bow and a second later received a terrific blast from a huge gun of the ram. But they were so near that the missile passed over their heads. At about the same time, Cushing, believing that the torpedo lowered on the end of the spar was in contact with the bottom of the ship, pulled the lanyard that exploded it. The great geyser of water that shot up nearly filled the launch. Escape in the launch was impossible. Several of the expeditionary party surrendered. Some were drowned in attempting to escape. Cushing succeeded in swimming to the bank below the city, and after hiding in a swamp slipped away the next morning in a skiff left by a picket party and slowly worked his way down the river. Before he had left Plymouth, he learned from a negro that his project had been successful and that the *Albemarle* was sunk. With this good news he rejoined the blockading squadron.

Operations off Savannah and Charleston (South Atlantic Blockade)

Early in 1862, Savannah had vied with Charleston in the commerce brought by the blockade runners, but when Fort Pulaski was captured, this greatly declined. An unsuccessful attempt was made in 1863 by the Confederates in Savannah to break the blockade. Taking an English iron steamer that had slipped in, they cut her down nearly to water level and, superimposing an armored casemate, mounted four Brooke rifles. The builders were confident that she would prove superior to any craft on the coast. Du Pont, who was in command of the South Atlantic Squadron with his station at Port Royal, obtained information on the progress of the *Atlanta,* as the new ram was called, and ordered the monitors *Weehawken,* Captain John Rodgers, and *Nahant,* Commander John Downes, to stand by and attack her on her first appearance.

Early on the morning of June 17, she was reported to be coming down the river. Rodgers at once beat to quarters and slowly steamed around the point to the entrance of the river. The *Atlanta,* lying athwart the channel, opened fire, but the *Weehawken* did not answer until she had reached a position 300 yards distant. Then she delivered an extraordinarily effective fire with her two huge Dahlgrens, one a 15-inch and the other an 11-inch. The fight lasted fifteen minutes, the *Weehawken* firing five shots. The first, a 15-inch cored shot, struck the shield of the *Atlanta* about the height of the ports, pene-

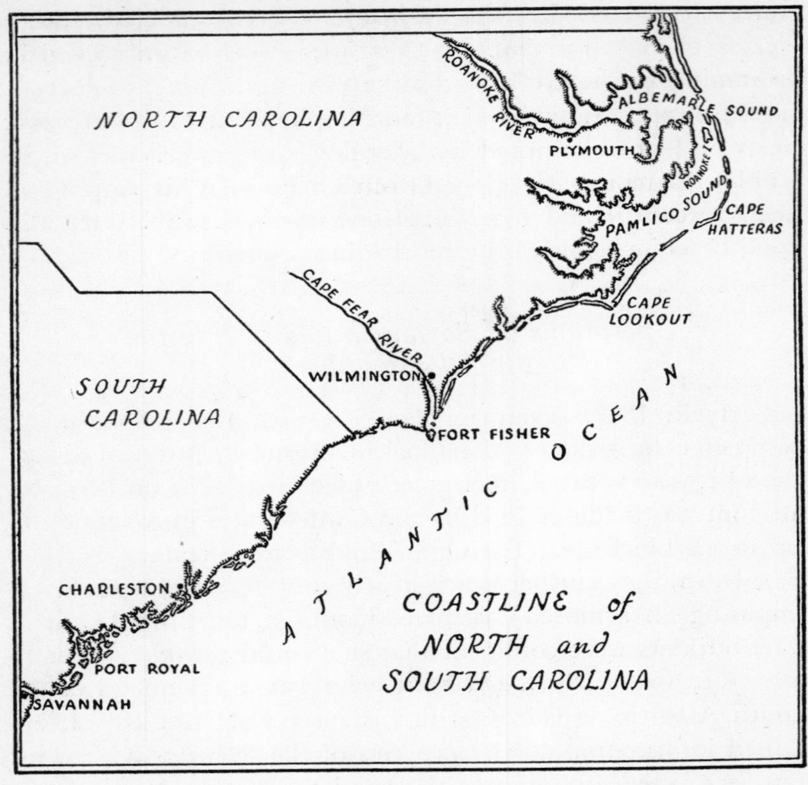

trated the armor, and smashed in the wooden backing, wounding several men with splinters of iron and wood. The next three shots also hit their mark and were almost equally effective. Thereupon, the *Atlanta,* which was aground, hoisted a white flag. A few hours later she was floated and taken to Port Royal.

At Charleston previous to this (January 31, 1863), two Confederate ironclad rams, the *Chicora* and the *Palmetto State,* made their attack on the blockade. Coming out of the harbor when only a light squadron was on guard, they caught the blockaders unawares. The action began at five o'clock in the darkness of a misty morning and continued until half past seven. One of the Confederate ships rammed the *Mercedita* before she could bring a gun to bear, and firing a shell through her port boiler opened up a hole in her side four or five feet square. After delaying a half hour to receive the surrender of the stricken ship and to arrange for the parole of her officers and men, she then made for the next Union ship, the *Keystone State*. The latter made a spirited resistance and even attempted to run down one of the rams. But she was unequal to her opponents. One shell pierced her boiler and ten shells struck her hull, most of them near or below the water line. About this time other Union ships, discovering that a battle was in progress, joined the engagement. Though their fire apparently did nothing more than to knock off the pilot house and flagstaff of one of the rams, they induced the ironclads to retreat to Charleston. The *Keystone State,* being relieved from further attention, raised her flag again—it was lowered when she had been rendered helpless, but no notice was taken and the firing on her had continued. Receiving assistance from the *Memphis,* she was towed to Port Royal.

The Union Squadron did not make a well-organized defense. The engagement is instructive, however, in showing the difficulties under which the blockading force labored. Their strong fighting units had been temporarily withdrawn. Such ships as were left were slow in joining the battle, for most of them supposed that the distant firing was only that often heard as a blockade runner attempted to run the gauntlet. On account of the haze and the utter lack of an adequate system of signaling, those farthest out had no knowledge for an hour or more of what was taking place. The Confederates planned the time and manner of their attack well, but when the advantage was all theirs, it is difficult to understand why they did not go ahead and sink many of the frail ships opposed to them. They returned to Charleston with no prizes, and the blockading force being quickly strengthened by several monitors the two rams made no further bid for glory.

As stated in an earlier chapter, if a small well-disciplined army had followed immediately on the heels of Du Pont's victorious force at Port Royal in November, 1861, it might have seized both Savannah and Charleston. The Confederates along the seacoast were panic-stricken and roads leading to the two cities were open. There were reasons convincing at the time, however, for not sending troops. The Regular Army was pitifully small and many months were required to bring volunteers to the point where they were ready for campaigning. General Sherman says in his *Memoirs,* "At the time of Mr. Lincoln's inauguration, viz., March 4, 1861, the Regular Army by law . . . [admitted] of an aggregate strength of 13,024 officers and men . . . ; but at no time during the war did the Regular Army attain a strength of 25,000 men." All the rest were militia and volunteers. That explains the disaster at Bull Run and the hard task McClellan had in training the Army of the Potomac.

So Charleston was not taken by the Army in 1861. Next year, however, the Navy Department was confident that the fleet would cause its surrender. Welles and Fox, stressing the defensive power of the *Monitor* when hammered by the guns of the *Virginia* and the success of Farragut in taking a fleet past Forts Jackson and St. Philip, believed that the Navy, with a squadron of monitors, could go anywhere there was a sufficient depth of water. Thus, early in 1863 Welles repeatedly urged Du Pont, in command of the South Atlantic Blockading Squadron, to steam past the forts defending Charleston and seize the city. Troops were not available for a joint operation. But in his opinion the Navy could accomplish the task unaided, and thus would gain the greater honor.

On the seventh of April, 1863, the *New Ironsides,* Du Pont's flagship, supported by eight monitors, advanced against the forts defending Charleston. The plan of battle closely resembled that employed by Du Pont at Port Royal. The ships of the squadron were slowly to steam forward, not replying to the batteries on Morris Island, but reserving their fire until they were abreast of Fort Sumter or had passed it. If they encountered no obstructions, they were then to attack the fort on its northwest face and to pound the walls with their heavy Dahlgrens until they had demolished them. But when the attack began at 1:15 P.M., the situation, as they soon discovered, was not at all like that of the earlier engagement. Then the Confederates had been unprepared. Their untrained gunners had been overwhelmed by the volume of fire of the wooden frigates and had been able to do nothing in return. At Charleston, on the other hand, the defenders had known for months what would be attempted. They had placed batteries at every conceivable point; the volume of fire was altogether in their favor; and their marksmanship was the best shown by the Confederates in any engagement in which the National Navy fought.

When the monitors had advanced to a position near the principal forts, they halted before some ominous obstructions from Fort Moultrie to Fort Sumter "marked by rows of casks very near together and in several lines"; beyond these were piles extending from James Island to the middle ground.[1] When the leading monitors stopped, they threw the rest of the squadron into confusion. The flagship, from her position in the middle of the column, could not bring her battery to bear on Fort Sumter without the risk of firing on the monitors. Meanwhile the forts, which had kept their large guns silent until the monitors were in close range—the *Weehawken* being only six hundred yards from Fort Sumter—let loose a devastating fire. The *Keokuk* was struck by ninety shots, nineteen on the water line. The *Nahant* was struck by eighty. The *Passaic* had her turret bent in by a single shot, so that it could no longer be operated. The *Keokuk* was so badly damaged that she sank that evening at 8:10.

It was a one-sided contest. The guns of the monitors, though of large caliber, were few in number, and they fired only 139

[1] H. A. Du Pont, *Rear Admiral Samuel Francis Du Pont*, p. 190.

shots against 2,200 discharged by the Confederates. They represented the heaviest naval ordnance of the time, but they made a poor showing.

Du Pont, seeing this, signaled at 4:30 for the fleet to withdraw, intending to renew the attack on the following morning. But during the night, when officers from the different units came aboard the flagship to report, they were unanimous in the opinion that Charleston could not be taken by the naval force. Having already reached the same conclusion, Du Pont abandoned the project.

A comparison of the attack of Du Pont on Charleston and that of Farragut on New Orleans is instructive. Farragut had accurate and complete information of obstructions he must pass and fortifications he must encounter. He would not begin operations until he had his squadron assembled and troops at hand in case they were required. After making every preparation and indoctrinating all his captains most carefully, he launched his attack under cover of darkness, when the aim of the enemy gunners was uncertain, and greatly reduced their fire by the concentrated fire of his ships. Du Pont plainly did not know what he had to meet and, making his attack under conditions most favorable to his enemy, was turned back by a force he could not cope with on account of its position and gun power. Comparison shows that Du Pont was not the equal of Farragut. But neither was any other officer of the United States Navy, or of any navy, at this time.

The Navy Department, disappointed by the lack of results, planned to relieve Du Pont by Foote, and when the latter died placed Dahlgren in command (July 6, 1863). Dahlgren, like his predecessor, felt the official pressure and also the popular desire voiced in the newspapers urging him on to action. But, with his officers, he felt the futility of attacking Charleston with the naval force unaided.

In the fall of 1864 and the following winter, General Sherman was making his well-known march to the sea, and the relation of the strategy of the Army to that of the Navy became evident. Taking Fort McAllister by assault, he opened communication with the fleet and compelled General Hardee to evacuate Savannah (December 20) and withdraw his troops to Charleston. Marching north, when he had occupied Columbia he again forced Hardee to fall back. In consequence, Charleston was abandoned by the Confederates on the eighteenth of February, 1865. This was a great blow to the Confederacy. Jefferson Davis wrote, "I had hoped for other and better results and the disappointment is to me extremely bitter." What the Navy had been unable to accomplish by direct attack, the Army, cutting lines of communication, accomplished without a battle.

The Capture of Fort Fisher

When the forts at the entrance of Mobile Bay had been taken and Charleston and Savannah were closely guarded, Wilmington took on supreme importance. It was for the Confederacy the chief and almost the only remaining source of supplies coming from Europe—the next being the ports of distant Texas.

The city of Wilmington is on the Cape Fear River, twenty-eight miles from its mouth. There were two entrances to the river which, though not more than six miles apart in a straight line, were separated by Smith's Island and the dangerous Frying Pan Shoals; and the actual entrances were only a little less than forty miles apart. At the mouth of the river were the strong fortifications comprised in Fort Fisher. These and the shallow water made a purely naval attack on the city impracticable. Its blockade had begun almost immediately on the first proclamation of blockade in 1861, but the blockading force never was able to maintain the close watch it kept over other ports until very near the end of the war, when Fort Fisher had been taken.

A combined Army-Navy attack on Fort Fisher had been planned for October, 1864, but was postponed, for troops at that time were not available. Rear Admiral David D. Porter was called from the West to command a large naval force concentrated at Hampton Roads and Beaufort in preparation. And General Benjamin F. Butler was given command of the troops who were to co-operate—brought by transports from Hampton Roads the last of December. Meanwhile, the Confederates had also been preparing, and General Bragg had been sent from Richmond to insure a successful defense.

The Union forces began the battle with the explosion of the *Louisiana,* a captured blockade runner which they had converted into a fireship, loaded with 3,000 barrels of powder. This project, proposed by General Butler, had been eagerly accepted by Admiral Porter, who was always looking for something new in warfare. A terrible disaster caused by an explosion in England had suggested the idea. The *Louisiana* was cautiously towed in on the night of December 23 and then proceeded under her own steam to a point 400 yards from the fort, where she was anchored and set on fire. All proceeded according to plan, and the explosion occurred in the very early morning at a quarter before two. The small force who had had charge of the last preparations aboard the fireship had fled in desperate haste, expecting a blast that would cause destruction for a mile or more. It was sufficient to break one or two glasses in the nearest Union vessels, but that was about the extent of the damage. Although Union officers for some days were certain that it had killed a large number of the defenders of the fort and demoralized others, they later learned that most of the Confederates were not aware of the explosion; those that had noticed it supposed that a blockade runner on being pursued had grounded near the fort and had set fire to herself.

At noon after the supposed panic occasioned by the explosion of the *Louisiana,* the fleet bombarded the fort, and Porter reported that in an hour he had silenced all the batteries. Six Parrott rifles in the fleet had burst, and the casualties resulting were considerably in excess of all those suffered in the fort as reported by Colonel Lamb. On the following day, when 3,000 troops brought by the transports had been landed, the Union fleet returned to the bombardment. Admiral Porter was sure

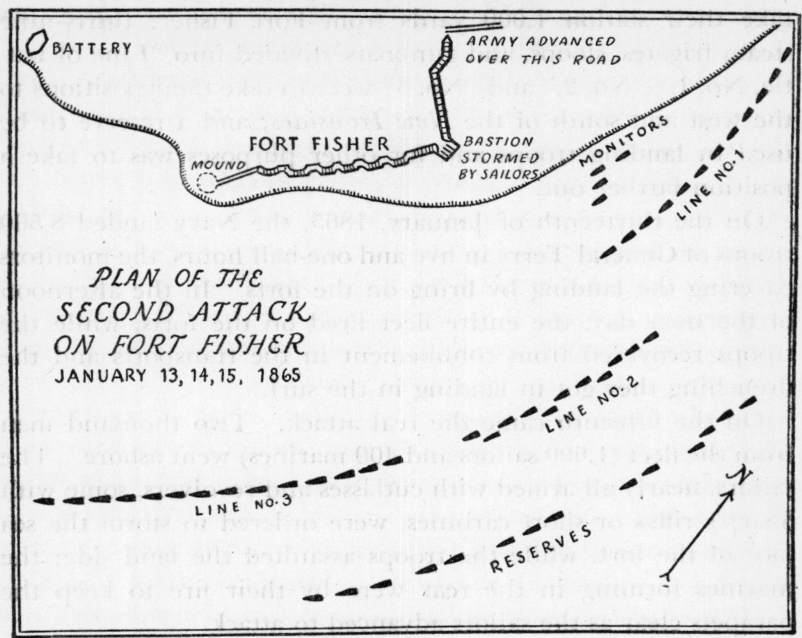

that Fort Fisher was practically demolished and would be theirs for the taking. But on making a reconnaissance, General Weitzel, who was in charge of the Union troops ashore, reported that the enemy fortifications were still intact. General Butler thereupon withdrew the troops and returned to Hampton Roads—much to the disgust of the determined and outspoken Admiral Porter.

A second attack was immediately planned, and for this Major General A. H. Terry was placed in command of the troops. No novel military ideas were tried, but sound preparation was made, and the co-operation of Army and Navy, which had been faulty in the previous operation, was now the best.

Porter had a naval force of over fifty ships, a force the like of which had never before been assembled under the American flag, and he most carefully studied out the position of each ship in the attack. The *New Ironsides* and four monitors were to take their station 1,000 yards from Fort Fisher; thirty-nine steam frigates, sloops, and gunboats, divided into "Line of battle, No. 1," "No. 2," and "No. 3" were to take their positions to the west and south of the *New Ironsides;* and a reserve to be used in landing troops and for other purposes was to take a position farther out.

On the thirteenth of January, 1865, the Navy landed 8,500 troops of General Terry in five and one-half hours, the monitors covering the landing by firing on the forts. In the afternoon of the next day, the entire fleet fired on the forts, while the troops recovered from confinement in the transports and the drenching they got in landing in the surf.

On the fifteenth came the real attack. Two thousand men from the fleet (1,600 sailors and 400 marines) went ashore. The sailors, nearly all armed with cutlasses and revolvers, some with Sharp's rifles or short carbines, were ordered to storm the sea face of the fort, while the troops assaulted the land side; the marines forming in the rear were by their fire to keep the parapets clear as the sailors advanced to attack.

At ten o'clock all the vessels had steamed to their stations, and opening a heavy fire continued the bombardment until three in the afternoon. Then, at a signal accompanied by the blowing of all the whistles, the ships changed the direction of their fire. This marked the moment for the assault by the troops and the sailors.

The sailors and a few of the marines had already worked their way along the beach to a position where they had dug in only 200 yards from the fort. Rushing through the palisades they tried to seize the strong bastion at the northeast corner of the fort. Suddenly, however, the parapets swarmed with defenders and a terrific fire of grape and canister opened upon the head of the column. Porter in his plan had relied on the marines with their rifle fire to keep the parapets clear. But at the last hour the marines were still awaiting orders—something had gone wrong and most of them took no part in the battle. Porter, terribly disappointed, spoke in no uncertain language of their failure to give protection; but it is doubtful if their small force could have changed the result. The few Union sailors that reached the parapet were quickly thrown back; the main column and rear then gave away. The naval attack was unsuccessful.

Meanwhile, the Army had assaulted the far end of the land side of the fort and had taken two traverses. As Colonel Lamb stated in his report, the Confederates, thinking that the main attack was that made by the sailors on the bastion, concentrated their strength at that point; and because of the diversion they did not make a strong resistance to the assault of the troops.

The land side defense of Fort Fisher consisted of seventeen bombproofs or traverses, each sixty feet long, fifty feet wide, and twenty feet high, mounting one or two heavy guns. The guns had all been dismounted or destroyed by the ships' fire, and for three days the Confederate troops had found no opportunity for rest, cooking, and refreshment.[2] The monitors continued to fire on the traverses still occupied, and the Union troops proceeded to take one after another. At ten o'clock that evening they were in complete control. The prisoners they took numbered 112 officers and 1,971 men. The gunboats could then advance up the river toward Wilmington, and as Porter announced, the place was "hermetically sealed against blockade runners."

The Strategic Value of the Blockade

Beginning with Jefferson Davis, Southern writers have had much to say of the ineffectiveness of the blockade. No more painstaking study of this has been made than that by Professor Frank L. Owsley in his *King Cotton Diplomacy*. Speaking of the herculean task of blockading a coast of 3,549 miles, he notes that if the 600 vessels of every kind and description in the Navy had been placed at regular intervals along the coast from Norfolk to the Rio Grande, there would have been only one for

[2] *Naval War Records*, XI, 593.

every six miles.[3] And there is something of post-war fire expressed in his comment on the "absurdity of the thing," which he characterizes as one of Lincoln's practical jokes. But we may well scrutinize the figures which he says he arrived at after a study of all evidences, showing the captures of blockade runners in comparison with those that escaped:

1861, not more than 1 in 10
1862, not more than 1 in 8
1863, not more than 1 in 4
1864, not more than 1 in 3
1865, not more than 1 in 2

Accepting these approximations as reasonably accurate, we still have reason for thinking that the blockade had great influence on the course of the war.

The British government early noted the inconsistency apparent in the protests made by Davis and the Southern emissaries in London and Paris, as they called attention to the injustice and wrong suffered by the South, on account of the blockade, and at the same time ridiculed its futility. This was when Davis was rendering great assistance to the blockade by withholding cotton from exportation. His reasoning was that, cotton being absolutely essential, the demand for it would compel foreign powers to seek relief and therefore they would give full recognition to the Confederacy.

Although a number of skilful and daring captains, sailing swift ships especially designed as blockade runners, repeatedly entered and left the blockaded ports, those less skilful and daring were captured or at least deterred. This is evidenced by the great rise of prices in the South in all foodstuffs, as well as manufactured articles: bacon, lard, and butter reaching more than twice their gold value in 1860; sugar and molasses, five

[3] The Navy Department from the beginning of the blockade followed a policy of placing a guard about the principal harbors and rivers and ignoring the long stretches of flat, sandy shores where no ships of size could make a landing. Therefore, Owsley's calculation is not convincing.

times; and coffee, eight times. Tobacco and cotton were the only commodities that fell below their gold value in 1860.[4] Cotton could be purchased in the Confederacy for eight cents a pound and sold in Nassau or Bermuda for six times that amount.[5] No wonder that the successful blockade runner made enormous profits and was reported even to have paid for his ship after two successful trips. But he was taking a chance. The yearly exportation of cotton from the Southern states, which in 1860 reached a total of 2,000,000 bales, finally fell to 13,000.

The South worked hard to discover substitutes for commodities previously imported. They made coffee out of grain and a variety of parched seeds; buttons of persimmon seeds; shoes of wood and canvas; writing paper of scraps of wallpaper. Many of the people, becoming inured to doing without, repeatedly denounced the importations as luxuries. Thus, the Confederate Congress passed an act, March 1, 1864, prohibiting the importation of a long list of articles. The blockade runners for the most part came from England, many financed by British companies or individuals in business. The result was not satisfactory. Naturally, in this time of dire need the South could not look calmly on the large profits carried away. The charge made in Richmond was that the traffic "depressed the currency, drained the country of specie, encouraged extravagance and speculation, and spread disaffection."

Consequently, although the reader may agree with critics like Owsley and Scharf that the blockade was far from complete, he may recognize its practicability and effectiveness. Professor Schwab of Yale in his scholarly study reached the conclusion that it "constituted the most powerful tool of the Federal Government in its effort to subdue the South." "It was the blockade rather than the ravages of the army that sapped the industrial strength of the Confederacy."

[4] J. C. Schwab, *The Confederate States of America, 1861–1865*, pp. 175, 178.
[5] J. T. Scharf, *History of the Confederate States Navy*, p. 482.

References

Lamb, William, Colonel, C.S.A., "The Defense of Fort Fisher," in *Battles and Leaders of the Civil War,* IV, 642–654.

Official Records of the Union and Confederate Navies in the War of the Rebellion, Vol. X, for Cushing's report of the destruction of the Albemarle; also *Battles and Leaders of the Civil War,* IV, 634–640.

Owsley, F. L., *King Cotton Diplomacy*: *Foreign Relations of the Cotton States,* 1931.

Schwab, J. C., *The Confederate States of America, 1861–1865*: *A Financial and Industrial History of the South during the Civil War,* 1901.

Selfridge, T. O., Captain, U.S.N., "The Navy at Fort Fisher," *Battles and Leaders of the Civil War,* IV, 655–661.

Soley, J. R., *The Blockade and the Cruisers,* 1883.

West, R. S., *The Second Admiral; A Life of David Dixon Porter,* 1937.

XVI BRINGING THE WAR TO AN END

In discussion of the Civil War, emphasis is often so largely placed on operations in Virginia or in Kentucky and Tennessee as to suggest that the fighting on these two fronts was very nearly the whole story. It is more logical to consider at least five strategic fronts: (1) military, (2) naval, (3) political, (4) economic, (5) moral or psychological. On all five the North obtained superiority before it won the final victory. There was much overlapping, and it is because the Navy influenced not only the military front but also the others that all should be briefly considered.

The Political Front

As we have already seen, the South, without a single warship at the outbreak of hostilities, was able to send out cruisers only with the aid of Great Britain. Such assistance would have grown to large proportions had it not been for our ministers in London and Paris.

On the political front, both abroad and at home, the North usually had the advantage. The Confederacy was handicapped in the beginning in having no constitution and established order to direct her executive and legislative departments. She had to improvise hurriedly. The system adopted was patterned after that which her statesmen had recently been a part of, but to duplicate this required time and effort.

President Davis was an able and experienced administrator, marked by strong character, intellect, and knowledge of military affairs, as well as those of state. He was a graduate of West Point, and had taken part in the Black Hawk War and in the War with Mexico. In the Civil War he regarded himself as the equal of any of the generals.[1] As Secretary of War under President Pierce and leader in the United States Senate he was a national figure when Lincoln was unknown. But he was not the latter's equal in sympathy and in understanding of men, and his acquaintance with military affairs too often tempted him to interfere with leaders in the field. When defeat followed, responsibility devolved on him, and in time criticism of him was widespread. The Confederate Congress was not noted for its harmony, and the contentions of Richmond were as acrimonious as those of Washington in the years previous to 1861. The executive and legislative branches often did not work well together; further, in their relations with the state governors they proved that whatever in normal times may be the argument for state rights, in time of war a highly centralized government has greater force.

If the government at Richmond had not been constantly embarrassed by the Union blockade and could have reported some outstanding naval victories at strategic moments, the political situation would have been vastly improved.

The Economic Front

Both North and South were rich in natural resources. The North had an advantage, however, due to the diversification of her industries, agricultural products, mines, timber, and manufactures—all stimulated by improved methods of transportation. As other wars have demonstrated, when in mili-

[1] "If I could take one wing and Lee the other, I think we could between us wrest a victory from those people." Quoted by Mrs. Davis in her *Memoirs,* II, 392.

tary and naval power two nations are not wholly unequal, the belligerent which has a preponderating economic and industrial superiority will win. The North had depended on the South for its cotton, tobacco, and rice. And the South had depended on the North and upon Europe for its ships and shipping, iron and copper manufactures, textiles, and shoes—as well as for its guns and munitions. The South was able, in the stress of war, to develop only a small part of the industries she suddenly had need of. Her warships suffered from lack of guns, and it is surprising that her people were as successful as they were in supplying ordnance, small arms, and powder for her military and naval forces.

Labor was another commodity unequally possessed. The North, notwithstanding the large number of soldiers and sailors in her armed forces, had a fairly ample supply. In this, immigration played an important part. It had greatly increased on the passing of the Homestead Act in 1862 and the throwing open of 2,500,000 acres to settlement at a time when there was great demand for all food products.

It happened also in 1862 that the crops in Great Britain and in large parts of Europe were a failure, and a protracted drought in Virginia reduced her yield of wheat to one-fourth of the normal. The consequences were highly favorable to the Union. The demand for wheat was not limited to one year but continued. Soon more was produced in the North than previously had been grown in the whole country, both North and South. Brought by the railroads and by the Great Lakes and Erie Canal, it reached the Atlantic ports to be forwarded to Europe. Wheat and beef defeated King Cotton and were of great aid in improving foreign relations. Lumber mills and the mines of the West were also rapidly developed and their output assumed a place among the leading exports.

Transportation had for the first time assumed a role of great importance in military operations as well as in commerce. Victory was no longer dependent solely on those who could march, for railroads and steamboats, taking combatants to strategic points and bringing up artillery and supplies, introduced a new factor. In the South the absence of railroad shops and manufacturing plants told disastrously. The railroads deteriorated and became less and less serviceable. To assist the railroads, Southern shipping might have been developed and might have become an important auxiliary, but the Union Navy with the constant patrol of rivers and inlets prevented this.

Breaking Down the Morale

What then was it that brought the long war to an end? Newspapers and contemporary records of 1864 show that there was apathy toward war quite as evident in the North as in the South. There were draft riots in New York, as well as food riots in Richmond. Editorials in leading newspapers and open forums on both sides discussed terms of peace that might be acceptable, ranging all the way from those based on complete victory to those of virtual surrender. But the North held grimly to its terrible task in the following winter and spring, and the South suddenly collapsed.

This is to be explained not merely by the military reverses. They were severe, and the losses in battle were enormous; still the South had a formidable number of trained soldiers surviving. If they had been assembled in organized units, they would have represented a force greater than Lee or any other general ever commanded at any one time. Early in April, 1865, 150,000 to 200,000 were supposedly answerable to the orders of the Adjutant General in Richmond. The Army of Virginia was fast dwindling, but fresh forces that occupied the important posts in Texas might have held out for months—led on by the hope of inducing the North to accept a negotiated peace, out of sheer war-weariness.

The demoralization of the South was undoubtedly increased

by hunger.[2] Though abundant food was to be found in many localities, the lack of it at essential points, even though temporary, was near to famine. The Confederate commissary, like the Confederate railroads, had broken down.

Physical hunger was destructive to morale—the last of the five fighting fronts and the one on which decision is finally reached. The fighting spirit of the South was gone. More and more her people felt the futility of further resistance. And their feeling of resentment against profiteering blockade runners, food speculators, and blundering administrators became scarcely less pronounced than that felt against the armed forces of the North.

A small group of men who fled from Richmond to avoid capture urged the transfer of the seat of government to Texas, where Confederate forces still held the field. But Lee and Johnston had a better understanding of the situation. They were conscious of the changed spirit of their armies and of the Southern people. The cause for which they had been fighting was hopeless. The people were hungry not only for food but also for peace.

The Navy's Part in the War

In wars fought by the United States subsequent to 1865 the Navy has been the first line of defense and has taken the initiative in offensive operations. In the Civil War it was different. The fighting was primarily on land. The South never had more than a shadow of a navy, and the brunt was sustained by their military forces. To get a complete picture, however, let us give the proper place to what was emphasized often by Grant and Sherman and also by President Lincoln: the Navy was of vital assistance to the Army in joint operations. The Navy was

[2] Dr. Basil L. Gildersleeve, an officer in the Confederate Army, later famous as professor of Greek in the Johns Hopkins University, wrote, "Hunger was the dominant note of life in the Confederacy, civil as well as military." *Atlantic Monthly*, Sept., 1897, p. 339.

most essential in winning the battles fought at Hatteras Inlet, Port Royal, Fort Henry, Fort Donelson, Shiloh, Island No. 10, New Orleans, Vicksburg, Mobile Bay, and Fort Fisher—and without these successes how could there have been the final victory in 1865? The Navy by successfully undertaking the task of blockade—which European neutrals regarded as impossible in accomplishment—from the beginning diminished foreign credits and checked the bringing in of arms and military supplies. Had it not been for the gradual closing of ports on the Atlantic and on the Gulf and the interruption of internal communications on the Mississippi and its tributaries, the provisioning of the Confederate Army and the supplying of food for their cities would also have been much simplified.

"To form a more perfect Union" had been proclaimed three-quarters of a century previous as one of the chief aims of the Constitution. This, in 1861, seemed to a great many people a task impossible of accomplishment, but the two great arms of the National Service recognized their mission and held faithfully to it.

References

Davis, Jefferson, *The Rise and Fall of the Confederate Government,* 2 vols., 1881.

Jones, J. B., *A Rebel War Clerk's Diary at the Confederate State Capital,* 2 vols., 1866.

Stephenson, N. W., *Lincoln,* 1922.

XVII
THE OLD NAVY, AND THE NEW

A Period of Decline

After the Civil War the Navy lapsed into somnolence for nearly a score of years. At the end of the war, with over seven hundred ships mounting 5,000 guns, and sixty-five of them ironclads, it was one of the strongest in the world; but within five years, more than two-thirds of this force was sold or otherwise disposed of. The wartime fleet of monitors was for the most part allowed to rot and rust away; on four of these, set apart for reconstruction in 1874, the work was not complete until after twenty years. In 1880 there were in our Navy only forty-eight ships that could fire a gun, and of these not more than thirty wooden corvettes and sloops were fit for service abroad. In naval strength we stood twelfth, after Denmark, Chile, and China. "Our most immediate need," wrote Commander E. J. King, U.S.N., in *Warships and Navies of the World* (1880), a book which drew attention to our naval deficiencies, "is a fleet of unarmored cruisers to replace the obsolete types that have neither guns to fight nor speed to run."

Naval vessels, it is true, still displayed the flag in ports visited by American commerce, and small squadrons protected American interests in distant parts of the world. In the late 1860's Admiral Farragut, commanding the European squadron, was royally welcomed in ports of England and of the continent as the outstanding naval leader of his time. But in these distant cruises of single ships or small squadrons there was little thought of co-ordinated operations of the Navy as an instrument of war. For long voyages, moreover, coal economy was essential, and on many ships, speed under steam was actually cut down to improve sailing qualities. Admiral Goodrich, in *Rope Yarns from the Old Navy*,[1] states that in those days "a captain was obliged to enter in the log book in red ink his reasons for getting up steam." Congressional appropriations were limited to repairs of old ships, and these repairs often mounted up to more than the ship's original cost. More is said to have been spent on two old wooden vessels, the *Omaha* and *Mohican*, than it would have cost to build a new steel man-of-war.

For this decline of the Navy, aside from the inevitable war reaction and the administrative laxity in the 1870's, the reasons are fairly clear. The national energies were wholly devoted to internal growth. In the postwar decades our frontiers were pushed to the Pacific. Four great railways were thrown across the continent. The prairies were opened up for an immensely increased agricultural production. Eastern capital was poured into this Western development and into the growth of industries to meet increased home and foreign demands. Between 1860 and 1890, while our population doubled from thirty to sixty million, our increase in manufactured products was five-fold, and in exports we rose from fourth to second place among nations. The country in these decades had reached its continental borders, but as yet had hardly looked beyond.

Another reason for failing naval interest was the fact that, despite the growth of foreign trade, the American merchant marine was in a steady decline. American capital found a far more profitable outlet in the industrial development just outlined than in building ships in competition with more advanced British iron ship construction, or operating them in competition with cheaper costs abroad. In 1860 American shipping amounted to over 2,500,000 tons. The loss during the war was nearly a million tons, of which 110,000 tons re-

[1] Quoted in H. and M. Sprout, *The Rise of American Naval Power.*

sulted from capture and the rest from transfer to foreign register.[2] From then on the decline was steady until the close of the century, when our total was less than a million tons, and only about 9 per cent of our foreign trade was carried in American bottoms. As Mahan admitted in his earliest volume, with a vanishing merchant fleet one of the chief motives for naval power was removed.

Other and even more basic motives for naval power are defense of the nation's sea frontiers and foreign interests. But internationally, in these postwar decades, the horizon was relatively clear. France, for various reasons, not least of which was an American army of 50,000 on the Texas border and an American fleet able to control the western Atlantic, had decided in 1866 to withdraw from her Mexican adventure; and after the Franco-Prussian War in 1870 her chief concern was in building up her army. The German Navy was still in embryo. With England, the war scare over the *Alabama* claims was disposed of in 1871 by peaceful settlement and payment of $15,500,000 —a settlement in which Britain was probably influenced far less by fears of a few fast 17-knot American cruisers of the *Wampanoag* type, as some supposed at the time, than by the advantage of establishing a principle which would bar the construction or fitting-out of commerce raiders in neutral ports. England's eight bases and thirty coaling stations in the western Atlantic were, as ever, a matter of some concern to our naval strategists, but not of serious alarm.

Yet, even in the 1870's there were diplomatic episodes which revealed our naval weakness, notably the *Virginius* Affair of 1873. The *Virginius,* while engaged in a filibustering expedition during the Cuban Rebellion of 1868–78, was captured on October 31 by a Spanish gunboat off Jamaica and taken into Santiago, where within a week fifty-three of her crew and passengers, including about thirty United States citizens, were put to death by what Secretary of State Hamilton Fish truthfully described as "brutal butchery and murder." Since the

[2] For the effect of the war on shipping, see Chapter XV.

ship carried American papers, and no formal state of war existed, both the seizure and the executions were illegal. Naval vessels were dispatched to Santiago and for a time war threatened, but upon the revelation that the ship was actually owned by the Cuban Junta and her papers were falsely obtained, the State Department consented to a settlement involving the surrender of the ship with the 102 remaining prisoners, and the payment of an indemnity. Naval significance lay chiefly in the fact that hostilities would have tested our aging monitors against Spain's new armored broadside ships of British build. Later, during the war between Chile and Peru, in 1882–83, there was some talk of intervention by the United States, but this met an effective damper when it was realized that Chile had four ironclads which were better than anything we could send to the scene of the war. Here also was an argument for rearmament that was used repeatedly during the next ten years.

The New Navy

In fact, no great argument should have been necessary—especially in those halcyon days of surplus revenues in the Treasury—to show the crying need for an American Navy more nearly correspondent to the nation's increased wealth and responsibilities. First efforts in that direction are credited to Secretary of the Navy Hunt, in the Garfield-Arthur Administration, who in 1881 named a naval board headed by Rear Admiral John Rodgers to consider the Navy's needs. Seen through these eyes, the Navy needed no less than thirty-eight new steel cruisers and twenty-five gunboats and torpedo boats. Congress, when it finally took action in March, 1883, reduced the cruiser program to a modest four—the unarmored cruisers *Atlanta, Boston,* and *Chicago,* of 4,500 to 2,500 tons, and the smaller "dispatch boat" *Dolphin.* These were the "A B C D's" of the White Squadron. A further step forward was made at the same time by limiting repairs on ships to 30 per cent, and later to 20 per cent, of their original cost, thus at once scratching forty-six veterans from the navy list and releasing funds for new construction. During Cleveland's administration, 1885–89, this progress was carried forward under the able Secretary, William C. Whitney, who secured some thirty-three ships aggregating 100,000 tons and ranging from our first modern battleship *Texas* (6,315 tons) to the highly original "dynamite cruiser" *Vesuvius,* pierced through the foredeck with three compressed air guns to throw dynamite bombs, and our first torpedo boat, the *Cushing*. After investigations abroad by a naval commission, the Washington Gun Factory was started in 1887; and the domestic steel industry received a strong impetus from contracts for steel armor and gun forgings given to the Bethlehem Iron Company in the same year. Other ships of the late 1880's were the *Charleston* (3,730 tons), the first to discard sail rig; the armored cruiser *Maine* (6,672 tons), with an armor belt; and protected cruisers such as the *Baltimore* and *Olympia,* with 3-inch steel decks. These, with the battleships *Indiana, Massachusetts,* and *Oregon,* authorized in 1890, the fast armored cruisers *New York* and *Brooklyn,* and the battleship *Iowa,* authorized in 1892, were the ships that formed the backbone of our Navy in the Spanish War.

The strategic idea behind the earlier unarmored cruisers of this program was primarily the old American policy of commerce destruction, which, as illustrated in the Civil War and earlier, seemed the only effective weapon against a superior sea power. As a supplement to these light raiders, the monitors and gunboats were to be used for harbor defense, in conformity with the popular view of a purely defensive war. But with the turn of the nineties, new and sounder strategic principles began to take control. Commerce destroying, whatever its nuisance value, had never won a war. Coast defense, with the increasing range of ordnance, could best be managed by guns on shore. Ships should operate not singly but in well-organized squadrons. (The first "squadron of maneuver," eyed dubiously by old-timers, practiced awkward evolutions in the year 1889.)

The battleships were now described as "*seagoing* coast-defense battleships," and their use was to be for an offensive-defensive, joined in a fleet sufficient to prevent blockade, and even to cope with such an enemy fleet as, in the existing European situation, a European power could afford to send overseas.

The War College and Mahan

There is good evidence to show that the chief source of these new ideas guiding naval construction was the Naval War College, established in 1885 at Newport, R.I., and its first instructor in strategy, tactics, and naval history, Alfred Thayer Mahan. For the establishment of the Naval War College, far earlier than similar institutions were established abroad, primary credit is due to Rear Admiral Stephen B. Luce, who conceived the project and worked unweariedly for its accomplishment in the face of departmental indifference and hostile service opinion. Luce also was responsible for the selection of Mahan, who was then, at the age of forty-five, on distant duty in the South Pacific. At that time Mahan was of note chiefly as a brilliant student at the Naval Academy, a capable lieutenant in the Civil War, and an officer of intellectual interests who had written a study of Civil War naval operations entitled *The Gulf and Inland Waters.* Mahan succeeded Luce as president of the college, and remained there through the vicissitudes of its first seven years, when it was sometimes without students, sometimes without funds. The product of his lectures and studies was his great book, *The Influence of Sea Power Upon History* (1890), which almost at once attained international fame, and which, with succeeding volumes and occasional essays, was destined to exercise a profound influence on naval and national policies both at home and abroad. As his friend Theodore Roosevelt wrote, "In the vitally important task of convincing the masters of us all—the people as a whole—of the importance of a true understanding of naval needs, Mahan stood alone." Highly important also, in a period when the best brains and energies of the Service tended to become preoccupied with the multitude of material problems raised by changes in ships and weapons, was the establishment of the War College for improving officer personnel in the art of war, and for establishing a sound body of naval doctrine based on historical study and practical experiment. Through its influence, as one officer has put it, the Navy experienced "an intellectual as well as a spiritual renaissance after an all-time low." [3]

The Nation Looks Outward

To understand American naval progress in the eighties and nineties and the shifts of national policy involved, one must bear in mind the profound changes then taking place in the international sphere. These decades marked the beginning of an intensified commercial and colonial rivalry, in Africa, in the Far East, and elsewhere, which led ultimately to the First World War and its sequel in our own time. This new imperialism, to use the term by which it is commonly known, was stimulated by the rapid industrial growth of both Germany and the United States and the resultant clash for foreign markets and sources of raw materials which threatened England's long dominance in these fields. It found a philosophical justification in popular evolutionary theories of the survival of the fittest (conceived generally in terms of might rather than right), and in the belief that nations, like other organisms, must either grow or decay. It found an idealistic appeal in the notion that the Western nations must take up "the white man's burden" and spread the gospel of Western civilization to the "backward races" of the world. And, as already suggested, it found its clearest exposition and most powerful propaganda in the works of the great American naval philosopher Mahan. Trade, shipping, colonies, navies—these were the keys to sea power and hence to world power.

---

[3] Captain J. M. Ellicott, U.S.N., "With Erben and Mahan in the *Chicago*," *Naval Institute Proceedings*, Sept., 1941.

In the United States the swing toward imperialism developed slowly, and was not fully manifest until near the close of the century; but throughout the period under study there were diplomatic episodes which involved the Navy, and at the same time raised questions of expansion and of new interests beyond our continental limits.

In the Far East, after trouble over the seizure and probable murder of American seamen shipwrecked on the Korean coast, Rear Admiral John Rodgers, with a squadron of five ships, visited the Hermit Kingdom in 1871, in company with the American Minister to China, for the purpose of securing a treaty. During preliminary negotiations, when two seamen of a survey party were killed by fire from a Korean fort and no apology was forthcoming, the Admiral adopted characteristic Western methods of punishment by landing a force of 650 men, which captured several forts and held them eleven days, inflicting an enemy loss of nearly 350, as compared with three Americans killed and ten wounded. Subsequently, Commander R. W. Shufeldt, U.S.N., after ineffective efforts to negotiate through Japan, gained the intercession of the powerful Chinese Viceroy Li Hung Chang, and thus in May, 1882, was able to sign a treaty with Korea which marked the beginning of that nation's contact with the Western world.

Acquisitions in the Pacific

In the mid-Pacific, the United States took possession of Midway Island in 1867, and later acquired rights to a coaling station at Pago Pago, Samoa, together with a kind of quasi-protectorate over the Samoan Islands, shared after 1880 with England and Germany. Thereafter, foreign agents, especially the Germans, interfered with the native government and made the islands a veritable hotbed of petty intrigue, with the result that in the spring of 1888 no less than three German, one British, and three American war vessels—the *Vandalia, Trenton,* and *Nipsic*—were assembled in Apia Harbor to protect rival national interests. In this tense situation the islands were struck with a terrific hurricane, in which the German and American ships were all driven ashore, with a loss of fifty-one American lives. Only the British *Calliope* had sufficient engine power to get out of the bay.

Sobered, perhaps, by this disaster, the three nations subsequently arranged a condominium over the islands, guaranteeing their autonomy and neutralization, which lasted until 1899. Then, after another upset, in which all three guardian nations used naval forces ashore, the islands were divided. The United States took Tutuila with its excellent harbor of Pago Pago and some smaller eastern islands of the group; Germany took those to the west; and Britain received compensation elsewhere. This arrangement continued until New Zealand forces seized the German portion of the islands in the First World War.

Like that of Samoa, the problem of Hawaii illustrated the uncertainties of American policy as to outlying colonial possessions—a policy strongly opposed to European acquisitions in the eastern Pacific or in the Caribbean, but divided as to the wisdom of assuming such responsibilities ourselves. Since first visited in 1825 by an American naval vessel, the schooner *Dolphin,* under Captain "Mad Jack" Percival, the Hawaiian Islands had been a resort for whalers, a center of American missionary and trading activity, and a favorite anchorage for American men-of-war. Our reciprocity treaty of 1872 with the islands contained safeguards against their passing under foreign control, and in 1887 a clause was added granting us the exclusive right to a fortified naval base at Pearl Harbor. Naval officers had already recognized the importance of the islands as a crossroads of Pacific trade and a vital outpost for naval defense of the Pacific coast and the western approaches of an isthmian canal.

On January 16, 1893, the native rule of Queen Liliuokalani in Hawaii was overthrown by a bloodless revolution, engineered chiefly by American residents and given strong support by the American minister, John L. Stevens, who probably prevented any defense on the part of the Queen's forces by requesting that a party of 150 marines and sailors be put ashore from the U.S.S. *Boston*. Stevens recognized the new government the next day, and two weeks later established a virtual protectorate. The forthcoming application for annexation was quickly approved by the Harrison administration in Washington, but the treaty was held up in the Senate until after the inauguration of President Cleveland in March. A staunch foe of imperialism, Cleveland recalled the treaty, sent an investigator to the islands, and soon withdrew the protectorate. But by this time the government under President Sanford B. Dole had become firmly established, and Hawaii remained a republic till July, 1898. Then, in the new situation created by Dewey's victory at Manila, the annexation was approved by a joint resolution of Congress, requiring only a majority vote.

Problems in the Caribbean

In the Caribbean, as early as Grant's administration, there had been tentative but unsuccessful moves to purchase the Danish Virgin Islands, and also to take over the Dominican Republic, with its attractive naval base site at Samaná Bay. Later on, when the French engineer De Lesseps started canal construction at Panama, Secretary of State Blaine, in the early eighties, tried to get England's consent to abrogation of the Clayton-Bulwer Treaty, which prevented exclusive United States control and fortification of such a canal. At that time England refused, for she could point to her own extensive possessions in the New World, and she did not see then—as she did later in 1901—the need of cultivating American friendship by such a concession.

Blaine was also greatly interested in trade relations with Latin America, and he was again Secretary of State when the first Conference of American Nations, for which he had extended invitations much earlier, met finally in 1889. The meeting was the first of a continuous series of such gatherings to promote inter-American co-operation, though its only definite accomplishment was the establishment of a Bureau of American Republics, later renamed the Pan-American Union.

Unfortunately, some injury to this movement for closer relations with Latin America resulted almost immediately afterward from trouble between the United States and Chile. United States representatives had incurred the ill-will of the successful Liberal revolutionary party in Chile by alleged favors shown to the opposition, and by chasing down and forcing the surrender of the merchant vessel *Itata,* which had escaped from California with a cargo of arms for the Liberals. Hence, when Commander W. S. Schley of the U.S.S. *Baltimore* permitted a landing party of 120 unarmed seamen in Valparaiso, on Oct. 16, 1891, there was a tavern row and a mob attack in which two sailors were killed and several injured. Commander Robley D. Evans, whose ship, the *Yorktown,* succeeded the *Baltimore* at Valparaiso, handled the local situation with tact and firmness, in disregard of Chile's superior naval force and threatening torpedo boat maneuvers, until the Chilean government finally offered apologies and reparations.

Probably a closer approach to naval war—and one for which our Navy was still almost absurdly inadequate—resulted from President Cleveland's vigorous assertion of the Monroe Doctrine in the British-Venezuelan boundary dispute. In this affair, as will be remembered, the President and Secretary of State Olney called for arbitration; and finally, in the extraordinary message to Congress of December 17, 1895, the President proposed to settle the boundary by an American commission and support its decisions, if necessary, by force of arms. The story of American boldness, bluntness, and even truculence in this dispute; of British indifference and condescension; and of the timely publication of the Kaiser's congratulatory message to President Kruger of the Boer Republic, which submerged British annoyance toward America in a wave of anger against Germany—all this belongs rather to diplomatic than to naval history. From the naval standpoint, the final British agreement to arbitrate ended the serious problem presented by possible hostilities with a nation having a battleship superiority over us of something like thirty to three. After this thunderstorm had cleared the air, it was perhaps natural that Anglo-American relations should steadily improve. Another possible, though unforeseen, result was that the patriotic enthusiasm aroused in the American people by the President's resolute action may have contributed to their bellicose temper in the approaching trouble with Spain.

In the Far North

Along with the main naval interests of the post-Civil War period, some mention should be made of the Navy's part in arctic exploration, which carried on the tradition established by the Wilkes Expedition in the Pacific and Antarctic, 1838–42, and the arctic expeditions of Lieutenant E. J. De Haven, U.S.N., in 1850–51,[4] and of Surgeon Kane, U.S.N., in 1853–55.

The *Jeannette* Expedition, 1879–82, though financed by James Gordon Bennett of the *New York Herald,* was commanded by Lieutenant G. W. DeLong, U.S.N., and included the naval officers Lieutenant Danenhower, Lieutenant Chipp, Naval Engineer Melville, and Surgeon Ambler in its personnel of thirty-three men. DeLong's plan was to enter the Arctic through the Bering Straits and drift toward the pole on the northeasterly branch of the Japanese Current. But after the *Jeannette* was caught fast in the ice pack on September 6, 1879, her drift was generally northwestward for the next twenty-one months, until she was finally crushed by the ice, June 12, 1881, some five hundred miles north of the nearest settlements in Siberia. With sledges and the three ship's boats, the party now undertook the arduous journey southward, hindered greatly by the northerly drift of the ice. On September 12, the boats were separated by a storm. One was never heard of again. The second cutter, under Melville and Danenhower, reached

[4] See page 125.

a Siberian village near the mouth of the Lena delta. The first cutter, under DeLong and Ambler, went ashore farther west, and thence the crew undertook to traverse, through swamps and snow, the estimated ninety-five miles or more to the nearest settlements. Short of provisions and weakened by illness and exposure, they fell short of their goal, though the two strongest, who had been sent ahead, managed to struggle through. When word reached Melville, he organized and led a searching party, despite the fact that he was suffering from frostbite and scarcely able to stand. The party was held up by a blizzard, and the bodies of DeLong and his companions were not recovered until the next spring. The leader's records had been kept faithfully almost to the end, and the body of the surgeon was found with those of the sick men for whom he had remained behind. Since the aim of the entire expedition had been primarily scientific, the carefully preserved records were of great value. It was the course of the *Jeannette* that suggested Nansen's later drift across the sea north of Siberia in the *Fram*.

It was also a naval expedition under Commander W. S. Schley which, on June 22, 1884, rescued at Point Sabine, Ellesmere Land, the leader and six other survivors of the American expedition under Lieutenant Greely, United States Army, when they were in the last stages of starvation. Several relief parties in the two preceding years had failed even to leave supplies.

Robert E. Peary was the first to reach the North Pole, August 6, 1909. He was an officer in the Civil Engineer Corps, U.S.N., who, while still maintaining his connection with the Service, was permitted to devote most of his later years to polar exploration. During his eight expeditions from 1886 on, he attained a degree of patience and thoroughness in preparation and such mastery of native methods of life and travel in the North, that his ultimate success seemed almost assured.

Still nearer our own time, Richard E. Byrd, a naval officer taken from the active list of the Navy for a slight physical disability in 1916, made a successful airplane flight over the North Pole with Floyd Bennett on May 9, 1926. He later applied modern equipment and skilled methods to exploration and scientific research in the Antarctic on such a scale that his work may be regarded as creating a new chapter in antarctic history. In 1929 Byrd duplicated his northern achievement by a flight over the South Pole. In the next year he was made a rear admiral. Subsequent well-organized antarctic expeditions under his direction, in 1933 and 1940, made notable contributions to scientific knowledge in geography, geology, meteorology, oceanography, and allied fields. To each of these expeditions the Navy made some contribution in planes, equipment, and personnel.

References

Bailey, T. A., *A Diplomatic History of the American People,* 1942, Chapters XXIII–XXX and references there cited.

Bennett, F. M., *The Steam Navy of the United States,* 1896.

Brodie, B., *Sea Power in the Machine Age,* 1941.

Davis, G. T., *A Navy Second to None,* 1941.

Mahan, A. T., *From Sail to Steam,* 1906.

Perkins, D., *The Monroe Doctrine, 1867–1907,* 1937.

Roddis, L. H., "The United States Navy in Polar Exploration," *Naval Institute Proceedings,* October, 1942.

Sprout, H. and M., *The Rise of American Naval Power,* 1933, Chapters XI–XIII.

XVIII OUR WAR WITH SPAIN

The Approach of War

In the preceding chapter some of the contributory factors in the origin of the Spanish-American War have already been indicated—notably the world trend toward imperialism, which inevitably found some reflection in this country, the increased American interest in the Caribbean and in the approaches to the Isthmus, and the perennial problems arising from Spanish misrule in Cuba, which had more than once, as in the *Virginius* Affair of 1873, brought us close to war with Spain. Revolt again broke out in Cuba in 1895, accompanied by the usual devastation of fields and destruction of property, concentration of the country people in towns, starvation, and brutal, indecisive warfare. American property interests suffered, and our trade with Cuba, amounting before the war to nearly $100,000,000 annually, was in large part ruined. Both the evils and the injuries of the war were exaggerated in the American press, which was ready enough to sacrifice facts for sensational news. Filibustering from the United States was renewed on an increasing scale, as evidenced by the fact that in the years 1895–98 there were seventy-one attempted expeditions, thirty-three of which were broken up by American authorities and only five by the forces of Spain. President Cleveland, after Spain had declined his offer of friendly intercession, gave warning just before the close of his administration that a situation might arise in which our obligation to the sovereignty of Spain would be "superseded by a higher obligation." President McKinley went even further, but his proffer of friendly services was also declined.

With the advent of a Liberal government in Spain late in 1897, the harsh regime of General Weyler in Cuba was ended, and his successor General Blanco was authorized to offer the Cubans a substantial measure of self-rule. This offer, however, came too late. It was scorned by the rebels, who by this time were counting confidently on American support, while, on the other hand, the pro-Spanish elements in Havana actually started riots against the new policy of concessions.

Intervention, toward which the United States Government was steadily being pressed, was made almost inevitable by two events which soon followed in close sequence. The first was the publication, in the *New York Journal* on February 9, 1898, of a private letter written by the Spanish Ambassador at Washington, Dupuy de Lome, in which he raised questions as to the sincerity of recent Spanish policy and also spoke disparagingly of President McKinley, describing him as "weak and a bidder for the admiration of the crowd." Spain quickly accepted the ambassador's resignation, instead of granting the American demand for his recall.

The second event, far more serious in its effect on popular feeling, followed from the sending of the U.S.S. *Maine* to Havana in late January, a measure which had been suggested by Consul General Fitzhugh Lee as possibly necessary for the protection of American interests, but which was taken in advance of his actual request. Tragic indeed, and wholly unexpected, in view of the correct though somewhat strained relations established by Captain Sigsbee of the *Maine* with the Spanish authorities, was the destruction of the vessel, at 9:45 on the evening of February 15, by a terrific explosion which shook the whole water front, and resulted in the loss of 266 out of the ship's complement of 353. The report of a United States naval court of inquiry—later substantiated when the wrecked hull was brought to the surface and then sunk at sea in 1911—was that the disaster had resulted from "a heavy external explosion as by a mine, which drove the bowplates inward," with probable subsequent explosion of the forward magazines. Though no clue to responsibility for the sinking was revealed then or later, the cry "Remember the *Maine*," raised by the American press and people, became a powerful incentive to war.

Both nations thereafter hastened military and naval preparations, and were partly guided by the progress of these preparations in their diplomatic moves. Spanish efforts were hampered by administrative laxity and limited means, and in inner government circles the disastrous results of a war were no doubt clearly foreseen. But national pride, together with fears of a revolt and overthrow of the dynasty, prevented full surrender to the American demands.

The American Congress on March 9 voted $50,000,000 for national defense. On April 11 President McKinley requested congressional authorization to use the military and naval forces "to secure a full and final termination of hostilities between the Government of Spain and the people of Cuba, and to secure in the island the establishment of a stable government." At the close of the message the President mentioned a Spanish proposal for cessation of hostilities on the island, of which he had been informed only the day before, and the possibilities of which he left for Congress to consider "in its solemn deliberations." The President had also received a few days earlier a note expressing hope for peace, which was presented by the ambassadors of the six chief European powers, chiefly on the initiative of Germany, who feared a war might upset her plans for purchase of Spanish islands in the Pacific.

Among historians the view has been very generally expressed that in these last weeks, despite popular and congressional sentiment for intervention, a strong Executive might have avoided war—in other words, that the conflict was a needless one, into which the Government was pushed by the extravagant accounts of Cuban atrocities in the yellow press, and by the activities of a few ardent expansionists headed by Theodore Roosevelt, Senator Henry Cabot Lodge, and Captain Mahan. While these forces undoubtedly played a part, it should be noted that the Spanish concessions toward the end came chiefly as a result of the certainty that the United States really meant war—a mere "bluff" would not have served. Furthermore, a peace with continuance of Spanish rule in Cuba would have meant a continuance of the existent evils, or their recurrence at some future time. The war that actually followed, to quote a vigorous critic of the Government's policy at the time,[1] "quickly ended the horrors and destitution of chronic insurrectionary hostilities and saved thereby the lives of hundreds of thousands, not only of Spanish soldiers, but of Cuban *insurrectos* and civilian population, men, women, and children. It was in this sense a merciful war."

In response to the President's message, Congress passed a joint resolution on April 19, by a vote of forty-two to thirty-five in the Senate and 311 to six in the House, which declared:

> First, that the people of Cuba are, and of right ought to be, free and independent. Second, that it is the duty of the United States to demand, and the Government does hereby demand, that the Government of Spain at once relinquish its authority and government in the island of Cuba and withdraw its land and naval forces from Cuba and Cuban waters. Third, that the President . . . is directed and empowered to use the entire land and naval forces . . . to carry these resolutions into effect. Fourth, that the United States hereby disclaims any disposition or intention to exercise sovereignty, jurisdiction, or control over said island except for the pacification thereof, and asserts its determination when that is accomplished to leave the government and control of the island to its people.

This last clause was the famous Teller Amendment, passed unanimously, which expressed the high sentiments with which

[1] S. F. Bemis, *A Diplomatic History of the United States*, p. 463.

the President, the Congress, and the great majority of the American people entered the war.

On April 20 the President signed the joint resolution and called upon Spain to accede to the demands therein expressed by noon of the twenty-third. A blockade of northern Cuba was proclaimed on the twenty-second, and on the twenty-fifth, in the absence of a reply from Spain, Congress declared a state of war to have existed since the twenty-first.

Comparison of Forces

It was evident to all that the war would be primarily naval, and would be decided in favor of the nation able to establish control in the waters around Cuba. This granted, and in view of the one-sided character of later naval events, it may seem surprising that even competent European critics, such as Admiral Colomb in England, should have prophesied a stalemate, "a long, desultory war."[2] On paper, however, there was no such disparity between the two navies as was afterward shown, for statistics did not reveal the bankruptcy of Spain's naval resources, the woeful condition of her ships, the lack of training of her crews, the absence of initiative, aggressiveness, or aught save high courage in her officer personnel.

Even on paper Spain had nothing to match the four new battleships which formed the backbone of the American fleet—the *Iowa, Indiana, Massachusetts,* and *Oregon,* each of about 10,000 tons and mounting four 12- or 13-inch and eight 8-inch guns. Other first-line ships were the armored cruisers *Brooklyn* (9,215 tons) and *New York* (8,200 tons), with a speed of over twenty-one knots, and the older battleship *Texas.* While Spain had a second-rate battleship *Pelayo* and an armored cruiser *Carlos V,* not in readiness for service, her major units actually available at the outbreak of war were limited to the four 7,000-ton armored cruisers of Cervera's squadron, *Infanta*

---

[2] Captain Mahan's forecast, "about three months," was very nearly accurate. See Puleston, *Life of Mahan,* p. 186.

Maria Teresa, Almirante Oquendo, Vizcaya, and *Cristóbal Colón.* The last named was a new Italian-built ship, rated better than the *Brooklyn*—if she had not sailed without her two best 10-inch guns. In lesser types the American superiority in protected cruisers was eleven to three; in unprotected cruisers and gunboats, twenty to twelve. Spain's only advantage lay in thirteen of what were then the larger type of torpedo craft, ranging from 750 to 380 tons, of which the United States had none completed; but this was more than counterbalanced by the six American double-turreted monitors, heavily armed and of considerable value in protected waters.

Initial Moves

In the first part of April the Spanish Admiral, Cervera, with the cruisers mentioned in the preceding paragraph, had joined a destroyer flotilla in the Portuguese Cape Verde Islands, some 1,500 miles nearer than Spain to the probable theater of war. His letters at this time and earlier reveal, and largely justify, his gloomy outlook on events to come. He lacked adequate charts, or news of the enemy's distribution and movements, or information of the Ministry's plan—if indeed it had a plan—for conduct of the naval campaign. The *Colón* was without her heavy guns; the *Vizcaya,* just returned from Cuba, was so foul under water that with a trial speed of twenty knots she could hardly make thirteen. In view of these conditions, Cervera and his captains unanimously favored taking a defensive position in the Canary Islands. But this would mean practically abandoning the colonies. In response to urgent calls for aid from the authorities in Cuba and Puerto Rico, the Ministry ordered the Admiral to sail on April 29 for the Caribbean with his four cruisers and the destroyers *Furor, Pluton,* and *Terror.* His force was spoken of as the "first division," and there was talk of others to follow. But, to quote a Spanish naval officer, "From the admiral down to the last midshipman, they knew perfectly well that there were no more fleets, no more divisions, no more vessels, and that these six [3] ships (if the destroyers may be regarded as such) were all that could be counted on to oppose the American fleet." Cervera's instructions were concerned chiefly with the defense of Puerto Rico. To the Americans, informed immediately of his departure by a cable from the United States consul in the islands, his destination and purposes remained a matter of surmise.

While the Spanish fleet was steaming slowly westward, the United States battleship *Oregon,* ordered from Seattle to the East Coast on March 7, was on the last stage of her famous 14,-700 mile cruise. Leaving San Francisco on March 21, she made the journey in the record time of sixty-six days, with an average speed at sea of 11.6 knots. The voyage, which ended with the ship in complete readiness for further service, was a remarkable engineering performance, and at the same time afforded an excellent argument against divided forces and in favor of an isthmian canal.

The *Oregon* joined the North Atlantic Squadron, based on Key West. Since January, this force had been operating in southern waters in increasing readiness for war. For reasons of ill health, the commander in chief, Rear Admiral Montgomery Sicard, was succeeded on March 26 by Captain William T. Sampson of the *Iowa,* whose appointment, over seventeen officers higher on the Navy List, was determined by careful departmental consideration of his outstanding record in the development of the new Navy. As one writer has put it, the Santiago campaign was won "by officers whom he had drilled, on ships that he had constructed and armored, equipped with guns that he had built." With something less of stiffness and reserve, which were increased by the tremendous strain of the ensuing campaign, Sampson might have been more readily accorded later the full recognition that he deserved.

Admiral Sicard was appointed to a "Strategy Board" in

---

[3] The *Terror* was left at Martinique because of boiler trouble. The quotation is from Tejeiro, *Battles and Capitulation of Santiago de Cuba,* published by the United States Office of Naval Intelligence, *War Notes,* No. 1, p. 28.

Washington, which included Rear Admiral A. S. Crowninshield of the Bureau of Navigation and Captain Mahan,[4] the function of which was to advise the Secretary on the general conduct of the naval war. Thus for the first time the Navy entered hostilities with a kind of improvised general staff, a body necessary since even then the development of modern communications tended to center the conduct of operations in the Navy Department rather than in the command at sea. For the brief period and limited problems of the Spanish war, the Strategy Board served reasonably well.

As early as March, plans were put into effect for separating the Atlantic forces into two divisions, of which the main part, including the *New York* (flagship), *Iowa, Indiana,* and later the *Oregon,* with the bulk of the minor units, was to operate under Sampson at Key West; while a so-called "Flying Squadron," consisting of the *Brooklyn* (flagship), *Massachusetts, Texas,* and the light cruiser *New Orleans,* under Commodore Winfield S. Schley, was based at Hampton Roads. Though seemingly a not unreasonable measure of precaution against a possible Spanish raid on the North Atlantic coast, this division was later condemned by Mahan and cited as an example of the evil effect that popular agitation might have on naval strategy. Upon news of Cervera's advance westward this clamor rose to ludicrous extremes, the press and people calling loudly for ships and guns in every port and bay. As a further concession, of little or no military value, a "Patrol Squadron" consisting of the *San Francisco* and several auxiliary cruisers was organized to cover the coast north of the Delaware capes.

The first hostile move was the advance of the Key West forces on April 22 for the blockade of Havana and about 140 miles of adjoining coast. Sampson had earlier urged upon the Department a plan for the bombardment of Havana, on the ground that its defenses could be reduced without serious injury to his ships and that the fall of the city would quickly end the war. Although his plan was based on careful study, and

---

[4] Appointed May 9, after his recall from a tour abroad.

might quite possibly have succeeded, the Department's reply took the sound strategic ground that the enemy squadron must be the first objective, and that our ships must not be risked against "strongly fortified ports" unless the Spanish fleet were within. It is not unlikely that fears of possible support for Spain by other European powers figured in this veto of the plan. Incidents of blockade enforcement now occupied Sampson's squadron until the news came on May 1 of the sailing of Cervera two days before.

Leaving the consequences of this move for another chapter, we may now turn to the stirring events which intervened in a far distant, and for most Americans wholly unexpected, theater of war.

The Manila Campaign

In the Far East, our Asiatic Squadron was under Commodore George Dewey, whose appointment, late in the preceding year, had been brought about largely through the skilful management of Theodore Roosevelt, then Assistant Secretary of the Navy. "I want you to go," Roosevelt had told Dewey. "You are the man who will be equal to the emergency if one arises." [5] Before leaving for the East, Dewey made a careful study of books and charts relating to his area of command, and saw to it that his ships should not lack a full supply of ammunition, though the second shipment reached Hongkong in the *Baltimore* only just at the outbreak of war. After February he kept his force of light cruisers in readiness at Hongkong. It included the flagship *Olympia* (5,870 tons), *Boston, Raleigh, Concord,* and the little gunboat *Preble.* The *Baltimore* (3,113 tons) joined on April 22, and the revenue cutter *McCulloch* a few days before.

On February 25 Dewey had received a message from Roosevelt, who on that particular day was Acting Secretary: "Keep

[5] For the quotation, as well as the politics in the appointment, see Dewey, *Autobiography,* p. 168.

full of coal. In the event of war with Spain, your duty will be to see that the Spanish squadron does not leave Asiatic coast, and then offensive operations in the Philippines." It was a significant order, made apparently without consultation even with Secretary Long, yet committing the nation to a campaign and possible conquests in a region which the President himself, as he confessed later, could not locate "within 2,000 miles." But the Commodore's preparations needed little prompting. As war approached, he purchased two British ships and loaded them with coal and supplies, dismantled the old gunboat *Monocacy* and distributed her crew among the other ships, and arranged for a temporary base at Mirs Bay, twenty miles distant in Chinese waters, where he would not be bothered by neutrality rules. Up to the last moment he was busy distributing the final shipment of ammunition, and painting his white ships a wartime gray.

On April 25 came the final stirring dispatch: "War has commenced between the United States and Spain. Proceed at once to Philippine Islands. Commence operations particularly against the Spanish fleet. You must capture vessels or destroy. Use utmost endeavor." In these orders, unlike those to Sampson, there were no restrictions against risks; and there was no hesitation in their execution, though it involved attacking an enemy fleet in a supposedly mined and strongly fortified harbor, with no assured base of supplies for the attacking force within 7,000 miles. Dewey moved to Mirs Bay on the twenty-fifth, and after waiting until the arrival of Mr. Williams, United States Consul at Manila, with latest news of Spanish preparations, he sailed on the twenty-seventh for the Philippines.

Throwing overboard all spare fittings and woodwork on the way, the squadron reached the Philippine coast early on the thirtieth. The next move was a thorough search of Subic Bay, near the entrance to Manila, which the Spanish force under Admiral Montojo had expected to occupy, but had abandoned just the day before. Dewey now planned to seek out the enemy at once by passing that night through the entrance into Manila

Bay. There was a council of captains on the flagship, but no written orders, for, as the commodore stated, "Every preparation that had occurred to us . . . had already been made."

The broad opening into Manila Bay is divided into two channels, the larger or Bocca Grande being about three and a half miles in width and seventeen to thirty fathoms deep. According to Dewey's calculations, the depth and currents would prevent effective mining by the methods of that day, while the width of the channel would prevent effective fire from the batteries on shore during a night passage.

With men at quarters and all lights extinguished save a single guide light at the stern, the column, led by the flagship, approached the entrance at about midnight. In the moonlight broken by passing clouds, the ships must have been visible to lookouts on shore. Signal lights were seen flashing, and shortly after twelve, when the leading ships had already passed the narrows, four or five shots were fired from a battery on the rock of El Fraile, on the south side of the channel. These fell wide but were answered by shells from the ships in the rear. There were seventeen heavy guns guarding the entrance, eight of which were modern breech-loading rifles. Three 6-inch rifles on Caballo and three 4.7-inch rifles on El Fraile bore directly on the Bocca Grande. There were launches and gunboats at Manila that might have been fitted out for torpedo attack. The ease of the entry was due to the almost complete failure of the Spanish to utilize available means of defense.

In his decision to enter the bay, the American commodore, as he writes in his *Autobiography,* was guided by his conviction that "the Spanish would stand upon the defensive . . . and the more aggressive and prompt our action the smaller would be our losses." In both thoroughness of preparation and resolute speed of execution, he profited also by the example of Farragut, under whom he had served in the Mississippi operations of the Civil War. On this we have his own testimony:

Whenever I have been in a difficult situation, or in the midst of such a confusion of details that the simple and right thing to do seemed hazy, I have often asked myself, "What would Farragut do?" In the course of the preparations for Manila Bay I often asked myself this question, and I confess I was thinking of him the night that we entered the bay, and with the conviction that I was doing precisely what he would have done.

With speed slowed to four knots, the squadron sighted the spires and shipping of Manila through the mists of early dawn. Montojo's ships were at first not in evidence, for to avoid injury to the city he had sacrificed the great military advantage of fighting under the support of the city batteries, which included twelve modern rifles, several of them superior to anything in the American squadron.

Instead, he had taken a position six miles to westward across the mouth of the bay between the Cavite Arsenal and Sangley Point. The seven ships there lined up constituted a motley collection, the largest of them being the flagship *Reina Cristina* of about 3,500 tons and the old wooden ship *Castilla,* unable to move under her own power but moored with springs and protected by stone-laden scows. The five others were small gunboats of from 500 to 1,100 tons, some of which are described as moving about during the battle "in an aimless fashion, often masking each other's fire." Some auxiliary vessels and four little torpedo craft were anchored closer inshore. There were no mines. The Manila batteries were too far distant; the two 5.9-inch guns on Sangley Point might have proved a menace, though it turned out that they could not be depressed to fire at the closer ranges of the action. The Spanish had only thirty-one guns afloat to the Americans' fifty-three, and nothing to match the combined battery of ten 8-inch guns in the *Olympia, Baltimore,* and *Boston.* Hence, there is truth in the English historian H. W. Wilson's comment that Manila was "a military execution rather than a real contest"—but truth also in Admiral Chadwick's remark that a reversal in marksmanship might have reversed the results.

Dewey had headed for the Spanish fleet. After closing to about 5,000 yards, at 5:40 A.M. he gave his often-quoted order

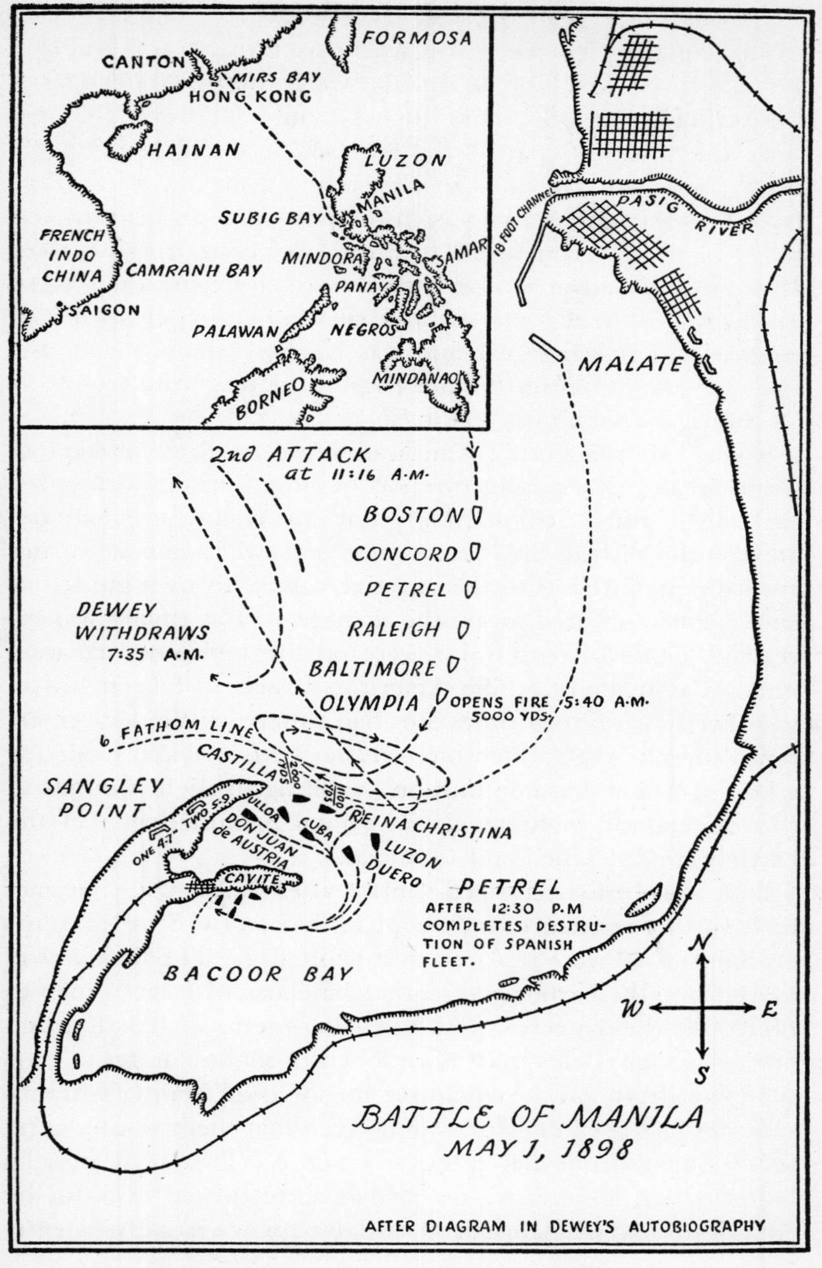
FORMOSA
CANTON
MIRS BAY
HONG KONG
HAINAN
LUZON
MANILA
SUBIG BAY
FRENCH
INDO
CHINA
CAMRANH BAY
SAIGON
MINDORO
SAMAR
PANAY
PALAWAN
NEGROS
BORNEO
MINDANAO
18 FOOT CHANNEL
PASIG
RIVER
MALATE
2nd ATTACK
at 11:16 A.M.
BOSTON
CONCORD
PETREL
RALEIGH
BALTIMORE
OLYMPIA
OPENS FIRE 5:40 A.M.
5000 YDS.
DEWEY
WITHDRAWS
7:35 A.M.
6 FATHOM LINE
CASTILLA
2000 YDS
1100 YDS
SANGLEY
POINT
ONE 4.7
TWO 5.9
ULLOA
CUBA
REINA CHRISTINA
DON JUAN
de AUSTRIA
LUZON
DUERO
CAVITE
PETREL
AFTER 12:30 P.M
COMPLETES DESTRU-
TION OF SPANISH
FLEET.
BACOOR BAY
N
W
E
S
BATTLE OF MANILA
MAY 1, 1898
AFTER DIAGRAM IN DEWEY'S AUTOBIOGRAPHY

to his captain, "You may fire when you are ready, Gridley." But firing did not become general until the ships had swung westward along the 5-fathom line, at about 4,000 yards. Thereafter the squadron passed the Spanish fleet and the Sangley battery at about six knots in long ellipses, making three runs from the eastward and two from the westward, and closing the range in the last run to 2,000 yards. At about 7:00 A.M., the *Reina Cristina* advanced gallantly as if to close with the American flagship, but was met by a terrific fire which crippled her engines and steering gear and was largely responsible for the total of 220 casualties on the flagship alone. Montojo soon afterward shifted his flag to the *Isla de Cuba.*

Shortly after 7:30, the American squadron drew off temporarily because of a mistaken report of ammunition shortage for the 5-inch guns. Up to this point the enemy fire had not greatly diminished, and Dewey was somewhat uncertain and even disappointed as to the effectiveness of his own guns; but as the smoke cleared away, the damage to the enemy was revealed. Some of their ships were on fire and some aground under Cavite Point. The American vessels had been hit altogether about fifteen times, but had suffered little damage except from one shell which pierced the *Baltimore* and exploded a box of 3-pounder ammunition, resulting in slight wounds to two officers and eight men. The total Spanish losses in the battle were 381 killed and wounded.

The squadron re-engaged shortly after 11:00 A.M., but met little further resistance, and about 12:30 P.M. the Spanish colors on the Arsenal were replaced by a white flag. The little *Petrel* moved into the harbor and sent a whaleboat with seven men to undertake the dangerous task of setting fire to some half dozen of the smaller enemy craft abandoned in shallow water.

In the afternoon the squadron anchored off Manila, after assurances had been demanded and given that there would be no further firing from the batteries on shore. Two days later the batteries at the entrance to the bay were turned over to the Americans and dismantled. Manila was now virtually defenseless, and its occupation awaited only the arrival of American troops. The cable from Manila had been cut on the night after the battle, but despite the first misleading reports the American public shortly had accurate news of the victory, and greeted it with a wave of enthusiasm which soon swept the Government into full acceptance of the Eastern war, with all the responsibilities entailed.

Pending the arrival of troops and of two monitors from the West Coast, Dewey was occupied with innumerable problems of blockade enforcement, dealings with the Spanish authorities and Philippine insurgents, defense against mines and torpedo attack, and the danger involved in the dispatch from Spain of another squadron under Admiral Camara. This force, which included the *Pelayo* and *Carlos V,* left Cadiz on June 16 and had reached Suez when it was called back because of an American threat against the coast of Spain.

Equally troublesome were the diplomatic problems which developed upon the arrival in the harbor of British, German, Japanese, and other foreign men-of-war. The Germans, though their trade and property interests at Manila were far less than those of the British, assembled there at one time a force of five ships under Rear Admiral von Diederichs, estimated as about 20 per cent stronger than that of Dewey. The Germans were not overtly hostile, but had come there with the idea that, if colonies were to be picked up, by transfer, purchase, or otherwise, they should not miss the opportunity. British and Japanese policy, on the other hand, far preferred that the islands should come under American rather than German control. Meanwhile, whether or not through unfamiliarity with international usages, the Germans landed forces for drills, carried on extended communications with the Spanish, and disregarded the American rules for identification of ships entering or leaving the port. When they remonstrated over the stopping of the *Irene* on June 27, Dewey declared that the German ships must reveal their identity, and that if they did not they would be fired on. "And I tell you," he added, "if

Germany wants war, all right, we are ready."[6] The first American troops arrived at the close of June. The German naval forces were later reduced, and the trouble quieted down.

At the occupation of Manila on August 13, the naval bombardment was only formal, as the Spanish had arranged to surrender after a mere show of resistance. In the movement of foreign naval vessels before the action, the British ships *Iphigenia* and *Immortalité* are generally stated to have taken a position between the Germans and the Americans, as a warning against interference. That the moves actually had this significance has not been fully proved.

The story of American naval operations during the Philippine Insurrection belongs to a subsequent chapter. The immediate effect of Dewey's victory was to project the United States vigorously into Far Eastern affairs, with new possessions, influence, and responsibilities, at a time when China appeared about to become a spoil of the Western powers.

References:

See end of Chapter XIX.

[6] As quoted by the German staff officer to whom the words were addressed. See T. H. Bailey, "Dewey and the Germans at Manila Bay," *American Historical Review*, Oct., 1939. Others present have quoted Dewey's statement in slightly different form.

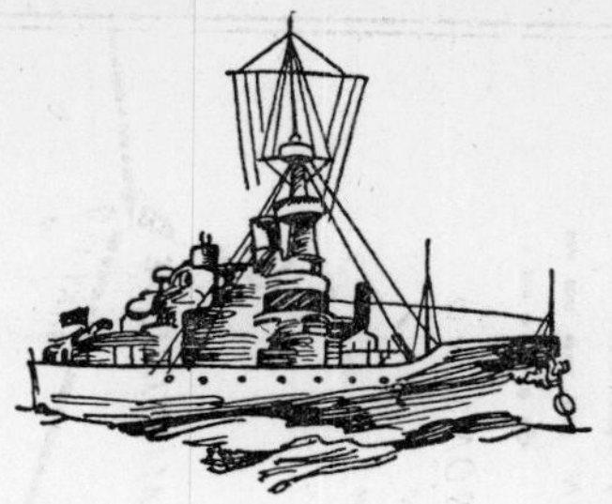

THE SANTIAGO CAMPAIGN

XIX

IMMERSED IN HIS own difficulties, the most immediate of which was constant boiler trouble in his destroyers and the necessity of towing them most of the way across the Atlantic, Admiral Cervera could hardly have imagined the problems which his approach raised for the American authorities. There was concern over the *Oregon,* whose arrival in the West Indies and that of Cervera would nearly coincide. There was the possibility that the Spanish cruisers would attempt a raid on East Coast ports and commerce—a possibility discounted by the Navy Department but good material for scareheads in the press. If their destination was the West Indies, it might be either Havana or the southern port of Cienfuegos, in Cuba, or more probably the intervening Puerto Rican base at San Juan. This advance of a European force into the western Atlantic, if new to American experience, was one which conceivably might be faced in later times, and for this reason the dispositions and movements before Cervera was actually cornered at Santiago have an even greater interest and significance than the subsequent blockade and destruction of his squadron.

When Sampson on April 30 received word that the Spanish squadron had sailed, he was convinced—rightly as revealed later by the Spanish orders—that its first objective would be San Juan. Accordingly, though in doing so he seriously weakened the blockade off Havana, he proceeded thither on May 3

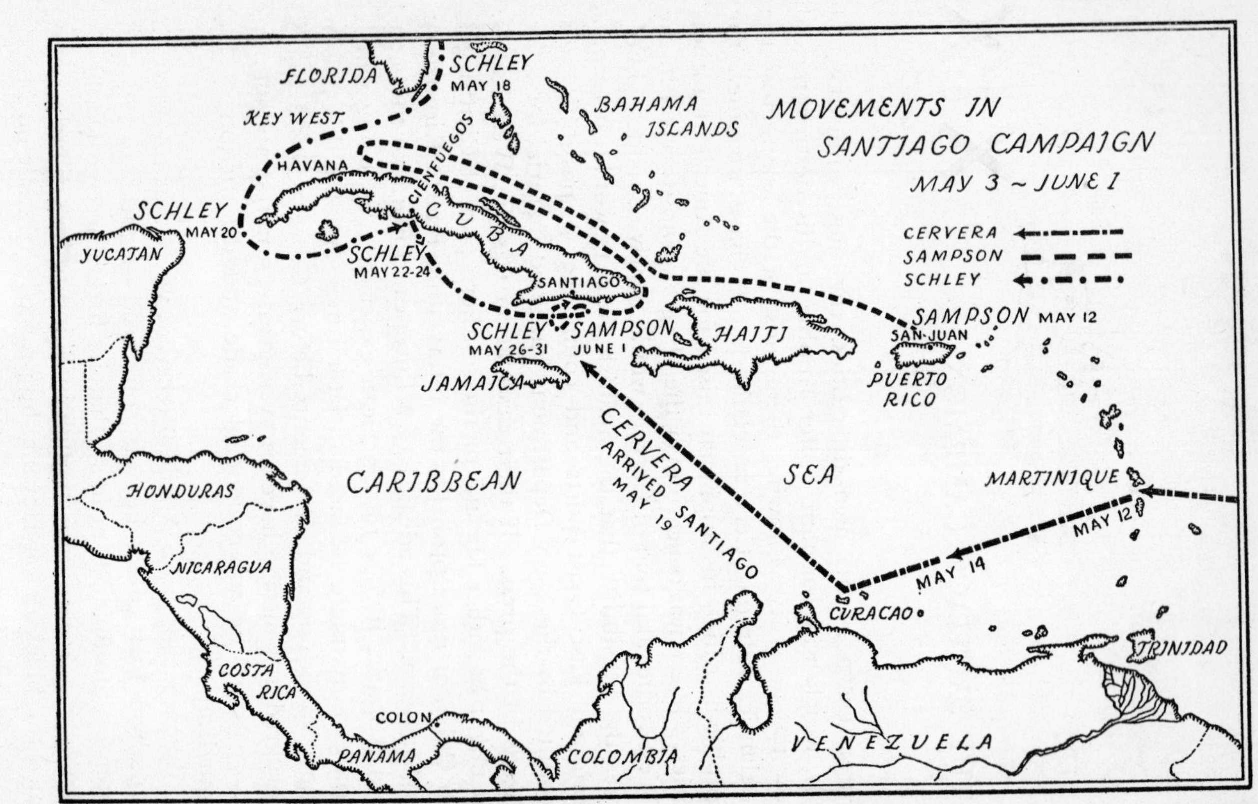
MOVEMENTS IN
SANTIAGO CAMPAIGN
MAY 3 ~ JUNE 1
CERVERA
SAMPSON
SCHLEY
FLORIDA
SCHLEY
MAY 18
KEY WEST
BAHAMA
ISLANDS
HAVANA
CIENFUEGOS
SCHLEY
MAY 20
CUBA
SCHLEY
MAY 22-24
YUCATAN
SANTIAGO
SAMPSON MAY 12
SAN JUAN
SCHLEY
MAY 26-31
SAMPSON
JUNE 1
HAITI
PUERTO
RICO
JAMAICA
CERVERA
ARRIVED
MAY 19
SANTIAGO
SEA
MARTINIQUE
CARIBBEAN
HONDURAS
MAY 12
MAY 14
NICARAGUA
CURACAO
TRINIDAD
COSTA
RICA
COLON
PANAMA
COLOMBIA
VENEZUELA

with the *New York, Indiana, Iowa,* two monitors, and some lighter craft. Like the Spanish destroyers, the monitors were an endless nuisance because they developed boiler trouble, and he was eight days covering the 960 miles. To his great disappointment, he found no signs of the Spanish ships. Next morning, after subjecting the San Juan defenses to a three-hour bombardment, he had no recourse but to fall back on Havana at best speed.

Cervera's Advance

The Spanish admiral, instead of steering directly for Puerto Rico, had taken a course considerably southward, and had escaped contact with the inadequate American scouting force, the converted liners *Yale, St. Louis,* and *Harvard,* which were cruising around Puerto Rico and east of the Lesser Antilles. On the very day of Sampson's arrival at San Juan, May 11, Cervera was off Martinique, and sent the destroyers *Furor* and *Terror* into Fort de France for news. On this same day, also, the *Harvard* chanced to put in at the near-by Martinique port of St. Pierre. American officers heard of the destroyers, caught sight of cruisers on the horizon, and soon had this all-important information on the cables for Washington.

The *Furor,* stealing out the same night, brought Cervera plenty of discouraging news—of the defeat at Manila, the blockade at Havana and Cienfuegos, the governor's denial of coal at Martinique, the presence there of an American scout, and finally (through a press leak which set Sampson more than ever against the swarming press flotilla) of the American ships at San Juan. Turning westward at eleven knots, Cervera put in on May 14 at the Dutch port of Curaçoa, where his arrival was again promptly cabled north. Thence, having managed to get enough coal for immediate needs, he steamed northwest for Santiago de Cuba, which seemed the last port open, and no doubt he gave fervent thanks when on the morning of the nineteenth he led his squadron through the tortuous channel into the bay. His freedom of exit was to remain completely unimpeded for the next ten days.

American Countermoves

What were the American countermoves during this time? Sent southward at the first news from Martinique, Commodore Schley's Flying Squadron reached Key West on May 18, and Sampson, who had received the message as he steamed westward from San Juan, was there on the same day. At this time the Department was under the influence of erroneous information that Cervera carried munitions essential for the Spanish forces at Havana, and must enter either that port or Cienfuegos, which had rail connections with the capital. Accordingly, Sampson resumed station off Havana, and the Flying Squadron, with the *Iowa* as a re-enforcement, was dispatched with all speed around the west coast of Cuba to Cienfuegos, where it now seemed certain the quarry would be run down.

Scarcely had Schley left when evidence began to accumulate that the Spanish squadron was actually at Santiago. On the night of the twenty-first Sampson wrote to Schley: "Spanish squadron probably at Santiago—four ships and three torpedo-boat destroyers. If you are satisfied they are not at Cienfuegos, proceed with all dispatch, but cautiously, to Santiago de Cuba, and, if the enemy is there, blockade him in that port."

Sent by the fastest dispatch boat available, this reached Schley on the twenty-third, the morning after his arrival. In fact, during the advance toward Cienfuegos, the Flying Squadron had proceeded slowly, and, both then and later, hardly lived up to its name. Commodore Schley could not get a view of the harbor from outside, but had seen "considerable smoke." He had been told of means of contact with the Cuban insurgents, who could have given exact information, but this means was not used until the twenty-fourth. Not until the evening of that day was the departure made for Santiago, and, owing to trouble of one of his gunboats with head seas, the 315 miles thither was covered at an average speed of only seven knots. Once there, on the afternoon of the twenty-sixth, he made contact with the scouts *Yale, St. Paul,* and *Minneapolis,* all of which had been off Santiago at various times since the twenty-first but had not sighted the Spanish ships or verified the reports that they were inside. Schley was greatly worried over coal supply, for, though he had a collier with him, he had been prevented by rough weather from coaling at sea. That night came his extraordinary order to the squadron to get under way—"destination Key West!" Not much progress was actually made, for there was further delay over engine trouble in the collier, and next morning the *Harvard* came up with a sharp message from the Department: "All Department's information indicates Spanish division still at Santiago. The Department looks to you to ascertain facts, and that the enemy, if therein, does not leave without decisive action . . ."

To this the Commodore replied in a dispatch sent by the *Harvard* from Jamaica. It emphasized the coaling difficulties and ended with regret that ". . . the Department's orders cannot be obeyed, earnestly as we have striven to that end. I am forced to return to Key West, via Yucatan Passage, for coal. Can ascertain nothing certain concerning enemy. . . ."

The westerly movement was resumed that afternoon, but fortunately, the weather moderating, coaling operations were found feasible, and next day (the twenty-eighth) the column turned toward Santiago, still only thirty-seven miles distant. That night Schley halted about ten miles off the entrance and sent the *Marblehead* to scout closer in. Next morning the *Colón* was plainly to be seen at the harbor mouth and another Spanish ship farther inside. For the next two days the American vessels cruised about near the entrance, but not until the thirty-first was the *Colón* fired on, by the *Massachusetts, Iowa,* and *New Orleans,* at ranges too great for damage to either side.

In view of the many problems faced by Commodore Schley, and the ultimate success of the campaign, it is unlikely that much criticism of his operations up to this point would have arisen, had it not been for the unfortunate Sampson-Schley controversy after the war, and the resultant court of inquiry. The court pronounced Commodore Schley's conduct of operations up to June 1 as characterized by "vacillation, dilatoriness, and lack of enterprise," basing their opinion largely on the slow movements of his squadron, the "retrograde" turn westward, the delay in executing the Department's order of the twenty-fifth, and the tardy and ineffective attack on the *Colón*.

Within Santiago, Admiral Cervera had found little help in the way of coal, supplies, or facilities for repair. On the twenty-fifth and twenty-sixth he was on the point of leaving for San Juan, and could freely have done so, though he was deterred by fears raised by the scouting vessels outside. As Captain Mahan remarked in his *Lessons of the War with Spain*, "We cannot expect ever again to have an enemy as inapt as Spain showed herself to be."

Blockade of Santiago

Sampson reached Santiago on June 1 and at once issued orders for a close blockade. The battleships were stationed in a semicircle about six miles (later reduced to four) offshore, with smaller cruisers and picket launches farther in. At night the ships were to move closer, and after June 8, a searchlight from one of the battleships, two miles distant, was held directly on the entrance, to reveal and hinder a night sortie. If the enemy made such an attempt, by night or day, the orders were to "close in and engage as soon as possible and endeavor to sink his vessels or drive them ashore." About a week after the beginning of the blockade, a marine force was landed at Guantanamo Bay, forty miles east of Santiago, and after some fighting on shore, a sheltered base was established there for coaling and repair.

From the outset the chief obstacle to an entry into Santiago was, not the relatively weak shore batteries, but the mine fields known to be planted in the narrow channel, and the impossibility of clearing these without a landing force sufficient to seize and hold the defenses on shore. Risking battleships by attempting to run through the mines was negatived not only by departmental orders, but by the danger that the sinking of a single ship might block the channel with part of the force outside and part within.

To end all chance of Cervera's escape, which still seemed a possibility by night or after a severe gale, plans were at once made to sink a blockship across the channel. Before dawn, on June 3, this operation was gallantly attempted by Assistant Naval Constructor Richmond P. Hobson and seven volunteers in the collier *Merrimac,* which was to be run ashore in the narrows and sunk by explosive charges as her stern swung across channel in the flood tide. The *Merrimac,* however, came under heavy fire from both banks, her steering gear was cut, and when finally sunk she had drifted beyond the point intended and presented no serious obstacle. With but two men slightly wounded after all the firing, Hobson and his crew were later picked up by Admiral Cervera himself in a steam launch. Word of their rescue was sent out to Sampson under a flag of truce, and the prisoners were well treated until their exchange on July 6.

The need for combined operations at Santiago, already indicated, offered a welcome opportunity for the expeditionary force under General Shafter, which had already been organized for a brief expedition to Cuba but not—in the summer heat—for a large-scale campaign. Seventeen thousand troops embarked at Tampa in thirty-two army transports, escorted by ten naval vessels under Captain Goodrich, and on June 20 reached Santiago.

Here the destruction of the Spanish fleet, as the sole objective of the operations, was apparently forgotten; the naval proposal for a limited combined attack on the defenses at the entrance was discarded for inadequate reasons, and the Army decided to march into the interior for investment of the city itself on the north and east. In disregard of useful experience gained in the Civil War, the combined operation ceased to have such a character, and provided, rather, an example to be avoided in later times. To quote Captain French E. Chadwick, Admiral Sampson's chief of staff and author of the standard history of the war: "The Army . . . finally did by brute force and much loss that which might have been accomplished with little loss had the operation been carried on with the assistance of a trained staff and the co-operation which the Navy was only too anxious to give." The cause, as Chadwick saw it, was "not want of good will, of which there was plenty," but chiefly "the want of a general staff system in both the War and Navy Departments, which prevented intimate understanding and mutual study of conditions as they arose."

The landing at Daiquiri, ten miles east of Santiago, and on the second day at Siboney, five miles east, was, as Colonel Theodore Roosevelt described it, "done in a scramble." Without naval officers aboard, most of the transports could not be induced to come within reasonable distance of the shore, and the disembarkation could hardly have been accomplished without naval supervision and provision of forty navy boats and twelve steam launches. Most of the troops were got ashore on the twenty-second and twenty-third, but not all of them until the twenty-sixth. In a letter of thanks, General Shafter frankly admitted that without naval assistance he "could not have landed in ten days and perhaps not at all." Fortunately, the landing was entirely unopposed. Naval artillery covered the disembarkation, but though available and within effective range, it was not utilized in subsequent army operations. By July 2 the Army had captured San Juan Hill and threatened the city, but had lost 1,475 killed and wounded, or 10 per cent of the forces engaged. Retreat was seriously considered. Though since the landing there had been no consultation between the army and navy leaders, General Shafter now wrote to the Admiral: "Terrible fight yesterday . . . I urge that you make effort immediately to force the entrance to avoid future losses among my men, which are already heavy. You can now operate with less loss of life than I can. . . ." Thus the Army, which had been brought to Santiago to help solve a primarily naval problem, was placing itself in an opposite role.

It was to consult with the General on measures to force the entrance that Admiral Sampson moved eastward toward Siboney in his flagship at 9:00 A.M. on July 3. But the problems of both Army and Navy were simplified by Admiral Cervera's choice of this very moment for his sortie.

The Spanish admiral had himself no relish for such a course, which he condemned as "a useless hecatomb . . . of lives sacrificed on the altar of vanity." But he was forced to it by mandatory orders from General Blanco in Havana. There was, in fact, some justification for Blanco's view, which was shared by Sampson and other American naval officers, that a sortie by night still offered possibilities; with guiding lights on shore to aid in navigating the entrance, and then a melee amid blinding smoke and confusion of friend and foe, it was thought that some at least of the Spanish ships might escape. Cervera, however, chose to leave by daylight.

The Battle of Santiago

For a day exit the time chosen was opportune, since the *New York* was off station and the *Massachusetts* was at Guantanamo for coal. The Spanish plan, if it could be so called, was for the flagship *Infanta Maria Teresa* to steer for the fastest American ship, the *Brooklyn,* at the west side of the semicircle, if possible injure her by gunfire or ramming, and thus open a gap for escape westward along the coast. As a last resort, captains were to sink their ships after running them ashore. At 9:35, as the *Teresa* came outside, her bugles sounded the call for battle, a signal which, as her commander Captain Conchas wrote later, meant that "four centuries of greatness was ended and that Spain had passed into the ranks of secondary powers."

Sighting the smoke of the *Teresa* even before she appeared, the *New York,* which was now five miles distant, hoisted the signal for action and at once turned westward. Men on the

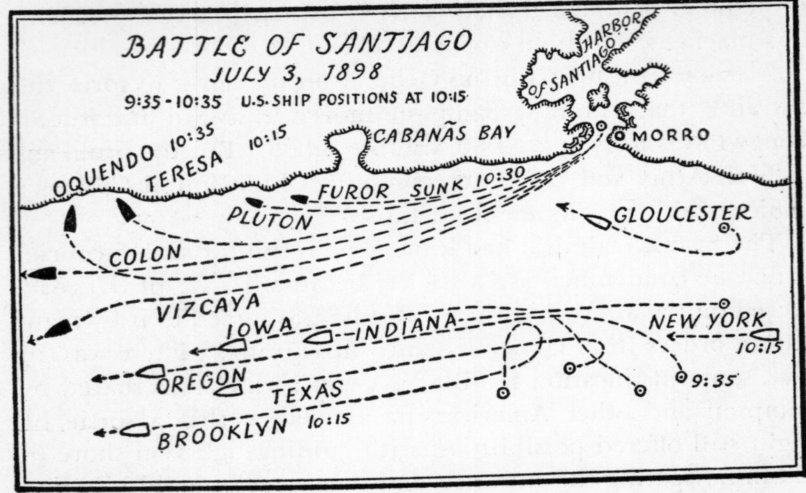

big blockaders ran to their stations, and forced draft was applied as the ships closed in. The *Brooklyn* at first was heading about north, but as the *Teresa* rapidly closed the range and seemed likely to ram or to put the *Brooklyn* in a blanketing position, the American cruiser swung around, not to the westward (left), but in the opposite direction, across the bows of her sister ships nearest by. Though there was some later conflict of testimony, officers of the *Texas* were convinced that only the quick backing of their ship prevented a collision. As the *Texas* checked speed, the *Iowa,* and next to her the *Oregon,* the latter with full steam pressure and high-grade coal, long saved for this emergency, surged by.

After nearly ten minutes the Spanish flagship was followed by the *Vizcaya, Cristóbal Colón,* and *Almirante Oquendo,* and last of all by the two little destroyers *Plutón* and *Furor*. In the initial concentration, the *Teresa* came under a hail of fire. With steam lines cut, main pump out of action, wooden decks and fittings burning fiercely, she turned slowly toward the shore at ten o'clock and grounded about four miles west of the entrance.

The American fire was next concentrated upon the last Spanish cruiser, the *Oquendo*. This ship, according to Lieutenant Eberle of the *Oregon*, "made the pluckiest fight and suffered the most severe punishment, as attested by her torn and battered hull," which about 10:35 finally rested on the beach half a mile west of the *Teresa*.

As smaller craft engaged in the work of rescue, pursuit now centered on the *Vizcaya*, about two miles distant, while the *Colón*, inshore and farther ahead, was still increasing her lead. Under heavy punishment from the *Oregon*, *Brooklyn*, and more distant ships, the *Vizcaya* turned shoreward just after eleven, her crew huddled forward, clear of the flames. Shortly after she struck, about fifteen miles from the entrance, a column of smoke was driven a thousand feet in the air by the explosion of her forward magazine.

The Spanish destroyers came under heavy fire from the *Indiana*, which had started from the east side of the entrance, and from the secondary batteries of other ships. They were finished off by the little converted yacht *Gloucester*, Lieutenant Commander Wainwright, which boldly closed in to six hundred yards and later sent boats for survivors. The *Furor* was disabled and sunk, and the *Plutón* blew up after running ashore.

After twelve o'clock the *Colón*, which up to that time had averaged nearly fourteen knots, began to lose distance, and about 1:15 the *Oregon*, at a range of 9,000 yards, placed a 13-inch shell just beyond her bow. Though scarcely injured, the last Spanish cruiser now struck her colors and ran ashore, where she opened her sea-cocks and went to the bottom that night, mostly submerged on a steeply shelving ledge. In her last dash she had run over fifty miles.

Of the rescue work which occupied the afternoon, Admiral Sampson remarks, "It was the occasion of some of the most daring and gallant conduct of the day. The ships were burning fore and aft, their guns and reserve ammunition were exploding, and it was not known at what moment the fire would reach the main magazines. In addition, a heavy surf was running just inside the Spanish ships." Admiral Cervera was among those picked up after swimming ashore. Of the Spanish total of 2,227 officers and men, 1,813 were taken prisoner and an estimated number of 150 escaped by shore to Santiago, which would make the reckoning of killed or drowned about 260.

Though the Spanish ships after coming under fire were quickly put out of action, the actual number of hits, so far as revealed later from an examination of the battered hulls, was disappointingly low—a total of forty-two hits out of 1,300 shots from guns of 4-inch and over, or only 3.2 per cent. There were also seventy-seven hits from 6-pounders. Probably the number of hits was twice that indicated, and obviously the smoke, haste, and confusion of battle presented conditions very different from target practice. Nevertheless, the figures made a good argument for increased attention to gunnery after the war.

Minor Operations

In the story of the Santiago campaign, some of the episodes of the Cuban blockade have been disregarded, notable among which was the cable-cutting exploit at Cienfuegos on May 11, in which 200-foot lengths were cut from two cables connecting Cuba with the outside world. Under the command of Lieutenant Cameron McRae Winslow, four launches from the *Nashville* and *Marblehead* were engaged in the operation for over three hours. They were covered by the ships' guns, but much of the time the men wielded axe and hacksaw while under sharp fire from rifle pits on shore. Two men were killed and seven wounded.

In an attack on Spanish gunboats and shore defenses at Cardenas, in northern Cuba, on the same date, the torpedo boat *Winslow* suffered injuries to her steering gear and was gallantly towed out of her dangerous position by the revenue steamer *Hudson,* then in the naval service. Ensign Worth Bagley and four others were killed in the *Winslow,* and three men were wounded.

A third exploit deserving mention was the outcome of mistaken reports of Spanish warcraft at large in eastern Cuban waters, which delayed the sailing of the army from Tampa for four days' time. To make positive that all Cervera's ships were at Santiago, Ensign (later Rear Admiral) Victor Blue volunteered, on June 11, for a dangerous two-day reconnaissance within the Spanish lines. Provided with a guide by the insurgents, he approached to a point where he had a clear view of all vessels within the bay, and then safely made his return.

Closing Events and Peace Terms

The destruction of the Spanish squadron firmly established American sea control and virtually ended the war. After some delay the Spanish military command in Santiago signed capitulation terms which provided for the surrender of 22,000 troops and the evacuation of the entire eastern end of the island.

In late July General Miles, with a naval escort under Captain F. J. Higginson in the *Massachusetts,* proceeded to occupy Puerto Rico, landing troops at Ponce and elsewhere on the south side of the island. The operations at these points involved little more than landing and taking possession. At the cessation of hostilities on August 12, the island was largely under American control.

The singularly one-sided character of the naval war is evidenced by the fact that in the entire conflict the American naval forces lost only eighteen killed, sixty-seven wounded, and six invalided from the Service. No ships or guns were surrendered and the crew of the *Merrimac* were the only men taken prisoner. With all due allowance for material superiority, the naval forces were in the main handled with energy and good judgment. The Navy largely avoided the difficulties created in the land forces by political pressure and the strain of sudden expansion, and it merited the popular acclaim and support it received.

After the surrender of Santiago, the Spanish government opened peace overtures through the French ambassador at Washington. In the treaty, negotiated at Paris and signed December 10, Spain relinquished sovereignty over Cuba and ceded to the United States the islands of Puerto Rico, Guam, and the Philippines. In compensation for government and other property in the Philippines, the United States agreed to pay $20,000,000.

These terms gave the United States increased protection in the Caribbean area, and a much more important role in Pacific and Far Eastern affairs. Over the acquisition of the Philippines there was strong opposition, but popular sentiment supported President McKinley's conclusion that the islands could not be returned to Spain, or disposed of to other powers, or left to shift for themselves. The apparently impending break-up of China and its division among the Western powers provided an additional motive for a vantage point in the East. The British (and the Japanese at the time) were glad to see the United States, rather than Germany, in the Philippines. Our presence there added to the increasing community of interests of the United States and Great Britain, and meant an increased American concern in the stability of the Eastern world.

References

Chadwick, F. E., *The Relations of the United States and Spain,* 2 vols., 1911.

Fiske, B. A., *From Midshipman to Rear Admiral,* 1919.

Goode, W. A. M., *With Sampson Through the War,* 1899.

Mahan, A. T., *Lessons of the War with Spain and Other Articles,* 1899.

Millis, W., *The Martial Spirit,* 1931.

Pratt, J. W., *Expansionists of 1898,* 1936.

Wilson, H. W., *The Downfall of Spain,* 1900.

XX

THE NAVY BACKS DIPLOMACY

THE DEFEAT OF Spain threw the United States into the full current of world affairs. The nation was faced with new responsibilities and new problems, in the handling of which the vital interdependence of our foreign policies and our naval strength was clearly revealed. As a preamble to what follows, it seems desirable to re-emphasize the significant features of this relationship.

In the first place, military (including naval) strength—actual or potential—is the ultimate sanction behind diplomacy, or in other words behind the attainment of national aims in the foreign field. Arguments based on legality or "rights" may serve in minor controversies between nations, in which both parties are eager to avoid conflict; but they are almost certain to be disregarded, or twisted to suit the national viewpoint, whenever major interests are involved. Hence the truth of the familiar saying that the diplomatic arm must not overreach the military arm. Hence also the conclusion that the phrase "renunciation of force as an instrument of national policy" is very nearly a contradiction in terms, or at best a renunciation of policy itself, so far as policy involves more than an acceptance of the status quo. And it is difficult to envisage a world of nations satisfied with things as they are. In short, however aided by the skilful bargaining of diplomats, by propaganda, or by economic pressure (in itself a form of force), the attainment of a nation's foreign policies is in the end dependent on its ability and willingness to support them if necessary by force of arms.

If this strength is clearly adequate, the policies involved are quite likely to be attained without resort to arms. Or, a mere show of force—the dispatch of a naval vessel, a concentration of the fleet, a note of warning—may suffice. There are many instances of such use of naval force in the period under study. On the other hand, if the opponents approach equality of strength, or vital issues are at stake, there arises the possibility of war. A point to bear in mind is that, whether the dispute ends at the council table or on the battlefield, the nation's armed strength is a factor involved.

It is an obvious corollary of this principle that the nature of a nation's foreign policies, and the extent of opposition they are likely to encounter abroad, will be primary considerations in determining the strength required in the nation's fighting arms. The policy will determine the strength; and vice versa, the strength will often guide or determine the policy.

Self-defense, or national security, including protection of home territory, colonial possessions, freedom of trade, and access to essential raw materials—this is the most fundamental of any nation's foreign policies. Under it may be included, or from it radiate, nearly all policies that are not frankly designs of aggression—and it is often so interpreted as to include even those. In the case of the United States, national security was the accepted basis for specific policies such as the construction and ownership of an isthmian canal, naval control in the Caribbean, the Monroe Doctrine, the extension of naval control in the Pacific, the "Open Door" in China, and a vital concern in any conflict in the Far East or Europe that might upset the world equilibrium and thus threaten our own interests. It may be added that the policies adopted by our political and naval leaders, in the post-Spanish War period, were in general justified by events of later years. Theirs was the difficult task, always involved in shaping foreign or military policy, of envisaging the distant shape of things to come.

Naval Expansion

The policies just mentioned all called for naval power, and explain why, contrary to precedents, our Navy after the Spanish conflict experienced, not a decline, but a steady expansion. The nation itself had increased immensely in wealth and world influence, and felt the need of corresponding strength at sea. The new bases in the Caribbean and Pacific, while increasing the effectiveness of naval action, were worthless unless protected and utilized by an adequate fleet.

Another motive for American naval expansion, though not perhaps fully realized at the time, was the relative weakening of British sea power, which for a century had served as a factor in world stability and in the security of the American continents. As a nation with sated territorial ambitions, Britain could be counted on to use her sea strength as a check on the possible designs of other nations, in the Americas or elsewhere. But now the rise of German economic, military, and naval power called for a concentration of the British fleet in home waters and lessened its influence in the outer seas. The new sea power of Japan became dominant in the western Pacific. Furthermore, the potency of sea power itself had already been somewhat lessened by new economic and technological developments—the increased industrial self-sufficiency of nations, which made them less subject to the strangling grip of blockade; and the development of mines and submarines, which made close blockade impossible and was later to put a dangerous weapon in the hands of the weaker naval belligerent. The effect of all these changes was a growing warmth and sense of community of interest in Anglo-American relations, and a tendency to measure our own naval needs by the rising power of Germany and Japan.

Whether Theodore Roosevelt be regarded as a fire-eating jingo or a farsighted statesman—or something of both—his advent to the presidency in 1901 accelerated the expansion of the

Navy to meet these new problems. No preceding President had had such enthusiastic interest in the Navy or such grasp of its functions and use in foreign affairs.

During his first administration, from 1901 to 1905, authorization was secured for ten new battleships, four armored cruisers, and seventeen smaller craft.[1] At the end of that time there were twenty-eight battleships, counting old-timers of the Spanish War period, and twelve armored cruisers. The first British all-big-gun dreadnoughts of 1906, with ten 12-inch guns, were matched by our *Michigan* and *North Carolina* of eight 12-inch guns, designed earlier but completed later than the British ships. Increased international tension and increased construction abroad kept our program of two battleships a year fairly steady up to the more rapid expansion during the First World War.

Equal progress was not maintained in cruisers, destroyers, and other auxiliary types, and not until 1909 were adequate funds provided for the development of bases at Guantanamo, Cuba, and at Pearl Harbor. Submarines, the first of which to be built for the Navy was the *Holland* in 1900, numbered twelve in 1906 and thirty-eight in 1914.

In the Roosevelt era much stress was laid on naval readiness for war. Flag-showing in distant ports was left to small cruisers, and the battleships were concentrated in a single Atlantic fleet, with a Pacific fleet of armored cruisers. The enlisted personnel was increased from 25,000 in 1900 to about 45,000 in 1909, but rapid wartime expansion remained difficult through lack of reserves and through the fact that the number of officers was kept far below the proportions maintained in foreign navies. Fleet gunnery forged ahead. Under the stimulus chiefly of Lieutenant (later Vice Admiral) William S. Sims, who had noted similar moves in the British Navy and had finally carried his proposals directly to the President, reforms in range-finding, spotting, and target practice were adopted with such success

[1] H. and M. Sprout, *The Rise of American Naval Power*, p. 260.

that gunnery improved at least 100 per cent within a few years after the first fleet target practice in 1903.

The first great peacetime test of this new Navy came in the World Cruise of 1907–09. This will be taken up in proper sequence in the following survey of naval activities in the Pacific and in the Caribbean.

The Navy in the Pacific

Only confusion could result from treating in detail the Navy's many operations during the Philippine Insurrection, 1899–1901. Since there was no opposing naval force, these operations consisted in general of aiding the Army in transport and escort of troops, bombardment and frequent occupation of shore positions, and patrol and blockade to cut off munitions from the rebels. After Admiral Dewey's departure for home in the *Olympia* (May, 1899), the eastern command went to Rear Admiral J. C. Watson, and later to Rear Admiral G. C. Remey. Most of Dewey's cruisers, monitors, and gunboats remained, and were augmented by the *Oregon,* a number of cruisers, and some seventeen small gunboats mostly taken over from Spain, the command of these last affording excellent experience for ensigns and junior lieutenants. To cite typical activities, naval fire on rebel trenches supported the Army in its first moves north and south of Manila; naval forces occupied the city of Iloilo; and in the autumn of 1899, ships, including the *Oregon, Baltimore, Charleston,* and *Concord,* bombarded and took over the naval base site in Subic Bay. Typical of operations ashore were those of the officers and men of the cruiser *Newark,* who, in the following winter, landed at Aparri in northern Luzon, received the surrender of insurgents in that area, and spent two weeks campaigning in the interior.

The naval operations were accompanied by much survey and hydrographic work, the scope of which is suggested by the fact that the 11,000-mile coast line of the islands is greater than that of the continental United States, and the need of which was indicated by the sinking of the *Charleston* in November, 1899, without loss of life, after striking an uncharted shoal. The insurrection, which had begun in February, 1899, was for the most part suppressed by the close of that year, though scattered guerrilla warfare continued until 1901.

Meanwhile, the attention of our eastern forces was drawn to the situation in northern China, where in the spring and summer of 1900 the Boxer Uprising threatened the safety of all foreign residents. While connected with earlier foreign aggressions in China, notably by the Russians in southern Manchuria and the Germans at Kiao-chau, this movement soon developed into a fanatical attack on all "foreign devils," with little opposition from imperial troops. In response to urgent calls from our legation at Peking, the cruiser *Newark* was dispatched to the mouth of the Pei-ho River, near the port of Tientsin, and on May 31 the *Newark* sent a force of fifty-three marines and three sailors by rail from Tientsin to the capital. These, with other foreign troops, maintained a heroic defense of the Peking legation quarter until its final relief in August.

Early in June, landing parties of American seamen, numbering 112 in all, were sent to join the naval forces of other nations assembled at Tientsin. On the night of June 9, after all communications with Peking had been cut off, the foreign commanders met to consider further moves. Their conference was stirred to action by the American leader, Captain McCalla of the *Newark,* who is reported to have declared, "I don't care what the rest of you may do, but my legation is in danger and I am going immediately to start for its relief." [2]

Under Vice Admiral Seymour, R.N., as senior officer, the expedition left by train next day. It numbered 2,078, with

---

[2] Captain J. K. Taussig, "Experiences During the Boxer Rebellion," *United States Naval Institute Proceedings*, April, 1927, p. 407. Taussig, who was wounded in the campaign, was later in command of the first destroyer flotilla sent to Queenstown in the First World War. In the British contingent were Captain Jellicoe and Lieutenant Beatty, World War commanders of the Grand Fleet. Jellicoe was severely wounded.

large British, Russian, and German contingents, and smaller representation, in the order named, of Americans, French, Italians, Austrians, and Japanese. The first day they covered forty-five of the eighty miles to Peking, but at the end of ten days they were still short of their goal. Boxers in ever increasing numbers swarmed along the railway, tearing up track in front and rear, attacking detachments left for its protection, and at one point fighting a pitched battle in which they suffered five hundred killed and inflicted considerable losses on the allies. With food and munitions running low, it was necessary to turn back, and there was further desperate fighting before the expedition was met by re-enforcements on the twenty-fifth just outside Tientsin. The American loss was five killed and twenty-six wounded. Captain McCalla was wounded three times but remained in command of his detachment, which had acted as an advance guard. In the international army of 18,000, which in August reached Peking by rail and relieved the legations, there were 2,300 American troops, including 900 marines.

Our military and naval participation in these operations added weight to the State Department's efforts to secure general acceptance of the "Open Door" policy in China. In a note of the preceding September, Secretary John Hay had suggested that the powers extend equal trading rights within their special concessions, and he now received at least a show of support for a proposal not only to "safeguard equal trade with all parts of the Chinese Empire" but also to "preserve Chinese territorial and administrative entity."

In its consistent pursuit of this policy, one of the chief concerns of our Government was to prevent a situation in which any one power, by gaining a dominant position in the eastern field, should threaten the position and rights of other powers. Thus, in the Russo-Japanese War of 1904–05, our sympathies were with Japan as the apparent defender of China against Russian aggression, and, according to his own statement, President Roosevelt even gave assurances of support for Japan if Russia secured European allies. At Japan's request, the President made the preliminary moves for the peace conference at Portsmouth, New Hampshire, and later, when the conference was deadlocked, he stepped in to gain acceptance of a settlement which gave Japan the southern half of Sakhalin, in lieu of a cash indemnity.

As usual after such intercessions, his guidance was viewed with some resentment in Japan. The island empire had won its first conflict with a Western power, and as time went on, it became increasingly evident that from Japan rather than elsewhere might come the next menace to the Pacific and Far Eastern status quo. Sharp friction, aggravated by yellow journalism on both sides, developed in the next year over the treatment of Japanese on our Pacific coast, and particularly over the segregation of Japanese students in the San Francisco schools. It was of this affair that the President wrote to Secretary of State Root: "I am more concerned over the Japanese situation than almost any other. Thank Heaven we have the Navy in good shape." A compromise was finally reached by which the city rescinded its action and Japan agreed to stop further labor emigration.

In the Japanese communications, however, the President thought he had detected a tone of "veiled truculence," and it was partly to add a touch of firmness to our Pacific diplomacy that he now determined to send the fleet on a world cruise. This was to be done not as a threat and hardly as a demonstration, and there were other excellent reasons for the move. As the President said, "It would arouse popular support and enthusiasm for the Navy," and it would afford a splendid test of naval equipment, efficiency, and morale.

Commanded by "Fighting Bob" Evans, and ready, as its leader said, "for a feast, a frolic, or a fight," the fleet of sixteen first-line battleships left Hampton Roads in December, 1907, and returned in February, 1909. Not until its arrival on the West Coast was it revealed that the ships would visit the Orient and continue around the world. At San Francisco, owing to Evans' illness and approaching retirement, the command was turned over to Rear Admiral Charles S. Sperry, who handled both the diplomatic and administrative parts of his duty with admirable skill. The fleet was warmly welcomed in Australia and New Zealand, and when it visited Yokohama on the invitation of the Japanese Government it was met with a genuinely enthusiastic reception. School children lined the streets singing "The Star-Spangled Banner" in Japanese!

As a diplomatic measure the cruise effectively served its mission of bettering relations with Japan. The Root-Takahira Agreement, in which Japan gave support to the Pacific status quo, the "Open Door," and "the independence and integrity of China," was signed in the same year. Returning through the Mediterranean on the last leg of its 46,000-mile voyage, the fleet showed marked benefits from the cruise. It had found itself, and got the sea habit. It had made improvement in maneuvering in formation, in coal economy, in gunnery, and in morale, though the need for distant bases and better collier and other supply service had also been shown.

The Navy in the Caribbean

Amid these events which proved the need of naval strength in the Pacific, the Roosevelt administration was striving to make this strength available by pushing forward the construction of the Panama Canal. The need for such a means of shifting naval force quickly to either coast was, it will be recalled, one of the striking lessons of the Spanish War. Britain, feeling the need of American friendship in her rivalry with Germany, was now ready to surrender her old rights, under the Clayton-Bulwer Treaty, to share in the control of an isthmian waterway; and in the revised Hay-Pauncefote Treaty of 1901, she agreed not only to American ownership of the canal but also (tacitly) to American fortification and defense. When Colombia, in 1903, held up the treaty conferring rights across the isthmus, the President took no pains to conceal his anger and chagrin. He wanted to "make the dirt fly," especially before the next election. And when the inevitable revolt was started in Panama, the United States cruiser *Nashville* appeared opportunely on the scene. On November 2, a Colombian gunboat landed 470 troops at Colon to put down the revolt; but a landing party from the *Nashville* was likewise put ashore to protect American interests and also, under old treaty arrangements with Colombia, to "prevent disorder on the isthmus." On the fifth the *Dixie* arrived with a battalion of marines. Panamanian representatives now crossed the isthmus for a conference, and by a mixture of threats and persuasion the Colombian troops were induced to re-embark. The revolutionary government in Panama was proclaimed on the fourth; it received recognition from Washington on the sixth; and a treaty with the new republic was soon negotiated which granted the United States a 10-mile wide strip from ocean to ocean for an initial payment of $10,000,000 and an annual payment of $250,000. Construction began in May, 1904, and the canal was opened for traffic in August, 1914. To assuage the ruffled feelings of Latin America over our "rough rider" diplomacy, there was the assurance that all nations would benefit from the completed canal.

Plans for a canal put sharpened emphasis on the Monroe Doctrine, particularly in its application to Central America and the Caribbean. Hence, when in 1902 England, Germany, and Italy took concerted blockade measures against Venezuela to enforce debt payments, President Roosevelt mobilized all available naval strength in Puerto Rican waters under Admiral Dewey. He then made an arbitration proposal which was quickly accepted. Some doubt has been cast on the story that the President delivered a virtual ultimatum to the German ambassador, but there is no doubt that the fleet gave weight to his diplomacy.

This was a period when Germany in particular was on the lookout for colonial footholds, and when all the major powers were inclined to drastic methods in dealing with the delinquencies of small states. To prevent such action in Central

America, involving possible challenges to our traditional policy, the President came to the conclusion that a kind of tutelary guidance might be needed for the weak nations of this area. As he put it in 1904, in what became known as "the Roosevelt Corollary" to the Monroe Doctrine, the United States might be forced, "in flagrant cases of such wrongdoing or impotence, to the exercise of an international police power."

When, in 1905, the Dominican Republic was thus threatened by European creditors, our Government negotiated a protocol —at first a *modus vivendi* but finally approved by the Senate in 1907—by which a virtual protectorate was established and American officials took charge of customs collections and debt payments. The system worked well, but when revolutionary disturbances broke out in 1916, the United States found it necessary to extend its control. Our marines carried out a campaign of pacification, and a military government was set up under Captain Harry S. Knapp, U.S.N., which continued for eight years. With graft and waste reduced, funds became available for a program of civic improvements, including 550 miles of macadam highway, enlarged port facilities, an increase in school enrollment from 18,000 to over 100,000, and better hospitals and sanitation.

In the neighboring republic of Haiti, a chronic state of disorder invoked similar action. On July 18, 1914, Rear Admiral Caperton landed a force of thirty-four bluejackets from the *Dolphin* at Port au Prince, where complete anarchy reigned and the mutilated body of the murdered President was being dragged about the streets. Later, some 2,000 marines suppressed banditry throughout the country, and a delegation of navy paymasters took charge of the customs and brought some order out of financial chaos. In 1932 a new treaty provided for reduced financial supervision and withdrawal of the marines.

The complicated story of our intervention in Nicaragua belongs largely to a later period. It may be noted here that in 1912, at the request of President Diaz, naval vessels were stationed off Nicaraguan ports and the ever-ready marines went to Managua to restore order and protect foreign lives and property. The marines were withdrawn—though not for long—in 1925. One of the measures in our financial dealing with Nicaragua was a treaty, ratified in 1916, by which, for a payment of $3,000,000, the United States received a perpetual option on the Nicaraguan canal route, a 99-year lease of Great and Little Corn Islands on the east coast, and the privilege, for the same period, of using Fonseca Gulf on the west coast for a naval base.

In our troubled relations with Mexico during these years, the most serious naval episode occurred in 1914. After refusing to recognize the "unspeakable Huerta," President Wilson had maintained naval forces on both Mexican coasts for the protection of American interests. "Watchful waiting" ended when on April 9 Mexican authorities at Tampico arrested and marched to jail an American paymaster and his party, peacefully engaged in putting gasoline aboard a launch from Rear Admiral Mayo's flagship *Dolphin*. Though the prisoners were soon released with "regrets," the Admiral called for a formal apology and a 21-gun salute to the United States flag. When Huerta refused the salute, President Wilson, with the approval of Congress, ordered the Navy to seize the customs house at Vera Cruz. A force of about 800 marines and seamen landed on April 21 and after considerable street fighting occupied the customs house and other structures near the water front. Extensive re-enforcements went ashore next day at dawn, supported by fire from the *Chester, Prairie,* and *San Francisco,* which during the night had entered the inner harbor, and the city was occupied before noon, with an American loss of fifteen killed and fifty-six wounded. Shore operations were later taken over by our Army. Mediation by the "ABC powers" (Argentina, Brazil, and Chile) soon followed, and Huerta left the country in July, but the American fleet remained off the Mexican coast until November.

Altogether, there were about thirty United States interventions in this part of the world in the first quarter of the new century, usually involving employment of the Navy and the Marine Corps, and there was United States financial supervision of varying degrees in fully half of the Central American republics. In these moves, our motives were partly to protect American and other foreign interests, but primarily, as already said, to prevent an extension of any form of foreign control. Fortunately, in more recent years changed conditions have made it possible and expedient to abandon the intervention policy for that of the "good neighbor," with co-operation of all the American nations in hemisphere defense.

The timely completion of the Panama Canal in 1914 facilitated defense of both our East and West Coasts, and made less dangerous a division of naval forces between the two. Concentration of our battlefleet was a cardinal principle of Mahan, who showed clearly that a united fleet on either coast was a better defense of both than was the same fleet divided between the two. This principle was strongly endorsed by President Roosevelt, who made it a last warning to his successor in 1909. The growing Navy of these peace years had retained its popularity, maintained its traditions of efficiency and service, and was in fair readiness for the rapid expansion and severe tests that came with the First World War.

References

Bailey, T. A., *Theodore Roosevelt and the Japanese-American Crises,* 1934.

Evans, R. D., *An Admiral's Log.*

Jones, C. L., *The Caribbean Interests of the United States,* 1916.

Latane, J. H., *The United States and Latin America,* 1920.

Long, J. D., *The New American Navy,* 2 vols., 1903.

Sprout, H. and M., *The Rise of American Naval Power,* 1933.

THE FIRST WORLD WAR

THE OUTBREAK OF WAR in Europe in August, 1914, might seem to have provided adequate warning to the United States Government to take thoroughgoing measures of preparation in every military arm. Particularly, it was a warning to put the Navy in readiness "from stem to stern," for it was evident that, even more than in the Napoleonic wars, our nation would be the chief neutral ocean carrier and source of supplies for the belligerents, and as such must expect violent disregard of its rights by both groups of warring countries. British blockade and commerce restrictions would halt our trade with Germany; on the other hand, our immense food and munitions exports to the Allied nations would be a cause of grievance and an object of attack for the Central Powers. In the end it was the violation of our neutral rights at sea that brought us into the war.

Moves for Naval Preparedness

Yet, with nearly three years' warning, our naval defense measures were incredibly slow. After the war, in 1920, Rear Admiral William S. Sims wrote a letter to the Secretary of the Navy entitled "Certain Naval Lessons of the Great War," in which, among other points, he stressed the delays due to unpreparedness in both matériel and personnel, at the outbreak of hostilities, and our lack of definite plans for effective, aggressive war. The resultant congressional investigation, with its 3,500 pages of testimony, had a value in its emphasis on errors and shortcomings, some of which at least were avoided when we faced a similar situation twenty years later, and the former Assistant Secretary of the Navy, Franklin D. Roosevelt, had risen to Chief Executive. The investigation in general bore out the Admiral's contention that, to cite definite figures, 66 per cent of the ships of our Navy, on April 6, 1917, were in need of more or less repair; that not more than 10 per cent of them were fully manned; and that only after several months of costly delay was our full naval strength thrown into the war. These shortcomings could be attributed partly to faulty naval administration, partly to defective departmental organization, but in large part also to difficulties inherent in our democratic form of government.

During this period of nonbelligerency, the nation was divided in sentiment, its dominant element doubtless pro-Ally in sympathies, but its great majority bent above all on keeping out of war. The Administration reflected these views; it was no more war-minded than the nation. In military matters, it favored "orderly, unhurried progress"; it felt that strenuous military preparations might savor of unneutrality, and incidentally, lose votes in the close elections of 1916. The Democratic Party, though its majority in Congress had approved the usual battleship increases in 1914 and 1915, was traditionally isolationist and anti-imperialistic; the Democratic Secretary of the Navy, Josephus Daniels, was rated a "big navy" man, but was more enthusiastic over the Navy's educational possibilities, its morals, and its social welfare, than its fighting efficiency. "He was," as an officer said, "greatly interested in many things that were good, but generally they did not affect the preparation of the Navy for war." Here again, the Secretary was but reflecting a national state of mind. The nation was not "interested" in war. But in the Secretary's preoccupation with other matters, important military needs were sometimes neglected or postponed.

The most notable step forward in departmental organization was the creation by Congress, early in 1915, of the Office of Chief of Naval Operations, which was to have direct control, "under the Secretary," of war plans and fleet operations, corresponding in its functions to a much needed general staff. During its first year, however, the Office was handicapped by lack of provision for subordinate officers, and by the resignation in April of its first chief, Admiral Bradley A. Fiske, on the issue of more vigorous steps toward preparedness. Fiske, the inventor of the torpedo plane, was a graduate of the Naval War College, and of high scientific attainments and progressive vision. His successor, Admiral William S. Benson, though inclined to more conservative courses, brought the Office into an efficient organization during the war years. An instance of the Department's slow progress, in this period, was its failure to oppose a congressional cut in the naval aeronautical appropriation in 1916 from $13,000,000 to $3,500,000, a sum manifestly inadequate in the light of aircraft developments even in the First World War.

To return to the Sims criticisms, it is difficult to find in the investigation testimony or elsewhere evidence of a plan which took full cognizance of the actual naval situation facing the Allies in April, 1917. Our initial measures included a patrol of the Atlantic coast, with the main fleet held in readiness at Hampton Roads (to meet a victorious German fleet if the Allies surrendered), and only limited aid overseas. In the light of the situation as Sims saw it when he reached London, with the German fleet held in check by the British Grand Fleet, but the submarine menace threatening to force England to her knees within a year, what seemed necessary was the throwing of every ounce of American naval strength into the anti-submarine campaign.

But realization of this situation, and of the need of an all-out effort, came only by degrees. When Admiral Sims was sent to London in March as our naval representative, following the severance of diplomatic relations with Germany, one of the parting injunctions to him was, "Don't let them pull the wool over your eyes. It is none of our business pulling their chestnuts out of the fire. We would as soon fight the British as the Germans." [1] This, however, was not the dominant sentiment even at that time.

Chiefly from the nation itself—the Navy League, the Security League, the United States Chamber of Commerce, defense organizations of all kinds, and pro-Ally leaders, such as Theodore Roosevelt and Leonard Wood—came the strong urge toward preparedness which resulted in the big naval appropriations bill of 1916. President Wilson's conversion to such a course had come early the year before, and it was at St. Louis early in 1916 that, albeit in unguarded impromptu phrasing, he had called for "incomparably the greatest navy in the world." The 1916 Naval Appropriation Act authorized a three-year building program which would provide ten new battleships, six battle cruisers, ten scout cruisers, fifty destroyers, and sixty-seven submarines. This was a long-range plan, inapplicable to the emergency, and, in 1920, three-fourths unfinished, for in 1917 most of it was wisely suspended to permit concentration on anti-submarine weapons.

Approach Toward War

Meanwhile, controversies with both belligerents over neutral rights at sea had brought the nation steadily closer to war. With England, the conflicts were concerned primarily with evasions or sweeping extensions of accepted principles of international law. Close blockade was no longer possible because of increased dangers from torpedoes and mines, but in March, 1915, in retaliation for the German-declared "war area" around the British Isles, England declared her purpose to cut off at the entrances to the Baltic "all goods of enemy destination, ownership, or origin." Our State Department accepted this "long range" blockade, and confined its protests to British inter-

[1] E. E. Morison, *Admiral Sims and the Modern American Navy*, p. 338.

ference with our legitimate trade with the Netherlands and the northern neutrals. That much of this trade—or its equivalent in goods of the importing country—had its ultimate destination in Germany was evident from our increased exports to these nations, which in 1915 were 75 per cent greater, and in 1916 nearly 50 per cent greater, than before the war. Cargoes stopped by Britain were generally paid for, but the new system of taking ships into British ports for search involved vexatious delays; and British "black lists" of American merchants supposedly engaged in trade with the enemy were an added irritant. England's constant endeavor was to keep all these disputes within the bounds of diplomatic note-writing, and in this she was aided by the sympathy of the American Ambassador at London, and perhaps even of our own State Department officials. It may be noted also that our exports to Britain and her allies had increased nearly fourfold, and credits of over two billion dollars to finance these purchases had further tied our interests to the Allied cause.

The more strenuous character of our protests to Germany was partly due to the fact that her infractions entailed losses, not merely of property, but of lives. Furthermore, they involved not extension but a complete disregard of established principles controlling sea warfare. To grasp this clearly, one has only to think of the seas as great common highways open to all, and at the same time an inevitable fighting arena of nations at war. The prime end and aim of each belligerent is to secure the free use of the sea for his own military movements and commerce, and to deny it to the enemy. As a compromise between the rights of the neutral trader and those of the belligerent, long custom had established the principle that the belligerent might use his naval strength against enemy and neutral trade in two ways: (1) to blockade enemy ports and coasts against all traffic, provided such blockade was clearly defined and effectively maintained; (2) to cut off by seizure on the high seas any contraband—i.e., goods useful for war and destined for the enemy—whether in enemy or neutral ships, with the provision that the visit, search, and seizure should involve no injury to passengers or crew of the ship submitting to search.

But it was the right and also the duty of a neutral nation to oppose a "blockade" extending over great areas of the high seas, maintained not by sea control but by a limited number of lurking submarines, which sank ships, belligerent or neutral, without warning, and which at any given time was not effective against more than 1 or 2 per cent of the passing traffic. "Without conceding her own impotency as a nation," in the words of President Wilson, "and endangering her own present and future security, no nation could suffer such restriction of the movement of her trade and her people over the sea highways."

Our first sharp protest, holding Germany to "strict accountability," followed her declaration, February 1, 1915, of a war zone in the waters around Great Britain and Ireland, including the whole English Channel, "in which area she would sink enemy ships without warning and would assume no responsibility for the destruction of neutral vessels." Sinkings of American ships and of Allied ships with American passengers soon followed and were climaxed by the torpedoing of the great Cunard liner *Lusitania,* May 7, 1915, off the Irish coast, with a loss of 1,198 persons, of whom 128 were Americans. Renewed protests resulted finally in a German promise to spare liners if they did not resist or attempt escape; and in May, 1916, after the *Sussex* sinking and further protests, Germany made a qualified agreement not to sink unresisting ships without provision for the safety of passengers and crew.

There ensued a limited respite, but in February of 1917 Germany tore up all pledges, and gambled on an unrestricted submarine campaign to bring England to surrender before the United States could put its full strength into the war. Ships were to be sunk in a vast "barred zone" extending from Holland around the British Isles to Cape Finisterre and including most of the Mediterranean (see map, p. 385). Under certain conditions an American ship could enter Falmouth once a week, and there was a narrow lane leading to neutral Greece.

With the nation now solidly behind it, the United States Government broke off diplomatic relations with Germany, armed American merchant vessels in March, and on April 6, 1917, with but seven Senators and fifty Representatives opposed, declared war. Thereafter, incidentally, it joined the Allies in putting into force most of the commercial restrictions —the extensions of contraband, black lists of neutral traders, and virtual rationing of supplies to northern neutrals—which it had hitherto opposed.

After the war, disputes over legal points involved in our entry tended to obscure the underlying feeling in the minds of most Americans at the time—that the security of our nation and of the Western Hemisphere would be gravely threatened by a Germany dominant in Europe, and able, by a victory over England, to extend her economic and political ambitions overseas. In short, they realized that America was no longer isolated, but vitally concerned in an upset of the European and world balance of power.

American Destroyers Overseas

After his arrival in England on April 9 and his talks with the First Sea Lord, Admiral Jellicoe, Admiral Sims was brought to a realization of the actual status—not fully revealed to the public—of the submarine war. Shipping losses had risen from 500,000 tons in February, and threatened in April to reach an unprecedented figure of nearly 900,000 tons. One-fourth of all tonnage available was gone. Continued sinkings on this scale meant that England must starve or surrender within a few months' time. "They will win," said Jellicoe, "unless we can stop these losses, and stop them soon." The outcome of the war hinged on quick coping with the submarines. On the date of Sims's first cabled appeal to Washington (April 14), a division of six destroyers was ordered to prepare for sea. On May 6, after a stormy passage, this first American squadron overseas approached the green-clad hills of the Irish coast, and was met out-

Courtesy U.S. Naval Institute

Top, UNITED STATES NAVY "BLIMP" AND CONVOY NEARING BREST, JUNE, 1918. *Bottom,* EXPLODING A DEPTH CHARGE, FIRST WORLD WAR.

side Queenstown by the British destroyer *Mary Rose* flying the signal, "Welcome to the American colors!" As they steamed up the swept channel, the American and British destroyers were sharply contrasted in arrangement of stacks, gun placements, and general contour; though less maneuverable and of greater fuel capacity, the American craft had at the same time more slender and graceful lines.

After the first greetings at Queenstown, the American officers ascended the hill to Admiralty House to meet their new commander, Admiral Sir Lewis N. Bayly, R.N.—taut, taciturn, but akin to the American temper in his quick intelligence and energy. Soon came the question, "When will you be ready to go to sea?" There were minor engine troubles not to be mentioned at this time. "We are ready now," replied the senior American officer, Commander Joseph K. Taussig, "or as soon as we have fueled."

They were given four days for repairs, and brief words of advice—no lights, no slowing below thirteen knots, no fixed system of patrol, the "art of irregularity," of untiring persistence and skill, in this sea game of fox and hounds. Though in general command of American forces in European waters, Admiral Sims adhered to the sound policy that his units should be closely integrated with the British, under co-ordinated direction. The relations between the American officers and their British chief developed into a close and warm understanding, expressed in the postwar message of Admiral Bayly, "To command you is an honor, to work with you is a pleasure, to know you is to know the best traits of the Anglo-Saxon race."

The first squadron was re-enforced by others until by July the number of American destroyers at Queenstown had reached thirty-four, at which figure or thereabouts it remained for the rest of the war. At the armistice we had seventy-nine destroyers in European waters. The British had some two hundred, but nearly one hundred [2] of these were with the Grand Fleet, and

---

[2] The argument that all American destroyers should have been sent at once to European waters to fight the submarine might apply equally to these British

most of the rest were in the Channel, the Mediterranean, and many other areas of vital concern. At Queenstown the British rarely had more than four or five. The system employed at first was to give each Queenstown destroyer about four days at sea and two in port, and assign to each a great patrol area of about nine hundred square miles. This, however, was soon replaced by the more effective system of convoy.

Long discussed by the Admiralty, and strongly advocated by Sims, the age-old convoy system was, in May, 1917, given a new trial. The objections to it had been many—the 20 per cent delay to traffic, the feeling of merchant skippers that they were unequal to the difficulties of steaming in close formation in zigzags and without lights, and the lack of sufficient escort forces, especially of cruisers to protect the convoys against surface raiders in the outer seas. Yet, it was a measure of concentrated and organized defense, which forced the submarines either to come within range of destroyer action or else confine their operations to attacks close inshore after the convoy was dispersed. The safe arrival of the first experimental convoy from Gibraltar on May 20, and of another four days later from Hampton Roads, may be said to have marked a turning point in the naval war. Before its close, 90 per cent of Allied traffic was in convoy, and losses, while ships were actually in convoy, and not after dispersal, were less than half of 1 per cent.

Control of this vast traffic was centered in a room of the Admiralty in London. Here, on a huge wall map of the Atlantic was plotted the course of every convoy and of every submarine located at sea. From departure to return, the movements of the U-boats were closely followed. Their daily communications with each other and with home bases were caught by British direction finders at various points, thus giving an accurate location. And these were supplemented by the prompt, though less reliable, reports of their contacts with

---

destroyers with the Grand Fleet, especially since the German fleet at this time had been largely relegated to the role of a base guard and source of manpower for the U-boats.

Allied ships. Thus, it was even possible by quick radio warnings to detour a convoy around an interposing submarine. Sydney (Cape Breton), Halifax, New York, Hampton Roads, Dakar (West Africa), and Gibraltar were the chief ports from which convoys converged on the British Isles.

For the American destroyers at Queenstown, as later at Brest and Gibraltar, the main task was to share with the British in the escort of convoys to and from points about two hundred miles at sea, or in other words, through the danger zone. Beyond, Allied cruisers brought them or took them on their way. Convoys of from sixteen to twenty ships were ranged in several parallel columns with escorts on the two exposed wings and perhaps a guard for stragglers in the rear. At first sight of a periscope, or other evidence of torpedo attack, the general practice was for escorts to dash to the spot at best speed and drop depth bombs where the submarine was indicated to be. The bombs, loaded with three hundred pounds of TNT, and set to explode at any desired depth, were run off the stern or dropped on either side from "Y" guns. In the later months, they were dropped in greatly increased numbers, creating an unnerving barrage for the quarry below. Among all the American escort forces in European waters there were 286 attacks, nearly two hundred of which were on actual U-boats. As a result, there were four to six verified sinkings and seventeen other encounters which caused damage necessitating return of the submarine to its base or internment in a neutral port.

Off Queenstown the *O'Brien,* on June 16, 1917, made a damaging contact of this kind with the *U-61,* and the *Wadsworth* and *Benham* in June and July scored similar blows. A typical contact was that which developed on October 19, 1917, out of the fight between the United States steamer *J. L. Luckenbach* and the *U-53.* Steaming alone for St. Nazaire, France, about ninety miles ahead of a convoy escorted by the United States destroyers *Conyngham* and *Nicholson,* the *Luckenbach* was shelled from 8:50 A.M. on by the U-boat, which could outrange the *Luckenbach's* guns. Having sent a radio call to the destroyers and received promise of aid, the *Luckenbach* pluckily kept up the fight, though she was hit nine times and set on fire. About 11:20, at the first shots from the approaching *Nicholson,* the submarine dived and got away.

That, however, was not the last of her, for late that afternoon the cruiser *Orama,* forming part of the same convoy escort, was suddenly hit by a torpedo. A periscope appeared for a moment to starboard, and as the *Conyngham* dashed toward the spot, the green, cigar-shaped hull was actually sighted below. Depth charges were dropped, scraps of wreckage shot upward, and after rescuing the crew of the *Orama,* the destroyers stood by for five hours. There were no further signs of the submarine. But that night London caught this message to Berlin: "Sank one 8,000-ton ship [the *Luckenbach,* which survived] with gunfire and one of 10,000 tons with torpedo . . . was attacked with waterbombs but escaped." The *U-53,* though badly damaged, was evidently able to limp home.

More successful a month later was the attack of the *Fanning* and *Nicholson* on the *U-58.* A convoy of eight ships had just formed outside Queenstown, and the *Fanning* was circling to a position on the flank when her bridge lookout sighted a "finger" periscope only four hundred yards distant. The *Fanning* made a quick, accurate turn at twenty knots and dropped a depth charge. Speeding directly through the convoy, the *Nicholson* did the same. For a few moments there was no sign. Then the stern of a submarine rose, tilted at a 30-degree angle; then the conning tower and part of the hull. As the destroyers opened fire, through the hatch appeared Kapitän-Leutnant Amberger and his crew, with hands up, calling "Kamerad." The first depth charge had wrecked the motors and jammed the diving rudders, and the commander, faced with death or surrender, had blown his tanks when two hundred feet down. The U-boat had now been scuttled, but the *Fanning* picked up four officers and thirty-five men who leaped into the sea as she went under. Two American seamen dived overboard to rescue one of them, but he was too far gone to be revived. Congratulations for the destroyers came from the Admiralty, and a message from Admiral Sims ending "Go out and do it again!"

References

See end of next chapter.

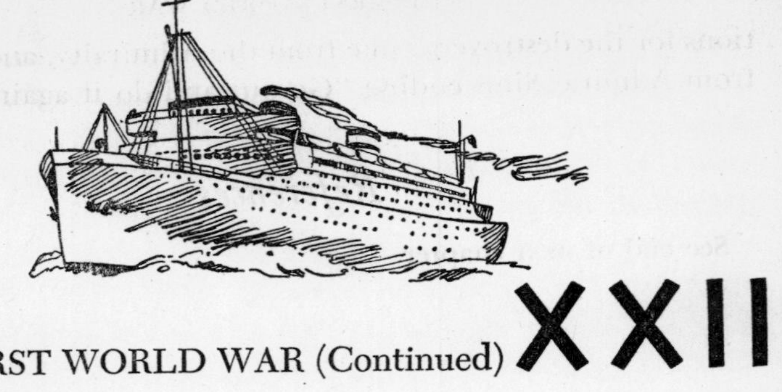

THE FIRST WORLD WAR (Continued) XXII

As already noted, Germany's unrestricted submarine warfare was based on the calculation that England could be starved into surrender before American forces could be brought effectively into the conflict on the Western Front. This meant that the opposed American naval strategy must be directed along two closely related lines: first, to check shipping losses by throwing the full strength of the Navy into the Allied anti-submarine campaign; and second, to provide quick, safe, and sufficient transport overseas for American troops and supplies.

The achievement of the first aim would contribute greatly to that of the second; and furthermore, the transport problem was less immediate, for our troops were still in training, and in fact up to the close of 1917 only 177,000 of our ultimate expeditionary force of 2,000,000 were carried overseas. To meet the submarine menace, the Queenstown destroyers, whose work has been described in the preceding chapter, represented but one of many widespread efforts, with weapons of every available type.

Continental Bases

At Brest, France, selected as a chief base on the Continent, a division of six converted yachts—increased by degrees to twenty in all—arrived on July 4, 1917. They were officered and manned largely by naval reserves, most of them with little sea experience and many of them fresh from college. To these men, serving in yachts, sub-chasers, aviation squadrons, and other branches of our vastly expanded Navy, Admiral Sims pays high tribute: [1]

> If there is anyone who still doubts what the American system of higher education is doing in our country, he should have spent a few days at sea with these young men. That they knew nothing at first about navigation and naval technique was not important; the really important fact was that their minds were alert, their hearts filled with a tremendous enthusiasm for the cause, their souls clean, and their bodies ready for the most exhausting tasks . . . I am sure [he adds] these reservists would be first to acknowledge their obligations to the loyal and devoted regular officers of the navy, who labored so diligently to train them for their work.

It is well to remember, as Sims here suggests, that the peacetime Navy forms but the firm skeletal structure upon which the vastly expanded wartime Navy is built.

Since, at Brest, the provision for tanks, docks, and other naval requirements was limited, American efforts were first directed toward enlarging facilities of this base and preparing it as a later main disembarkation port for troops and stores. Most of the early convoy work was with coastal traffic, but as the base was enlarged and destroyers added, it had as its chief task the escort of overseas troop and supply ships through the danger zone. Under the energetic direction of Rear Admiral H. W. Wilson, Commander of American Naval Forces in France, our strength at Brest and elsewhere on the Biscay coast increased rapidly, until at the armistice it included about forty destroyers, many auxiliary craft, and an operating body of 12,000 men. In 1918 it escorted over 90 per cent of the convoys that entered the Atlantic ports of France.

No tougher service can be pictured than that of these light escorts, operating in all seasons in the severe Biscay gales. The

[1] *The Victory at Sea,* p. 176.

yacht *Alcedo* was torpedoed and two others were wrecked. One of the notable successes of the force was that of the little yacht *Christabel,* in May, 1918, against the *UC-56.* While escorting a British merchant vessel which had lagged behind a convoy, the yacht sighted a periscope about two hundred yards distant, and dropped two depth charges, set to explode seventy feet down. After the explosion of the second charge, a third underwater explosion was heard, and scraps of wreckage were blown to the surface. Though the submarine was seen no more, it was seriously damaged, and a day or two later it crept into Santander, Spain, where it was interned.

Similar American support was extended to the British at Gibraltar, where our forces under Rear Admiral Niblack ultimately numbered about forty ships, including light cruisers, gunboats, coast-guard cutters, and four or five antiquated destroyers. These last were 420-ton craft which their senior officer, Lieutenant Commander H. R. Stark—Chief of Naval Operations twenty-four years later—had brought 12,000 miles from the Philippines; with only self-provided overhaul they steamed on escort duty 48,000 miles more. Operating in both the Atlantic and the Mediterranean, our Gibraltar forces gave protection to about a quarter of the local and three-quarters of the ocean convoys in this area. The yacht *Venetia,* left to watch the scene of an attack on a Gibraltar-Bizerte convoy, had the credit of spotting her prey, injuring it with depth bombs, and forcing it to enter Carthagena to be interned. Another submarine sinking in the same waters was credited to the United States yacht *Lydonia* and the British destroyer *Basilisk,* though in this instance it was three months before the Admiralty authenticated the claim.

Submarine Chasers

A special type for commerce protection was the "sub-chaser," an expertly designed, quick-turning wooden boat of 60 tons,

110 feet overall, and equipped with a 3-inch gun, depth charges, and listening devices perfected by American physicists in the earlier period of the war. About four hundred of these were built and nearly two hundred were sent overseas under their own power, crossing the Atlantic in the stormy winter months of 1917–18. Some thirty-six of them, based on Plymouth, England, went to work in the western reaches of the Channel, which had heretofore been a happy U-boat hunting ground for ships dispersed from convoys. The chasers, operating in trios, would use their highly sensitive hydrophones to spot their prey, and then edge slowly closer, until at last they would dash in and bombard it with depth charges. Off Plymouth and elsewhere this system worked with some success. The sub-chasers cleared the stretch of Channel so thoroughly—chiefly by frightening submarines out of the area—that not a ship was sunk in the six weeks they were there.

Another thirty-six of the sub-chasers went in the summer of 1918 to the Straits of Otranto, where they joined with British and Italian destroyers, drifters, kite balloons, and a net barrier in efforts to block enemy submarines in the Adriatic. Here their listening devices and depth bombs proved an added menace. A few German U-boats still got past, but nearly all were bombed, and at this stage of the war the Austrians refused to venture through.

Early in October eleven of the chasers acted as a screen for British and Italian cruisers in an attack on the Austrian base at Durazzo. "It's going to be a real party, boys," said the senior officer, Commander C. P. ("Bully") Nelson—and so it proved. While the cruisers demolished port structures and shipping, the scurrying chasers fell upon two submarines. A shot from *No. 215* hit a periscope, and subsequent depth bombs blew metal plates and wreckage into the air. Another submarine was apparently accounted for by *No. 129,* just as the sub-chaser's own engines stalled. "Their conduct," wrote the British officer in charge of the operation, "was beyond praise. They all returned safely without casualties. They thoroughly enjoyed themselves."

Submarines against Submarines

Probably the most effective weapons employed against the U-boats were craft of their own kind.[2] Though most American submarines were small coast defense types, a flotilla went to the Azores in October, 1917, and another of seven boats struggled across the Atlantic in the depths of the winter to a base in Bantry Bay, for operations on the Irish south and east coasts. Here their chief value lay in keeping the enemy out of the immediate area, for the U-boats, spending much time on the surface to save batteries, feared especially an attack from their own kind. "We got used to your depth charges and did not fear them," said a captured German officer, "but we lived in constant dread of your submarines."

The most extraordinary contact made by one of our submarines was that of the *AL-2,* Lieutenant Paul Foster. While approaching at periscope depth to investigate a suspicious object, the boat was shaken by a terrific explosion, not more than fifty yards distant, and a periscope appeared for an instant at the same spot. Propellers were heard, but soon stopped completely, though the American boat searched the vicinity for several hours. Some light was thrown on the mystery when British intelligence reported three months later that the *UB-65* had been located that day near the indicated point, but had never been heard from again. Apparently her torpedo, fired at the American submarine, had either exploded in the tube or made a complete ricochet and hit the boat from which it came.[3]

---

[2] In support of this view, Admiral Sims states that "The Allied destroyers, about 500 in number, sank 34 German submarines with gunfire and depth charges; auxiliary patrol craft, such as trawlers, yachts, and the like, about 3,000 in number, sank 31; while the Allied submarines, which were only about 100 in number, sank 20." —*The Victory at Sea,* p. 224.

[3] See C. S. Alden, "American Submarine Operations in the World War," *United States Naval Institute Proceedings,* June, July, 1920.

The Northern Mine Barrage

In view of the tremendous and seemingly disproportionate effort required to combat the U-boats, there was a very general feeling both in this country and abroad that the best way to deal with them would be to "destroy their nests," or "block their bases." In line with this idea, the suggestion of a mine barrage closing the North Sea from Scotland to Norway had a very natural appeal. An operation of this nature was planned and broached by the Ordnance Bureau of our Navy Department, but was regarded by the British Admiralty as unfeasible, chiefly because of the 150-mile stretch of sea to be covered, the depths ranging to more than nine hundred feet, the vast number of mines required, and the difficulties experienced with all existing types of mine. The Germans constantly swept channels through British mine fields in Helgoland Bight, and even in the narrow Straits of Dover the mine fields had not proved fully effective. The American authorities renewed their proposal, however, after successful tests with a new type of "antenna" mine. Its novel feature was that it was exploded, not by contact with "horns" projecting from the mine itself, but by contact of any metal object (and metal only) with a long copper wire antenna extending either above or below the mine, thus rendering dangerous an area as great as the mine's explosive force would cover. With its anchors and antenna, the mine could be dropped as a unit, and anchored automatically at any desired depth. Furthermore, the American Bureau of Ordnance, headed by Rear Admiral Ralph Earle, undertook not only to produce the mines at the rate of 1,000 a day, but to transport and lay them. At the end of October, 1917, the project was fully approved.

The whole undertaking gave excellent scope for American skill in organization and mass production. Contracts for mine parts were distributed among as many as five hundred different firms. A plant was built at St. Julien's Creek, Norfolk, where the mines were assembled at the rate of one every two minutes, loaded with three hundred pounds of TNT, and rolled in cars to the pier. Twenty-four Great Lakes freighters were secured to transport the mines to the Scottish west coast, whence they were taken by rail or the Caledonian Canal to the two east coast bases established at Inverness and Invergordon on Moray Firth. Our mine-laying force, consisting of the old cruisers *San Francisco* and *Baltimore,* was expanded to ten by the purchase and conversion of eight coastwise vessels, which were fitted with tracks and elevators for quick handling of mines. The mine layers were assembled at the Scottish bases by May of 1918. The mine-layer force was commanded by Captain R. K. Belknap, and the general operation overseas by Rear Admiral Joseph Strauss.

The first mine-laying operation, or "excursion" as it was called, took place on June 7, and the ensuing twelve occurred at average ten-day intervals until late October. Delays between excursions were due to the need of securing protective patrols from the Grand Fleet and timing the movements to coincide with those of British mine layers. The whole dangerous undertaking was carried through without losses from accident or enemy action. Despite fogs and adverse weather, the ships would keep station in line abreast at a speed of over twelve knots, laying mines at the rate of five a minute, and as many as 5,000 in a single day. Of about 70,000 mines laid, 56,600, or 80 per cent, were American mines, laid by the American force.

Even before the mines were extended entirely across the passage—with six to ten lines of mines near the surface and three to four below—the barrier had become a serious menace. The *U-86* was injured in July and forced to accept internment in Norway; the *U-113* suffered similarly in August; and in September there were several losses, including the big *U-156* returning from American waters. Altogether the barrier was credited with probably seventeen U-boats sunk or seriously damaged. It served further as a powerful deterrent by its effect on enemy morale, contributing thus to the decline of submarine activity in the final months, and perhaps to the mutinous attitude of German crews.

U-Boats on the American Coast

The *U-156,* just mentioned, was one of a half dozen large, long-range submarines which operated, not more than one or two at a time, on the American east coast in the last summer of the war. As a diversion to hold American forces on this side of the Atlantic, such a move might have been most effective a year before, but in 1918 it failed of this purpose and indicated rather the effectiveness of Allied counter-measures in waters nearer their home bases. The first and most successful of the raiders was the *U-151,* which in June laid mines off the Delaware and the Chesapeake, operated later between New York and Hatteras, and sank twenty-three vessels in its entire three months' cruise. The most notable exploit of the *U-156,* a converted "merchant submarine," was the laying of mines off Fire Island, near New York, one of which sank the old armored cruiser *San Diego,* of the Transport Force, with a loss of six men. The *U-140* was across on our Atlantic coast in August but returned in damaged condition after rough contacts with the destroyer *Stringham* and with two armed merchantmen with naval crews. Other boats sent into the western Atlantic had more limited activities, which were cut short by their recall in the last days of the war. Altogether they sank about 200,000 tons of shipping, or a fifth of the total losses in the last five months of submarine activity.

Naval Aircraft

Though the airplane was an American invention, and the first successful hydroplane was developed in this country by Glenn H. Curtiss in 1911, the Navy had taken only first steps in aviation before the World War. It was a great event in naval aviation history when, in November, 1910, Eugene Ely flew a biplane from the deck of the cruiser *Birmingham* at Norfolk, and a still greater one when, two months later, the same pilot made a successful landing on the battleship *Pennsylvania* at San Francisco. He landed on a wooden platform 130 by 50 feet, sloping slightly aft, and was checked by 100-lb. sandbags rigged to be caught by hooks in the lower framework of his plane. The aircraft carrier was thus assured for the future, and the aircraft as an arm of the fleet.

In March of 1911, the Navy contracted with Curtiss for two planes and with the Wright Brothers for another, and in October, 1912, Lieutenant Ellyson, the first qualified naval aviator, was successful in flying a plane shot from a compressed air catapult, mounted on a barge in the Potomac. The first naval aviation unit, organized by Ellyson, John Rodgers, J. H. Towers, Victor Herbster, and other pioneer aviators, had a camp in 1912 at Greenbury Point near the Naval Academy, and in 1913 a station and school were established at Pensacola. In this year, Towers made the first scouting flight for the fleet, and in the next year, for a six-week period, planes scouted over the city during the operations at Vera Cruz. All these were highly risky first experiments in aviation. Appropriations were far below the requirements, even for experimentation, and the Navy had only thirty-nine qualified pilots and about fifty planes when we entered the war.

Thus our extensive wartime aviation overseas, though organized and commanded by naval officers, had to start from insignificant beginnings in personnel and planes. The Yale University Aviation Unit of twenty-nine members, under Trubee Davison, formed the nucleus of the Naval Reserve Flying Corps, whose later recruits were drawn largely from college men and civilian flyers. A group of seven officers and 122 men of the corps, landing at St. Nazaire in early June of 1917, was the first American force to reach France. At Killingholme on the English east coast, and at Dunkirk, where our Northern Bombing Group was established, American naval aviators worked as subordinate units under the British. At Killingholme, they were occupied chiefly in anti-submarine patrol and protection of North Sea shipping. In France, in addition to the large naval and marine force at Dunkirk, eleven seaplane stations were set up on the Atlantic coast, as well as a gunnery school and repair base, and there were five stations in the British Isles and two in Italy—all serving effectively in the protection of coastal commerce.

In the chief naval aviation center at Pauillac, France, accommodations for 20,000 men were constructed and a big aircraft factory was set up, which, like many other aviation installations, was just approaching effective operation at the armistice. Captain Hutch I. Cone had general charge of overseas naval aviation, and Captain T. T. Craven did excellent work as Aide for Aviation in France. At Dunkirk, Killingholme, and elsewhere, naval aviators had their full share of thrilling action. As a single instance, Lieutenant Commander A. L. Gates,[4] at Dunkirk, received both British and American decorations for the heroic rescue of a British crew off Ostend, and for many flights over the enemy lines, in one of which he was finally shot down and made prisoner. Of thirty-nine direct attacks made by our naval aircraft, ten were pronounced in varying degrees "successful." Between the beginning and the end of hostilities the naval aviation force increased from 54 to 2,127 planes and from 39 to 1,656 aviators.

Battleships Overseas

Consideration has now been given to the many types and weapons—destroyers, yachts, mines, subchasers, submarines, and aircraft—employed to maintain sea communications against the U-boat menace. In this warfare the major surface

[4] Gates was a member of the First Yale Aviation Unit. He was made Assistant Secretary of the Navy for Air in 1941. Other distinguished members of this group were their leader, Davison, who was Assistant Secretary of War for Air in 1926–32 and a colonel on the Army Staff in the Second World War; David S. Ingalls, spoken of by Admiral Sims as "the Naval Ace of the War," who was Assistant Secretary of the Navy for Air, 1929–32; and Robert A. Lovett, who became Assistant Secretary of War for Air in 1940. See R. W. Paine, *The First Yale Unit.*

fleets on both sides may seem to have played a subordinate role. Yet it should be borne in mind that the German High Sea Fleet, by preventing a close blockade of the German coast, made the submarine campaign possible. And without the Grand Fleet at Scapa Flow, guarding the entrance to the Atlantic and maintaining surface control, all British resistance would have been quickly at an end. Even with this protection, there were fears that, as the great troop movement overseas got under way, German surface raiders or even battle cruisers might elude the blockade and wreak havoc on whole convoys. As a further guard against such attacks, which fortunately did not eventuate, three of the faster American battleships, the *Nevada, Oklahoma,* and *Utah,* under Rear Admiral T. S. Rodgers, were stationed, toward the end of the war, on the extreme southwest coast of Ireland at Bantry Bay.

In December, 1917, a squadron of five of our coal-burning battleships, the *New York, Wyoming, Texas, Florida,* and *Delaware,* under Rear Admiral Hugh Rodman, joined the Grand Fleet in the bleak northern base of Scapa Flow. This new Sixth Squadron of the Grand Fleet served as a tangible evidence of Allied solidarity and a most helpful re-enforcement in the British tasks of patrol, commerce protection, drill, and ceaseless vigil in northern waters.

In February, while the *Florida* and *Delaware* were engaged in protecting a Scandinavian convoy, a U-boat fired four torpedoes at the first-mentioned battleship and two at the second, all of which were avoided by skilful use of the helm. On another occasion, the flagship *New York* actually ran down a submarine in the entrance to Pentland Firth, coming into collison with it on her starboard quarter and hitting it a probably fatal blow with a propeller. Two blades of the propeller were broken off. While proceeding to drydock at twelve knots, the *New York* was again attacked, but all three torpedoes fired passed across her bow.

Our main fleet on the American east coast, under Admiral Henry T. Mayo, had to combine the tasks of maintaining con-

Top, courtesy U.S. Naval Institute; *bottom,* official U.S. Navy photograph

Top, ADMIRALS SIMS AND RODMAN ON THE U.S.S. NEW YORK, 1918. *Bottom,* CAPTURE OF THE U-53 BY THE U.S.S. FANNING. From a photograph taken aboard the *Fanning*.

stant readiness for action and at the same time training great numbers of new recruits for subsequent dispatch overseas. Both Admiral Mayo and the Chief of Operations, Admiral Benson, made tours of inspection in England and France in the autumn of 1917, and their visits increased the effectiveness of our participation by giving the American authorities a clearer appreciation of the scope and exigencies of the naval war. As in all modern warfare, the nerve center of naval activities was the Navy Department at Washington, where all larger questions of policy and strategy were decided, and where each bureau was immersed in the problems of furnishing personnel, munitions, supplies, and repair for the far-flung operations. In London, Rear Admiral Sims's staff, which for four months at the beginning had consisted of one aide, was enlarged to 1,200 officers and assistants.

The Transport Service

While grappling with the submarine to keep down shipping losses, the Navy was also primarily concerned in providing ships and protection for the transport of an American Expeditionary Force—in sufficient numbers and in time to turn the balance of the land war in favor of the Western Powers. This unprecedented overseas troop movement was ultimately carried out on a scale and with a speed far beyond the expectations of the Germans or our allies. General Joffre had counted on only 400,000 men. "It appears impossible," wrote the British Admiral Beresford in July, 1917, "to provide enough ships to bring the American Army overseas in hundreds of thousands . . . and supply the enormous amount of shipping which will be required to keep them full up with munitions, food, and equipment." [5]

Nearly 7,000,000 tons of shipping had been lost up to April, 1917. To overcome the resultant shortage, large-scale con-

[5] Vice Admiral Albert Gleaves, *A History of the Transport Service*, 1921, p. 22.

struction had been started in this country for some time before our entry into the war. The Shipping Board had been established, with its branch the Emergency Fleet Corporation, whose special task was to increase ship-building to the limit. From a prewar construction of 300,000 tons, production rose to 1,300,000 in the year ending June 30, 1917, and in the next year this figure was more than doubled. In the great newly completed shipyard at Hog Island, near Philadelphia, simply designed, largely prefabricated steel ships were built and launched from fifty ways, while as many more were under completion at the piers.

But a more immediate answer to the pressing transport needs was found in the 600,000 tons of German and 300,000 tons of Dutch shipping lying interned or idle in American ports. On the engines of the German liners their crews had done an expert job of sabotage, but by the then novel use of electric welding, the cylinders and boilers were repaired in record time.

Ships from these sources, together with about twenty American liners and two naval transports, the *Henderson* and *Hancock,* brought the total available up to forty-five. These troopships, which were soon taken over by the Navy and manned by naval crews, together with twenty-four cruisers and other escort ships, formed the Cruiser and Transport Force, commanded by Rear Admiral Albert Gleaves. For supply ships, the Naval Overseas Transport Service was established under the Navy Department late in 1917, and at the armistice was operating a cargo fleet of 450 ships, with a naval personnel of 5,000 officers and 45,000 men.

For troop transport, British liners were also made available. The records show that of the 2,079,880 troops sent abroad, over 46 per cent were carried in American ships (practically all naval transports), 48 per cent in British or British-leased ships, and the small remainder in ships of other allies. For the entire troop movement, American naval vessels provided about 86 per cent of the escort protection.

The first troop convoy went over late in June, 1917, but the big troop movements were concentrated in the spring and summer of the next year, culminating in the transport of 311,000 men in July. It was highly difficult to launch a successful U-boat attack on the fast moving, well-guarded convoys, which, when routed directly for France, followed a course somewhat to southward of the usual submarine hunting grounds in the traffic lanes to the British Isles. From the ships under American escort, not a man was lost by enemy action on the outward voyage.

Partly because they were necessarily less carefully routed and guarded, the westbound troop ships were not equally immune. The *Antilles* and *Finland,* both torpedoed in October, 1917, were homeward bound and not far from the French coast. They were still manned largely by civilian crews, with a small naval contingent to man the guns and act in emergencies. From the *Antilles* about 70 per cent were saved, and were again sailing westward in the *Finland* at the time of the second attack. In this instance an incipient panic was suppressed by the naval men on board, and the damaged ship was brought back to Brest.

The *President Lincoln,* attacked in May, 1918, was cleverly picked out of a group of four transports which the escort destroyers had left near the edge of the danger zone the night before. The submarine had been able to get ahead in the darkness and at dawn fired three torpedoes from eight hundred yards off the *Lincoln's* port bow. All struck, but though the ship went down quickly she was abandoned with excellent discipline and of the 715 on board, all but twenty-six were rescued later from boats and rafts. Lieutenant E. V. Izac, U.S.N., was picked from one of the rafts by the submarine, the *U-90,* and taken to Germany. With valuable information thus gathered, he later joined with other Americans in a thrilling escape from the Villingen prison camp, short circuiting the lights, scaling the barriers, and finally swimming the Rhine to Swiss soil.

The *Covington,* a former Hamburg-American liner of 26,-

000 tons, was sunk July 1 by a single torpedo fired at night while the ship was still in convoy. All but six men were saved. The last transport to suffer attack, the *Mt. Vernon,* lost thirty-seven men out of 1,450 on board, most of them killed by the explosion. Two compartments were flooded by a hole nineteen feet wide amidships, but the ship was finally brought into Brest by the splendid work of her engine-room force and the entire crew.

Naval Service on Shore

In addition to its service in assuring "the bridge to France," the Navy contributed to the land campaign by constructing railway mounts for a number of big 14-inch guns, originally intended for new battleships, and operating these guns with naval crews overseas. Under the general command of Rear Admiral C. P. Plunkett, five of the guns, with trains of fourteen cars for each, were in action on the Western Front from mid-September until the armistice. With a range of thirty miles, they fired a total of 782 rounds, doing serious damage to railway junctions and ammunition dumps well behind the enemy lines.

Throughout the American participation, also, brigades of the Marine Corps fought with typical courage and endurance. The severity of their fighting at Chateau Thierry, Belleau Wood, St. Mihiel, and elsewhere is indicated by the fact that of 8,000 men engaged, 1,600 were killed and over 2,500 wounded, or more than half of the total force.[6]

Finale

The task of our Navy in the First World War, like that of navies in most wars, lay in maintaining sea control and sea communications; and its great achievements were its effective

[6] For further account of the work of the Marines in France, see H. Metcalf, *A History of the United States Marine Corps,* 1939.

support for the British in combating the submarine and its major part in transporting our army overseas. In estimating these achievements, allowance must be made for the advantages we enjoyed—our remoteness from attack, time for preparation, participation with strong naval allies, and entry at a time when both sides had been worn down by nearly three years of exhausting conflict. It should be no cause for boasting or undue confidence that in these conditions our fresh forces turned the scales in favor of the Allies. But great credit may be taken for the energy, the spirit of co-operation, the magnitude of effort with which, once the need was clearly realized, American resources and manpower were thrown into the war.

On October 21, 1918, as a result of preliminary negotiations with President Wilson, the German Government agreed to abandon submarine attacks on passenger ships, and this practically ended the submarine campaign. There was talk of a last desperate sortie of the High Sea Fleet, but this was halted by mutinies among the seamen at Wilhelmshaven and Kiel. On November 21, in accordance with the armistice terms, the bulk of the German fleet—nine dreadnoughts, five battle cruisers, six light cruisers, and fifty destroyers [7]—steamed through the Grand Fleet, with the American Sixth Squadron, drawn up in two long columns at the Firth of Forth. At sunset, from the masts of this great naval force intended as a potent instrument for world conquest, the German flag was lowered for the last time.

References

Belknap, R. R., *The Yankee Mining Squadron,* 1920.

Daniels, Josephus, *Our Navy at War,* 1922.

Gleaves, Albert, Vice Admiral, *A History of the Transport Service,* 1921.

[7] The armistice terms called for surrender of ten battleships, six battle cruisers, eight light cruisers, fifty destroyers, and all submarines. The submarines and some of the larger types were surrendered elsewhere.

Knox, Dudley W., Captain, *A History of the United States Navy,* 1936.
Miller, H. B., Lieutenant, *Navy Wings,* 1937.
Morison, E. E., *Admiral Sims and the Modern American Navy,* 1942.
Sims, W. S., Vice Admiral, *The Victory at Sea,* 1920.

THE NAVY BETWEEN WARS (1918–1941)

DURING THE PEACE years between 1918 and 1941, the actual operations of our Navy were relatively unimportant, or at least were thrust into the background by the determined moves for international reduction of naval armaments. These moves, ending at length in failure and rearmament on an unprecedented scale, may seem today unimportant. Yet, at the time, they were a dominant element in American foreign policy; they have been the subject of voluminous study; and in both naval and diplomatic history they have a continued significance, illustrating, if nothing more, the difficulties of arms limitation until the more fundamental causes of war have been removed.

It would be difficult to overstress the feeling of revulsion, in the postwar period, against war and all the instruments of war. It was felt by both victors and vanquished—in the Old World, which had suffered most from war's ravages, and in the New World as well. Faith in the possibility of ending wars was even stronger in the New World, perhaps because of its more youthful, hopeful spirit, its less sharp realization of the age-old animosities and rivalries dividing the nations and classes of men. To all, the idea of reduction of armaments combined an emotional and practical appeal. If nations A, B, and C had a naval armament, say, of 20, 20, and 10 ships respectively, would they not be equally well prepared, and at much less expense, if their relative strengths were reduced to 10, 10, and 5? The idea seemed eminently reasonable. Yet, the point might be made that in establishing such a ratio, the A and B nations were seeking to impose a permanent inferiority, or impotence, on nation C. In other words, the same objection might be brought against arms limitation as against the League of Nations, that it sought to perpetuate the status quo. It would be accepted unwillingly, or with reservations, or only for temporary advantage, by nations resolutely bent on changing their position in the world.

There was another line of argument against arms limitation which, especially to those immediately concerned in American defense problems, seemed to have much validity. One of the lessons to be drawn from the conflict of 1914–18 was that future wars, unless prevented altogether, would no longer be "limited," but would be on an intercontinental or world scale. By keeping out of the League, the United States had weakened the machinery, feeble and faulty at best, for preventing war. Hence neither pacifists nor isolationists could feel much assurance that there would be no future wars, or that this nation would not be drawn in. A superior Navy, made possible by our wealth and resources, would be the best insurance against involvement, and against defeat if we became involved. The danger of war was increased when nations controlled wealth and resources which they lacked strength to defend. Between nations with no conflict of national interests, arms limitation might be easy; it would be difficult when deep-seated conflicts of policy were concerned.

These general considerations for and against arms limitation may well be borne in mind in reviewing the specific conditions that led to the Washington Conference on Limitation of Armaments in 1921–22.

The Washington Conference

After 1918, the United States, Britain, and Japan were the only important naval powers. It was perhaps inevitable that the peace should bring discord and incipient rivalry among these victors and former allies. Before America entered the war, such possibilities were evident in British interference with neutral trade, and in the American decision to build "a navy second to none." In 1918, this aim at naval parity with Great Britain was again evident in the policy of the Wilson administration, not only to maintain a strong merchant marine, but to complete the immense naval construction program of 1916. This meant that to the United States battle line of sixteen dreadnoughts, plus three others of the 1915 program nearly completed, would be added no less than ten battleships and six battle cruisers, all embodying postwar improvements in protection and armament. Against such a fleet England's forty-two ships of older design would have a doubtful superiority. The British had a preponderance of cruisers but not of destroyers, and, in their economic straits, they were carrying out wholesale demobilization and cutting naval appropriations to the bone. Hence, they viewed the possibilities of a new naval rivalry with resentment and dismay. On this subject there were hot conflicts between the American and the British delegations at Paris. It seems clear today that the Wilson administration was supporting the big naval program, not with complete sincerity, but as a makeweight to gain British support for the League Covenant, just as the same threat of immense naval appropriations was used later in this country to induce acceptance of the League. At Paris a truce was arranged in April, 1919, by which, in return for British support of the League, President Wilson agreed to put some brakes on new construction, with apparently a tacit understanding that the problem of relative naval strength would be settled in a separate conference after the peace treaty went through.

Between the United States and Japan the trouble went deeper. When Allied fears of Russia had led to the dispatch of Japanese troops into Siberia in the summer of 1918, we had approved reluctantly, and had sent our own forces there chiefly as a check on the Japanese. There was the problem also of the

Japanese occupation of Shantung and further designs on China embodied in the notorious "Twenty-One Demands." There was the transfer to Japan of the former German Caroline and Marshall Islands in the Pacific, only doubtfully restricted by League supervision, and affording opportunity for air bases and submarine nests athwart American communications with the East. There was finally the Anglo-Japanese alliance, which England might now value chiefly as a check on Japan, but which would certainly affect British action if the United States and Japan became involved. This was seen clearly in Canada, and the ending of the alliance was strongly advocated by the Canadian Premier at the Imperial Conference in London in June, 1921.

On both sides of the Atlantic, there was a strong demand for reduction of naval armaments by joint agreement, and a realization that this must be accompanied by an ending of the Anglo-Japanese alliance and a general settlement of Pacific problems. In America especially, after the abandonment of the League, political leaders saw the advantage of American sponsorship for a striking move toward world peace. These were the circumstances in which the Harding administration, only slightly anticipating a projected British proposal of the same nature, on July 11, 1921, invited Britain, France, Italy, and Japan to a conference in Washington, the scope of which would include not only "limitation of armaments" but "Pacific and Far Eastern problems." As nations with Pacific interests, Belgium, the Netherlands, Portugal, and China were included in subsequent invitations, but not Soviet Russia, which was still regarded as outside the diplomatic pale.

In preparation for the conference, there was intense activity at Washington in the State and Navy Departments. Naval needs, actual tonnage afloat, ships built and building—these were considered as bases for reduction proposals, and the last was adopted as fairest and most likely to lead to acceptable ratios. Detailed proposals were largely worked out by Assistant Secretary of the Navy Theodore Roosevelt, Jr., the Chief of Naval Operations Admiral Koontz, and his assistant Captain Pratt. Though Secretary of State Hughes, former Secretary of State Elihu Root, and Senators Lodge and Underwood were the chief American delegates, the naval advisers were constantly consulted and had an important part in the negotiations.

Rarely in diplomatic assemblages has there been a more striking scene than that at the first plenary session of the conference on November 12, in which Secretary Hughes presented the American proposals for sweeping nearly two million tons of ships from the world's chief navies. "Was this the face," so ran the caption, quoting the famous lines of Marlowe, under a contemporary cartoon of the distinguished Secretary, "was this the face that sank a thousand ships!" It had been expected that the opening session would be confined to generalities. There was scarcely concealed satisfaction on the faces of foreign delegates as the Secretary gave a detailed list of American ships to be scrapped, but expressions changed when he turned to the navies of Britain and Japan. Briefly, the United States was to scrap fifteen ships built and fifteen building or projected, amounting to nearly 846,000 tons, Britain was to scrap about 583,000 tons, and Japan about 449,000, leaving their capital ships in a ratio of 5–5–3. As finally arranged, with adjustments to enable the Japanese to keep the newly completed *Mutzu,* the ratios and tonnages were:

Nation	Ratios	Capital Ships	Aircraft Carriers
United States	5	525,000	135,000
Great Britain	5	525,000	135,000
Japan	3	315,000	81,000
France	1.75	175,000	60,000
Italy	1.75	175,000	60,000

As additional "qualitative" restrictions, battleships were limited to 35,000 tons and 16-inch guns, carriers to 27,000 tons and 8-inch guns, and cruisers to 10,000 tons and 8-inch guns. For the major powers, there was to be no replacement of battleships until 1931; the treaty was to remain in effect until December 31, 1936, and thereafter unless two years' notice was given.

Into the subsequent difficulties and intricate bargaining of the conference it is unnecessary to go in detail. Angered at her relegation to an inferior position, France made it clear that she would not accept the inferior ratio in auxiliary types, and she set her submarine needs at the high figure of 90,000 tons. With support from the United States and Japan, France also rejected the British proposal to abolish submarines altogether. A separate protocol was adopted prohibiting gas warfare and limiting submarines to action in accord with established international law, but this was rendered ineffective by the subsequent failure of France to give it ratification. The French attitude afforded England a justification for refusing—as she would have done in any event—to accept application of the ratios to cruisers and other lesser types, and the net result was that the United States, having sacrificed most heavily in capital ships, found that she would get no compensation in reduction of cruisers, where the other powers had a preponderance.

Japan, having entered the conference with some reluctance, and a fear that her political policies would be subjected to joint pressure of the Western nations, was able to drive a good naval bargain. In point of fact, the 5–3 ratio still gave her naval predominance in Eastern waters, and ended possibilities of an armament race in which she would have been outclassed. She was able also to secure in the naval treaty a most valuable "standstill" agreement on the fortification of Pacific islands. Each nation specified the island possessions to which stoppage of defense measures would apply:

For the United States—the Philippines, Guam, and the Aleutians, but not Hawaii or islands adjacent to Alaska, the Pacific coast, and Panama.

For Great Britain—Hongkong, but not Singapore or islands adjacent to Canada, Australia, or New Zealand.

For Japan—Formosa, Amami-Oshima, the Kuriles, Bonin, Loochoo, and Pescadores Islands, and any others afterward acquired, but not the homeland or islands adjacent.

The important point was the American pledge not to increase the fortifications of the Philippines or Guam. This the senators on the American delegation readily conceded, in the belief—doubtless justified—that Congress would never in any case approve the expenditures or political commitments which the full fortification of these bases would involve. Yet the pledge, along with the established ratios, ended the ability of the United States, single-handed, to give effective support for its Far Eastern policies. Henceforth, so long as the agreements remained in effect, trust in treaty promises must take the place of force. It was a trust not justified by the event.

The promises in question were embodied in a number of political agreements. The "Four Power Treaty" (United States, Britain, France, and Japan) ended the Anglo-Japanese alliance and substituted therefor a pledge of the signatories to respect each other's insular possessions and to confer in the event of a Pacific controversy. The "Nine Power Treaty" (including all the nations at the conference) bound the signatories to observe the "Open Door" policy, "respect the sovereignty, independence, and territorial integrity of China," and not take "advantage of conditions in China to seek special rights and privileges." This treaty, as well as League pledges, was violated by Japan in Manchuria in 1931, and consistently thereafter.

Significant for the future was the weakening of American and British influence in the Eastern sphere, unless the two nations should act in concert and be unhampered by pressure in the West. Yet, the general fairness of the naval agreements was perhaps evidenced by the complaints of each nation concerned. Britain had submitted to parity, Japan had lost face by accepting an inferior ratio, the United States had made the chief sacrifices. But the sacrifices of the United States were of ships and fortifications the completion of which was at least problematical. Meanwhile, the immense savings were obvious to all.

Later Moves for Naval Limitation

The United States hoped the ratios would soon be applied to all types, and limited new construction accordingly, but the other powers observed no such restrictions. Thus, the figures for new construction in the years 1922–27 stood as follows: United States 120,000 tons, Great Britain 285,000, Japan 339,000.[1] Somewhat alarmed at this situation, and after unsatisfactory results from co-operation with the League in disarmament efforts, President Coolidge proposed a second naval conference at Geneva in 1927. France and Italy declined to attend and the conference ended in failure, largely as a result of British insistence on a large number of cruisers and their limitation in size to 7,500 tons, with 6-inch guns. The American delegates were equally insistent on 10,000-ton cruisers with 8-inch guns, suited for long range operations with a limited number of bases, and having a clear superiority over converted liners.

With the passage of time, the closeness of Anglo-American interests became clearer and the need of co-operation more urgent. In the London Conference of 1930, this resulted in a compromise agreement by which each nation was permitted to build a preponderance of the type of cruiser desired, within a common global limit of about 330,000 tons. Limits were also set on destroyer and submarine tonnage, and the holiday in battleship construction was extended to 1936. France and Italy were unable to compose their difficulties and join fully in the agreement, and Japan was brought in only by conceding her a 7–10 ratio in cruisers and equality in submarines. The limitations were:

Types	United States	British Commonwealth	Japan
Cruisers (guns over 6.1 inch)	180,000	146,800	108,400
Cruisers (guns of 6.1 inch)	143,000	192,200	100,450
Destroyers	150,000	150,000	105,000
Submarines	52,700	52,700	52,700

[1] Figures from G. T. Davis, *A Navy Second to None*, p. 314.

The Japanese coup in Manchuria came in 1931; the rearmament of Germany, in defiance of League restrictions, had been gathering headway since 1928; and Italy undertook the conquest of Ethiopia in 1935. Clearly, international relations were rapidly deteriorating, and the end of arms limitation was at hand. With the advent of the Roosevelt administration in 1933, the United States undertook increased naval construction, and in 1934 the Vinson-Trammell Act authorized a long-range building program to provide a Navy of full treaty strength by 1942. In negotiations in 1934 preparatory to another naval conference, Japan was willing to abolish capital ships altogether, but demanded nothing short of parity in all types retained. This refused, she gave the required warning that she might drop treaty restrictions at the end of 1936. The new treaty signed by the United States, Britain, and France in 1936 retained only a shadow of limitations. Aircraft carriers were limited in size to 23,000 tons and submarines to 2,000 tons, but the agreement was sprinkled with escape clauses which were soon utilized, as the danger of war became imminent. With some oversimplification, yet with a measure of truth, it might be said that the relaxation of force by the chief naval nations, in these decades, had contributed toward outbreaks of violence all over the world.

Fleet Operations

In the postwar period, the American Navy was at first fully occupied with tasks growing out of the war. These included the transport home of troops from Europe, in which battleships as well as troop ships were utilized and which in June, 1919, reached a peak of 341,000 men; the sweeping up of mines in the North Sea, in which eleven lives were lost and twenty-three ships injured; and the support of American Army forces in northern Russia and Siberia. In August, 1919, Rear Admiral Mark L. Bristol was made United States High Commissioner at Constantinople, and continued in this duty until

1927, rendering aid in American relief work and protecting and forwarding American interests throughout the Near East. As American representative at Lausanne in 1923, he was instrumental in arranging a final settlement between Turkey and the Western powers. The two cruisers and the destroyers under his command brought away thousands of refugees from Russian ports on the Black Sea, and supervised the evacuation of 262,000 Greeks from Smyrna and elsewhere, after the Turks had routed Greek forces in Asia Minor. For several years American naval officers also administered former Austrian territory along some three hundred miles of the east Adriatic coast. The rapid postwar reduction of the Navy brought its enlisted strength from 497,000 men in 1918 to an authorized 86,000 in 1922, in the neighborhood of which figure it remained until the expansion of the late thirties.

A significant change in the strategic disposition of American naval forces came in 1919 with the decision to create two main fleets, one in the Atlantic and one in the Pacific, and to concentrate the newer ships on the West Coast. Though not so explained, this was a recognition that American foreign policy would face its chief problems in the West. At the close of 1922, the two fleets were combined as the United States Fleet, under unified command, and the battle strength was thereafter, for the most part, concentrated in the Pacific, with only minor forces on the East Coast. This continued until 1939, when three older battleships were brought to the East Coast to form the nucleus of an Atlantic Patrol Force, later further expanded and organized as an Atlantic Fleet.

In view of disturbed conditions in China, the Yangtse Patrol was strengthened in 1922 and placed under flag-officer command. During the civil conflict in China and in the warfare after July, 1937, between China and Japan, our naval forces were constantly employed in the protection of American lives and property. The sinking of the United States gunboat *Panay,* December 12, 1937, was but one manifestation of the open purpose of the military faction dominant in Japan to break down British and American treaty rights and interests in the eastern sphere. The little river gunboat, which with three Standard Oil tankers had moved some twenty-eight miles up the Yangtse to avoid the fighting at Nanking, was attacked by Japanese aircraft with bombs and machine guns and sunk with a loss of two killed and fourteen injured. The immediate apology and offer of reparations by Japan was accepted by the State Department in Washington, but not the Japanese version of the attack that it was unintentional.

Fleet exercises in this period centered chiefly on training for the co-operation of all forces in a major fleet action, with full utilization of improvements in ships and weapons, but with the universal human tendency to build on past experience rather than on an imaginative prevision of the future. Yet while the Navy remained well below treaty limits it could scarcely have planned in any case to cope with the exigencies of naval warfare and commerce protection, not only on two oceans, but extended over the seven seas. With the reduction of ships, fleet exercises and war games became increasingly strenuous. In routine practice and training four submarines were lost and many aircraft, with an attendant loss of personnel pioneering in these experimental fields.

Naval Aviation

American naval aviation was universally regarded as outstanding in progressiveness and efficiency. Its beginnings and expansion in 1914–18 have already been outlined.[2] Thereafter it was cramped somewhat by limited appropriations and the general tendency to underestimate its importance in future war. On the other hand, it gained from its complete integration with the fleet. Its pilots were almost entirely line officers with fleet experience, and its training was for co-ordination with fleet action. The pilot training at Pensacola maintained the most rigorous standards. By 1921 the force had been re-

---

[2] See pages 357–359.

duced to about 300 officer pilots and 4,000 men. Appropriations ranged from about $13,000,000 in the twenties to $40,000,000 in 1936, after which they surged upward. In 1926, an Assistant Secretary of the Navy for Aviation was appointed, and a five-year production program was instituted which reached its goal of 1,000 planes in 1931.

During this period much of the work was necessarily experimental, a testing out of types of planes and their most effective use with the fleet. A notable flight was that of three Navy Curtiss (NC) boats from Long Island to Newfoundland, thence via the Azores to Lisbon, and then to Plymouth, England, in May of 1919. The three NC's were selected from several big "flying boats" designed for direct wartime flight to England, but not ready before the armistice. In the actual flight, in which Commander J. H. Towers was senior officer, sixty destroyers and other surface craft were stationed along the course. Two of the planes were damaged by heavy seas in landing at the Azores, but the NC-4, Commander A. C. Read, completed the 4,500 mile flight in fifty-four flying hours. It was the first transatlantic flight in aviation history. Naval and Marine Corps flyers also made early experiments in dive-bombing in 1926–27, and it was Admiral Bradley A. Fiske, U.S.N., who invented the torpedo-plane before we entered the First World War.

In the long-standing aircraft vs. battleships controversy, the aircraft had early naval supporters, including senior officers such as Admiral W. F. Fullam and Admiral Sims. "Command of the air," in Sims's view, gave "command of the surface, whether it be sea or land." The aircraft bombing tests in 1921 on the ex-German dreadnought *Ostfriesland* and on several smaller naval vessels were not fully conclusive, though most of the ships were finally sunk. The official report declared that battleships must still be regarded as "the backbone of the fleet," and that while there should be "the maximum possible development of aviation," it had not simplified but "added to the complexity of naval warfare."

For the progressive spirit and high morale of American naval aviation, much credit belongs to Rear Admiral William A. Moffett, who was Chief of the Bureau of Aeronautics from 1921 until his death in the *Akron* disaster in 1933. By the early thirties naval aircraft of all types were operating with the fleet, not only from carriers but from all battleships and larger cruisers. The employment of huge dirigibles was an essential part of the experimental work in aviation, but was ended by successive disasters. The *Shenandoah* broke in three parts during a thunderstorm in Ohio, in September, 1925, carrying to death her commander and fourteen of her crew of forty-nine; the *Akron* went down in bad weather off the Jersey coast, April 3, 1933, with the loss of all but four of her crew; and the *Macon* ended her career off the West Coast in 1935 with a loss of two men.

The Navy had but one aircraft carrier, the *Langley,* until the conversion of the partly completed battle cruisers *Lexington* and *Saratoga* after the Washington Conference. In 1941, it had seven in service and twelve under construction. In that year the number of naval planes was increased from 2,500 at the beginning of the year to about 5,000 at the close, and the number of pilots was increased from 3,639 to 6,900—a creditable approach toward the projected figures of 15,000 planes and 12,000 pilots. The use of aircraft with the fleet represented a new element in sea power, and the beginnings of a change perhaps as revolutionary as that in the nineteenth century caused by the introduction of steam.

The American Merchant Marine

The experience of the United States in 1914–18, both as a neutral and as a belligerent, strongly emphasized the need of an adequate merchant fleet under the national flag, to insure the transport of products, maintenance of markets, and supply of essential goods from abroad. With the nation at war, this need was made greater by the demands of the Navy for sea-going personnel and for ships of all types as transports and auxiliaries. Furthermore, in the postwar period there was an increased trend abroad toward national control of shipping and its use as a weapon for trade expansion. The great obstacle to a large American merchant marine was, as in the past half century, the fact that foreign ships could be built and operated at much lower cost. This applied, of course, only to our ships in foreign trade, and not to the great bulk of our fleet which operated on the Great Lakes and in coastwise traffic. Completion of the wartime building program left the United States with a greatly increased tonnage of ocean carriers, and the fixed government policy was to maintain this advantage, while transferring the ships, so far as possible, to private hands.

In 1921, American ships carried about 40 per cent of our foreign trade, but the proportion fell to an average of around 35 per cent in the rest of the decade, with a shrinkage also in volume. This was due largely to the general decline of international trade, resulting in idle ships, and sharper competition with foreign carriers. Even with the aid of profitable government mail contracts, sale of ships at nominal prices, and government loans for new construction, the Shipping Board met only limited success in its policy of establishing foreign shipping services, building them up if possible to a paying basis, and then turning them over to private companies. Thirty-eight such services were established and twenty-two disposed of. The Shipping Act of 1936 abolished the system of subsidies disguised as mail contracts and put into the hands of a newly created Maritime Commission of five members the task of awarding straight subsidies on both construction and operation, sufficient to compensate for higher costs abroad. Ships built with government aid were made to conform to requirements suiting them to conversion for naval use in war. The officers and at least two-thirds of the crew were required to be American citizens. With the Government paying up to one-third of the cost, and further aid in the form of low-interest loans, an energetic program of construction was undertaken; but before the new system could be fully tested, the approach of war upset peacetime plans and demanded construction on an immensely increased scale. Aircraft also, as a means of passenger, mail, and even freight transport abroad, were entering into the complicated problem.

The End of Peace

It might be assumed that the strong anti-military sentiment prevailing in America during the decades after 1918, and the sharp restrictions placed on new construction, would have some adverse effect on naval morale and on the quality of men attracted to the naval service. Yet labor conditions, together with the attractions and positive benefits of naval training, made it possible to bring into the Navy a far higher quality of enlisted personnel, in health, intelligence, and educational background, than the men of an earlier day. Each year, under the four-year enlistment system, the Navy took in from 15,000 to 20,000 young men and returned an equal number to civil life, the latter benefited not only by military discipline but by instruction and practical training in many trades which could be taken up as a lifework. Increased stress was also placed on the advanced training of officers at the Naval War College, at the Postgraduate School in Annapolis, and in engineering schools. In the act of 1925 reorganizing the Naval Reserve, provision was made for the establishment of Naval Reserve Officer Training Courses in six universities, and the number of these was greatly increased with the renewed threat of war. Taken as a whole, the Navy enjoyed—and merited—a high degree of public confidence when it was called upon once more to provide the backbone, training, and morale for an immense wartime expansion.

References

Buell, R. L., *The Washington Conference,* 1922.

Griswold, A. W., *The Far Eastern Policy of the United States,* 1938.

Johnstone, W. C., *The United States and Japan's New Order,* 1941.
Simonds, F. H., *American Foreign Policy in the Post-War Years,* 1935.
Sprout, H. and M., *Toward a New Order of Sea Power,* 1940.
Spykman, N. J., *America's Strategy in World Politics,* 1942.

THE SECOND WORLD WAR (1939–1941)

American Measures Short of War

Of the conditions and actions which led to American participation in the second world conflict, it seems needful to stress here only those relating more especially to commerce and warfare at sea. The larger issues of the European struggle which began in September, 1939, were similar to those of 1914–18. In the later period, the American desire to keep out of war was no doubt equally strong, but the feeling against the aggressor nations was more general and unrestrained. This feeling was fully shared by the Administration, and, profiting by the lessons of the earlier conflict, it took energetic steps of military preparation, while shaping its policy increasingly toward "all assistance short of war" against the militant dictatorships.

A Modified Neutrality

The "keep-out-of-war" sentiment had found its strongest expression in the neutrality legislation of 1935 and 1937. The Act of 1937, suspending to a large extent the rights traditionally assumed by a neutral, provided that, in a war in which the United States was not a participant, this Government in its relations with the belligerents should (1) forbid the export to them of any arms, munitions, or implements of war; (2) halt

American loans or other financial aid; (3) forbid Americans to travel on their ships; and (4) at the President's discretion, require that exports of any kind to them should be on a "cash and carry" basis, that is, the goods must be sold before shipment and must be carried in other than American vessels. A Munitions Control Board was also set up to control the manufacture and export of war materials. In this legislation the arms embargo in particular, closing the doors to American sources of supply, put a severe handicap on those nations that had not planned and geared their whole national economy for war. A fact also disregarded—in this effort to legislate the United States out of future trouble—was that the effects of the law would vary greatly in different wars. Thus in the Chino-Japanese War, which broke out a few months later, its provisions almost wholly favored Japan. In this instance, with full popular support but with only the slender excuse that there had been no war declarations, the President refrained from putting the law into effect.

Soon after the outbreak of the war in Europe, the Neutrality Act was altered fundamentally by the new Act of November, 1939. This, while retaining other provisions of the old law, dropped the arms embargo and permitted "cash and carry" traffic in goods of all kinds, including arms. Obviously, the law would now favor the nations controlling the sea, able to purchase the goods and take them away. Furthermore, to ease the injury to American shipping, the cash-and-carry requirement was not in general applied to belligerent territories outside the European area. Thereafter, the President by proclamation excluded American ships from belligerent ports in Europe and also from a "danger area" east of 20 degrees west longitude and extending from the Bay of Biscay to Norway (see map, page 385).

As a means of securing inter-American solidarity in the world crisis, representatives of the twenty-one American republics, meeting at Panama in October, 1939, pledged co-operation in all problems raised by the war, and set up a "safety belt" in the

Official U.S. Navy photographs

Top, U.S.S. HOUSTON AT HONOLULU. *Bottom,* FORMATION OF MOTOR TORPEDO BOATS.

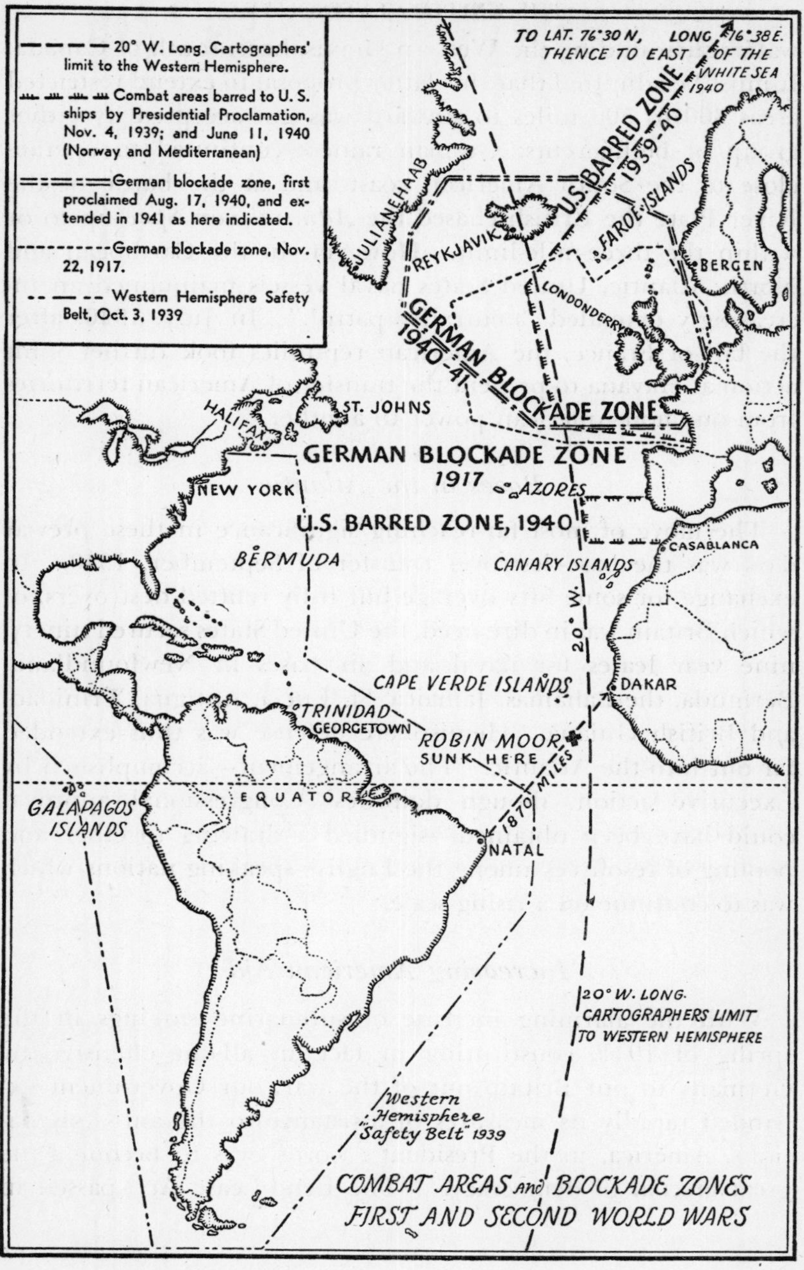

20° W. Long. Cartographers' limit to the Western Hemisphere.
Combat areas barred to U. S. ships by Presidential Proclamation, Nov. 4, 1939; and June 11, 1940 (Norway and Mediterranean)
German blockade zone, first proclaimed Aug. 17, 1940, and extended in 1941 as here indicated.
German blockade zone, Nov. 22, 1917.
Western Hemisphere Safety Belt, Oct. 3, 1939
TO LAT. 76°30 N, LONG. 16°38E.
THENCE TO EAST OF THE WHITE SEA
1940
U.S. BARRED ZONE 1939-40
FAROE ISLANDS
JULIANEHAAB
REYKJAVIK
BERGEN
LONDONDERRY
GERMAN BLOCKADE 1940-41
BLOCKADE ZONE
HALIFAX
ST. JOHNS
GERMAN BLOCKADE ZONE
1917
AZORES
NEW YORK
U.S. BARRED ZONE, 1940
BERMUDA
CASABLANCA
CANARY ISLANDS
20° W.
CAPE VERDE ISLANDS
DAKAR
TRINIDAD
GEORGETOWN
ROBIN MOOR
SUNK HERE
870 MILES
EQUATOR
GALAPAGOS ISLANDS
NATAL
20° W. LONG.
CARTOGRAPHERS LIMIT
TO WESTERN HEMISPHERE
Western Hemisphere "Safety Belt" 1939

COMBAT AREAS and BLOCKADE ZONES
FIRST AND SECOND WORLD WARS

waters surrounding the Western Hemisphere, south of Canada. It must be admitted that this latter proposal to extend restricted areas 300 to 500 miles to seaward was not accepted by either group of belligerents; German raiders continued to operate close to the South American coast, and at the battle of the River Plate the British chased the *Admiral von Spee* up to or within the three-mile-limit. However, in the Caribbean and North Atlantic, United States naval vessels maintained an increasingly extended "neutrality patrol." In July, 1940, after the fall of France, the American republics took further joint action at Havana to prevent the transfer of American territories from one non-American power to another.

Bases in the Atlantic

The move of most far-reaching significance in these prewar days was the base-destroyer transfer of September, 1940. In exchange for some fifty overage but fully refitted destroyers, of which Britain was in dire need, the United States secured ninety-nine year leases for naval and air bases in Newfoundland, Bermuda, the Bahamas, Jamaica, St. Lucia, Antigua, Trinidad, and British Guiana. Hemisphere defense was thus extended far out into the Atlantic. The arrangement—accomplished by Executive action, though doubtless Congressional approval could have been obtained—signified a drawing together and pooling of resources among the English-speaking nations which was to continue on a rising scale.

Increasing American Aid

With the alarming increase of submarine sinkings in the spring of 1941, constituting in fact an all-out offensive by Germany to put Britain out of the war, our Government expanded rapidly its measures of assistance to the anti-Axis nations. America, in the President's words, was to become "the great arsenal of democracy." The Lend-Lease Act, passed in

March, ended the problem of immediate payments; the President could sell, lease, lend, or otherwise transfer arms, implements of war, ships, and "defense articles" of all kinds to "any country whose defense the President deems vital to the defense of the United States." The Act even permitted the repair of such articles—including battleships—in American ports.

In June, our Government ordered the closing of German and Italian consulates in this country, froze all remaining assets of the Axis or Axis-controlled nations, and put into service some eighty or more ships of these nations which had been seized in American ports. Further to replace shipping losses, the Maritime Board was already supervising an immense program of new construction, which added a million tons of new ships in 1941, eight million tons in 1942, and had for its goal sixteen million tons in 1943. Fifteen hundred Liberty ships were to be built by mass production, each to be completed in a little over a month's time.

Since early spring, the American naval patrol had been extended further into the Atlantic, with orders to protect American shipping anywhere outside the prescribed danger zone. This single measure put a serious curb on the submarine campaign, for Germany was especially anxious at this time to avoid clashes that would bring the United States fully into the war. In April, by an arrangement with the Danish minister in Washington (later disavowed by the Nazi-controlled authorities at Copenhagen), the United States took over the protection of Greenland for the duration of the war, and in July, American military forces were sent to share in the occupation of Iceland, with instructions to "insure the safety of communications between Iceland and the United States." Partly as a result of these measures, the summer months brought a sharp decline in submarine sinkings, which in April had reached the dangerous figure of nearly 600,000 tons. For this year, the "Battle of the Atlantic" was won. To all intents and purposes, also, the American Navy was now fully in the war.

Actions in the Atlantic

Meanwhile, American merchant vessels, though kept outside the danger zone, had not escaped destruction. A flagrant instance was that of the *Robin Moor,* torpedoed in May in the South Atlantic with complete disregard for the safety of passengers and crew, who were adrift in open boats for many days. This the President branded as "the act of an international outlaw." In September came definite orders to American naval vessels to fire on submarines engaged in such attacks on ships whether of American or other nationality. Shortly before this order, the United States destroyer *Greer,* while co-operating on September 4 with a British aircraft in locating a submarine, had used depth charges after avoiding two torpedoes fired by the U-boat. Before dawn on October 4, the new United States destroyer *Kearny,* coming to the defense of a heavily engaged convoy, was attacked by a submarine which fired three torpedoes simultaneously while running only partly submerged. One of the missiles hit and exploded with heavy damage near the forward fireroom, killing or blowing overboard eleven men and wounding seven more. Despite stalled engines, flooded compartments, and innumerable other injuries, Lieutenant Commander Daunis was able to get his destroyer under way and to bring her finally into Iceland. On the way, a surgeon transferred from another destroyer saved a petty officer's life by a blood transfusion with plasma dropped from an airplane. After six months for repairs in Boston, the *Kearny* was again at sea. A worse fate awaited the older destroyer *Reuben James,* broken in two and sunk two weeks later, also in Iceland waters, by a single torpedo which exploded a magazine. Of the crew of 145 only 44 were saved. American escort ships were now taking an active part in guarding the Atlantic passage. Up to December 21, according to Secretary of the Navy Knox, American naval vessels had sunk or damaged at least fourteen submarines in the Atlantic.

Naval Expansion

Much earlier than this time, an unprecedented program of new American naval construction had been put under way. The Vinson-Trammell Act, as noted earlier, had provided for a "treaty navy" by 1942. But these modest limits for new construction were pushed upward by 20 per cent in 1938 and again by 11 per cent in June of 1940; and a month later, after the surrender of France, Congress authorized a 70 per cent increase which by 1946 would provide the nation with an immense "two-ocean" navy. As compared with the 1941 strength of about 350 ships of 1,368,000 tons, the new fleet would include over 700 ships of something like 3,500,000 tons. There would be 32 battleships, 18 aircraft carriers, 91 cruisers, 365 destroyers, and 185 submarines. Of the new capital ships, the *Washington* and *North Carolina,* of 35,000 tons, with nine 16-inch guns in triple turrets and over twenty-seven knots speed, were ready in the spring of 1941, and four others of this type were completed in 1942. Keels were laid for four 45,000-tonners of the *Iowa* class, and seven still larger *Montanas* were projected, with a displacement of perhaps 60,000 tons. The cruisers for the most part were to be light and heavy types of 6,000 to 10,000 tons, though there was provision for six "super-cruisers" of over 20,-000 tons. In the war exigency, cost was hardly a controlling factor; the expenditure for new surface ships and aircraft might run far above $10,000,000,000.

Despite the pressing demand for new merchant tonnage and the vastly increased requirements for shipyard facilities and trained workmen, such progress was made in naval construction that in 1942 carriers, cruisers, destroyers, and auxiliary types were sliding off the ways well ahead of schedule, and there was a prospect that the bulk of the new Navy might be ready as early as 1944. But since the war was begun with the Navy of 1941, the following figures are those for July of that year for this country and Japan.

Types	United States			Japan		
	Built		Building	Built		Building
	Number	1,000 tons	Number	Number	1,000 tons	Number
Capital ships	17	544	17	12	381	10(?)
Aircraft carriers	7	155	12	7	75	3(?)
Cruisers (8 inch guns)	18	171	14	12	108	?
Cruisers (6 inch guns)	19	158	40	26	157	?
Destroyers	175	225	197	133	173	?
Submarines	115	115	74	84	120	?
Total	351	1,368	354	274	1,014	

Though the new construction went rapidly forward, it was certain that radical changes in the program would be dictated by new developments in the war. Even the first few months of fighting indicated the special need for escort ships of all types, for increased submarine construction, for more aircraft carriers, for the utmost expansion of aircraft strength, including both ship- and shore-based planes.

In June, 1942, legislation was adopted providing for suspension of work on the big *Montana* battleships, still in the blueprint state, and for the additional construction of 500,000 tons of aircraft carriers, 500,000 tons of cruisers, 900,000 tons of destroyers and escort vessels, and some 1,300 small motor patrols, torpedo boats, and mine craft. To combat the submarine menace in the Atlantic, there was a special need for escorts of a larger, faster type.

In aircraft, the problem was one of building up to already recognized needs. The 1940 program had set a goal of 15,000 planes. But, after practically doubling its strength in the course of the year, the Navy had only about 5,000 planes and 6,900 pilots at the close of 1941. In the autumn of 1942, funds were voted for 13,500 additional naval planes. At the close of 1941, the naval personnel in active service, including reserves in active status, numbered about 32,000 officers and nearly 300,000 men, to which should be added 20,000 officers and men of the Coast Guard, which in October of 1941 was put under naval control. These numbers grew rapidly. At the end of 1942 the Navy mustered between 1,000,000 and 1,500,000 men.

Official U.S. Navy photographs

Top, THE 35,000-TON U.S.S. WASHINGTON STEAMS THROUGH HEAVY SEAS. Six of the battleship's nine 16-inch guns are visible. *Bottom,* ANTI-AIRCRAFT PROTECTION ON A MODERN BATTLESHIP. Dual purpose 5-inch 38's firing.

War Clouds in the Pacific

Since their unhampered coup in Manchuria in 1931, Japanese leaders had felt increasing assurance that their schemes for expansion in Asia or elsewhere could be pushed forward without effective interference from the Western nations. The deliberately provoked war with China in 1937 had given them a hold on the Chinese maritime provinces and enabled them to set up a puppet rule at Nanking, though it had aroused a stubborn and seemingly unconquerable resistance from the Chinese Government and armed forces under Marshal Chiang Kai-shek. Since British or other aid for China was largely held up by the threat of war in Europe, Japan was quick to see that her immediate interests corresponded with those of the Axis powers. She already had a tie with Germany in the Anti-Comintern Pact of 1936, and in September, 1940, after the fall of France, she threw aside doubts and misgivings and in the Tripartite Pact linked her destinies with those of the German and Italian dictatorships.

This pact, while giving its blessing to the "new order in Europe" and a "greater East Asia" dominated by Japan, pledged all three nations to full political, economic, and military assistance if another nation, not already involved, should enter the war in either the East or the West. Obviously, this was primarily a threat to keep the United States out of the war. Its underlying policy was also sufficiently clear—once British opposition was broken down, America could be dealt with later on.

Up to this point, though the sympathies and interests of the United States and Britain lay wholly with China, their closely concerted Far Eastern policy had been in general one of appeasement, based on the idea that more was to be gained than lost by delaying a break with Japan. Though probably expedient in the circumstances, it was a policy that weakened their aid for China and enabled Japan, from American, British, and Dutch sources, to lay in heavy stock piles of scrap iron and steel, fuel oils, lubricants, and other strategic materials. In July of 1940, however, the United States placed restrictions on gasoline exports, and gave six-months' notice of its intention to abrogate the Japanese-American commercial treaty. In October following, restrictions were also placed on the export of American scrap iron and steel.

After the occupation of the Netherlands and the conquest of France, the eyes of Japan were more than ever turned toward the golden opportunities for expansion southward, into the rich eastern colonies of these powers. Demands on the Vichy French government in the spring of 1941 gave Japan practically a free hand in French Indo-China, with naval and air bases pushed closer to the Philippines and the British stronghold at Singapore. At this point, in July, 1941, the American, British, and Dutch governments, acting again in concert, froze Japanese assets and virtually suspended trade relations. There could be no further doubt that the vital interests of these nations, in Asia and throughout the Pacific area, were directly menaced by the advancing flag of the Rising Sun.

In Japan, the new ministry formed in October under General Tojo put the long dominant militarist faction in still more complete control. Diplomatic negotiations which were continued thereafter in Washington may be regarded chiefly as a cover for final Japanese military preparations. Certainly, when special envoy Saburo Kurusu arrived in Washington on November 20, the initial moves for Pearl Harbor were already under way; and the Japanese envoys were presenting another note to our State Department an hour after the attack of December 7 began.

The Attack on Pearl Harbor

In view of Japan's surprise moves against China in 1894 and against Russia ten years later, American military authorities were well aware that Japan, like her Axis partners, would be

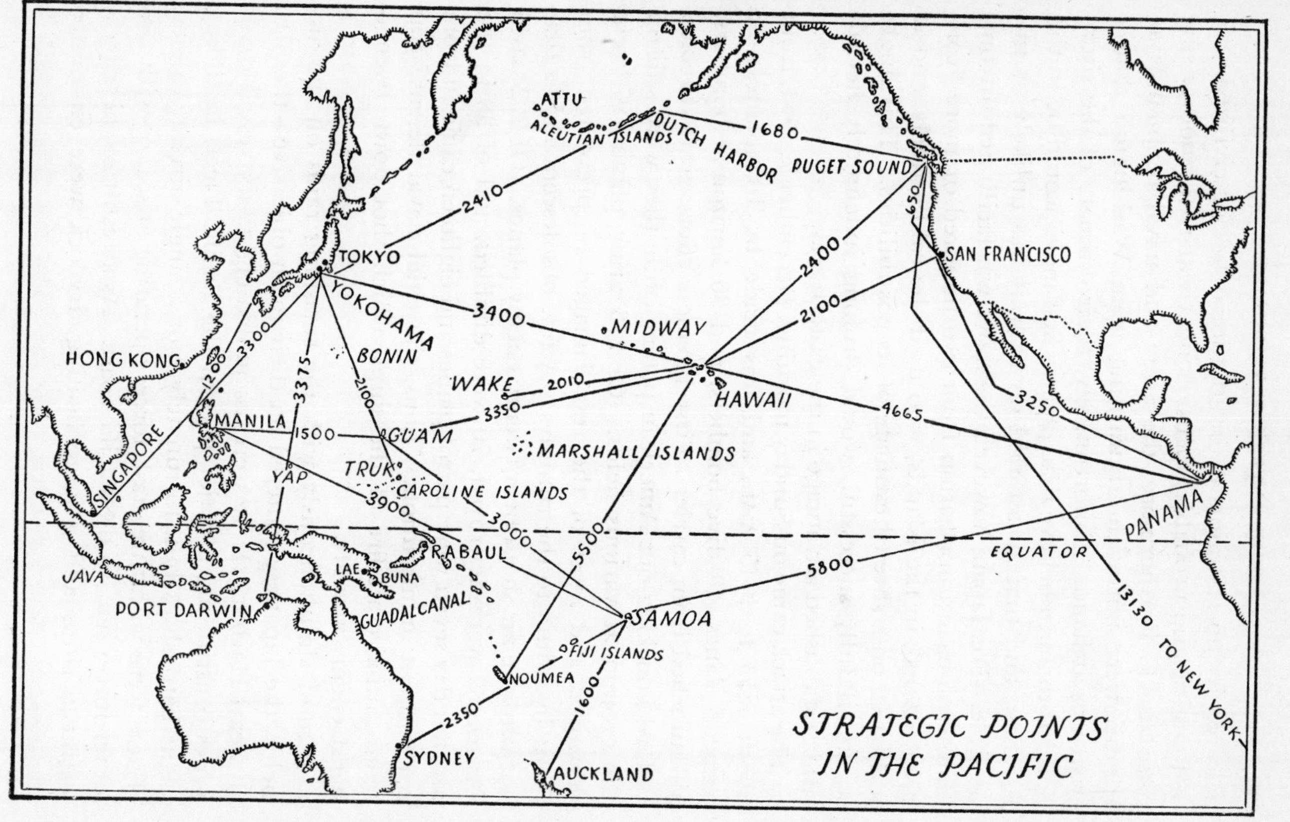
STRATEGIC POINTS IN THE PACIFIC
ATTU
ALEUTIAN ISLANDS
DUTCH HARBOR
1680
PUGET SOUND
650
SAN FRANCISCO
2410
TOKYO
YOKOHAMA
2400
2100
3400
MIDWAY
HONG KONG
1200
3300
3375
BONIN
2100
WAKE
2010
HAWAII
3250
4665
MANILA
1500
GUAM
3350
MARSHALL ISLANDS
SINGAPORE
YAP
TRUK
CAROLINE ISLANDS
3900
3000
5500
PANAMA
EQUATOR
RABAUL
JAVA
LAE
BUNA
5800
PORT DARWIN
GUADALCANAL
SAMOA
FIJI ISLANDS
13130
TO NEW YORK
NOUMEA
1600
2350
SYDNEY
AUCKLAND

deterred by no restraints of international law or civilized custom, and would probably open her next war with another surprise attack. Furthermore, the army and naval commands at Hawaii were not without warning from Washington that a crisis was at hand. Unfortunately, their estimate of the situation led them to believe that Japan's first move would be in the Far East, and that an air raid on Hawaii was unlikely or impossible. For Japan, however, the move was facilitated by complete espionage information from two hundred or more "consular agents" in the islands, who used the cables freely, and it was based on a shrewd estimate of its possibilities. This single stroke, if fully successful, would prolong indefinitely her already established advantage in the eastern seas.

The attack came on Sunday morning, December 7, 1941, from about 7:55 to 9:45 A.M., and was made by 105 planes—21 torpedo-planes, 48 dive bombers, and 36 horizontal bombers, all launched from carriers. First Japanese efforts were directed toward knocking out American planes while they were still on the ground at various fields. Of 273 army planes, 97 were destroyed and most of the rest damaged or prevented from flight by injury to the runways. A few obsolescent *P 38's* that got into the air shot down twenty enemy planes. Of 202 naval planes, 80 were destroyed, 70 were disabled, and of 38 in the air that day seven were patrol planes and eighteen came in from sea without ammunition. Thus, the chief naval defense was from anti-aircraft fire of the ships, which shot down twenty-eight enemy aircraft.

Almost simultaneously with the smashing raids on the airfields, the Japanese centered on their main objective—the fleet in Pearl Harbor. Here were assembled eighty-six vessels of all types constituting a major part of the Pacific Fleet, including eight battleships but, fortunately, not a single aircraft carrier. These were with three task forces operating at sea, or with two other forces sent to the Pacific coast. As a result of the attack, eighteen ships and a large floating drydock were either destroyed or damaged. Of the eight battleships, the *Arizona* was blown up by a bomb—a "hit in a million"—which went down her stack and exploded a forward magazine. The *Oklahoma* capsized after repeated hits, but could be righted and repaired. The *Nevada* was beached, and the *West Virginia* and *California* suffered heavy damage and settled at their berths. The other three escaped with minor injuries. Two cruisers were hit by torpedoes and a third by a bomb, and three destroyers were at first counted as lost. The destroyer *Shaw,* in drydock, received severe bomb hits, but was again at sea in July with a new bow. The *Cassin* and *Downes* were sunk, but their machinery, about 50 per cent of their value, was later recovered. Other losses were the old target ship *Utah* and the mine-layer *Oglala,* which had the ill luck to be in a berth marked by the Japanese as usually occupied by aircraft carriers. The repair ship *Vestal* was saved from destruction by the energy of her commander, who, though blown overboard by a bomb, swam back to his ship to direct salvage. The seaplane tender *Curtiss* was hit but soon repaired. The Navy suffered a greater loss of personnel than in all its fighting since the Civil War—3,077 killed or missing and 876 wounded. The Army's loss was 306 killed and 396 wounded.

After the attack the harbor was a scene of devastation, the waters covered with wreckage and burning oil, the skies overshadowed with smoke from ships in flames. Undoubtedly, the Japanese did not at once know the extent of damage inflicted. But the aircraft losses were soon replaced, and repairs were put under way. The naval report a year later declared the Pacific Fleet to be stronger than the year before, "partially because of the magnificent job of salvage carried out by Americans who were undaunted by their task."

Though the surprise was complete and an all-important factor, in view of the air defenses otherwise available, all fleet anti-aircraft batteries were brought into action within four to seven minutes after the first alarm. As stated in the report of the

Roberts Commission of Investigation,[1] "both officers and enlisted men, defending against the attack, demonstrated excellent training and high morale." The earlier report of Secretary of the Navy Frank Knox also cited many instances of heroic conduct—such as that of Captain Bennion of the *West Virginia,* who, though severely wounded, continued to direct operations from the bridge until he perished in an inferno of flames; of a bluejacket who manned a 5-inch anti-aircraft gun after ten battery mates had been shot down; of survivors of the *Oklahoma* who swam through blazing oil to climb aboard other ships and join gun-crews; of an officer who leaped from a hospital bed to cross the navy yard and join his ship, where he "fought with such gallantry and zeal that his captain recommended his promotion."

Among the weapons employed by the Japanese in the assault were several tiny two-man submarines. One of these was sunk by a destroyer and an aircraft outside the harbor, though the report sent in at 7:12 was not taken as a warning. Two others were destroyed inside the harbor, to which they had penetrated through the gate in the protective net at the entrance, left open after the passage of mine sweepers at 5:00 A.M. The submarines carried two 18-inch torpedoes and had a cruising radius of two hundred miles.

The findings of the Roberts Commission were that the preparations at Hawaii were inadequate, in view of the warnings given from Washington, and that Lieutenant General Walter C. Short, in command of the Hawaiian Department, and Admiral Husband E. Kimmel, Commander in Chief of the Pacific Fleet, were guilty of dereliction of duty in this respect and in not having consulted with each other regarding defense measures taken and required. According to the report, there was no naval distant air reconnaissance and no army inshore patrol operating on the morning of the attack. Though an anti-

[1] This commission, which presented its report on January 23, 1942, was composed of Justice Owen D. Roberts of the Supreme Court (Chairman), Admirals W. H. Standley and J. M. Reeves, and Generals Frank R. McCoy and J. T. McNarney.

aircraft warning system had recently been installed by the Army, it was operated only from 4:00 to 7:00 A.M., and the report of aircraft turned in shortly afterward by an inexperienced observer was disregarded.

Wake Island

With insignificant defenses, Guam was taken by the Japanese on December 11. At Wake Island, 2,000 miles west of Hawaii, a Marine garrison of 439 men under Major James P. Devereux, with twelve planes under Major Paul Putnam, beat off repeated Japanese attacks from December 8 to 22. In the first raid of twenty-four Japanese land planes, probably from the near-by mandate islands, seven American planes were destroyed on the ground and another was injured. On the eleventh the garrison repulsed a full-scale landing operation by waiting until the enemy were within 5,000 yards, and then pouring in a fire with their 3-inch and 5-inch guns which sank two destroyers and a gunboat, while the three planes still in operation sank a light cruiser and left another ship in flames. After severe losses, including more than half the air personnel and all the planes, the garrison surrendered. But the surrender was accomplished at a cost to the enemy of a cruiser, three or four destroyers, a gunboat, a submarine, and a dozen or more aircraft.

War Declared

The destruction at Pearl Harbor was heavy, in men, ships, and planes, but it is not evident that, even if these losses had not occurred, American naval strength would have been sufficient to prevent the Japanese advance in the southwestern Pacific. On the other hand, this treacherous attack on a nation still at peace may have lost for Japan more than it gained. It served as nothing else could to arouse the American people, unite them in the war effort, and drive home a realization that our own national security was at stake in the world conflict.

Japanese declarations of war were issued sometime on the

day of the attack. The American and British declarations against Japan came on the next day. Germany and Italy, on December 11, joined Japan in declaring war on the United States, and the Senate and House, on that same date, with no dissenting votes, passed a joint resolution declaring a state of war with the two Axis powers. On January 2, 1942, twenty-six governments, including the United States, the Soviet Republic, China, six states of the British Commonwealth, eight exiled governments of Europe, and nine states of Central America and the Caribbean, joined in a pact of the United Nations, giving pledges to employ their full economic and military resources against the members of the Tripartite Pact with which each government was at war, and to make war and peace together.

Early in 1941, the United States Fleet had been divided into three fleets, the Atlantic, Pacific, and Asiatic. After the outbreak of war, the President again placed all fleets and operating forces under a single Commander in Chief, United States Fleet, and designated Admiral Ernest J. King for this most important duty. Admiral Thomas C. Hart retained command of the Asiatic Fleet, Admiral Chester W. Nimitz was appointed to command the Pacific Fleet, and Admiral Royal E. Ingersoll was assigned to command of the Atlantic Fleet. In March following, to avoid conflicts and divided authority, Admiral King was also made Chief of Naval Operations, thus combining the two offices of highest responsibility in the Navy under one man.

References

For naval events:

Cant, Gilbert, *The War at Sea,* 1942.

Shubert, Paul, *Sea Power in Conflict,* 1942.

For diplomatic background:

Bailey, T. A., *A Diplomatic History of the American People,* Second Edition, 1942 (with references to further sources).

Johnstone, W. C., *The United States and Japan's New Order,* 1941.

THE SECOND WORLD WAR, 1942 XXV

IT MUST BE UNDERSTOOD that during a large part of the first year's operations in the Pacific the United Nations were fighting a defensive and delaying warfare, against Japanese forces bent on exploiting speedily and to the utmost their superiority at the time in the western Pacific theater. The fact of this superiority, viewed primarily from a naval standpoint, arose from a variety of causes, some dating far earlier than the war—the restrictions on our naval strength imposed by the Washington treaties and our national policy of arms reduction, the consequent inability to develop adequate bases in the western Pacific, the later transfer of a considerable part of our Pacific forces for the protection of commerce in the Atlantic, and finally the raid on Pearl Harbor, which heightened the difficulty of re-enforcing our slender fighting strength in the Far East. At the same time, the splendid resistance of those forces was of the utmost value, for it slowed the Japanese progress and brought closer the time when the immense armament production and resources of America and her allies would come in play.

In this lies the inestimable service of the last-ditch defense at Bataan and the heroic struggle of the United Nations cruisers in the Java Sea. Likewise, the two-month campaign in defense of Singapore, which fell finally to land operations on February 15, had an important part in the saving of Australia.

It may be noted further, as an example of the interlinking of operations in this world conflict, that the weakening of our Pacific force by retaining the *North Carolina* and the *Washington* in the Atlantic enabled the British to send the new battleship *Prince of Wales* and the battle cruiser *Repulse* to the East. Operating without air protection, these big ships were sunk December 9 by an overwhelming and skilfully handled Japanese air attack, while they were engaged in a gallant effort to strike at enemy troop movements to Malaya. Their loss facilitated the Japanese land campaign against the great British naval base at Singapore, which had been counted on as a bulwark for United Nations defense.

I. THE INVASION OF THE PHILIPPINES

The Japanese struggle for the Philippines was coincident with the Malaya campaign and was prolonged for two months after Singapore had fallen. On December 10 came the first bombing of Manila and the naval base at Cavite, in which the destruction of army planes on the ground was a crippling blow to Philippine defense. Most of the American naval forces based on Manila, including the heavy cruiser *Houston* of 10,000 tons, the older *Marblehead* of 6,000 tons, thirteen destroyers, and twenty-seven submarines, were operating at sea. The submarine *Sealion* and other craft in dry dock were damaged beyond repair. The destroyer *Peary,* though badly injured, escaped from Manila later and struggled through to Port Darwin, Australia. The day following her arrival, this much harassed boat went down in the big air raid of February 19, her few guns blazing to the end.

Before the surrender of Manila on January 2 the navy yard had been demolished, and naval personnel joined the Army on Corregidor and Bataan, where the old submarine tender *Canopus* was beached and used as a repair base, and other naval craft, including four mine sweepers, three China river gunboats, and six motor torpedo boats, had a share in the subsequent defense. Until the fall of Bataan, the sweepers and

Official U.S. Navy photographs

THE U.S. AIRCRAFT CARRIER LEXINGTON. *Insert,* BATTLE OF THE CORAL SEA. JAPANESE CARRIER (SORYU CLASS) BURNING FURIOUSLY AFTER AN ATTACK BY UNITED STATES NAVY TORPEDO PLANES.

gunboats protected the shore flank and maintained communications in the bay. Without adequate fuel for escape, they were destroyed after a hot fight with enemy aircraft on April 9. The naval contingent numbered about 2,275 officers and sailors and 1,570 marines, or approximately a third of the non-native forces, and all of these took a full part in beach and jungle warfare. Admiral Thomas C. Hart, in command of our Asiatic Fleet and for a time commander in chief of all United Nations naval forces in the East, shifted his headquarters to Java before the close of the year, effecting the transfer by submarine.

Meantime, making full use of their air and naval superiority, the Japanese in the latter part of December undertook landing operations at various points on the north, south, and west coasts of Luzon. For such purposes, bases in Formosa, only 240 miles distant, had been in preparation for several years. Typical landings were made after air reconnaissance, at dawn or high tide, with destroyers and gunboats about five miles out to cover the landings by a barrage, heavier naval vessels some five miles further out, and the transports and aircraft carrier, if present, between the two lines. A landing-boat carrier might be used, from which big barges laden with men, light tanks, or guns could be slid into the sea through side hatches. The Japanese were well equipped with fast, up-to-date motor landing boats which had protection at bow and stern and a hinged ramp forward for quick unloading.

Opposing landings in the Lingayan Gulf on the west coast, MacArthur's men sank 150 boats, and it was here on December 15 that Lieutenant Colin P. Kelly, Jr., in an army plane dropped three bombs on the battleship *Haruna,* and naval planes severely injured another battleship. But the Japanese pressed their attacks regardless of losses, and after capturing airfields in the north at Aparri and elsewhere they could still more fully dominate the air. The landings in fact demonstrated that the traditional advantage of the defensive in such operations may be overcome by a mobile naval force, with air cover, capable of feints and quick shifts from one point to another, especially in a large territory without swift means of shore transport. Once beach-heads were established, troops in overwhelming numbers poured into the island, and General MacArthur was forced to retreat for his desperately sustained defense in the strong natural position of Bataan, with Corregidor protecting his southern sea flank.

The naval air force at Manila was limited to forty-two slow patrol bombers, highly useful for reconnaissance but with limited defense against fast enemy fighters. Though they took a toll of enemy ships and planes, "Patwing 10" was reduced to half its strength when after a week or so in Bataan it flew south for operations in Java, and only three planes survived the fighting there. Fortunately, the losses in personnel were far lower. It was in this earlier period that the *Heron,* one of four tenders attached to the squadron, fought off a series of attacks by fifteen Japanese planes, shooting down one and damaging others, and came through a bombardment of forty-four bombs.

Before shifting to Java bases in early December, American cruisers and destroyers were for some time engaged in escorting valuable shipping from Manila southward, and, throughout the East Indies campaign and later, American submarines operated in their own effective fashion against Japanese shipping and transports. To quote from Admiral Hart, "The sum total of their bag of enemy ships equaled that of all other units which were brought against the Japanese during that entire Far Eastern campaign."[1]

Of the exploits of Lieutenant John D. Bulkeley, his officers, and some seventy men in their six motor torpedo boats of Squadron 3, the story is well known, and reveals the possibilities of these fast 45- to 60-knot torpedo craft. On January 19 one of the plywood 70-footers stole into Subic Bay, located its quarry, which proved to be a cruiser, and then, turning on its tail, sent two torpedoes racing toward the vessel, one of which set her in a blaze. On the twenty-second Bulkeley and Lieuten-

---

[1] "What the Navy Learned in the Pacific," *Saturday Evening Post,* Oct. 3, 10, 1942.

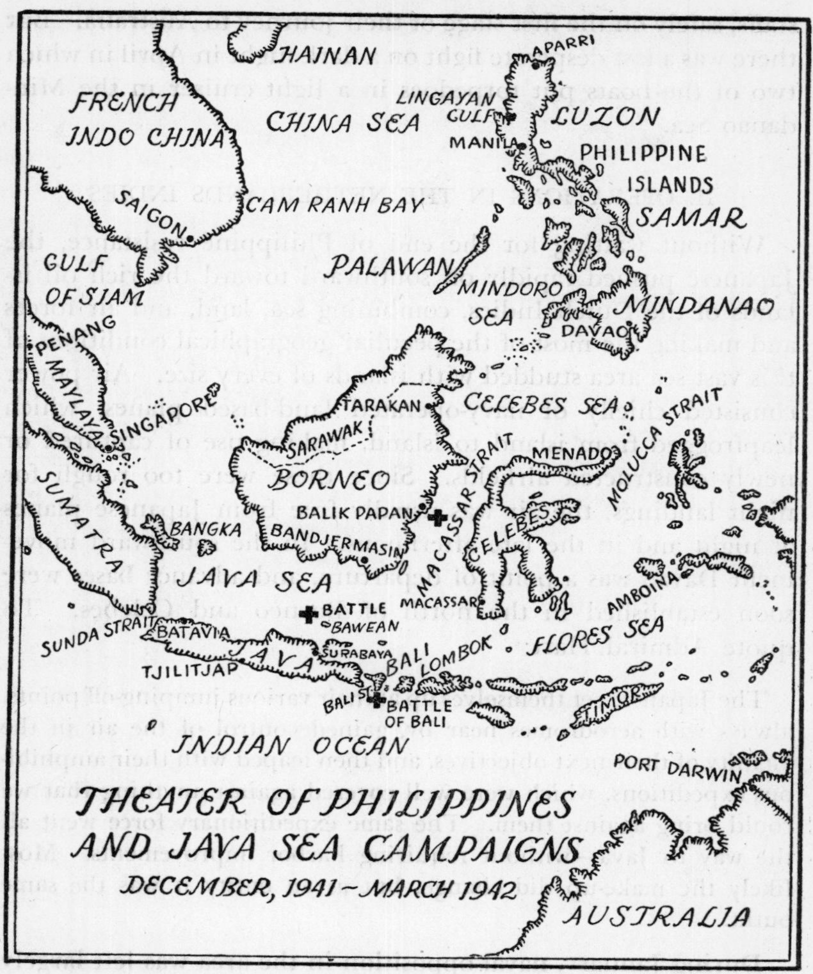

ant R. B. Kelly used machine guns to sink two barges loaded with troops, and two days later they torpedoed a 5,000-ton transport. The M.T.B.'s were "expended," but in Bulkeley's words they "probably sank at least one hundred times their tonnage in enemy warships." On March 14 the four remaining boats went south, carrying General MacArthur and Rear Admiral Francis W. Rockwell, commander of the Cavite base, with their staffs, safely on the first stage of their journey to Australia. But there was a last desperate fight on a dark night in April in which two of the boats put torpedoes in a light cruiser in the Mindanao Sea.

II. OPERATIONS IN THE NETHERLANDS INDIES

Without waiting for the end of Philippine resistance, the Japanese pushed rapidly on southward toward the rich oil islands of the Dutch Indies, combining sea, land, and air forces and making the most of the peculiar geographical conditions of this vast sea area studded with islands of every size. Air power consisted chiefly of navy-operated land-based planes, which leapfrogged from island to island, making use of captured or newly constructed airfields. Since these were too rough for night landings, the air was usually free from Japanese planes at night and in the late afternoons. In the southward movement Davao was a point of departure, and advance bases were soon established in the north of Borneo and Celebes. To quote Admiral Hart:

> The Japanese set themselves up at their various jumping-off points, always with aerodromes near by, gained control of the air in the vicinity of their next objectives, and then leaped with their amphibious expeditions, which were well covered against anything that we could bring against them. The same expeditionary force went all the way to Java—without requiring harbor improvements. Most likely the make-up did change, but as an entity it was the same outfit.

During January, naval opposition in the area was left largely to the American forces, for the Dutch and British were occupied with throwing re-enforcements into Singapore. As already noted, Admiral Hart's command included the *Houston, Marblehead, Boise* (soon disabled by striking an uncharted reef), and thirteen destroyers; the Dutch had the light cruisers *Java* and *De Ruyter* and six destroyers; and the British added the heavy cruiser *Exeter,* the *Perth* (Australian), and seven destroyers more. Of the submarines, which operated independently, the United States had twenty-seven, the Dutch nine, and the British three. All of the American destroyers were old boats of 1920 vintage, much in need of overhaul, and mounting only four-inch guns. This "ABDA" force (American, British, Dutch, Australian), while handled by able personnel in each national group, worked under the difficulties of a combined command, speaking two languages, with little opportunity to co-ordinate the different systems of signaling and tactics. In the Java Sea battle, Admiral Doormann put his light cruiser flagship at the head of the line, for the only signal he could be sure of making clear was "Follow me."

Macassar Straits

The first check on the Japanese advance was applied to a big troop convoy of forty or more transports and escorts pressing southward through the Straits of Macassar, along the Borneo shore. On three successive days these were harried by Flying Fortresses and Martin bombers from Java, and on the night of January 23, off Balik-papen, they were attacked by four American destroyers under Commander Paul H. Talbot—the *Ford* (flagship), *Pope, Parrott,* and *Paul Jones.* Knowing the coast from previous visits in December, Talbot about 3:00 A.M. swung through the slowly moving convoy, passing close to an enemy destroyer squadron without being detected, and then in a kind of clover-leaf pattern, made four high-speed runs up and down the Japanese formation, firing his torpedoes into the closely bunched transports. On the last run, with torpedoes gone, the destroyers opened with their guns. In the darkness and drifting smoke, the Japanese at first apparently mistook the attackers for parts of their own force. Their fire was wild, and the division, having suffered but one hit, got safely away. "I felt," writes Lieutenant W. P. Mack, gunnery officer in the *Ford,* "as if we had jumped on a merry-go-round, grabbed a handful of brass rings, and then jumped off without paying for our ride. It was hard to believe that four rickety, rusty old four-pipers could do such things."[2]

Damage to the convoy could not be accurately reckoned, but next morning a Dutch submarine, which had been lurking inshore, counted only twelve transports where twenty-one (those remaining after the air attacks) had been the night before. The convoy was halted for re-enforcements. But, for the Japanese, ships and men were expendable, and they were soon south of the straits, with bases on the Java Sea. An overwhelming air raid on the Dutch main base at Surabaya (February 3) did much damage to shore installations and to the limited supply of land-based planes.

The Marblehead

On the next day a force composed of the two American and two Dutch cruisers, with nine destroyers, under Rear Admiral Doormann, was hit hard by an attack of thirty-seven bombers. The *Houston,* though her anti-aircraft fire proved most effective in this and later contacts, was hit by a 500-pound bomb which killed sixty men and disabled the after turret for the rest of her brief career. The old *Marblehead* was more severely damaged by a bomb which shattered her steering gear and another which burst in the wardroom. Leaking badly, down by the head, and steering only by her screws, the *Marblehead* two days later staggered into Tjilitjap, Java's small south coast base. Thence, with leaks patched, she made for Ceylon, then to dry dock in Capetown, and at last home, in three months' time. Like that of many another American ship in the war, her survival was, in the words of her commander, Captain Arthur G. Robinson, "a tribute to the courage, stamina, and resourcefulness of the American bluejacket . . . and the rigid technical training which prepared her officers and crew for the demands of war."

---

[2] Narrative to be published in the *United States Naval Institute Proceedings.*

Bali and the Java Sea

By mid-February Singapore had fallen and the Japanese threatened Java from a wide stretch of bases extending eastward from Palembang in Sumatra to Amboina and Timor. Possibly in view of the Dutch interests immediately at stake, Admiral Hart had been succeeded as commander in chief by Admiral Emil Helfrich of the Netherlands Navy, and Vice Admiral William O. Glassford, Jr., had taken over the American command. With Allied approval, Admiral Helfrich's policy was to venture everything in resistance to the enemy advance.

There was temporary encouragement in a naval operation on February 19 against Japanese forces assembled off the island of Bali—a confused night action which began when the two Dutch cruisers, with the destroyers *Piet Hein* (Dutch), *Ford,* and *Pope,* in that order, swung in from the south about 10:45, attacking with torpedoes and gunfire the transports and cruisers lying near the airfield at the southern end of the island. The *Piet Hein*[3] cut across the bows of enemy cruisers and was destroyed by salvos at close range, but the *Ford* and *Pope,* though under heavy fire, circled southward again, and were confident of hits on an enemy cruiser and destroyer. Some hours later, the *Tromp* (Dutch) and four more American destroyers,[4] under Commander T. H. Binford, U.S.N., coming from the north through the narrow strait between Java and Bali, saw firing ahead—apparently the Japanese in a little battle of their own—and were soon in the midst of enemy ships. After a confused melee this force also got away, the *Stewart* being hit twice by 6- and 8-inch shells. The attacking force had registered at least eight torpedo hits and claimed the sinking of probably

[3] The commander of the *Piet Hein* escaped in a boat which had been dropped by accident from an American destroyer. Two days later he appeared (like a ghost) at Surabaya, and offered the American skipper profuse thanks for the thoughtfulness shown.

[4] The *Stewart, Parrott, Edwards,* and *Pillsbury.* The *Stewart* later capsized in dry dock and was demolished at the evacuation.

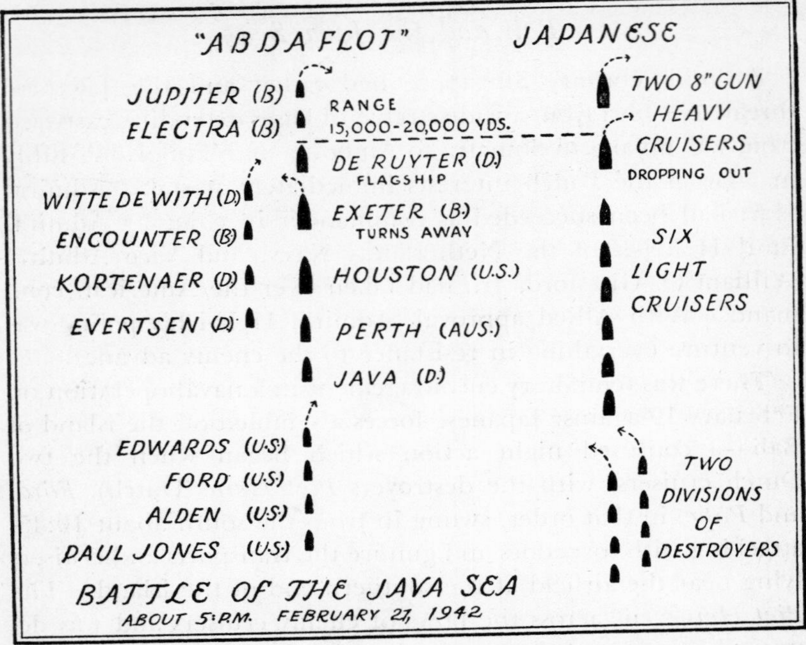

This diagram shows the strength and composition of the two squadrons, but gives only a general idea of their dispositions and movements. Acknowledgment is made to the excellent article by Fletcher Pratt, "Campaign of the Java Sea" (with four diagrams), *Harper's Magazine*, November, 1942.

four enemy vessels. But the Japanese were still in strength at Bali.

The ABDA fleet, with its limited air force gone, except for a few patched and battered PBY's, was now virtually "without eyes." The submarines were still active, and the old carrier *Langley* was on the way from Australia with more planes—but destined never to arrive.

Still, there were five cruisers left, and destroyer supports. It was this force, returning toward Surabaya on the afternoon of the twenty-seventh after an all-night patrol, that was turned back by radio to search for a big transport fleet sighted near Balean Island to northward. Contact was made at 4:15 P.M., not with the transports but with a covering force of eight Japanese cruisers, led by two 8-inch gun "heavies," and two divisions of destroyers. The action opened on parallel courses, as shown in the accompanying diagram, Admiral Doormann taking the lead by choice and as the surest means of guiding tactical moves. For a half hour there was at least an even exchange. Doormann had closed the range to about 15,000 yards, and the two Japanese leaders, on which the *Houston* and *Exeter* had concentrated, were seen to be on fire and swinging out of line. But a last shot hit the *Exeter* squarely, penetrating the boiler room, reducing her speed, and forcing her to turn away. A Japanese destroyer division had meanwhile made a sortie and scored one torpedo hit which sank the Netherlands destroyer *Kortenaer.* The *Jupiter, Electra,* and another destroyer counterattacked, and the *Electra,* in the words of the official report, was "not seen after she disappeared into the smoke screen." Before the action was broken off the American destroyers also attacked and fired their torpedoes into the Japanese cruiser formation, which had shifted course to eastward. The enemy losses could not be certainly known; a heavy cruiser was hit aft and burning fiercely, a light cruiser was also on fire, and two destroyers were reported sunk.

Aside from the *Kortenaer* and *Electra,* the ABDA Force losses all came later. That night, sweeping westward along the coast, both the *De Ruyter* and *Java* were sunk within two minutes by underwater explosion, in all probability by torpedoes from Japanese submarines. The *Jupiter* had been lost by torpedo a little earlier, a number of survivors reaching the coast. With these losses, there was no recourse for the remaining ships but to seek escape southward toward Tjilitjap, out of the Java Sea. The *Houston* and *Perth,* trying to get through Sunda Strait, were concentrated upon and sunk on the night of the twenty-eighth off its entrance, and of possible survivors there has been no later word. The damaged *Exeter,* with her escorts the *Pope* and *Encounter,* suffered the same fate early next day.

Without specific orders, five American destroyers struck east from Surabaya and reached Australia. But in the meantime there had been other losses—the *Langley,* 11,050-ton aircraft tender, sunk on the twenty-seventh with her cargo of planes, by bombers; the tanker *Pecos,* which had picked up survivors from the *Langley,* sunk next day with a loss of about half of those aboard; the destroyers *Edsall* and *Pillsbury* and gunboat *Asheville,* all lost during the retreat from Java. Admiral Glassford flew to Australia in a last plane of Patwing 10. The unequal struggle had been fought bitterly to the end, but now Japan had got her hands on an empire producing 85 per cent of the world's rubber and 94 per cent of its tin—for how long remained to be seen. This, as Admiral Hart remarked, "was just one campaign."

III. THE CENTRAL PACIFIC

Considerably before the fall of Java, the Japanese had pressed southward from their main base at Truk in the Caroline Islands to occupy bases and airfields at Lae and Salamaua, on the northern coast of New Guinea, and the excellent harbor of Rabaul in New Britain. This extension of control served a double purpose. Offensively, it threatened Australia and the American supply route thither. Defensively, it prolonged the barrier, the "fence [5] of island bases," which would protect the communications of Japan's newly grasped conquests in the Philippines and Dutch Indies.

On the other hand, Admiral King in December had issued the order to American forces in the Central Pacific to "Hold the Hawaiian Islands area on the Midway line at all costs," and to "Hold the communication line to the Southwest Pacific [Australia] on the Samoa-Fiji line and extend it to New Caledonia." [6] Thus, clearly, the frontiers of the United Nations and Japan

[5] The "Suetsugu Fence," so-called from Admiral Suetsugu of the Japanese Navy, a prominent advocate of such a chain of island defenses for a Japanese hegemony in the South Seas.

[6] From a press interview, quoted in *Time,* Dec. 7, 1942, p. 21.

met—and the area of conflict lay—along the line extending from the Aleutians to Midway and thence to the Coral Sea. Australia must be held as a great bastion for future offensive moves. This general view will suggest the significance of the ensuing engagements and of the Solomons and New Guinea campaigns.

In January of 1942 President Roosevelt and Prime Minister Churchill, in conferences at Washington, had set up a United General Staff of American and British military leaders, and in each theater of war had taken highly desirable steps toward unity of command. In the Pacific, General MacArthur was given supreme command of land, sea, and air forces in the Australian area; and Admiral Nimitz was accorded similar authority in the central Pacific, with headquarters in Hawaii. The division line between their two spheres, as finally set, ran close to the eastern coast of Australia.

Raid on the Marshall Islands

The opening months of 1942 were marked by a number of raids on Japanese island bases, limited in scale but highly promising. The first, on January 31, carried out by a task force consisting of the carriers *Yorktown* and *Enterprise,* four cruisers, and eight destroyers under Vice Admiral William F. Halsey, Jr., was directed against five points in the Japanese-held Marshall Islands and Makin Island in the near-by Gilberts. Since the objectives were spread over an area some 400 miles square, the force was divided into two groups centered about the carriers, the one to the south being under Rear Admiral Frank J. Fletcher. The most accurate timing was called for to make the attacks simultaneous at each point. First the planes swept in to bomb and strafe; then the surface craft blasted ships and shore structures with gunfire; and finally torpedo planes went in to complete the destruction. The chief concentration of ships was found at Kwajalein Atoll, and the only noteworthy air resistance at Taroe Island. Here, out of about thirty bombers and fighters, all but seven were put out of action, mostly on the ground, and three of the remainder were shot down in their efforts to get at the American carrier. Altogether, about 100,000 tons of naval and merchant vessels were destroyed, including a big 17,000-ton ex-luxury liner, a modern light cruiser, two submarines, three 10,000-ton fleet tankers, at least five cargo vessels, and numerous auxiliaries. Tanks, hangars, fuel and ammunition dumps, and other base facilities were demolished. Most of the thirteen American planes lost in the operation went down in a severe wind and electrical storm in one area. The natural encouragement over this success was tempered by a realization that it was but a minor stroke against bases that threatened our new supply lines, and by reports very shortly that the persistent enemy were moving back in.

Raids on Wake and Marcus Islands

Within the next few weeks an American task force including the same carriers subjected Wake and Marcus Islands to similar raids on a smaller scale. At Wake Island the American planes in a surprise attack at dawn of February 24 wrecked hangars, runways, fuel and ammunition dumps, and other defenses which the enemy "had worked feverishly to strengthen." There were seven heavy explosions, the first described by a correspondent aboard the cruiser *Salt Lake City* as "a bulbous blast of orange that billowed out mushroom-like hundreds of feet in the air." The planes were supported by accurate fire from the ships, some of which closed up until their secondary batteries were in range. Of three enemy planes that got into the air, one was shot down. Later in the day, as the force was withdrawing, a few bombers from the near-by Marshall Islands made scattered and ineffective attacks.

At Marcus Island, 760 miles to the northwest and only 1,000 miles from Tokyo, the visit on March 4 was a predawn affair, limited to planes, which had little difficulty in wrecking the radio station, a partly completed airfield, and other structures.

Our aircraft losses at Wake and Marcus were only two planes, one in each raid. Aside from the damage caused, these early operations provided most valuable war experience and useful tests of the performance in action of ships, planes, and personnel.

IV. CAMPAIGN AND BATTLE OF THE CORAL SEA

In the sea area northeast of Australia an attempted surprise raid on Rabaul by a task force under Vice Admiral Wilson Brown was called off after Japanese air scouts had discovered its approach. In a subsequent counterattack on February 20, by eighteen Japanese planes, at least sixteen were shot down in the course of the day, and Lieutenant Edward J. O'Hare made his extraordinary record of destroying five enemy bombers and crippling a sixth, before other flyers could come to his support. "As we closed in," said his senior officer, Lieutenant Commander Thach, "I could see O'Hare making his attack runs with perfect flight form. . . . I could see three blazing Japanese planes falling between the formation and the water—he shot them down so quickly. How O'Hare survived the concentrated fire of the Japanese division I don't know." [7] In these four minutes he had stood between the carrier and possible disaster.

The *Lexington* and *Yorktown,* with supporting forces, joined afterward to the south of New Guinea and sent their flyers over the 12,000-foot-high mountain range for a swoop on the Japanese bases at Salamaua and Lae, March 10, which resulted in the sinking of three cruisers, a destroyer, and five transports, aside from many other craft left in flames. Earlier and later, these bases had also been pounded hard by American and Australian land-based planes.

Despite these severe setbacks, the Japanese remained persistent in their determination to push into the islands and waters to southward. It was their final full-scale advance in this di-

[7] Quoted from Stanley Johnston, *Queen of the Flat-Tops.*

rection that brought about the five-day series of actions known as the battle of the Coral Sea, "the first clash in history between aircraft carriers, and the first defeat ever inflicted on the Japanese Navy." [8]

Into these waters in the first days of May moved once more the two forces centered about the *Lexington* and *Yorktown*, now combined under the senior officer, Rear Admiral Frank J. Fletcher. Learning by reconnaissance of a large concentration of enemy transports and escorts at Tulagi, just north of Guadalcanal Island, Fletcher on the night of May 3–4 steamed northward at high speed and before dawn sent thirty-six bombers, torpedo-planes, and fighters over the Guadalcanal mountaintops to strike at the Japanese twelve miles beyond. The surprise was complete; in the initial attack and two "wipe-up" flights later in the day at least twelve of the fifteen ships in the group were destroyed, including four patrol vessels, two destroyers, a tender, and a transport. Three American planes went astray and were lost, but the crews of two were saved.

Though still unknown to the Americans, two strong Japanese forces were at this time moving into the Coral Sea area, one coming directly south toward the Louisiade Archipelago just east of New Guinea, and the other skirting much farther to eastward around the Solomons. Fletcher's first word was of the force nearer the Louisiades, with a reported strength of one carrier or perhaps more, five cruisers, and several destroyers. Toward this he steamed, and in the early hours of May 7 launched seventy-six planes all told—thirty-six scout- and dive-bombers, twenty-four torpedo-planes, and sixteen fighters. After the scouts, the dive-bombers and torpedo-planes came in together, concentrating upon the enemy carrier, with little heed to Zero interceptors and "ack-ack" fire. It was pronounced "a most successful co-ordinated attack." The two squadrons *VB2* and *VT2* from the *Lexington* did not lose a single plane. Within five minutes the big new carrier, identified at the time

[8] Captain (later Rear Admiral) Frederick C. Sherman, as quoted in the press, June 22, 1942.

as the *Ryukaku,* was a sinking wreck from the hits of fifteen bombs and ten torpedoes. Caught at a disadvantage as she turned to launch her planes, she went down with most of them still aboard. At least one cruiser was also sunk. A young pilot who decided not to waste his bomb on the carrier picked this cruiser instead, and dropped his "egg" squarely on her quarter-deck. "A moment later there was a tremendous explosion and she vanished from sight." In the day's fighting the score was twenty-five enemy planes shot down to six of our own. It was in the midst of this action that Lieutenant Commander Robert Dixon, commanding the *Lexington's* scout-bombers, radioed his terse message, "Scratch one flat-top. Dixon to carrier. Scratch one flat-top."

On the next day, contact was made with the second force coming in from the eastward, which included probably two carriers. Each side, Japanese and American, located its opposition and launched its planes at about the same time. In the thick mist and rain clouds which enveloped the Japanese squadron, the attack of the seventy-three American planes was less closely co-ordinated than that of the previous day. Not all planes were engaged, and not all centered on the same target, but a carrier, believed to have been the 14,000-ton *Shokaku,* was left ablaze and settling in the water, after five torpedo hits and at least three hits by 1,000-pound bombs. Though her sinking was later denied, American flyers at the time felt assured she would not fight again.

The attack on the *Lexington* and *Yorktown,* about 11:15 to 11:30, was delivered by some eighty Japanese planes divided nearly equally between the two. Through the interceptor fighters and the heavy anti-aircraft fire—what Stanley Johnston describes as "the wham-wham of the 5-inchers, the staccato bark of the 1.1-inchers (37 mm.), and the rushing yammer of the 20 mm. batteries"—of both the carrier and her supports, the Japanese got through to the *Lexington* to make two torpedo hits, one 1,000-pound bomb hit, and two with smaller bombs. The *Lexington* still maintained over 20-knot speed, the list to port was soon corrected, and within an hour's time excellent work of the damage crews had brought the resultant fires under control. From about 12:45 on, however, there ensued a series of increasingly severe explosions, caused chiefly by concentration of gasoline fumes in closed compartments. These wrecked light and power lines, and, despite the most heroic efforts, made repairs impossible because of the fumes, flames, and danger from recurring explosions. Shortly after 5:00 P.M., Rear Admiral A. W. Fitch quietly passed the word to Captain Sherman to "get the men off," which was accomplished with perfect discipline. Of about 1,900 men on board, 92 per cent were saved, all the losses having occurred in the action itself or in the salvage efforts during the afternoon.

Owing apparently to more effective interception, the damage to the *Yorktown* was limited. Aside from the *Lexington,* the only United States losses in the five-day action were the tanker *Neosho* and her escort destroyer *Sims,* caught by aircraft on the sixth at a point distant from the main engagement. As already noted, the enemy losses in these five days were far more severe. For the whole campaign from March 10 to May 8 the official United States Navy communiqué of June 12 listed fifteen Japanese ships sunk, including a carrier, three heavy cruisers, one light cruiser, and three destroyers; more than twenty others severely damaged, including a carrier and three cruisers; and the loss of more than 100 aircraft. By blows chiefly to its air power, a decisive check was put on whatever offensive purposes this heavy Japanese concentration had in view.

V. THE BATTLE OF MIDWAY

From subsequent events it might appear that the Japanese operations in the Coral Sea, like the occupation of islands in the Aleutians, could be regarded as subordinate, flanking, or even diversionary in relation to the main advance attempted later through the center—an advance which, judging by its size, was directed at objectives even beyond Midway Island. Though

Official U.S. Navy photographs

Top, THE BATTLE OF MIDWAY. A Japanese bomber scores a direct hit on the U.S. Aircraft Carrier *Yorktown,* despite a tornado of anti-aircraft fire. *Center,* U.S. HEAVY CRUISER SALT LAKE CITY. *Bottom,* A JAPANESE HEAVY CRUISER (MOGAMI CLASS) AFTER BOMBING BY UNITED STATES CARRIER-BASED AIRCRAFT IN THE BATTLE OF MIDWAY.

this operation has been spoken of as highly risky, it would appear to have been justified by the Japanese strategy of rapid movement and by the superior naval strength which they possessed in that area at the time.

Reports from submarines and other sources had given warning of the heavy preliminary concentrations in Japanese bases, and with correct foresight American naval forces were deployed in the area between the Aleutians and Midway, with precautionary measures as far in the rear as the Pacific Coast and Panama. Like the Coral Sea action, the coming battle was to be novel in sea warfare, a battle having as its first objectives the destruction of enemy air power, fought chiefly by land- and carrier-based planes, in which the surface vessels never came in contact with each other or exchanged gunfire. Yet it was to be a battle which in extent of losses and significance in sea control might rank with the great sea fights of history.

The story of Midway, as of the later battles in the Solomons, can as yet be told only in general terms. The American forces engaged have not been fully revealed, though it may be assumed that major battleship forces were not at hand or they would have been used potently on crippled enemy ships after air control had been won. The Japanese story has not been told, and may never be fully known. Even were the facts all available, no brief account could do full justice to all participants, or to the many striking and heroic exploits in this far-flung battle of the air.

June 3.[9] The first actual contacts preceding the battle were made by naval scouting planes at 9:00 A.M. of June 3, about 700 miles west of Midway. The Japanese were advancing in five columns numbering about eighty ships, including battleships, carriers, cruisers, destroyers, and numerous transports and cargo vessels, bent evidently not on a raid merely but a full-scale occupation of Midway. These were not all in one body. A main

---

[9] The following account is based largely on the full résumé of the battle given in the United States Navy communiqué of July 14, 1942, and on other official data.

striking force of four carriers with heavy supports was discovered later about 150 miles northwest of the island. On the third, the more distant ships were attacked by Army Flying Fortresses from Midway, which scored several hits on a cruiser and a transport, and that night by four Catalina flying boats, also from Midway, which made torpedo hits on two large ships, one of which was believed to have sunk.

June 4. Next morning all available Army and Marine planes from Midway made a total of five attacks, pushed fiercely through a heavy screen of Zeros and a curtain of anti-aircraft fire. In bare summary, the first, by four Army torpedo-bombers, scored probably one hit on a carrier and lost two planes; the second, by six Marine torpedo-planes, was believed to have made a hit, with a loss of five planes; the third, by sixteen Marine dive-bombers, made three hits, probably on the carrier *Soryu,* and lost half their force; the fourth, by eleven of the same type, reported two hits on a battleship, left "smoking and listing"; and the last, by sixteen Fortresses, made three hits on carriers, one of which was "left smoking heavily." The losses thus inflicted were not regarded as a decisive check. Of the eighty ships, only an estimated ten had been damaged. Later, however, it was learned that after the attacks, between 8:30 and 9:30 A.M., the enemy had shifted course and begun a retirement to the northwest.

Earlier that morning, while the Midway planes were thus engaged, the island itself was subjected to a heavy enemy air attack. There were twenty-five Marine fighter planes available for defense, and in a desperate encounter with over 100 enemy aircraft, the planes and ground defenses shot down forty-three, while losing thirteen. Of the eighty-four Marine pilots and gunners in both the bomber and fighter squadrons at Midway, thirty-eight were reported missing and seventeen wounded at the end of the five days' fighting. All were accorded decorations, of which many were posthumous. The damages to runways and shore installations, "though serious, were not disabling," and they remained available for use.

Meanwhile, naval task forces, which included the *Hornet, Yorktown,* and a third carrier, had been brought into position and at about 7:00 A.M. had launched their planes. Of these, some groups failed to reach their targets, owing to the Japanese shift of course, and either searched until compelled to descend at sea, or refueled at Midway. Fifteen torpedo-planes finally located the enemy and delivered an attack without fighter protection of any kind. Not a plane returned. The single survivor of the thirty men in the planes, Ensign G. H. Gay, Jr., wounded and clinging to his life raft, saw three Japanese carriers ablaze. Gay was picked up thirty hours later by patrol planes, which repeatedly swept over the area for survivors.

By this time other carrier planes, directed to the enemy location, were pressing their attacks, the torpedo-planes so engaging the enemy's defense that dive-bombers were able to score hit after hit without serious interference. The result of these and the earlier attacks was the destruction of the two new carriers *Kaga* and *Akagi,* which burned until each went down, while the smaller *Soryu* was sunk by an American submarine as she was being taken in tow. Two battleships were hit, and one was left burning fiercely.

In the afternoon, planes from the *Yorktown* (the attack on which will be described later) located a part of the enemy force steaming northward, including the carrier *Hiryu* with accompanying battleships and cruisers. The *Hiryu* was thereupon so battered by planes from the American carriers that she sank next morning, and a heavy cruiser was also severely punished and probably destroyed.

By sunset of the fourth the American forces had gained full control of the air. With the enemy now divided and in full retreat, bad flying weather that night and next day made pursuit difficult, but Army Fortresses made fatal hits on one enemy cruiser and injured two others.

June 5–6. Through the night of June 5–6, the carrier planes pushed their pursuit westward, and in a series of attacks on the sixth sank the heavy cruisers *Mikuma* and *Mogami,* as well as a destroyer. Attacks continued until 5:00 P.M. The verified losses of the four-day action were:

1. Four carriers sunk, the *Kaga, Akagi, Soryu,* and *Hiryu.*
2. Three battleships damaged, one severely.
3. Two heavy cruisers sunk, three others damaged (one or two severely), and a light cruiser damaged.
4. Three destroyers sunk and several damaged.

It was estimated that 275 enemy aircraft were destroyed and 4,800 Japanese killed or drowned. The American losses, including those in the *Yorktown,* were about 600.

Loss of the Yorktown. The attack on the *Yorktown,* shortly after 2:00 P.M. of the fourth, illustrated the difficulty experienced in beating off a large-scale aerial assault resolutely carried out. Yet the *Yorktown* survived two attacks and might have pulled through had not her loss of propulsion exposed her to attack by submarine. Of eighteen bombers from the *Hiryu* which first approached the *Yorktown,* eleven were shot down by fighters before they got in range. Of the seven that broke through, perhaps four finally escaped—with no place to fly to—after scoring three hits.

Energetic repair work soon cleared the flight deck, and the *Yorktown* was again making fair speed when, about 5:00 P.M., from twelve to fifteen enemy torpedo-planes flew in. Only five were able to launch torpedoes, two of which crashed into the carrier amidships near the same spot. The damage was terrific. Almost immediately her engines stopped and she took a heavy list to port. The ship was soon abandoned, but she remained afloat for thirty-six hours longer. Plans were made for towing. Captain Buckmaster returned with a salvage crew, and the destroyer *Hammann* came alongside to supply power. But as they were starting pumps and cutting away guns, a lurking submarine struck a fatal blow with two torpedoes and also sank the *Hammann.* The hard-fighting carrier, which in her brief career had seen action at the Marshalls, Salamaua, and Lae,

Tulagi, and the Coral Sea, went down with colors flying. Of her complement of 2,072 all but 300 survived.

The significance of the Midway victory cannot yet be clearly weighed. Certainly a reversal of fortunes would have pushed American defenses back to Hawaii or even to the West Coast, for the Japanese at the time were undoubtedly aware of the incomplete repairs at Pearl Harbor. Fortunately, the actual result was a crippling blow to Japanese air power, with injury to morale and heavy losses of skilled personnel. The engagement also found our land, sea, and air forces working together in successful co-ordination. In the words of Admiral King, "Things began to break our way at Midway. . . . After the Midway action we told ourselves, 'Now is the time to hit the Jap in the southwest Pacific.' "[10]

VI. SOLOMON ISLANDS: GUADALCANAL

In the interview just quoted, Admiral King stated that the date for the Guadalcanal occupation was early set for August 1, and the operation actually began on August 7. It was "our first assumption of the initiative and the aggressive." Of its objectives, he added: "That campaign did two things. It made our line of communications [with Australia] that much more secure, and it took something away from the Jap that he had. The virulent, violent reaction was greater than we expected, so the attack must have stung him to the quick."

A glance at the map on page 422 will show the strategic location of the Solomons in relation to the line of communication with Australia, the struggle going on in New Guinea, and the protection of the Australian east coast. The Japanese reaction to our seizure of the base and the airfield 85 per cent completed at Guadalcanal was evident in their subsequent bitter struggle to break our hold. Only the toughest of fighting at first enabled us to hang on. But as time went by it appeared that Guadal-

[10] Press interview, quoted in *Time,* Dec. 7, 1942, p. 21.

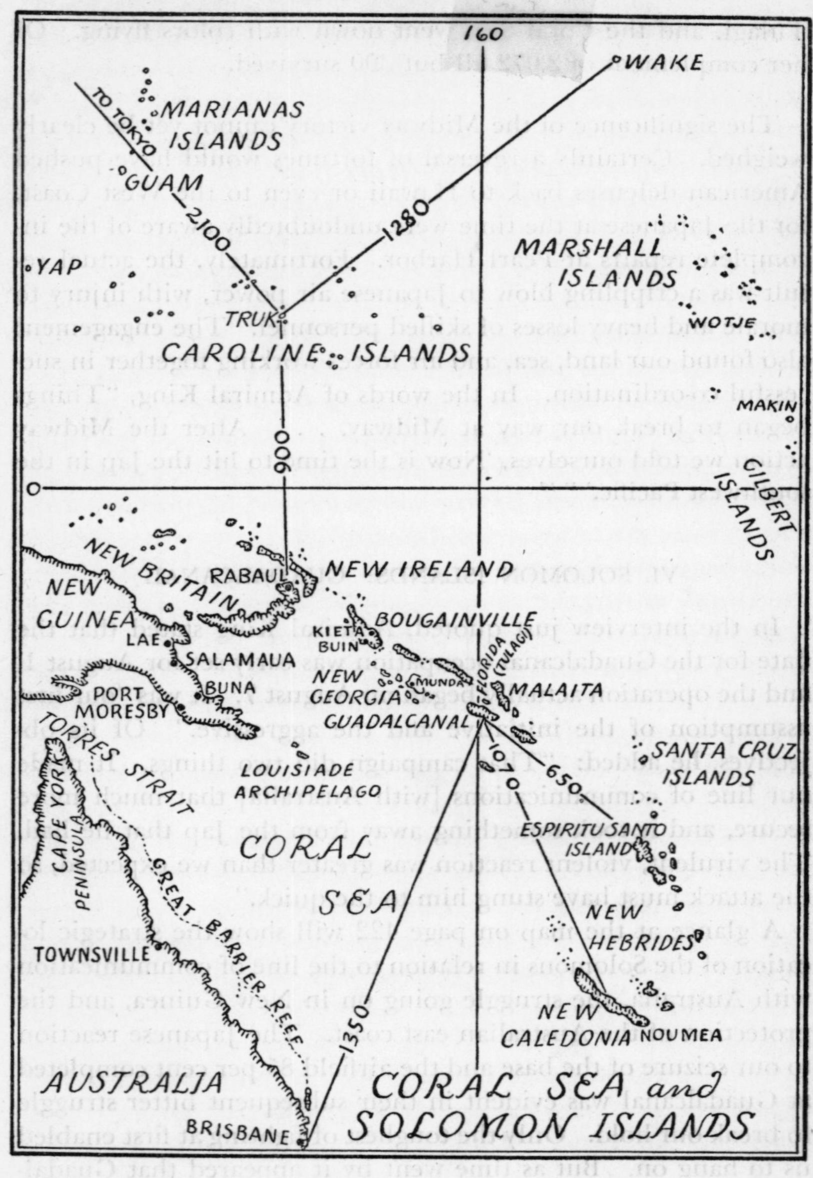
160
WAKE
TO TOKYO
MARIANAS ISLANDS
GUAM
2100
1280
MARSHALL ISLANDS
YAP
TRUK
WOTJE
CAROLINE ISLANDS
MAKIN
900
0
GILBERT ISLANDS
NEW BRITAIN
RABAUL
NEW IRELAND
NEW GUINEA
BOUGAINVILLE
KIETA
BUIN
LAE
SALAMAUA
NEW GEORGIA
MUNDA
FLORIDA (TULAGI)
MALAITA
BUNA
PORT MORESBY
GUADALCANAL
TORRES STRAIT
1010
650
SANTA CRUZ ISLANDS
LOUISIADE ARCHIPELAGO
CAPE YORK PENINSULA
ESPIRITU SANTO ISLAND
CORAL SEA
NEW HEBRIDES
TOWNSVILLE
GREAT BARRIER REEF
1350
NEW CALEDONIA
NOUMEA
AUSTRALIA
BRISBANE
CORAL SEA and SOLOMON ISLANDS

canal had become a vantage point, against which Japan felt bound to strike furiously, with futile and costly expenditure of men and materials.

The Occupation.[11] The landing at Guadalcanal and near-by points on August 7 was a thoroughly planned joint operation of Marine Corps units under Major General A. A. Vandegrift, naval transports under Rear Admiral R. K. Turner, and supporting ships under Vice Admiral Fletcher, the whole operation being under Vice Admiral R. L. Ghormley, who then commanded our naval forces in the South Pacific. Naval bombardments prepared the way for the landings, and carrier-based aircraft covered all movements, attacking shore batteries, supply stations, and centers of enemy resistance. Because of the complete surprise, on Guadalcanal itself there was little immediate opposition. Light artillery and amphibian "alligator" tractors were quickly put ashore, and by nightfall the Marines held a strong beach-head, extended next day to include the airfield. The initial enemy air raids cost only one transport and the destroyer *Jervis.* The stiffest fighting came at Tulagi and at the seaplane base at Gavutu, to northward, where over 1,200 of the enemy were killed and eighteen planes were destroyed before they got into the air. During the seventh and eighth further supplies were landed, and by the ninth the transports had left the area.

Cruiser Losses. On the night of the eighth–ninth, in an effort to interrupt these operations, Japanese naval forces scored one of their few notable successes of the campaign. Swinging in to the south of Savo Island, their cruisers and destroyers apparently took by surprise the two groups of cruisers patrolling east of the island, and at 2,000 to 3,000 yards sank in quick succession the Australian heavy cruiser *Canberra* and the American heavy cruisers *Quincy* and *Vincennes.* A fourth, the *Astoria,* burned through the night. Of about 3,500 men aboard these

[11] The story of the operation is summarized in the naval communiqué of Aug. 29, 1942, and in many press despatches. See also Richard Tregaskis, *Guadalcanal Diary,* 1943.

ships, a majority were rescued. It was a hit-and-run affair, in which the Japanese, missing their chance to strike at the transports in the harbor, made off to the north of Savo, with injuries unknown but probably not severe. As in subsequent night actions, in which the Japanese suffered, success came to the side taking the aggressive and gaining the initial advantage of surprise. It was stated later that the flag officer in command of our cruiser division had been called away, and that there was some uncertainty as to the tactical command. Our scouting was inadequate, and forces were operating at low speed.

Repulsing Re-enforcements. As already noted, our occupation of the Guadalcanal airfield, renamed Henderson Field, with adjacent territory and coast, spurred the Japanese to supply and re-enforce the former garrison, now driven back into the hills and jungles of the eighty-mile-long island. Patrol of the shores was inadequate to prevent night landings, such as that of August 20, for example, when 700 men got ashore, though in this instance 670 were soon killed by the ever-ready Marines, and the rest were made prisoner. In patrol and similar operations there was a considerable attrition of American destroyers—the over-age *Gregory, Little,* and *Calhoun,* and the newer boats *Blue, Jarvis,* and *O'Brien,* lost chiefly as a result of aerial action or attacks by superior force.

Though these landings by stealth, air raids, and sorties by both sides went on continually, the campaign from August to December may be said in general to have moved in a series of major crises, in which the Japanese marshaled their forces for all-out attack, with intervals of recoupment and relative quiet between. In these crises, the naval actions often took the form of sharp, hard-hitting encounters of surface ships fought at night and at high speed.

While attention is here centered largely on these more strictly naval engagements, it should be kept in mind that they were always part of the operations as a whole, linked closely with the fighting on land, the destructive raids of General MacArthur's Australian air forces on Japanese bases and con-

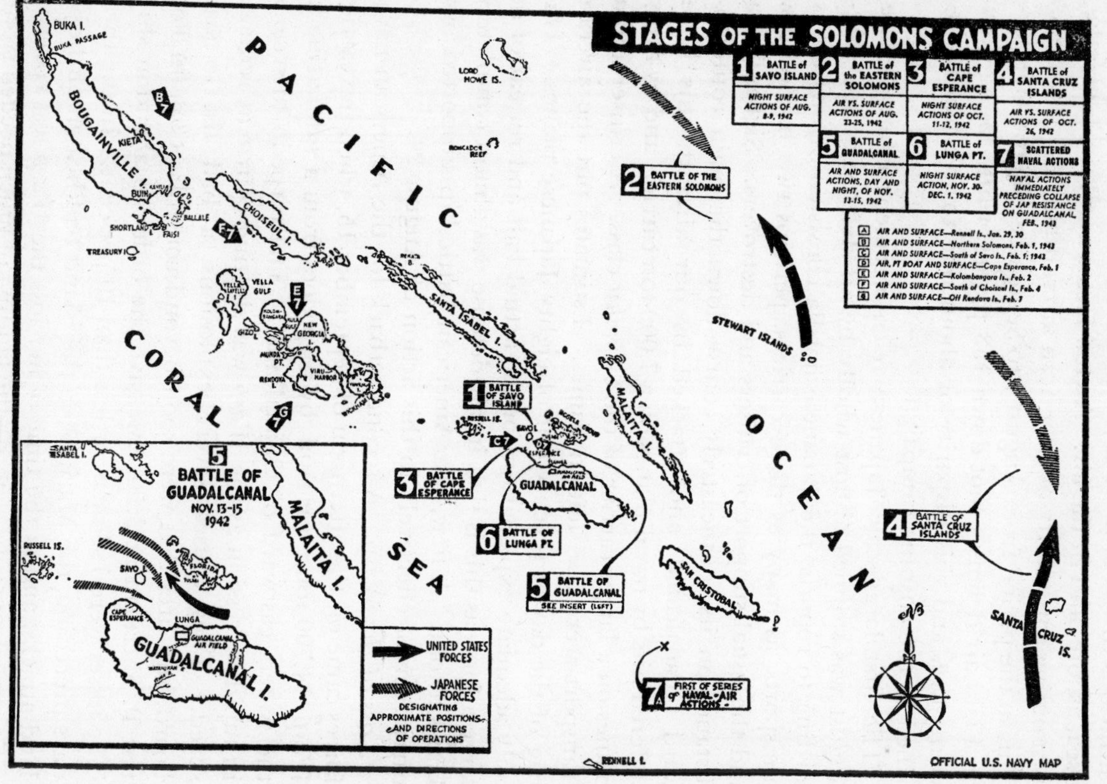
STAGES OF THE SOLOMONS CAMPAIGN
1 BATTLE of SAVO ISLAND
NIGHT SURFACE ACTIONS OF AUG. 8-9, 1942
2 BATTLE of the EASTERN SOLOMONS
AIR VS. SURFACE ACTIONS OF AUG. 23-25, 1942
3 BATTLE of CAPE ESPERANCE
NIGHT SURFACE ACTIONS OF OCT. 11-12, 1942
4 BATTLE of SANTA CRUZ ISLANDS
AIR VS. SURFACE ACTIONS OF OCT. 26, 1942
5 BATTLE of GUADALCANAL
AIR AND SURFACE ACTIONS, DAY AND NIGHT, OF NOV. 13-15, 1942
6 BATTLE of LUNGA PT.
NIGHT SURFACE ACTION, NOV. 30-DEC. 1, 1942
7 SCATTERED NAVAL ACTIONS
NAVAL ACTIONS IMMEDIATELY PRECEDING COLLAPSE OF JAP RESISTANCE ON GUADALCANAL FEB., 1943
A AIR AND SURFACE—Rennell Is., Jan. 29, 30
B AIR AND SURFACE—Northern Solomons, Feb. 1, 1943
C AIR AND SURFACE—South of Savo Is., Feb. 1; 1943
D AIR, PT BOAT AND SURFACE—Cape Esperance, Feb. 1
E AIR AND SURFACE—Kolombangara Is., Feb. 2
F AIR AND SURFACE—South of Choiseul Is., Feb. 4
G AIR AND SURFACE—Off Rendova Is., Feb. 7
PACIFIC
OCEAN
CORAL
SEA
BUKA I.
BUKA PASSAGE
BOUGAINVILLE I.
KIETA
BUIN
BALLALE
SHORTLAND
FAISI
TREASURY I.
CHOISEUL I.
VELLA GULF
NEW GEORGIA I.
MUNDA PT.
RENDOVA
VIRU HARBOR
SANTA ISABEL I.
LORD HOWE IS.
RONCADOR REEF
STEWART ISLANDS
MALAITA I.
SAN CRISTOBAL
RENNELL I.
SANTA CRUZ IS.
GUADALCANAL
RUSSELL IS.
2 BATTLE OF THE EASTERN SOLOMONS
1 BATTLE OF SAVO ISLAND
3 BATTLE OF CAPE ESPERANCE
6 BATTLE OF LUNGA PT.
5 BATTLE OF GUADALCANAL SEE INSERT (LEFT)
4 BATTLE OF SANTA CRUZ ISLANDS
7A FIRST OF SERIES OF NAVAL-AIR ACTIONS
5 BATTLE OF GUADALCANAL NOV. 13-15 1942
SANTA ISABEL I.
RUSSELL IS.
SAVO
FLORIDA
TULAGI
CAPE ESPERANCE
LUNGA
GUADALCANAL AIR FIELD
GUADALCANAL I.
MALAITA I.
UNITED STATES FORCES
JAPANESE FORCES
DESIGNATING APPROXIMATE POSITIONS AND DIRECTIONS OF OPERATIONS
OFFICIAL U.S. NAVY MAP

centrations to northward, and the innumerable minor clashes at sea, ashore, and in the air. A vital factor at all times was the outstanding superiority of American aircraft and air personnel. Thus in the period from August 7 to September 17, the Henderson Field air defenses shot down 133 planes, while losing only twenty-five, and this disparity of about one to five was maintained in the ensuing campaign.

The first large-scale Japanese re-enforcement effort in late August was stopped almost wholly by air defense at sea. According to reports, the Japanese flotilla consisted of numerous transports, as many as three carriers, perhaps two battleships, and the usual support of cruisers and destroyers. Sighted at a distance on its southeasterly course down the main route toward Guadalcanal, and attacked by our aircraft, this force suffered hits by naval planes on a 7,000-ton carrier, and by army planes on a larger carrier of the *Syokaku* class. A cruiser and a transport were also left in flames. Estimates put the aircraft bag of the day at seventy out of eighty Japanese planes. The only adequate explanation for the actual halt and retreat of so large a force as this is that its air defense was almost completely knocked out. A new, fast American battleship supported our carriers most effectively in this action of August 24.

Loss of the Wasp. A second setback for the American naval forces came on the afternoon of September 15, when the carrier *Wasp,* 14,700 tons, was sunk by torpedoes from a submarine in the waters eastward of Guadalcanal. The torpedo hits came in rapid succession as the *Wasp* was shifting course at reduced speed. They caused severe explosions, a bad list to starboard, and fires that were soon beyond control. Captain Forrest P. Sherman at 3:50 P.M. gave the order to abandon ship. The losses were 193 men, or less than 10 per cent. In the three days preceding, the Marines on the island had beaten off heavy land attacks, and at the time of her loss the *Wasp* was covering —in very dangerous waters—the landing of much needed troops and supplies.

Top, U.S. Marine Corps photograph; *bottom,* official U.S. Navy photograph

Top, HENDERSON FIELD. Showing steel mat (removable in small sections) laid to facilitate the landing of large planes such as the Army B-17 shown here. *Bottom,* LANDING BEACH AT GUADALCANAL. Taken several weeks after the occupation.

Battle of Cape Esperance. The action off Cape Esperance, in the waters between Savo Island and Guadalcanal on the night of October 11–12, was another clash of cruisers, like that of August 8–9 but with reversed result, in which a squadron under Rear Admiral Norman Scott met enemy forces of considerably greater strength—six cruisers, six destroyers, and a transport—engaged probably in covering Japanese landings. Complete surprise was a chief factor in this swift half-hour action. In one minute a Japanese heavy cruiser was burning fiercely, and four minutes later another was sunk by a destroyer's torpedo. "We caught them at five-mile range," said the commander of one of our cruisers, the *Salt Lake City,* "and hit some ships before they could open fire. . . . We capped their T. They were going toward Guadalcanal at a right angle to our course. The Jap ships turned in utter confusion, each ship taking its own course and trying to bring the action parallel. . . . The action was in spurts of from three to ten minutes with both forces moving at top speeds."[12]

After the first ten minutes the American force shifted to a southwesterly course to close the range. It was at this time that the *Boise,* 10,000 tons, was hit heavily forward, with fires on the forecastle burning so fiercely she appeared a total loss. Yet she pulled through, with a loss of 107 men, after firing over 1,000 rounds; and five weeks later she hauled into an American east coast port for repairs. After a second shift of course the enemy fire was silenced, and the American cruisers withdrew. That night, and in air attacks on the cripples next day, the enemy lost four cruisers and four destroyers, while another cruiser was badly damaged. The American suffered damage to two cruisers and the loss of one American destroyer, the *Duncan.*

---

[12] Captain Ernest G. Small, Associated Press Report, Nov. 2, 1942. The *Salt Lake City* later steamed between the damaged *Boise* and her opponent, and, though silhouetted by flames, completed the destruction of the enemy heavy cruiser with four 8-inch salvos.

Battle of the Santa Cruz Islands. The next fortnight was marked by intensified activity, during which the Japanese succeeded in landing some tanks and light artillery. On October 24 and 25 our Marines and Army re-enforcements withstood heavy attacks, supported by planes from Japanese carriers. The assaults twice pierced the American lines but were finally turned back.

During this very critical period, on October 26, the naval forces met in heavy air combats near the Santa Cruz Islands, east of the Solomons. This action resulted in the loss of the United States carrier *Hornet,* 19,900 tons, and the destroyer *Porter.* The *Hornet* came through two bomber and torpedo-plane attacks, shooting down fifty out of fifty-four planes, but was so badly damaged that she was sunk some hours later by her own force. From her deck, in April preceding, had flown the sixteen army bombers that first raided Tokyo. In this engagement the new battleship *South Dakota,* commanded by Captain Thomas L. Gatch, successfully fought off sustained aircraft attacks and gave protection to a second carrier. The defense indicated the increasing possibilities of a heavy and well-managed anti-aircraft fire. In the first onset of twenty bombers, from 11:12 to 11:30, "all were shot down"; and the second flight of forty torpedo-planes and bombers was met, according to press descriptions, by "a curving wall of glowing steel from the great ship." One torpedo-plane got through but made no hits. In a third assault the battleship was hit by only one 500-pound bomb.

On the Japanese side, though no ship was actually seen to sink, the damage inflicted must have been severe. American aircraft were credited with four to six hits by heavy bombs on a carrier, two medium bomb hits on a second carrier, heavy bomb hits on a battleship, and torpedo and bomb hits on five cruisers. A pilot reported that the deck of a carrier was completely smashed and that she appeared to be sinking. At the close of the month the Japanese fleet also suffered from heavy raids on their advance bases at Buin, on the island of Bougainville.

About this time it was announced that Vice Admiral Halsey, after a period ashore, had relieved Vice Admiral Ghormley in the South Pacific command.

Battle of Guadalcanal. The most outstanding in this crescendo of Solomons naval battles, and the last of consequence for 1942, saw battleships pitted against each other in gunnery action for the first time in the Pacific war.

On November 11 and 12 considerable American re-enforcements had again been thrown into Guadalcanal, despite Japanese harrying from the air. The superiority of the Henderson Field air defenses at this time is indicated by the report that on the twelfth, out of twenty to twenty-five Japanese bombers which attacked, not one reached the transports, and only one survived.

The re-enforcements were timely, for again Japan was organizing an expedition on a still larger scale, involving what was reported as no less than three divisions in eight large transports, with a cover or striking force which included not only the customary cruisers and destroyers but several *Kongo* class battleships. Naval engagements with these forces, or parts of them, occurred on three successive nights.

The first, on the night of November 12–13, was with a strong advance force—reported as two battleships, two heavy cruisers, four light cruisers, and about ten destroyers—approaching the Henderson Field roadstead with the evident purpose of clearing out naval opposition, bombarding the base, and softening it up for a general assault. Their guns were loaded with high explosive rather than armor-piercing shell. Against them the Navy went in with all it had available—two heavy cruisers, three light cruisers, and eight destroyers. As the Japanese approached in three columns, the American squadron plunged between two of them, firing on both sides at almost point-blank range. Judging from the outcome, the effect of this daring move was to confuse the enemy and throw off his fire. Toward the end of the engagement, according to the official communique, "two of the three Japanese groups were firing on each other."

Early in this attack, though not until after she had scored eighteen hits on an enemy battleship, the heavy cruiser *San Francisco,* flagship of Rear Admiral Daniel J. Callaghan, was hit on the bridge by a 14-inch shell, which killed the Admiral and Captain Cassin Young. Though temporarily stunned, the senior officer still alive on the bridge, Lieutenant Commander Bruce McCandless, held the flagship on her course. Of the maneuvering in this furious night action little is certainly known. Destroyer commanders pressed their attacks on the Japanese battleships with reckless daring. As a single instance, Lieutenant Commander W. E. Hank, in the *Laffey,* fired all his port torpedoes at a battleship at close range, and then, after cutting close across her bow, demolished her bridge with his 5-inch guns. The losses tell a part of the story. For the Americans the toll was two light cruisers, the *Juneau* and *Atlanta,* and seven of the eight destroyers—the *Cushing, Benham, Preston, Laffey, Barton, Monssen,* and *Walker.* The *Atlanta,* Captain Samuel P. Jenkins, was a fast, heavily gunned but lightly armored type, completed in 1942. According to Secretary Knox,[13] "she took everything the Japanese had and in return sent two Japanese ships to the bottom." At dawn her flag was still flying, and she was sunk by her own men. The Japanese lost a battleship, two heavy and three light cruisers, and five destroyers. The battleship was not actually sunk that night. Next morning, creeping off at five knots, she was set upon in a whole series of aircraft attacks and took eleven torpedo hits and six bomb hits before her crew had to scuttle her.

On the next night, the thirteenth–fourteenth, a second spearhead, still preparing the way for the main advance, approached Guadalcanal and at about 2:00 A.M. bombarded the base for

[13] Speech, March 12, 1943, accepting funds from the people of Atlanta, Georgia, for a new cruiser of the same name.

forty minutes. Motor torpedo boats were at this time the only naval defense at hand. Whether or not they forced the enemy's withdrawal, they put a torpedo into a cruiser and so slowed her down that, with another cruiser escort, she was sunk by aircraft next day.

On the fourteenth the transports, which the day before had been sighted steaming in from the eastward, were attacked from the air while still 150 miles from their goal. With courage and dogged persistence, they kept plugging on toward Guadalcanal. Before the day was over, the transports had been abandoned by their escorts, and all eight, loaded with troops, were sunk, together with four cargo ships. Four American planes were lost.

Finally, on Saturday night the fourteenth, there was another naval action off Savo, in which two 35,000-ton United States battleships, one of them Captain Gatch's ship, under Rear Admiral W. A. Lee as force commander, were ready to meet the four battleships opposed. If the Japanese had set a trap, as seems possible, it must have been for much smaller game. In the melee of destroyer clashes and sweeping searchlights, 16-inch guns soon brought decisive results. While there were no American losses, those of the Japanese included a battleship, three cruisers, and a destroyer, with damage to ships of each of these types.

Out of the big armada that had set out from Japanese bases several days before, only four cargo vessels finally ran ashore at Tassafronga, a few miles east of Henderson Field, and these were gutted by our aircraft before their munitions could be brought to land. The total Japanese naval loss was reckoned as sixteen naval vessels and twelve transports.

It was of this series of actions that General Vandegrift wrote his message to Admiral Halsey: "We lift our battered helmets in admiration for those who fought against overwhelming odds and drove the enemy to crushing defeat." "Let us thank God," added President Roosevelt later, in a speech quoting the General's message, "for such men as these. May our nation continue worthy of them." [14]

VII. AMERICAN SUBMARINES IN THE PACIFIC

Admiral Hart, as already cited, spoke of the injury to enemy shipping by the twenty-seven submarines under his command as equal to that inflicted by all his other units combined. Working later from Java and Australia, and throughout the year from the main base at Pearl Harbor, the expertly handled American "pig boats"—mostly large 1,500-ton craft capable of the 4,000-mile cruise to enemy home waters—maintained a steady attrition on the Japanese naval and merchant ships. Lurking off Japan's harbors, preying upon coastal trade and especially upon vital communication and supply lines, the American submarines at the end of 1942 had a record of 112 ships sunk, 22 probably sunk, and 29 damaged, amounting, at an average of 6,000 tons per ship, to a total probably well over 700,000 tons. At the opening of the war Japan had a merchant fleet of about 8,000,000 tons and a normal annual construction rate of not over 500,000 tons. In view of her immensely in-

[14] Quoted in the *New York Times,* Dec. 18, 1942. There was a subsequent furious surface action off Lunga Point on the night of November 30–December 1 in which the Americans lost the light cruiser *Northampton,* and the Japanese lost six destroyers, two transports, and a cargo ship. The final elimination of Japanese forces from Guadalcanal was completed on February 7, 1943. According to a United States Navy summary made public March 13, 1943, the naval losses at Guadalcanal up to February 7 were as given in the following table:

Type	United States			Japan		
	Sunk	Damaged	Total	Sunk	Damaged	Total
Battleships	0	0	0	2	6	8
Carriers	2	0	2	0	4	4
Heavy cruisers	7	2	9	12	25	37
Destroyers	14	3	17	26	51	77
Miscellaneous	11	0	11	0	4	4
Total			39			130

In addition, Japan lost 24 or 25 transports and cargo ships sunk and 27 damaged.

creased wartime shipping requirements, the loss of 700,000 tons by submarine, coupled with at least equally heavy losses of tankers, transports, and cargo ships in other forms of sea warfare, might well prove a crippling blow.

In one notably successful cruise toward the close of the year Lieutenant T. B. Klakring sank eight ships totaling 70,000 tons. Naval as well as cargo ships were included in the pig boats' haul. In operations around Java submarines claimed three cruisers sunk and a large aircraft carrier put out of action. In a July raid on Kiska in the Aleutians they sank three or four enemy destroyers, and in the course of the year a half dozen more. At Midway it was a submarine that gave the carrier *Soryu* her *coup de grace,* and a submarine under Lieutenant Grenfell waylaid and sank an enemy submarine in mid-Pacific. The citation accompanying the award of the Navy Cross to Grenfell and three other submarine skippers, Parks, White, and Mosely, read in part:

> All [the enemy ships] but the submarine credited to Lieutenant Commander Grenfell were sunk in Japanese waters, and in all but that instance the attacks were driven home in the face of intensive air and surface patrols. Only one of our submarines was damaged —the damage was slight—while there was no injury to personnel.

The skilful conduct of these operations is evidenced by the fact that the year's losses were kept to five submarines—one destroyed in dry dock at Manila, one sunk in collision near Panama, and only three, the *Perch, Shark,* and another, destroyed presumably by enemy action. In contrast, aside from a flurry of activity on the American West Coast early in the war, Japanese submarine accomplishments against merchant shipping were negligible. The immense traffic over Pacific supply lines remained secure.

The Aleutians

Japanese occupation of Kiska, Attu, and Agattu in the outer Aleutian Islands was accomplished in early June, 1942, coincident with the advance toward Midway. The purposes behind this move, whatever they may have been, remained undeveloped, and though at the year's end the Japanese were still at Attu, their ships, planes, and troops had served chiefly as a target for destructive air raids from the American base at Dutch Harbor.

VIII. THE WAR IN THE ATLANTIC; FIGHTING THE SUBMARINE

"Without merchant shipping all the actions of the naval war are crippled or doomed in advance." Though these were the words of a German naval spokesman, Admiral Lützow, they well expressed the vital dependence of the United Nations on shipping, not only for naval but for all military operations—in Asia, Australia, Africa, Russia—all relying on ships and sea communications for every kind of supply. In the Atlantic, in 1942 as earlier, the chief threat to ships and communications was the Axis submarine. The partial mastery of the U-boat menace in 1941 has already been recounted, but the problem had to be faced again at the close of that year, when the entry of the United States into the war ended all restraints and offered a wide new field for attack. The sinking of two tankers in mid-January, 1942, just off the port of New York, gave first warning of the shift of U-boats from the stiffly protected overseas convoys to the happy hunting ground for unguarded shipping on the American East Coast.

In commerce destruction of the Second World War, one must note at the outset that the U-boat enjoyed great advantages as compared with 1914–18. Instead of having its bases limited to home ports and a bit of Belgian coast, with narrow exits to the high seas, it could now operate from a coast line extending from the North Cape of Norway to the French-Spanish frontier. With the spread of submarine activity to the American coast, the Caribbean, the Mediterranean approaches, and the South Atlantic, most of the German boats operated from well-located bases on the Biscay coast, such as L'Orient, Brest, and St.

Nazaire. Here there could be no question of bottling up their exits by mines; and against air bombing the bases were given protection by heavy shelters of concrete.

As the war went on, the Germans speeded up submarine construction and made notable improvements in design. Many submarines of the 1942 model were increased from 500 to 880 tons, with a 14,500-mile cruising radius, five tubes and a larger supply of torpedoes, and a surface speed as high as 18 knots, enabling them to overtake most merchant ships and convoys. There were also larger submarines of 1,060 tons, and some use was made of submarine barges or storeships for supply at sea. Strengthened construction gave better protection against depth bombs, and permitted dives as deep as 600 feet, which increased the chances of surviving a depth-bomb attack.

When improved sonic detection devices made daylight attacks increasingly dangerous, the Germans devised the so-called "wolf pack" tactics, in which several submarines would follow on the skirts of a convoy by day and attack at night with hulls awash for better vision and speed. Sometimes they would attack in the midst of a convoy, or they would so time their approaches that the escort ships, concentrating on the first submarine sighted, would leave the others free to attack.

Defense methods were correspondingly improved, especially by increasing coastal aircraft patrols and extending them farther to sea, and by use of fighter planes for convoy protection, operating either from small carriers or from transports. With blimps or planes guarding a convoy, submarines could be kept sufficiently distant in the daytime to prevent their attack at night. For coastal patrol, blimps proved an effective weapon, able to cover wide areas, hover at critical points, and keep submarines below the surface. Depth bombs were also given heavier charges and were spread more freely. The arming of American merchant vessels was undertaken early in the war, and in time nearly all American ships were provided with guns and naval guncrews. In general, no better plan of defense was found than the convoy system, which necessitated, however, a vast increase in the number of destroyers, corvettes, and smaller escort craft of all types and sizes. As noted earlier, congressional appropriations in June, 1942, provided for 900,000 additional tons of destroyers and other escorts, and big increases in smaller craft. Yet, at the close of the year the demand still far exceeded the supply.

At the outbreak of the submarine campaign on the East Coast in January, 1942, the defense provisions were at first meager indeed, being limited to perhaps a dozen Coast Guard cutters, a few PC boats, a squadron or so of army and naval planes, and four blimps. It was well understood, moreover, that there could be no transfer of protection from the all-important convoys overseas. But as sinkings multiplied and spread up and down the coast from the St. Lawrence to the Gulf, the anti-submarine campaign also gathered headway. An Eastern Sea Frontier command was established under Rear Admiral Adolphus Andrews, and all defense organizations were placed under naval control. Private yachts and aircraft were pressed into service, a few old flush-deck destroyers as well as some British corvettes and trawlers became available, and finally, in mid-May, a convoy system was started from the Gulf to northern ports.

As the U-boats spread their activities into the Caribbean, concentrating especially on tankers and cargoes of war materials, the convoy system was also extended to Texas, Trinidad, and Aruba, and a Gulf Sea Frontier was set up with Rear Admiral James L. Kauffman in command. Mexico, declaring war on the Axis in June, and Brazil, joining in August, added their naval contingents to the sea patrol. The efficacy of the convoy system was demonstrated by the fact that of 1,800 ships convoyed along the coast up to the close of July, only four were lost. The convoy control room in New York, like the famous control room at the Admiralty in London in World War I, had its immense wall map, its affixed movable models representing submarines, convoys, and patrols, and its swift communications with forces at sea. Sinkings in the western Atlantic mounted steadily to a total of slightly over 100 in June. Thereafter they showed a rapid decline, but rose again late in the year with the increased troop and supply movements to North Africa.

Throughout the year American naval and air forces joined with the British in protection of trans-Atlantic convoys and supply lines to the ports of northern Russia, and extensive American naval bases and repair stations were set up at Reykjavik in Iceland and Londonderry in northern Ireland. While the Atlantic traffic moved with fair security, and large bodies of troops reached Ireland and England without losses, the Murmansk convoys received rough handling. German aircraft, submarines, and surface vessels concentrated upon them in their passage close to the Norwegian coast. In the long days of summer, when the drift ice pushed the convoys closer to the coast, the losses were especially heavy, and a September convoy was considered fortunate when 70 per cent of its cargo got through. Yet the convoys continued to move "on schedule," carrying a total, up to the close of 1942, of 2,600 American planes, 3,200 tanks, and 81,000 "jeeps," trucks, and other military rolling stock for the Russian war.

It would be impossible to chronicle in a brief space the many desperately fought actions in defense of convoys, the instances of individual fortitude and heroism, in this long-sustained struggle to maintain the flow of supply by sea, a struggle in which the hardships and dangers were shared alike by merchant sailors and naval crews. Estimates at the end of 1942 gave a total of 3,800 ships and over 63,000 merchant seamen of many nationalities lost in commerce warfare. The United States Merchant Marine lost 3,200 men in 1942, or nearly 4 per cent. German sources claimed the sinking in 1942 of nearly nine million tons of enemy shipping; but in the same period American ship construction alone amounted to just over eight million tons, and total construction represented a net gain.

Among American naval losses in 1942 were the Coast Guard cutter *Alexander Hamilton,* torpedoed off Iceland in February; the old destroyer *Truxtun* and cargo vessel *Pollux,* wrecked in the same month in a gale off the Newfoundland coast, with losses of nearly 100 men from each; and two other old four-stack destroyers—the *Jacob Jones,* torpedoed in March off the Delaware coast with only eleven survivors, and the *Sturtevant,* sunk in May off Florida.

At the close of 1942, submarine construction in Germany was believed to be from twenty to thirty a month, and since the destruction of submarines ran considerably below that figure, it appeared not improbable that the Axis might have from 400 to 600 submarines in action during the next year. In Germany submarine construction was given highest priority for materials, and Admiral Doenitz, while retaining his former post in charge of U-boat activities, succeeded Admiral Erich Raeder as Commander in Chief of the German Navy. For the United Nations, halting the submarine menace remained the gravest problem of the naval war.

IX. THE MOVEMENT OF FORCES TO NORTH AFRICA

Decided upon in June and planned beforehand in the utmost detail, the overseas movement of American and British forces to French North Africa in November, 1942, was undoubtedly the largest of its kind ever carried out in a single operation. It called for about 500 troop and supply ships and 350 naval units. Its purpose was to open a second front against the Axis in the only theater deemed feasible that year; and in view of the leading American part in its preparation and composition, Lieutenant General Dwight D. Eisenhower, United States Army, was assigned to chief command. Rear Admiral Henry K. Hewitt, United States Navy, commanded the American forces engaged in the transport and landing of troops.

The contingent from the United States, under American naval protection, sailed for ports on the West African coast. Two big convoys from England, under British naval escort and carrying both British and United States forces, swung first wide into the Atlantic, then toward Gibraltar, and finally entered

Algiers, Oran, and other French African ports on the Mediterranean. Landings at all points were made simultaneously in the early hours of Sunday, November 8.

The expedition had been kept secret, and apparently the Axis had insufficient knowledge of its purpose or precise objectives to assemble large submarine forces in advance. Only one American ship, sailing in a Mediterranean convoy, was torpedoed before the landing, and the troops of this ship got safely ashore. In all, five American transports were sunk later, totaling 53,000 gross tons. The British reported the loss of ten small naval vessels, including three destroyers (one of them Dutch), a small converted carrier, and two former United States Coast Guard cutters, most of which were lost in the breaking of booms and harbor fighting at Algiers and Oran. British transport losses were not published, but were described as "considerably less than anticipated."

The American landings at Safi, Fedhala, and Medhia in Morocco were little opposed and were well covered by aircraft from carriers, which knocked out 100 French planes on the ground and twenty-six in the air. The chief fighting centered at the port and naval base of Casablanca, where the 35,000-ton battleship *Jean Bart* (with five of her eight 15-inch turret guns mounted), together with cruisers, destroyers, submarines, and shore battleries, offered for a time a stiff naval opposition. A light cruiser and three destroyers standing out of the harbor were driven ashore by gunfire and carrier aircraft. Aided by aircraft spotting, a United States battleship was reported to have made hits on the *Jean Bart* at a distance of 26 miles, but most of the bombardment was at much closer range. The *Jean Bart's* last turret gun was not silenced till after a dive bomber attack on the tenth.

Admiral Darlan, Vichy representative in Africa, had surrendered at Algiers on the evening of the eighth, and subsequently, as chief authority in the French colonies, Darlan made arrangements for the co-operation of all French forces in North and West Africa with those of the United Nations. Upon the capitulation of Casablanca on November 11, resistance ended and French military and civilians at once fraternized with the Anglo-American troops. Later in the month, the surrender of Dakar gave the United Nations control of this important stronghold on the West African coast, together with the very considerable French naval force based there. The subsequent destruction, November 27, of the sixty or more French naval vessels at Toulon, by order of their commander to prevent their capture by Germany, ended the possibility that this force might be taken over by the Axis powers. Aside from its immediate results, the establishment of the North African front raised prospects of re-opening the short supply route to the East through the Mediterranean, and of a future invasion of the European continent from the south. The United Nations were in position for aggressive warfare in 1943.

References

At the time this chapter was written, the chief sources available were official communiqués, news reports, and data supplied by the Navy Department. The following books were also most helpful:

Casey, Robert J., *Torpedo Junction,* 1942.

Cope, Harley F., Commander, U.S.N., *Serpent of the Seas*: *the Submarine,* 1942.

Johnston, Stanley, *Queen of the Flat-Tops,* 1942.

Pratt, Fletcher, "The Campaign of the Java Sea," *Harper's Magazine,* November, 1942, and later articles in the same magazine.

INDEX